BURIED PLEASURE

THE GOLDEN CARPET by SOMERSET de CHAIR

'One of the most brilliant enterprises in military history is worthily described in this notable book, which is as sure of a place in war literature as was T.E. Lawrence's famous work.' *Daily Telegraph*

'This author has made in *The Golden Carpet* something that is significant, symbolic and satisfying. For all the comradeship of all war, all its hazards and heroisms, the strange interludes of beauty that it may have, are here, in the small space of this adventure, held up for our regard.'
Howard Spring in *Country Life*

'When Lawrence of Arabia anti-climaxed a mighty career by crashing to death on a motor cycle in a quiet English lane in 1935, it seemed incredible that within a comparatively short period another man could cross the desert where he once roamed and produce a modern, abbreviated counterpart to *The Seven Pillars of Wisdom*. ... In the Lawrence of Arabia style is Somerset de Chair's graphic record of war in Iraq.' *News Review*

'The only leader in the last war whose deeds grew into a popular legend after the war had ended was T.E. Lawrence. ... The desert had a lot to do with investing the story of the Arab Revolt with the old heroic quality of the Odyssey and the Siege of Troy. ... A glittering book from the desert has just been published by a Member of Parliament, not so long and not so grandly epic as Lawrence's *Seven Pillars of Wisdom*, but written with a touch of the same inspiration. ... *The Golden Carpet* places Mr. de Chair at once among the literary luminaries of Parliament.' *Evening Standard*

'Captain de Chair writes magnificently and does not neglect either humour or beauty.' *Punch*

'After spending the greater part of last evening enthralled by Mr. de Chair's narrative, I do not think that any of the eulogies was overstated. Mr. de Chair is, I should say, one of the most remarkable young men in the present Parliament: poet, author and man of action.' *Eastern Daily Press*

'Here is the whole story now made available to the general public for the first time, and it is a story in the tradition of T.E. Lawrence, and one worthy to take its place in the history of the British soldiers' heroic campaigns in the Near East.' *Spectator*

'This is an enthralling book and Captain de Chair is a gallant and engaging writer. I read this volume with more interest than any other recent campaigning record.' *Manchester Guardian*

Published by Faber and Faber Limited

The Author photographed by Lord Killearn on one of the lions in the British Embassy at Cairo, Boxing Day 1945.

BURIED PLEASURE

by

SOMERSET de CHAIR

For
Ginny Clark,
affectionately
Somerset de Chair

MERLIN BOOKS LTD.
Braunton   Devon

BY THE SAME AUTHOR:

Historical Fiction
Enter Napoleon
The Story of a Lifetime (Limited Edition, 100 copies only)
Bring Back the Gods
Friends, Romans, Concubines
The Star of the Wind
Legend of The Yellow River (1979)
Contemporary Fiction
Red Tie in the Morning (Satire)
The Teetotalitarian State (Satire)
The Dome of the Rock
1939-45 War
The Golden Carpet (Limited Edition)
The Silver Crescent (Limited Edition)
(Published jointly in the public edition as The Golden Carpet)
A Mind on the March
Historical
(As Editor and Translator)
The First Crusade (Limited Edition only)
Napoleon's Memoirs (Limited and Public Editions)
Supper at Beaucaire (Limited and Public Editions)
Julius Caesar's Commentaries (Limited Edition only)
Biographical
(as editor)
The Sea is Strong
The Naval Memoirs of Admiral Sir Dudley de Chair,
KCB, KCMG, MVO
Political
The Impending Storm
Divided Europe
Drama
Peter Public
Poetry
The Millennium
Collected Verse

ISBN 0 86303 239-7
Printed in England by Maslands Ltd., Tiverton, Devon

Captain de Chair's sequel to *The Golden Carpet* begins with his convalescing in Jerusalem from wounds sustained in the assault on the desert fortress of Palmyra, held by the Vichy French Foreign Legion. He is invalided back to his home in the wintry Western Isles of Scotland in time for Christmas, 1941. After a short spell at the War Office in Military Intelligence dealing with the Middle East, he receives a letter headed 'Chequers, Aylesbury, Buckinghamshire', which he at first thinks is the address of a pub, but which asks him to resume his parliamentary duties as Parliamentary Private Secretary to a member of the War Cabinet (Oliver Lyttelton), Minister of Production. His 2½ years in that capacity is punctuated by operations on his wounds in 1943, over which Winston Churchill expresses his concern, as he had hoped to include him in his government in a more advanced capacity.

Mr. de Chair sees a lot more of Mr. Churchill in the 1950/51 parliament, when Churchill accepts the dedication of his *Julius Caesar*. 'I so much enjoyed your masterly *Julius Caesar*,' writes Churchill to him, and says that he has spent so much of his life correcting proofs that he cannot resist marking the points as they occur to him, and sends his proof corrections to Mr. de Chair. Subsequently he invites Mr. de Chair to lunch at 10 Downing Street when he is Prime Minister, and reads out large passages of the Vol. 1 of *The History of the English Speaking Peoples* to him, and asks Mr. de Chair to check Vol. 1 for him.

The intimate glimpses of Sir Winston described by the author bring the great man into much sharper focus than all the lengthy biographies put together.

Parallel with his political activities, we find the author living in some of the most spectacular houses in Britain. After the island of Gigha, there are Chilham Castle in Kent, Trerice Manor in Cornwall (which he sold to the National Trust), Blickling Hall in Norfolk, (formerly the home of Lord Lothian, Britain's

Ambassador to the United States), and St. Osyth's Priory in Essex, built twenty years before Christopher Columbus set sail for America.

Mr. de Chair was also asked by the War Office to lecture to the three Services in Egypt, Tripolitania and the Sudan in 1945/6 and in Singapore, Malaya and Hong Kong in 1948. His travels in these countries form a fascinating part of the book.

His account of winning a Parliamentary election in London while leading a double life under another name on the other side of the Park (the rich side) is hilarious.

Forty-four years on from the capture of Baghdad in 1941 and three wives later, Mr. de Chair's life has never been dull.

ERRATA

Page 149, line 24:
for Lady Anne Cavendish-Britol
read Lady Anne Cavendish-Bentinck
Page 366, line 1:
for Jeal Paul Getty
read Jean Paul Getty

CONTENTS

	ı	7
	ce	11
	f Gigha	18
	ʔroduction	27
	ld Parliament	59
	ı Kent	69
	ɔr	79
	ɪe Middle East	82
		111
9	Tripolitania	118
10	The Mystery of Sarah Aaronsohn	123
11	The Greatest of These . . .	144
12	Singapore	152
13	Bangkok	166
14	Madame Eu Tong Sin and Others	171
15	The Story of Allison Owens	182
16	Malaya	194
17	Strange Goings-on at No.10	205
18	The 1950 Parliament	212
19	Chenonçeaux	239
20	The Navigation of the Bure	242
21	Winston Churchill	251
22	The Still Afternoon	270
23	The Harebell	278
24	Kung-Hai-Fat-Choy	290
25	St. Osyth Priory	301
26	Journeys in Morocco	323
27	Egypt Revisited	329
28	Travels with Tessa	339
29	The Farm in New York	346
30	Paul Getty	366
	Postscript	376

When it was all over, I lay in the hospital at Jerusalem, staring at the electric light shade over my bed: watching the dust on it daily accumulate. A pretty young V.A.D. flirted around the room with a duster and the fitter officers. She passed by my gaunt face, plastered leg, bandaged arm and hand and hip and shoulder; smitten all over, it seemed, by bullets and fragments of air-cannon shell. The dust accumulated and my tonsils turned septic.

The septic condition yielded to the second course of M & B; and in a few days I was sitting up cheerfully enough. My neighbour was a Padre in the Air Force, Padre Barr, operated on for gallstones which were removed in metallic lumps from his interior. He held his side painfully when I made him nearly split it with laughter. Across the room Siepmann complained that ever since I recovered, the ward had resembled an Oriental bazaar, with Armenian traders coming in to discuss the sealing and licencing of marble busts for export, or Arabs accompanied with all their male relatives to lend their support, standing round my bed to conclude the purchase of my motor car. Presently I was allowed to sit in a wheeled chair outside, under a scarlet blanket, and Armenian priests, with huge round black hats and deep black beards paused at my feet in greeting. There was a charming young Sister, in charge of the officers' ward; a red-headed Irish girl, who had little authority over the tougher Sisters in her charge. One of these we knew as 'heavy tanks' — she charged into the ward, during her night rounds, violently disturbing us from any slumber we might get; but all were kind at heart; and very few of us died, once they reached that sanctuary. Araminta McMichael, daughter of the High Commissioner came as a part-time V.A.D. to read our pulses and make other records of our doings. She became confused one day and entered me on her chart as having a pulse of 2 and bowels opened 64 times.

It was a happy day when I was transferred to the Red Cross

11

Convalescent Home, started by and named after Araminta's mother, Lady McMichael, amid the olive groves of Talbieh, within a stone's throw of the King David Hotel.

This officers' Convalescent Home was a pleasant little stone house, comfortably provided with a bathroom and with running water in the bedrooms. The officers dined at small tables in the dining-room and there were gathered in the first casualties of Wavell's scattered campaigns in Libya, Abyssinia, East Africa, Iraq and Syria. I sat at a table for two with an officer called Meynell, who had inherited a perfect castle on some Tyrolean crag. The agent, he said, had done his best to keep it from harm when the Nazis moved into Austria. What had happened to it and its fourteenth century frescoes he did not know. Another officer was Peter Lee, whose hand had been crushed when his armoured car turned over north of Damascus. All agreed that the Vichy French had fought with unexpected valour and ferocity; much bitterness being added to their defence by the inclusion in our forces of a Free French contingent.

I was able to walk now, on crutches, swinging my left leg in white plaster, and gripping the crutch handle, with a left hand still bandaged. I swung my way thus uphill to the King David Hotel, where the Swiss proprietor Hamburger and his striking looking wife, very reminiscent, I thought, of the Duchess of Kent, were kindness itself to me, and welcomed me in their private suite to read and write. On my birthday, the 22nd August, porters staggered down to Talbieh, with a seven-tiered cake, white with icing sugar and friendly greetings, the gift of Mr. and Mrs. Hamburger. There are some moments in our life, not many, when every man's hand seems to be for us; everyone is on our side. And it is this overflowing kindness that makes the convalescent period at Talbieh one of the happiest of my life, in retrospect.

My wife, in her distant island, had seen the Postmaster, Wilkinson, come up the drive towards the house, himself, where the rhododendrons were still in bloom, and hand her with sad, but composed countenance, the War Office telegram. It was a relief, fumbling to open it, to read that I was only wounded. Yet would it not have been better for her, if I had been reported dead? No long delayed reunion with a ghost; no severed nerves, and drugs to dull the throbbing pain; and the slow twisting round of character in a tormented frame; no long drawn parting in less noble circumstances at the end.

Life drifted by happily enough in Talbieh; where the climate was like an English summer's day; for Jerusalem, as we all know, is set upon a hill — 2,000 feet high. I began to make friends in Jerusalem. Clarissa Graves and her brother Richard, lived in a house in the German quarter. Richard Graves was a half brother of Robert Graves, the author. One evening I went out to their house, The Villa Rosemary, where it stood in the moonlight with pantiled roof, among cypresses — and heard, with surprise, on the silvery night, the strains of Elizabethan madrigals, pouring from the windows. They had a party of songsters practising these old English songs, which sounded so strangely on the air of Palestine. Clarissa had published a book of poems, which she lent me, and listened to some of mine, with a politeness not perhaps usual in fellow writers. She came to tea at the Convalescent Home, and said that my poem on Death —

'I thought that Death would have a face'
thrilled her right down to her ankle bones. To Talbieh came also another poet, Altounyan, whose home was at Katamon in Jerusalem, where he had an English wife, whose father had written a biography of Ruskin. Altounyan was Armenian, a sensitive soul, who still mourned the passing of his friend T. E. Lawrence; and ran eagerly into battle for the second time in his life. He had been decorated at Passchendaele in the First World War; and had now been Medical Officer to Glubb's Arab Legion in Syria, where he learnt a lot about air attack on ground troops. His father was a famous surgeon in Aleppo; and there had Altounyan practised also. When he heard of Lawrence's death he began to write sonnets about him, and these he shoved daily in a drawer, as he went into the operating theatre, until there were enough for a book, the *Ornament of Honour*, published by the Cambridge University Press. Altounyan was conscious of emulating the Shakespearean series and drew one parallel: "They too were written about a man. And just as in the case of my sonnets about Lawrence, they too were not in any way homosexual."

I read my own poems to Altounyan, and noted those which he praised. When I came, in the poem on Narvik to —

'Death is a lesson that is hard to learn'
he said, dreamily, gazing as if at some distant object through his owl-like glasses, "Ah, that is a good line."

It did not seem odd, in my febrile wounded condition at the Lady McMichael Home, to read my poems to Altounyan, although I would recoil now at reading them to any man.

I had no energy to keep a diary: I was content to live. But I did some writing of a disjointed kind: 'The philosophy of a wounded man.' I met Sir Harry Trusted, the Chief Justice under the Mandate, and he lent me a book of profound influence at such a receptive moment. *The Mind in the Making* by James Harvey Robinson, the gist of which is that the mind of man is a growing thing subject to the same evolution as any animal and is no more a truth-testing instrument than the snout of a pig; and depends very much on healthy food, not on biased, inherited notions, but clear and independently attained conclusions. He drew sharp distinctions between the real reasons for people's actions and the good or sufficient reasons which they advance for them, to deceive themselves or others. He aimed at securing for social and political systems the sort of honesty in thought which has characterised the steady build-up of the sciences.

One day I was astonished while Somerset Maxwell, my friend and neighbouring Member of Parliament in Norfolk, was visiting me, to learn that Sheik Hassan Suhail had arrived. He had made the journey from Baghdad, which he represented in the Iraqi Parliament, as he had affairs of his own to advance, in which he felt that I could get the army's help. He overrated my influence; but I rose, with difficulty, under the pillared semicircular portico to greet him warmly, and he came into the cool house; an impressive figure in his white robes, and Keffiyeh bound upon his head with the golden ropes of the Aqual. His family had presented me with gifts in Baghdad and I had none with which to repay him now. I asked Chris Thursfield of the Wilts, who also happened to be in the house, to go up to my room and bring down a parcel newly arrived from England. In it, wrapped in black tissue paper, were new gold braided stars, with the Garter crown of red, in a blue border, brightly woven. I handed them to him with deference; telling him that as soon as I returned to England I hoped to despatch a more appropriate gift. I did in fact send out to him, by the hand of the Regent of Iraq, no less, a copy of the limited edition on hand-made paper, bound in blue morocoo of *The Silver Crescent*, which reproduced upon a single page his impressive black bearded face, and Arabic signature. Hassan Suhail unfolded to me his story.

As I no longer kept a diary I have forgotten what his complaint was; but believe that it concerned some property which had been confiscated from him by the Iraq Government. I promised certainly to do all I could; and indeed urged Sam Maxwell, who was a Colonel, and who was departing forthwith, to have the matter raised at Force Headquarters. But Sam, alas, died of wounds received soon afterwards in Libya, and there is little more than his shield, in argent or in or, upon the walls of the new House of Commons to testify that he served the constituents of King's Lynn overseas.

Hassan Suhail departed, whence he had come, to Baghdad, and I hope that my intervention on his behalf with the Regent, whom I saw later on in England, a dapper young man in Western garb, at Claridges, secured for my old friend some redress of his grievances. At least he got the book, for he wrote to tell me so.

I have told the story of Helena of Abu Sinan, the nine-year-old Arab prophetess and healer, in *A Mind on the March*. She had given herself up to the nuns of the Russian Orthodox Church in Gethsemane, to be educated at the school in Bethany, when I knew her. The convent was in the charge of a Scots Abbess, Mary Robinson, born in Glasgow.

The Abbess was anxious to find some benefactor who would pay the very modest fees, £20 a year, required for Helena's education, as she said she did not want her to be sponsored by some wealthy local Arab who would want to show her off. I agreed to do it for the time being; and for three years after I left, I heard regularly from the Abbess and received formal school reports of Helena's progress.

'Mathematics fair', 'Russian good', that sort of thing. I was, in the reaction from wounds, passing through a deeply spiritual phase and saw, possibly, in Helena a portent of religious significance. But I heard less from the Abbess after I stopped contributing to Helena's education in 1944.

During this phase I lived like a saint, wrapped in a cloud, if not of repentance for past sins, at least of strong resolves about the present. And this lasted all the way home. At one stage I almost yielded to the temptation of an inner call to remain in the Holy Land and preach the gospel. But to whom?

The director of the Rockefeller Museum, Iliffe, had been to see me in hospital, and was willing to take delivery of the Beth

Shan bust, for which he would have to issue an export licence before I could take it out of the country. At his house I met the officer, Baxter, who dealt with officers' baggage; and he arranged to send a lorry to Ohan's shop, take the crate down to the Museum for licencing and sealing, and then, have it shipped as wounded officer's baggage to me in England.

I was given sick leave and went up to Nahariya, on the coast, north of Acre.

At Nahariya the sea beyond the sand was dark as indigo — almost the wine dark sea of Homer, and a pale blue banner of some kind fluttered on a flag staff. I was well looked after in a Jewish pension, where other officers on sick leave had been before me. And I began to write again — building upon my reading of *The Mind in the Making*. Was it perhaps possible to apply the methods of science to human affairs, and by a lucid and impartial scrutiny of the facts of history and life upon the planet, arrive at logical solutions of our affairs? J. H. Robinson wrote: 'As we grow up we simply adopt the ideas presented to us in regard to such matters as religion, family relation, property, business, our country and the state. We unconsciously absorb them from our environment. They are persistently whispered in our ear by the group in which we happen to live. When therefore we find ourselves entertaining an opinion about the basis of which there is a quality of feeling which tells us that to enquire into it would be absurd, unnecessary, unprofitable, undesirable, bad form or wicked, we may know that that opinion is a non-rational one, and probably, therefore founded upon inadequate evidence. Opinions, on the other hand, which are the result of experience or of honest reasoning do not have this quality of "primary certitude".'

He described the self-exculpation which occurs when we feel ourselves or our group accused of misapprehension or error, as 'Rationalising'.

'And now,' he went on, 'the astonishing and perturbing suspicion emerges that perhaps almost all that had passed for social science, political economy, politics and ethics in the past may be brushed aside by future generations as mainly rationalising. This conclusion may be ranked by students of a hundred years hence as one of the several great discoveries of our age.'

I proceeded therefore on the formula recommended in *The Mind in the Making*. I would set down the facts — first about myself, so that the reader would know what prejudices of heredity or environment to discount; next about the history of the international situation in my lifetime; (I brought this up to 1941, the time of writing); then of the national situation in my own country, Britain. Next the economic situation. Then, reviewing these factors, I would draw the great deductions.

I am inclined to think, even now, that this book, entitled 'The Facts' or perhaps, 'Mankind Revolts', although short, would stand publication on its own one day.

I paused in South Africa again on the way round the Cape. Aunt Beta, worn out with voluntary work for the war, and torn inside by cancer, was dying at Ida's Valley; but she looked lovingly and I thought proudly at her nephew from her sick bed. Uncle Charles's daughter Diana was growing up, disturbingly, and I sailed on to Trinidad, where I was lucky to get a day ashore; and met the Colonial Secretary of the Island. It was pleasant to see the smiling faces of the West Indian Negroes, along the roads bordered by tropical vegetation; and hear once again the crooning voices of native boatmen sing,

"She comes from Trinidad; because she's so bad.

Take a leaf of the famos tree,
It will cure all yo miserie.

Oh mama, she got no pease, no rice, no coconut oil,
All she got is brandy brandy off the ice."

and from there, across seas shadowed by the shapes of submarines, I reached home in time for Christmas 1941.

After acquiring the Island of Gigha from my sister in the early part of 1940 I was preoccupied as a junior subaltern in the army with the duties which fell to the army during the Battle of Britain. As these consisted of carrying out patrols in Windsor Park all night and training soldiers to be ready for battle all day I got very little sleep, and eventually collapsed and was ordered complete rest for ten days by the Medical Officer. This gave me the opportunity to visit the island which I had recently acquired, and to make arrangements for the conversion of a long grey farmhouse at the remote northern tip of the island called Kinnerarach, where a beach laved on both sides by the Gulf Stream ran out to a rocky headland. Admittedly the Gulf Stream was a little chilly by the time it had reached Scotland from Bermuda but the island was indeed a paradise. Another disused farmhouse half-way down the island called Cairnviscoye was to be converted by my parents for their use. In the meantime they continued to live in the rambling Victorian house called Achamore and Thelma lived with them there, bringing up the boys, the elder of whom, Rodney, attended the village school.

My mother's own house in Surrey had been requisitioned by the army and was in fact used as part of Montgomery's H.Q. to organise the invasion of Normandy later on. Jean Legge-Bourke had also come up to the island with her young children and occupied Cairnviscoye as soon as it was ready. I visited Harry Legge-Bourke at Heliopolis just after he had had parts of a bomb extracted from his arm following the campaign in Greece, and his principal concern was for his wife's safety in the London area which was being heavily bombed. I was able to reassure him, having just received an airgraph from Thelma that Jean was with her in the Western Isles. It was not until I was invalided back to England in November 1941 that I returned to Gigha.

I came loaded with gifts, painstakingly sought in the Middle

18

East: a necklace of Bahrein pearls for Thelma, as well as a surprisingly Parisian evening bag bought in Jerusalem. For my mother and sister, bracelets of Persian miniatures painted by Imami — each a gem of surprising detail. The pearls I had worn round my neck, under my shirt in case of shipwreck, which had seemed probable at one time with six U-boats in the path of the home-coming transport liner. Also I had brought this infernal crate of oranges which had plagued me with its bulk on the prolonged railway journey from Liverpool to the Western Isles in my lame condition, without porterage.

So here we were, approaching the island at last. I could have wept with emotion and exhaustion. For this moment I had been passed through thirteen Military Hospitals and travelled half-way round the world, crossing the Equator twice. I had warned Thelma by telegram not to come to the boat but to wait for me at Kinnerarach in the far north of the island where we had planned our house. But she was waiting on the quay at West Loch Tarbert. For some reason I felt that if I could see my father and mother first, who lived now in wartime in a small house half-way down the island, the one I have referred to as called Cairnviscoye, I would be able to draw enough strength from them to face the ordeal of meeting my wife again after all that had happened. For, of course, much had happened besides the battles and the wounds. Eighteen months is a long separation in wartime and I feared that the shock at seeing me returning from the Middle East was too much for her. When she had last seen me on the way out to war I had been a robust young subaltern and this pale ghost, returning almost from that undiscovered country from whose bourne no travellers are supposed to return, seemed to disturb her.

"I have bought some surprises for you," I said. "I am so glad that I have got here in time for Christmas. It will be wonderful to spend it at Kinnerarach."

"Well, actually," said Thelma, "we shall not be spending it here. I thought you would like to be in a cheerful party."

"Oh God!" I groaned aloud.

"You see," she changed her tack, "I didn't know for certain, till your wire arrived from Liverpool, that you would be back in time — so as Meg and Helmut Schroder invited all of us to stay at Dunlossit I thought, for the boys — "

"Yes, of course," I agreed, "for the boys. How are they?"

"Rodney is getting very Scottish at school – but I don't think it's doing him any harm. It's not the same thing as going to a village school in England at all. And, of course, Peter is running about now. You will love him."

I supposed that I would. He had been just over a year old when I left, still in his pram.

"You find that you can manage them all right?" I asked.

'Oh yes. One must not expect too much in wartime. And then there is Pat – "

My brother's wife? "Graham's wife?" I asked. "Is she here?"

"Yes. You see, as we did not know whether you would really be sent home or not, we agreed to share expenses at Kinnerarach, and have been moving in this last few days."

"You are actually in the new house then? And where is Graham – at sea I suppose?"

"No, he has leave, so he is here too."

"What! Both of them and their two children?"

"Well what I've arranged," said Thelma practically, "is for you to see your parents for a few minutes on our way up the island: then we can have one night at Kinnerarach alone with Rodney and Peter – Graham does not get leave till Christmas Eve, which is tomorrow, and Pat has gone to meet him. Of course we shall have their two children to keep an eye on, but they really all help to look after each other. And then," she went on hurriedly, seeing no doubt the look of exhausted anguish in my eye, "we can catch the afternoon boat, by which Graham and Pat arrive tomorrow, and we will go on for Christmas at Islay with Meg. It will just give you a chance to wish Graham a Merry Christmas on the pier."

All very sensible no doubt. And yet – was it really fair? Could I be expected to face any of this? I sighed inwardly for the kindly, robust matrons of convalescent homes I had visited in the Middle East.

The island loomed up in the rain like a whale, six miles long. It took an hour to pass down its eastern coast – a fact which had surprised me when I first saw the place. It looked unprepossessing from the raw grey sea of December, yet I knew that once upon its shores, enviable vistas of the neighbouring islands and the mountains of Kintyre would show up.

"I hope the pier is still standing up to the gales," I said.

"McSporran thinks we shall have to put in some more piles at the far end sooner or later. But Dada has got all the baulks you asked him to send for, and these have been laid in place of the rotten ones along the top."

The estimate for putting in one of the main piles, driven into the sea-bed, was £2,000. So I said jokingly, "We shall have to sell the island when McSporran's nerve finally cracks."

McSporran was the general store-keeper, Postmaster and Pier-master of the island. He had taken advantage of my sister's departure to import a motor van for delivering the letters — it was an ordinary shooting brake. But it violated the serenity of a motorless island. Yet, alas, it was useful. I had hoped to be met in the open buggy, drawn by Old Bill, the perennial horse, which I had bought along with the island and the contents of Achamore House. Old Bill was known to be thirty years old. Some said fifty. He still jogged happily along between the shafts.

"I thought," Thelma explained, "as you might be tired after the journey, we ought to go up to Kinnerarach in McSporran's van: it would take an hour or more otherwise. And the rain . . . . "

"One gets used to the rain in these parts" — I sighed. "And after the desert — but still — you are quite right: I expect Dada and Mother will be impatient to see me."

We had rounded the south-eastern headland and the village of Ardminish came into sight. Half a dozen houses and a small hotel. In front of it was one of the beaches, looking grey and rather sodden. The woods of Achamore could be seen, through the rain-streaked windows of the saloon, as a green smudge against the bleak moorland hills behind it. The roofs of Home Farm, long lines of wet slate, could just be seen above the woods. From there on fine days, views of almost tropical splendour greeted you at the crest of the path. And there I had last seen McLean, who rented the Home Farm (and sold cheeses, now, to the Milk Marketing Board). He had been weighing potatoes in sacks, against seas of intolerable blueness, while my father, in his grey Homburg hat stood switching the flies away from his face with a frond of bracken.

We were coming into the lea of the pier now: there was McSporran and his son running along the slippery planks with thick coils of rope, looped at the end. Against the side of the pier were the inevitable fenders of old motor tyres. The ship came alongside with a formidable crash as the seas lopped her up against the piles. I thought 'Some millionaire will have to deal with this soon.' The pier had been built in Victoria's reign by a previous owner, without permission of the Lords of the Admiralty and a law suit had ended, agreeably, in their Lordships' conveying to the owner 'All that bed of the ocean belonging to Queen Victoria' on which the pier stands. The bed of the ocean belonging to Queen Victoria now belonged to me — but it was not an easy couch to rest upon.

We were already on deck, looking across at the people in their shining oilskins on the pier. I looked into McSporran's weather-beaten old red face, and to my horror it suddenly dissolved into tears. He was looking at me, the young laird as he was pleased to call me, as if he had seen a ghost. It was disconcerting to have this effect on people. First Thelma, now old McSporran. I began to wonder how my parents would react.

We went ashore, down the gangway. The rubber tip of my stick (an implement given me on my way home by an uncle in South Africa) slipped on the wet ramp and Thelma gripped me quickly, while the Chief Officer of the boat, propped me up on the other side. My green canvas bedroll and the case of oranges followed me on to the jetty and I shook McSporran by the hand.

"It is good to see you back — alive," the old man declared, while he buried his face in the coiling of ropes on bollards. It had been he, in his capacity as Postmaster and Postman, who had carried up to Achamore the telegram from the War Office announcing that I had been wounded. It had been a shock to Thelma, no doubt. All the same she had held her head high. Indeed she had worn my wounds like feathers in her cap.

They all helped me into the front seat of the car, beside the driver's seat: the luggage was piled into the back over the flap. The steamer was already pulling away into the driving rain, bound for Islay, and we were soon passing the gates of Achamore, now unoccupied, and heading northwards along the single island road.

The car passed the gates of the big house and went on up the road to the dripping village, where McSporran got out to leave the mail and the newspapers which had arrived by the steamer.

"I hope you will like the alterations to Kinnerarach," Thelma said, somewhat apprehensively. "Of course Arnott's a fool" — she was referring to the builder: "but in wartime we are lucky to get anything done at all, I suppose. We probably would not get the licence at all now. Timber and all materials are much scarcer now. Your big window was done in cedarwood: but it really looks very nice."

We had intended to do it in oak. I had left with such high hopes of this house with the great mullioned window fifteen feet long by seven feet high to look right over the sea. But already I was aware of an extraordinary indifference to it all. What did it matter? What did anything matter? Was it wise to have come home? I had not the strength to cope with pleasurable surprises.

McSporran re-emerged from the village store, which also formed the post office, and we drove off.

"It'll no be verra long noo, afore ye clap een on the Admiral," he said cheerfully.

The road was bordered here by old iron park fencing, and a hundred yards away on the right was the Manse, set about with dark, damp fir trees.

"The Meenister will aye be glad to see ye hame safe," he added.

We passed various low crofts, with stone walls; the substantial cone of Creag Bhan rose from heath and bog on our left, its lowly summit hidden in mist. There were no majestic peaks here; but on fine days, the Paps of Jura would show up across the waters of the loch and the sea beyond it.

At Ballatyne's farm, the main road petered out and, passing through the farmyard, was resumed as a stony track dwindling in importance, till we reached the wilder parts of the island; the road was closed by gates every mile or so; and McSporran had to get out and open them. The small converted farmhouse where my father and mother were now living stood a few yards back from the road. They were already on the look-out, standing in the doorway.

"McSporran will take me to Kinnerarach," said Thelma, "and come back for you." She helped me out and I hurried as fast as my leg would permit up the narrow path to the house.

My father still had the look of an admiral, with his keen blue eyes, which ranged far horizons. His hair, what was left of it, was now almost white. He clapped a hand on my shoulder. "Well done," he said. So far I had, in his eyes, done nothing discreditable for an Admiral's son. My mother was very flushed in the face, which was broad and rather masculine at sixty years of age. She had been a great beauty in her youth, but her Dutch blood had allowed her to put on weight with the years. She presented a somewhat stubbly chin for me to kiss, and her expression was one of horror, rigidly controlled. Thelma left us quickly together with some fluttering comments and a wave of the hand, darting back in her white mackintosh and scarf-covered head to the van.

"Come in," my father said, "and we'll have a yarn."

This was just the right attitude. He expected an interesting tale, and would not be over-sentimental about it.

My mother, on the other hand could not resist violent outbreaks such as, "It's absolutely damnable — how could they do such a thing? — And in an ambulance, too — weren't they marked with Red Crosses?"

"Oh, yes, they were marked clearly enough," I said drily.

It would nevertheless have been a very good thing if I could have stayed there with my parents, and gone no further that day. I had gone far enough. Half-way round the world had I been and whatever strain there may be at times in the relationship between mother and son, there are times — and this was one of them — when we are a little boy again with his knee gashed and a little bandaging and cosseting will put us right.

My father talked about the war. "I can't understand what happened to the *Prince of Wales* and the *Repulse*, sunk like that. It seems as if the Japs are just making fools of us."

"People are only just beginning to wake up to what aeroplanes can do," I said feelingly, having been left myself without air-support.

But he was still puzzled. "And Singapore falling like that, without a shot." He belonged, in fact, to an era when such positions had been fought for more robustly. "At this rate it will take us another three years to win the war." As usual he was right.

McSporran returned in the van. It was already dark outside. My mother had been waiting for me to comment on the house she had converted. "Achamore was too big for wartime," she explained. "You father and I are very snug here."

I looked round — it was well enough. I had not been enthusiastic about her idea because it meant one of those inter-family leases which always turn out wrong — where the question of who pays for the improvements when the lease is given up, as it eventually would be after the war, was bound to cause hard feelings. But I said, "You have made something out of nothing as usual."

McSporran came up to the door, and my mother said, "Shall I help you down?"

I said, "No, McSporran will guide me."

"It seems a pity you could not have stayed longer," my mother pointed out. "But I suppose you want to hurry on to Thelma."

"I haven't seen the house yet."

"No of course not" — and my father added, "well, goodbye, old chap. Come and see us again tomorrow: and get a good sleep — you look tired." He waved from the doorstep as the van drove off, and my mother turned her stiff broad back abruptly, to hide her feelings.

Suddenly I felt very angry: one ought to be killed or cured. This dragging out of existence was not going to be a success. Perhaps I should have fallen overboard into those heavy grey seas in the Atlantic.

Kinnerarach was nothing but a long low outline in the dark. Inside, it was a flimsy house — the draughts whined under doors: the great hall, which I had last seen as disused stables, seemed a vast and bleak apartment. The window I had designed so carefully was uncurtained and presented a black and chilled rectangle of glass; broken up by unduly red cedarwood mullions.

"What do you think of it?" Thelma enquired.

"Very impressive."

A large Verdure Tapestry had been hung on the adjoining wall, at right angles to the window and covered most of the end wall. A flimsy gallery ran along the north wall, overhead, leading to what was supposed to be my dressing-room — over what had once been the cow byre. It was all a remarkable achievement in wartime: and I should have been overjoyed. But somehow nothing registered at all. It was as if somebody were going through all the motions of taking a photograph, but had forgotten to take the cap off the lens. The result was a blank negative.

The fireplace had been made with a single block of granite across a large opening. A fire burned in it, but did little to warm the room: and Thelma had dotted paraffin stoves about the floor, which was sparsely covered with rugs. It would no doubt be splendid in the summer, but as a winter home-coming for one from whom the last drop of blood seemed to have been drained, it was not a success.

"Mary McVean has come in to help with the dinner and bath the boys," Thelma explained. "I thought you would like to see them when they are in bed."

"Oughtn't I to see them now?"

"Of course, if you feel you can manage it."

Rodney was now six years old: and already out of the windswept bath, drying himself. His teeth were chattering.

"Hullo Daddy — did you kill a German?"

"No" — I laughed: "he nearly killed me."

"I would have shot him, if I had been there."

"I expect you would."

Peter, a baby when I left, was now two, and very amusing he appeared to be, in the bath, splashing away.

"I'm cold," he said. Mary McVean, the amiable Scotswoman from a neighbouring croft, was scrubbing his hands and face, till they were crimson. He was putting up a good-natured struggle. I could not recognise in him the infant I had last seen.

Dimly I felt this should be such a wonderful moment, such a happy home-coming: but it was all like a dream, through which the wind shrieked.

"Couldn't Arnott have made all this a bit more draught proof?" I suggested.

"Och," said Mary McVean, "it's evident ye hae no had much experience o' the Western Isles in winter" — she laughed. "There's nae draft in here."

The whole house seemed very dimly lit — here and there a naked bulb gleamed. But it was something to have got an electric light plant installed at all. What was wrong with me?

The dining-room ceiling was very low and once again I had a feeling of a dark room, pierced by a gleam of light, leaving cold dark corners.

My dressing-room when I got to it was very nearly freezing in spite of a paraffin stove.

CHAPTER 3

After our sunlit campaigns in the Levant, the home-coming was painful. Within two days of Christmas, the wounded were hounded into a hospital outside Liverpool, which had formerly been a Lunatic Asylum; the doors had been removed from their hinges; and I did not hesitate to use my influence as a Member of Parliament to get all the men medically boarded, in time for them to get home on Christmas Eve.

I forwarded a letter of introduction from Elphistone to the D.M.I. General Davidson, and he invited me to luncheon at his club; when I should come south. He was very interested in all I had to say about Intelligence in the Middle East. There was snow on the ground, and I still walked with the rubber tipped stick which Uncle Charles had helped me to choose in South Africa. Nearing the D.M.I.'s office, Davidson said to me without warning, "Gavarite-li po-Russki?" Somewhat startled I replied "Konyechno" and we went into his room. I went to see Margesson, now Minister of War and all he could say, when I described the scene at Palmyra was, "Bloody. Absolutely bloody." Could any description have been more literally accurate? He sat at his desk looking more than ever like a Red-Indian scalp hunter carved out of teak. And of Sidi Rezegh, he said to me, "We got a bloody nose." I learnt later that it was he who went along to the D.M.I., who was already well enough disposed, and asked if there were no suitable post for me in the M.I. Department. I was appointed G.S.O. III in the Middle East department, and given Palestine, Syria, Transjordan and Iraq to look after. On the opposite side of my desk, sat a 'J.C.A.' – or Junior Civil Assistant, Constantia Rumbold. At another desk James Pope Hennessy brooded over Persia and we were intelligently and congenially controlled by Larry Kirwan, who had served in peacetime in the museum at Cairo. We were a happy band and I learnt a lot more in a few weeks about how we conducted the war than in all the rest of it. During my brief time there, I evolved the

28

plan for establishing a local Palestine Regiment; and supported it subsequently in the House.

When I saw Beverly Baxter, he asked what I was doing. He was incredulous. "You are sure you mean the Middle East," he said, "not the Middle West? It sounds too like a square peg in a square hole to be right for the War Office." People drifted in to ask detailed questions about the route from Baghdad south of Lake Habbaniya. I gave them feeling answers; or about the effectiveness of the black basalt, boulder-strewn plain in Transjordan as a tank obstacle. I ventured an opinion. But suddenly into this congenial atmosphere came a telegram from Brendan Bracken, saying that Oliver Lyttelton, newly returned from the Middle East, where he had been Minister of State, to take over from Beaverbrook the inception of a Ministry of Production, wanted me to be his Parliamentary Private Secretary. It seemed to be an appropriate move in all the circumstances. I went along to see Davidson. "We shall be sorry to lose you," he said. "But I will not stand in your way."

Now why was Brendan so solicitous on my behalf? I did not know him and we must assume that 'the patronage Secretary's' intervention was not wholly altruistic. Perhaps he had listened to my speech in the House, on returning from the Middle East; when I cried cheerfully, "A roseate glow of self-complacency casts its softening influence over Westminster, Whitehall, Cairo, Suez and Singapore. What is the origin of this phenomenon, Mr. Speaker? It is the last bloody glimmer of the sunset of the old school tie." I could see Mr. Speaker trying to restrain his mirth at this subtle introduction of an unparliamentary adjective, and two Australian seamen in the gallery, put there by Alan Lennox-Boyd, who had hitherto regarded my speech as the product of a normal guards officer nearly fell over the rail into the Chamber as I went on, "Thank God my old school in New South Wales has not got a tie." Brendan possibly thought that this sort of thing should be brought under control. Or perhaps Oliver, who had a habit of sending for dark horses, asked him to sound me. I telephoned Brendan to know what it was all about and he said, "Oliver Lyttelton has a cold. But have a talk with him when he gets back after Easter"; and into Oliver's improvised office, in the improvised Ministry of Production on the corner of George Street and St. James's Park, I was accordingly ushered.

He looked what he was, an ex-Grenadier; burly and boyish, slightly freckled and he had a knack of putting one at ease instantly by leaning forwards, elbows on knees, and speaking ruminatively, as if one were already in his confidence.

"Why do you send for me?" I asked. "I don't know anything about nuts and bolts."

"I know all about them. But I have to make speeches, and they tell me you know all about the House. This is all beginning. All I have taken over from Beaverbrook is an armchair and a secretary. You will probably feel, at the end of the day, that we have been beating a very large lake with a very small paddle. But it ought to be fun and you will gain experience. And the idea is partly that you are one of our bright lads and will be given office yourself later on."

"I could only work with you," I pointed out, "if I was in your complete confidence. As you know I am in M.I.2 at the War Office now, so I know what is going on."

"I could not work in any other way," said Oliver quickly, but without, quite rightly, having the slightest intention of revealing any inner secrets from the War Cabinet.

"I have spoken to the D.M.I.," I said, "and he is willing to let me come to you. He made it clear that they would not have released me to anybody else; but they have a great regard for your work in the Middle East."

"Have they?" laughed Oliver. "That's news to me. But at least I did not try to trip them up. When I was sent out, the Generals eyed me a bit askance. But I told them I would not report on any of them behind their backs without their seeing what I sent home. After that it was a love feast."

I left Oliver, who told me to turn up after Easter; and in the private office, I had a word with an elegant youth, who was his assistant Private Secretary. This was Lord Moore,* and he had recently been retrieved by Brendan Bracken from some anti-aircraft battalion and after a spell on the *Financial Times*, was posted to Oliver. Garret Moore, lean dark and aesthetic, looked somewhat fragile for total war, even at the Ministry of Production; and being a friend of Oliver's, somewhat resented, I felt, the arrival of a parliamentary aide who would have the Minister's

*Later Earl of Drogheda

private ear. However, he said, "I heard you speaking in the House the other day. On the Middle East. It seemed to be very well received."

The Principal Secretary, Poynton, was a very different type; a career civil servant, very tough, taken over with the armchair from Beaverbrook. There was a touch of the Brigade Major and the Intelligence Officer in our relationship, all over again. But I was delighted with this unexpected new opening; and in truth, I had found the hours of work and the close confinement to an office, under artificial light in the War Office; more than my physical capacity could stand at once. I was actually to find the constant shuttling between the Ministry and the House even more wearing; but the variety was an easement. And I liked Oliver at once. His total absence of pomposity or side was engaging, and he brought to his task a fresh, but by no means open mind. He had many enemies in the established supply departments, who resented the Commons insistence on setting over them a super Minister. But Oliver smiled with no — concern.

"The ultimate test," he said softly, "is who gets carried off in the ambulance." And he did not look in the least like being carried off in an ambulance.

I may not have been able to obtain an audience with Dr. Benes at the Castle of Hdracin in 1929 but he was glad enough to see me in Eaton Place in June 1942. I found this gristly veteran, presiding over the exiled Czech government.

During my conversation with Benes I got him to explain three things; his standpoint at the Munich crisis; his opinion of the denouement of the war; and his ideas for a peace settlement of Europe in general and Czechoslovakia in particular.

"At the time of Munich," he said, "the Russians urged me 3 times to fight and said that they would stand by me. But I saw that France and England were not prepared to fight and I did not want to fight with only Russia. Germany would have defeated Russia and the French and British would have said 'this beast is going East.' Then later he would have turned on the West and it would have been the end of Western Europe. And therefore although I realised the terrible sacrifice for my country, although I knew that the war would come in 6 to 10 months, I preferred to make this agreement."

Throughout this diagnosis Benes referred to the incredible

blindness of people here and in France then.

When he came to England he said, "It was very difficult for me. Everyone was suspicious that we were the advance point of Bolshevism."

I said, "But surely you never had any difficulty with Eden and Churchill over that?"

He replied, "Oh no."

On the subject of the war itself, Benes startled me by saying that in 1940 France, (Daladier) wanted to form an alliance with Finland in her war against Russia and that this would have meant an end of the war between France and Germany who would also have turned against Russia.

Did he think the war with Germany would finish in 1942? No. But it could not go on beyond May of the next year.

Why not? Fuel?

"Fuel, transport, morale, everything will be gone by then."

He did not rule out the possibility of the war ending in 1942 if we could start a second front, and send over some more raids like the ones on Cologne and Essen.

Benes told me that he had received from Berlin detailed information by May 1st (1941) of the date of the German attack on Russia and the exact plan following 'the Grechischen Gegenstand'. He had given this information to our Government and Intelligence. This fitted in with the fact that I was handed this information at Habbaniya, in the Iraq campaign on May 18th, and it may well have been his information passed on. We knew nothing of the well-guarded secret of 'Enigma' in those days.

The Anglo-Russian pact was, he said, his great ambition, and would give to Europe during the period of chaos after the war, the 20 years of security necessary for readjustment. There was going to be appalling chaos in Europe after the war; and civil wars. At the end of the last war everybody was idealistic; "Now they are all realistic, too realistic, disillusioned." There would be too much hatred – of a kind which had not existed in Europe at the conclusion of the Great War. He instanced what the Germans were doing to Czechoslovakia; what the Magyars had done to the parts they had taken over; what the Poles and the Russians would feel. In such circumstances he thought it impossible to expect such nations to collaborate in a United States of Europe. He believed in the idea of a United States of Europe – it was on this point I was pressing him — and he believed that it would come but it would require twenty years to prepare for it.

On the subject of specific frontiers, he said "From a moral point of view it is essential that no country which has made the aggression shall be rewarded. Of course my people, they demand the whole of the pre-war Czechoslovakia. But we are in some ways to blame. For 300 years we have been a subject people. In the moment of liberation we perhaps perform excesses. But I would agree that if we get our frontiers back in principle, then I am prepared to consider certain readjustments, not only of population but of territory. Yes of territory."

He produced a little map from his pocket book, on which the Czech statistics of the Magyar, German and other minorities were shown. He said, after this war all minorities must be solved on a basis of exchange of populations. There would be too much bitterness for such peoples to live side by side.

He went to his desk, picked up a paper knife and pointed to a large wall map which showed the mountains:

"For every one German whom I am prepared to give up with land, two must go without land."

"Will that enable you to keep your mountain barrier?" I asked. "Yes."

"In the south there are 750,000 Magyars living with 400,000 Slovaks." (The figure of 1,300,000 Magyars given by Hungarians was, he said pure propaganda.) "There are also some Slovaks on the Hungarian side of the frontier. I am prepared to make readjustments of the frontier here and here — " (he indicated on his small map pockets densely populated by Magyars — 80% - 100%) " — but on condition that all Magyars leave. We do not want any minorities. We want only Czechs and Slovaks."

On the subject of post-war diplomacy he said that England would always be confronted by two evils — whether to give the Polish Corridor to Germany; whether to give East Prussia to Poland. And so on. His task would be to throw his weight into helping us make a right decision.

My position as P.P.S. to Oliver Lyttelton necessitated my spending a large part of the day at the Ministry of Production.

The Civil Service idea of keeping the Parliamentary Private Secretary in his place was to give him the dingiest office possible, with no carpet; everybody being graded in their eyes according to the salary he drew. Thus a Member of Parliament drawing £600 per annum, was a six-hundred-a-year-man. The fact that I was doing the job at the Ministry for nothing, led them at first to think that I should have no office. But when the other dollar-a-year-men moved in, expecting large desks and furry carpets, they realised the weakness of this logic. I tried to liven up my own office, with a couple of Old Masters, one of which was an attractive portrait of Princess Mary, the daughter of Charles I, at the age of 12, on the occasion of her betrothal to the Prince of Orange. She was wearing a gold brocade dress, which cheered up the sombre room. The Assistant Establishment Officer Crawley looked at it disapprovingly. It was not in keeping with the grade of dog kennel prescribed by him. He sat on my desk telephoning about some new arrival, 'a thousand-a-year-man' for whom carpets, big desks and all the rest of it must be provided at once.

When Oliver moved from his own rather poky office overlooking George Street, to a sumptuous apartment in the Regency style, decorated in robin's-egg blue, overlooking the park, I was shifted to an even dingier office on the floor below. Oliver took one look inside the door, and sniffed. "A bit reminiscent of the last act of the Constant Nymph." But he made no effort to have it changed.

I had the services of a Secretary from the typing pool, upstairs, a bright and efficient young thing, called Miss Kurland. Chegwidden, after I had limped out of hospital for the second time, so far unbent as to have me collected every morning from my house in one of the cars at the disposal of the higher civil servants. I used to arrive at five minutes to ten, and wait for Oliver in the Private Office, gossiping about the war, with Denis Rickett and Barbara Adam. She had come from the Awards and Decorations Department of the Admiralty. She thought Oliver one of the few people left in England with something of the grand manner. Oliver would arrive, with the chauffeur and the messenger overspilling the small office, shedding an enormous blue overcoat and his black 'Anthony Eden' hat and furled umbrella. He would be helped out of them by Eke, the faithful messenger, who carried on his chest some good First War ribbons. Then Oliver and I would go into his office and review the political aspects of his work for half an hour; unless there was a speech to prepare, in which case, Miss Bradshaw, his chief typist, a buoyant and efficient redhead, would be called in, and we would fling ideas about the room until something emerged.

34

Only on one occasion did I prepare a speech for Oliver which he delivered word or almost word for word. And that was when he had to speak at Aldershot and he simply had no time to work on a speech. He did not attach undue importance to this speech in his constituency, but because of a single phrase which he injected into it, the speech became sensational. After speaking on the stresses which we were surviving — the Battle of the Atlantic, where "the sea is shadowed by the shapes of submarines", I went on, for him to say, "If we can survive the next three months, we shall have got over the worst." This was in July 1942. Oliver liked the speech but said, "Let's point that up a bit. Let us make it the next eighty days." This was certainly more arresting. But it suggested that at the end of the specific period of 80 days, some miraculous salvation was in sight, unknown to others, but known to him. There were headlines — 'The Next 80 Days'; and even a cartoon of Lyttelton in a tin hat, crawling with John Bull in battledress through the barbed wire entanglement of the next 80 days in no man's land. What Oliver had in mind possibly, was the Alamein offensive, due in October, which was in fact a turning point. But when 79 days had elapsed the newspapers began ringing up; to know what was going to happen on the morrow in fulfilment of his prophecy. Personally, as his political advisor, I was in favour of any wide public interest in his utterances; and he was able to shake the eightieth day off his broad shoulders with a good-natured grimace. Not so easily did he shake off an impromptu interpolation to the assembled American correspondents at a luncheon of the American Chambers of Commerce. Suddenly laying down his notes and putting his hands on his hips, he said, "Of course America was never really neutral. She went on provoking Japan until Japan had to attack her at Pearl Harbor." When he saw the American reporters look up startled, with poised pens, he said, "I repeat. America was never really neutral."

I was sitting between Lord Riverdale, a shipping magnate, and Childes of our Supply Mission in Washington. They stiffened in their places like gaffed salmon. After the speech Oliver came round, quickly to my place, as usual to ask how I thought it had gone. "It was all right," I said, "except for the bit about America. Whatever persuaded you to say that?"

"Oh. That's ancient history. Everybody knows that."

"Well," I said, "it is the first time an English Minister in the

War Cabinet has said it."

When we arrived back at the Ministry in his car, he put a call through to the Public Relations Officer.

"Somerset thinks I have made a major international floater. What do you say?"

"With any luck," was the reply, "the speech about Britain's contribution to wartime inventions and production which was circulated to the American Press in advance will be printed in that form."

But by nightfall the wires were humming. Halifax in Washington was on the transatlantic telephone, asking what really had been said.

Next morning Oliver was a little subdued on arrival at the office.

"The flying bombs don't keep me awake," he said ruefully, "but this did. I have prepared a short apology for the House of Commons this afternoon. It is no use pretending that I was mis-reported." Just then the telephone rang. Dennis Rickett's brow furrowed thoughtfully as he answered it and he said to Oliver, "A summons from The Head. He wants to see you at once."

Driving over to the Commons which was meeting at Church House, on account of the flying bombs, he told me of his interview with The Head.

"What on earth did you want to say that for?" Winston had demanded.

"Because I was a bloody fool. That's all," replied Oliver. It was by far the best answer. And Winston after a growl or two read through his apology, and added a line of his own. I sat behind Oliver, as usual, when he rose, by leave of the House, to make a statement. It was a sincere apology; and took the wind right out of the sails of his critics. They liked the fact that he did not try to blame it on the reporting, as most Ministers do in such circumstances. And when he added that however unfortunately he had expressed himself, his words had been well-meant, he secured a cheer and closed the matter.

There was one other speech which had a sensational impact, for which I was partly to blame.

"I know where the blow will fall," he said before the landings in Sicily. I thought this a legitimate twist in the nerve war; giving the Germans, for a change something to think about. But Winston disapproved. "It sounds so boastful," he complained.

On the whole Oliver's speeches went over very well with the press and the public. But he still needed time to adjust himself to the unique atmosphere of the House of Commons where one must speak distinctly without tub-thumping; expertly without being boring; wittily without losing dignity; conversationally without being careless; wisely without being patronising; and good-naturedly without being weak. He accepted my verdict on his performances with alarming readiness; perhaps because he knew I would tell him the truth; and was not easily impressed. It is not easy to impress a Member who has listened to Lloyd George, Churchill, Maxton, and Cripps, who were each masters in their different ways. But Oliver was impressive, in spite of his inability to express himself, and the House treated him with respect. I was reminded of an anecdote about him in the First War. He had been running up a trench, tin-hatted and laden with hand grenades and so forth, when he encountered forty Germans running down the trench from the opposite direction. To his surprise they put up their hands and surrendered to a man. Oliver could never see why.

Oliver's only concession to the flying bombs, when they arrived, was to move his desk between the windows.

After the war both Eke and Miss Bradshaw (whose name changed by marriage, I could never remember) moved with Oliver to his office at Crown House in Aldwych when he became Chairman of the Associated Electrical Industries; and it was refreshing, visiting him there, for luncheon with his fellow directors in a suite on the top floor, to find these old friends from the Ministry of Production days.

Oliver was a great bridge-player, and found some relaxation over the game in the evenings at the Turf Club. He played seriously and well.

Gomer Kemsley, and his exotic wife Edith from Mauritius, with her charming French accent, did a certain amount of entertaining at weekends; and invited my wife and myself when *The Golden Carpet* was coming out. Oliver was there also and he and Kemsley formed the core of the bridge table. Bill Mabane, the under Minister for Food, another guest, seemed to have attached himself firmly to the Kemsleys and acquired a permanent position on the Kemsley Press when his ministerial days were over. The very Sunday I was staying with the Kemsleys, an ex-bombardier happened to write with unconscious tact to one of their newspapers, in which *The Golden Carpet* was being serialised, to say that he had often wondered what had happened to me, as he was wounded in the ambulance with me later. I had often wondered what had happened to him also, and to the other man shot inside the ambulance when it was torn apart round us by machine-gun bullets.

I received a letter from a society calling itself The Society for the Friends of the Genius of France. Would I join this society? I replied:

'Sir, having been shot twice by the French, I do not think I am yet quite ripe to join your society. But I should not like you to think that I am fundamentally prejudiced.
Yours, etc.'

Oliver Lyttelton asked me what I thought of one of the junior Members of the Government.

"Baldwin Vintage, 1924," I suggested.

"Rather corked," added Oliver, looking out of the car window as it glided from the gates of New Palace Yard.

He told me how he had entered politics.

Oliver was unlucky in these matters, for later in the war he was confidently tipped for the Chancellorship of the Exchequer when Sir Kingsley Wood died. Eden meeting him in the corridor said, "The Head wants to see you."

"For a caning?" Oliver asked.

"No," Eden replied, "the fifth form essay prize." But, the prize eluded his grasp, as it was to do again in 1951, when the Conservatives returned to power; and on this earlier occasion it went to Sir John Anderson.

Oliver could have had the vice-royalty of India, half-way through the war, and I urged him to take it. But he was reluctant to leave all his friends in London. "I am a gregarious animal," he said. The post went to Lord Wavell. If Oliver had accepted, he would probably still have been in Delhi when the Labour Government came to power; and it is difficult to see him handing over the Raj with the same alacrity that Lord Mountbatten did. He could probably have been another Lord Lloyd and returned home in disagreement with the government. Yet it would certainly be rash to judge this issue yet. It was no small achievement to have retained Pakistan within the Commonwealth for a time. And if the Indians in India are being more Irish than the Irish, their relations with Great Britain offer some scope for satisfaction. I certainly doubt whether any constitutional settlement agreed to by Lyttelton would have sanctioned the obliteration of the princely states and their treaties with the Crown. In fact there would have been an entirely different approach to Dominion Status; but possibly very real trouble as well. The fact that we are all playing cricket together in closely watched Test Matches, is probably the most significant commentary on the British Raj, since the dust of Partition and Transfer has settled down.

Life now began to resume something of its normal pattern for us. As P.P.S. to Oliver Lyttelton, I was expected to introduce him, over the port, to some of our colleagues in the House, whom it was desirable to charm. Very good he was at it. He belonged to an old family, which was strange in one who moved so rapidly with the times. He knew or conveyed the impression of knowing everything about everything. If it was a cursory glance at the Isphahan rug brought home from Cairo, he would say, "Have you seen Chester Beatty's ones?" On pictures he was very nearly infallible. When I stayed with him, on his rounds of factories, at the most suitable house in the neighbourhood — at Blagden in Northumberland with the Ridleys, at Himley near Birmingham with his old friend Eric Dudley; or at Hagley with his cousin Cobham; Oliver would go like a homing pigeon towards the pictures. "I like your Zoffany." In conference with business men he was equally at home; and never better than when talking after dinner behind closed doors with no reporters present. How could a body of Civil Engineers resist a Minister who told them the story of a man in correspondence with a rival? "Sir, I have your letter of yesterday's date. Its tone is such that I have no option but to put it in the hands of my solicitor." And the reply, "Sir, I have your letter of even date. You may put my letter in the hands of your solicitor or into such other part of his anatomy as your ingenuity or his complacency may suggest."

My first task was to advise him of an address to an all-party meeting of the House in the big Committee Room 14 upstairs. He had just returned from the Middle East, where our troops were being soundly beaten by Rommel. He had visited the Western Desert. But he proposed to talk of his work as Minister of State, in organising the civil side of that theatre of operations. "That is not what they want from you," I assured him. "What they expect to hear from you is what you think of Rommel. You are a soldier. You have studied the ground. You do not think Rommel is a great General. They fear he may be. You do not think he can defeat us in the Desert. They fear he may. Tell them what you think."

Sir George Schuster, father of my friend Dick, killed near me in the Desert, happened to come to the office and Oliver said, "Somerset here thinks I have got it all wrong. He wants me to talk about Rommel. Do you agree?"

"Certainly," said Sir George.

Oliver spoke accordingly, with tremendous effect. The Members buzzed out speaking of him as a possible Prime Minister. But unfortunately it was also on my advice that he put his stock down again. For, dining at 92, Eaton Place, Sir George Schuster, Jay Lewellyn (then Minister of Aircraft Production and not perhaps the best person to advise the Minister of Production when to make a speech) and I, all urged him to open the impending debate on the Fall of Tobruk, and meet the critics of our undergunned tanks, in debate. But Winston, who was to wind up the debate, reserved the strategic issues for his own inimitable presentation, and left Oliver to open the batting exclusively on the very sticky wicket of the 2-pounder gun. No sooner had Oliver got into his stride; and he was not too self-confident on the floor of the House yet; than Dick Stokes, himself an old soldier as well as an armament manufacturer, was on his feet heckling him with deadly fire. There was in fact no adequate answer to the charge that our men had been slaughtered with inadequate weapons in their hands; and none knew this better than Oliver — but it was not his fault. It was part of the long history of pre-war neglect — and had he been entitled to rise above the level of this debate and carry the House into the future, where he did in fact send our troops in Sherman tanks armed with the lethal 17-pounder gun, into the Normandy battles and complete victory, there is no doubt that he would have established himself next to Churchill in the esteem of the House. But Oliver was new to the House and lacked the soul-grinding apprenticeship of those who have sat on back benches, waiting to deliver polished speeches which are not delivered in the end at all. And at first, I warned him, he had a psychological resistance to heckling. "You are like an Alsatian wolfhound in an assembly of cats. Your hackles rise at once. Not until you are prepared to play kitten with them and chase their particular ball of string too, can you hope to lead them."

I thought of trying to speak later in the debate myself. The Government's critics were confined to a small group of discontented politicians, about 30 in number, whose attitude to the conduct of affairs would have been appreciably altered if they had been absorbed into the administration.

"I am going to call them the hard core of the unemployed," I told Oliver.

He liked that. "It would be more accurate to describe them as the hard core of the unemployment problem," he suggested.

After the debate, as we were moving down the green coconut matting, between the front benches below the gangway in the House of Lords Chamber, towards the voting lobbies, the Prime Minister turned to me and said, "You did not speak after all?"

"No. I did not try. I thought it a bit difficult as Oliver's P.P.S."

"I heard about your *mot*," he smiled.

Evidently Oliver had passed it on with relish.

I like to think that my work with him was as helpful to him as it was instructive to me. In the end I asked to be released, six months from the impending election, to attend to my own constituency, instead of looking after his, and devoting myself exclusively to his speech-making and Ministry affairs. He tried very hard to dissuade me, and when I persisted, suggested after a talk with Brendan Bracken, that I should do a spell in the Whips Office.

"It isn't much to start with. But it means a seat on the Front Bench, and the fact is you would do it frightfully well."

"No," I replied. "After two years in purdah, you want me to take the veil." And laughing, we left it at that.

The fact of the matter was that I found the strain of keeping up with him, for all his consideration, difficult. For during this period I had two operations on my leg wound. And I felt keenly the charade of being kept in his confidence, while the real secret conduct of the war had to be kept from me. I had no idea for instance when D-Day was to take place, nor would it have been desirable for anyone to know, unnecessarily.

My early troubles with the Civil Service, had smoothed out. Oliver had quickly dispensed with both Poynton and Moore and replaced them by Dennis Rickett, a congenial Fellow of All Souls, and Barbara Adam, the daughter of Sir Ronald Adam, in the private office. I never had a cross word with them. Soon after my appointment the question arose of appointing a Parliamentary Secretary to the new Ministry. Some thought I would be given this job. But in a Coalition Government the Socialist element soon made it clear that if the Minister was a Tory the junior Minister should be a Socialist. I was consulted as to the best choice and of those mentioned liked best the name of Garro-Jones, who had served with distinction in the Air Force in World War I, and had a flexible mind. Later he was made Lord Trefgarne and became head of the Colonial Development Corporation. I got on very well with him from the first. But there was Chegwidden, one of the first of the higher Civil Servants. And the incident of the Colourdex.

Alfred Edwards came to me as soon as Oliver was appointed and said the Minister ought to have an up-to-date method of keeping statistics. The Colourdex system would enable him to see the whole field of armament progress at a glance. I had a shrewd suspicion, from what Alfred Edwards said, that the Colourdex was going to be a substantial erection, about seven feet high and five feet wide; and this suspicion was confirmed when I telephoned the company and learnt that it cost about £200. But I did not want to cloud the issue and rang up the stationery department which authorised the issue of office equipment and told them that Mr. Lyttelton wanted a Colourdex and that I would arrange for delivery of this, if they would issue the necessary authorisation; which they did. They imagined, possibly something in the nature of a wall chart in the room adjoining Oliver's office. I realised that if workmen arrived and much hammering went on there would be doubts; and there would be no Colourdex; and Alfred Edwards would put it about the House that the new Minister was old-fashioned and incapable of moving with the times. So I told the company that they must come with their machine, and their steel blind, and their cupboards and their workmen during the luncheon hour, when the Civil Servants would be out to a meal. So, as soon as Chegwidden's large limousine had disappeared in a cloud of exhaust smoke, and the humblest official had mooched off; I signalled the Colourdex gang, and they marched through the dim portals with their drills and their bradawls; their tubular scaffolding and their hack-saws; their multicoloured labels and aluminium pegs; their paint pots and their brushes; their putty; and their bits and pieces. All that they needed I told them to bring; and I had given them two hours to finish the job. No burglars cracking a safe worked with greater stealth or despatch. For two hours there was the muffled sound of sawn metal and hammering. When I came back from luncheon the thing was there immovable as the Rock of Gibraltar; and it was more conspicuous than a Colourdex in any ordinary office, for the absolute secrecy of its records required a steel roll-shutter with padlock at the foot; and all this involved casing the contraption in; instead of merely sheltering it behind some velvet curtain. The machine dazzled like a Christmas tree. Upon a thousand branches hung gaudy labels, red or green, showing the numbers of items of equipment of any kind in production; green ahead of schedule; red behind. The Minister had only to stare upon this forest of colour and see whether the Churchill tanks were bobbing off the lines nicely; or whether a new aircraft-carrier had been completed.

"Put it on the wall next door," Oliver had said, and there it was. The Civil Servants were aghast. The mere fact that during luncheon an erection which the Ministry of Works would have taken eleven weeks to install had been plugged to the wall, immovably, housed in steel, and painted over all — "Do not approach too close Chegwidden," I cried, "the paint is still wet" — this violated all their sacred instincts of Civil Service procedure.

And there was more to it than that. The Ministry's entire system of statistics would have to be revolutionised to feed the Moloch and keep it up to date. The boyish streak in Oliver came to my rescue. "Well, there it is," he told the crestfallen officials, laughing. "We shall have to use it now." Alfred Edwards was of course delighted; and went up and down the corridors of the House saying that the Minister of Production was a live wire. Promptly upon his heels came to me some Members interested in getting a synthetic rubber plant built; all they wanted was the Minister's authorisation for a certain company to get the necessary allocation of steel and materials. They were a forceful group of Members, who were capable, if Oliver did not approve of the manufacture of synthetic rubber in England, of asking him a barrage of questions on such remote but inconvenient subjects as tanks in Libya. I warned Oliver that he must take the House of Commons as he found it; and believing also that it would be a good thing for us to make our own synthetic rubber, instead of letting the Americans do it, I put in a memo, advising him to sanction the project. The Civil Servants reacted smartly. They did not greatly admire the group supporting the project; and probably wondered why I urged it on the Minister. The idea that I was keen to win the Minister all the support in the House he could get, probably did not occur to them. They asked to see the formula for making the synthetic rubber, which was said to be so much cheaper than the raw product. But the company, through their representatives in the House, explained to me patiently, in the smoking room, as one might explain the workings of some dangerous machine to a child, that all their rivals in I.C.I. had been recruited into the Ministry of Supply — the Ministry of Supply say aye — and that if they divulged the formula to the Ministry of Production, this would be food and wine to their rivals. These were deep and shark-infested waters, to me. But I explained that the Minister's technical advisers must be satisfied with something, so they produced long-winded technical documents. And these were examined by C. R. Morris, who was our chemical expert, and had fortunately been one of my tutors at Balliol, and could therefore, possibly, reassure Chegwidden that, (a) I was not a Jew and (b) not at all likely to be in the pay of Jews. And that my urgency must be set down to the keenness of a P.P.S. and the impatience with Whitehall which was characteristic of young men who had been obliged to move about very swiftly on the battlefield. But they stuck on the need to see the formula and so for the present, there was no synthetic rubber plant; and Oliver became mysteriously unpopular at question time, when a number of Conservative Members asked him awkward questions about obscure matters. It was all this sort of thing that got the Tory Party so disliked towards the end of the war; and thrown out with such a purifying jerk in 1945. The trouble arose from the fact that all private firms were now doing work of national importance, although quite capable of keeping an eye on their competitive position in the post-war world; but under the cover of the national need their directors in the House of Commons had no hesitation in championing their needs, without even bothering, as in peacetime, to declare their interest. The most respectable and distinguished members would urge the need for adding a couple of bays to their factories for the production of some warlike equipment.

And upon these scenes of industry came Mr. Kendall and the

Hispano-Suiza automatic gun. This man, with his silk shirts and blue bow ties, his good, dark looks, and compelling eye, would have appeared quite at home in any Chicago gang. He had got himself elected as Independent Member for Grantham where his works were situated; and he was thought by our experts to be extremely capable in the matter of producing automatic guns. The trouble started when he refused to disclose his accounts to the Income Tax Authorities; and there was an inquiry into his affairs by the Public Accounts Committee. He managed to convince them that his gross profit for the year amounted to about £189.14.2. They went away scratching their heads; and Mr. Kendall went on escorting the more beautiful cousins of Dukes into the Ladies Gallery to hear him speak. Gradually Oliver began to make changes in the Civil Service. Upon Chegwidden − 'The White Rabbit' − was superimposed a permanent under secretary, Sir Henry Self. And he in turn was replaced by a man much more congenial to Oliver − John Henry Wood, who limped painfully from the effects of wounds in the First World War. Norman Kipping was brought in from the business world to plan production; he later became chairman of the F.B.I. Sir Thomas Barlow of the Metal Box Company was given a post; and Ivan Spens, an old business friend of Oliver's, was also given an advisory role. All these powerful industrialists and business men worked without salary − they were what the Americans call dollar-a-year men − and they tactfully bought the expensive limited editions of my books, as they came out. They were certainly very much easier to get on with than the regular Civil Servants. But these, in the person of John Henry Wood, the Permanent Under-Secretary and Dennis Rickett the Principal Private Secretary, proved as congenial and efficient as any of the people nurtured in private enterprise and brought in for the duration. It became a happy family.

There was much visiting to do in the Norfolk constituency, after so long an absence in the Middle East; and with Necton, our own house still in the army hands, we were welcomed to make our headquarter at Narford. Carlo Fountaine, who had volunteered at once on the outbreak of war for service at sea, had been strenuously commodoring convoys across the Atlantic, in all weathers, and in the path of many a U-boat. But the strain had told on him, and he had not seen eye to eye with the Lords of the Admiralty on the methods of signalling in convoys north of

Ireland. So he was now back at Narford, dozing by the fire in the khaki uniform of a Major in the Home Guard. His inventive mind turned upon the equipment for the Home Guard.

"Why no three-inch mortars?" he asked.

I explained that there was said to be a bottle-neck in the manufacture of the dial sights.

"Dial sights!" ejaculated Carlo. "I'll give 'em dial sights. Send me one of the things to experiment with and I'll soon eliminate the dial sight – and guarantee to fire it just as accurately."

I explained to Oliver Lyttelton that we had in Norfolk a remarkable man, who had been on the Ordnance Committee of the Admiralty and now wanted to modify the three-inch mortar, so that it could be mass produced for the Home Guard. "He wants a specimen to work on."

Oliver who had a flexible mind said, "All right. You write out a chit and I will sign it."

'Deliver to Vice-Admiral C. A. Fountaine, C.B. at Narford Hall, King's Lynn, Norfolk, one three-inch mortar complete with dial sight, and ammunition.'

In no time all this metallic junk piled up in the porch at Narford, and Carlo brooded over it with the help of a small engineer from Lynn.

He stared incredulously at the bi-pod. "Whatever do they want to lug this weighty contraption about for in the army?"

I told him, having borne the burden and heat of it at Bir Salim for three weeks, that they did not want to lug it about in the army.

Accordingly he eliminated the bi-pod, and slung the barrel from an overhead gallows, welded to the ends of the base-plate. On top of the gallows he placed a large round compass card, about 8 inches in diameter, marked in 360 degrees. The barrel was marked boldly in yards; 220 yards, 200 yards, 600 yards, etc. with a big pointer which could be slid easily, by elevating or depressing the barrel, to the required range. This was controlled by a cord, quickly attached to a cleat on one side of the gallows. Another cord swung the barrel according to the pointer on the compass above; and could be attached to the cleat with equal deftness. This was the Fountaine mortar and if the engineer in Lynn had put it all together a little more securely, it might well have gone into mass production. Carlo demonstrated it to me on the lawn in front of the front door at Narford.

"Too easy. Right four degrees," (a tug on the port string, and the compass pointer swings 4 degrees, till Carlo fastens the cord).

"Up 400," (a tug on the other string till the pointer has shot up four marks on the barrel. A twirl on the starboard cleat).

"Fire."

Now this was the operative part of the test.

"You're the last from school. You know the drill," Carlo said.

So we aimed the mortar up a wide grass ride opposite the front door, which was crossed, unfortunately, a hundred yards away by the side road from West Acre to Narborough. "Don't worry about that," Carlo said, "very little traffic passes along it anyway. And the odds against hitting the baker's van are hundreds to one."

"This is heavy ammunition," I pointed out, balancing a three-inch mortar bomb, capable of destroying about six Germans, in my hands; and eyeing the flimsy erection on the base-plate somewhat uneasily.

"Of course," Carlo pointed out, "this is only a mock-up mounting. If it works, we can have a more solid job done for general purposes."

"Here goes," I said. "Left two degrees, up three hundred (we must clear the passing traffic)." Carlo was in a flurry of ropes. "Fire." And, kneeling with some difficulty in the approved manner, I dropped the hideous projectile down the barrel, to be fired on the striking pin at the bottom.

There was a deafening explosion as the projectile went off and the machine broke up all at once. I found myself gazing, dazed, down the mouth of the smoking barrel, which had lurched drunkenly round my way.

"Don't worry," cried Carlo. "The projectile had gone long before the barrel hit you in the eye. This is poor workmanship." He stooped to examine the broken welding, where the gallows had been jerked off the base-plate.

And thereafter there was a general inclination to let the Fountaine mortar rest for a bit. It remained in the high arched porch, with its boxes of unused ammunition. But the idea was possibly sound, and in some future war, perhaps the Home Guard will be liberally supplied with Carlo's version of the three-inch mortar, mass-produced without a dial sight.

Carlo, for all his bluff and breezy countenance, read sensitively the changed lineaments of my own face. And when some Australian airmen, from the neighbouring aerodrome at Marham, came, as so many of them did, to dine at Narford, he introduced me to them. "Here is a man who has been through hell."

There was one Australian airman, at whose ribbons I stared with awe. There were only three but they were the V.C., the D.S.O., and the D.F.C. I was not in uniform and my only decorations were hidden deep, upon my skin. He had a poor opinion of the British Army.

"It is yellow," he said.

"What about Alamein?" I ventured; for this was a recent achievement.

"Alamein? A skirmish."

Carlo was deeply pained by this exchange; but was too courteous a host to a Commonwealth guest to do more than hurry the party in to dinner.

Later in the year, barbed wire began to encircle Narford and weird rumblings could be heard from the deep reaches of the lake screened by its trees. There were sounds as of primeval monsters wallowing. And a Major Bain, dark and brawny, appeared with his officers, around the Georgian mahogany table, drinking Carlo's port with approving sounds. A secret weapon was being tried out. It was the amphibious tank, with its apron, which swam, on the whole successfully, to the Normandy beaches.

I could not spend much time at Narford, except during periods of convalescence, because the work of the Ministry of Production seemed to me to have a very high priority over the task, on which my Socialist opponent remained for ever bent, of nursing the constituency in wartime.

With Oliver, Norman Kipping, and Dennis Rickett, I flew to Northern Ireland, on a visit to factories there. We toured the yards of Harland Wolf, and inspected other aspects of the Irish war production. We were entertained by the Prime Minister, Sir Basil Brooke; and had some difficulty in returning, for all the aerodromes in Britain were fog bound; until some clearance was reported at Prestwick, and we landed there. It was a congenial party. Oliver buoyant throughout. Kipping tall, smooth and imperturbable as if the planning of war production was an easy matter. Dennis Rickett, cultured to the fingertips, with his fellowship of All Souls. And myself. God knows what they made of me. In the car driving from Prestwick to Glasgow, the talk turned on the more unusual aspects of feminine charm. And I proffered my eye-witness account of Hedy Lamarr's violet eyes, in Vienna, as a feature unique in my experience. Oliver snorted good-humouredly, and said, not to be taken too seriously: "Why? I knew three women at one time in Paris, with violet eyes."

Over a very good dinner and liqueurs at the Malmaison Restaurant in Glasgow, we discussed the characters of the War Cabinet in terms of vintages.

Winston — Kipping insisted that he was Old Burgundy. (I should have thought Napoleon Brandy). And after some discussion we agreed roughly on the rest:

Attlee	— Quinine tonic
Sir John Anderson	— Vintage Port
Bevin	— Porter
Herbert Morrison	— Port and Lemon

Eden — (Oliver was emphatic about this) Château d'Yquem. Of present company we said nothing, but Oliver would I think, in his absence have gone down as Whisky and Soda. Or perhaps just Whisky.

We returned to London in a jocund mood.

I was not so fortunate when I flew with Oliver and Jay Lewellyn, the Minister of Aircraft Production, round England on a tour of aircraft factories. It was a bumpy day, of cloud and rain; and I had gastric flu, which prostrated me with sickness in the aircraft, until I was a vacuum to the elements and prayed for death. I had not got a good stomach for the air at that time, and after taking off at Hendon and flying for three-quarters of an hour, it exhausted my limited endurance to find that we had been circling round the same aerodrome all the time, as one leg of our Proctor would not retract. So I was quickly incapacitated when the real journey began to Babington in Gloucestershire; and by the time we reached the Rolls Royce works at Hucknall, somewhere in the North, I was almost a stretcher case, and was sent home by train.

"If you ever give any trouble," laughed Oliver, "I know how to deal with you. I shall take you up in an aeroplane."

I have not since been as seedy a traveller as this on my flights across the world, although I found bumping high over the air pockets of India in hot weather almost as bad as this rainstorm in England.

Oliver from time to time gave me tasks which tested my capacity for dealing with other departments. There was a certain secret weapon which I found languishing and which seemed to have been discouraged, unaccountably by the War Office. My attempts to hot them up almost led to inter-departmental warfare — I had much to learn about the technique of the slow approach and the blessed word 'consultation' at all levels — I was impatient; and it seemed to me that Hitler would not delay his own preparations while we stood upon ceremony. The V.C.I.G.S., General Weeks, himself an engineer, came to see Oliver and gave cogent reasons for the obstruction. He spoke, in front of me, of other and even more promising weapons of the same kind. And I was satisfied. Indeed I must say that my experience of the War Office both from inside and from outside, viewed thus at close range, has left me with a healthy respect for that much abused institution which has won two wars. The joke, current during the war, about the man going down Whitehall who asked someone, "Which side is the War Office on?" and received the reply, "Ours, I hope," was not really called for. I have not been able to elaborate upon the secret weapons Weeks was talking about because at the time of writing, 1952, they were still, surprisingly enough, a secret. But Oliver was not enthusiastic about P.P.S.'s knowing too much. He feared that the knowledge would be pumped out of them by Members of Parliament in the smoking room. That is why he had the Colourdex locked up, like a phosphorescent skeleton, in the cupboard. "It is not the fifth column I am frightened of," he said, "it is the sixth."

"Which is the sixth?" I asked.

"The House of Commons." But it was not said unkindly; and no one would have suggested that visiting Members of Parliament, and a substantial stream came to see the Minister on my recommendation, should also have been able to study the secrets of our production.

The episode of the Colourdex settled any lingering question as to who was to be the new under Minister.

"You certainly do not do anything to help yourself," said Oliver, ruefully nodding in the direction of Chegwidden's office. And I was able to get away in August (1942) to Gigha, and write my account of the Iraq Campaign.

This was a moment, in the House, of supreme goodwill towards me, not since paralleled in my experience. Maurice Webb, who

50

borrowed a copy of my war book, *The Golden Carpet*, said quite simply, "If I had written that one book, I should die content."

Even Eden, who as the second member of the Tory triumvirate in the War Cabinet could scarcely view Lyttelton's P.P.S. with whole-hearted approval, caught me by the arm when he saw me slip in the Central Lobby and said, "Having got you back at last, we don't want to lose you now." And he went on to say with what excitement in the War Room they had watched the flags, marking the progress of our column move out across the desert, pause before Ramadi, creep round Lake Habbaniya, and reach Baghdad.

There were august recipients. Princess Elizabeth* accepted a copy on coming of age.

Then there was Churchill, to whom, like Oliver, I gave one of the special thirty copies, bound in full green morocco. The Commons were sitting, since their own Chamber was blitzed, in the House of Lords, and approaching it one day from the Central Lobby, I passed Winston on his way out. I nodded deferentially in passing, wondering whether he had in fact seen the copy at all. He passed on, deep in thought. As I neared the swinging glass doors which gave access to the Peers Lobby, I saw Harvie Watt, Winston's jolly red-headed P.P.S. ahead of me, waving in a most peculiar fashion. He seemed to be gesturing at something behind my back, and turning slowly round I beheld — astonishing sight — the Prime Minister sprinting (there is no other word for it) the full length of the lobby towards me. He caught up with me, just as I turned and reversed direction quickly to accompany him back towards the Central Lobby.

"I got your book," he said. "What fun you must have had."

There was a gleam in his eye, which seemed to take his mind back from his great preoccupations to Omdurman, and the charge against the fuzzy-wuzzies, when he shouted to the N.C.O. beside him as he drew rein, "I hope you enjoyed that."

No wonder Leo Amery said that Winston's genius was primarily a genius for leadership. This was in 1943 and it is possibly the last time I or anyone else was to see Winston actually running.

I quoted in the introduction to *The Silver Crescent*, the speech made by Winston on the remarkable and unexpectedly quick

*Subsequently Queen Elizabeth II

transformation in our position in the Middle East caused by the Iraq and Syrian campaigns; and went on, with his permission, to record my first meeting with him on my return. Seeing me with a rubber-tipped stick in the smoking room he said, "Have you had an accident?"

I replied, "Yes, in a way. I was wounded." His eye lit up at once.

"Where was that?"

"Palmyra."

"Ah," he said, "that splendid affair amid the noble ruins."

It was this awareness of the drama of events and his quick solicitude for those who had participated in spirited affairs, that gave to his war leadership that phosphorescence which had not been known since the Premiership of Chatham; and further back the sovereignty of Queen Elizabeth. I did not see enough of him, amid his high preoccupations in the war, to be able to attempt a close-up portrait of him at this period. It was not until the Parliament of 1950, and after, that I had any dealings with him direct and his conversations at that time, which I have recorded, come later in this book. But I found that dealing with Mr. Churchill was rather like coming to terms with a mountain. Its size and might are often clear and recognisable at a distance, but as you approach it seems wrapped in mists. Then suddenly the fog clears, and you are in an arresting and sparkling landscape. Many Members of Parliament who have engaged him in conversation in the smoking room have heard his thoughts, like the gushing of a torrent, near at hand, but hidden from view. But awaken his personal interest; and suddenly all is changed. There is the brisk exchange of detailed information; the probing for more information, the winning smile; the rare favour of private consultation, enhanced by rolling, unforgettable phrases edged with the waved cigar; a startling flow of letters personally signed; and even telegrams. The mild deafness which is such a convenient sound barrier to boredom among men of his age, is abruptly put aside. But this sketchy outline can only be filled out in the chapter dealing with a later period. There is a design in these things; not accidental.

From time to time during the war he asked how my ankle was getting on. I told him, "Like the Churchill tank; effective enough but its radius of action is limited."

The War Cabinet offices were in the same building as the

Ministry of Production on the corner of St. James's Park and George Street. One day, in cold weather, as Oliver and I were descending to the entrance, which was baffled by concrete against the blast of bombs, Oliver nodded ahead and said, "There he is;" and silhouetted against the baffled light, loomed the broad, heavy, top-coated figure of the Prime Minister with a white silk scarf about his throat; somehow, in the cramped space of the entrance to the War Cabinet building, an overpowering figure, waiting for his car to take him to the House of Commons. And I was reminded, by Oliver's brief reference to him, of the way the French spoke simply of Napoleon as The Man.

Sometimes I used to ascend in the lift with Lord Bruce of Melbourne, the former Australian Prime Minister whose eloquence at the opening of Parliament in Canberra had first interested me in the political life. I told him this and he smiled. "Don't try to blame it on to me."

Oliver was a congenial person to work for, not only because he treated me thus publicly, as if I were a younger brother of whom he had reason to be rather proud at that moment, but because he had himself been gassed and wounded in seventeen places during the Battle of the Somme, and knew how little could be expected of me. He nursed me along like a brother – and kept my job open for weeks at a time when I had to go into hospital or retire to the Western Isles in convalescence. Indeed he saved me from a dire experiment which a Canadian Army doctor was trying on me at the Millbank Hospital. For, one day I tottered into Oliver's office, quite done in.

"Someone is playing you up at that hospital," he observed shrewdly. "You had better go and see my friend Rowley-Bristow."

Bristow was head of orthopaedics to the Army, but also practiced in Harley Street, where I found him wearing what appeared to be, and in practice was, a butcher's apron. When I told him what was happening he snorted, "That man is a quack. I will soon stop that."

I had in any case only one more appointment fixed to see this particular quack but he telephoned to say he had to go to the War Office as one of his army patients had complained to his Member of Parliament about the treatment. I very nearly said, "That's two Members of Parliament you will have after you." But I refrained and never saw him again. He was shipped back to

Canada. Yet his treatment was well meant; and not, I am sure, sadistic. I was merely, like the man who complained to his Member of Parliament, an unfortunate guinea pig. It is true that very little was known about nerve surgery at this time. One man, later on, at the Radcliffe Hospital at Oxford, recommended beating the end of the severed nerve with a hammer for 20 minutes every day, and strapping a golf-ball on to it; but he was suppressed by Girdlestone. The difficulty lies in preventing the nerves from growing again, in awkward filaments. Cutting is no good. They grow again like vegetables, and if they cannot be sutured − joined up again − the only way to discourage them seems to be to beat them, painfully at first, into insensibility. But this Canadian M.O. had a bright idea − to explode the end of the nerve. For this purpose he laid me upon a couch, and feeling for the tender spot, which when pressed with a thumb, could make me leap four inches, from the horizontal lying position, (surely an Olympic record?) he then began to prod about with the point of a hypodermic needle, asking me clinically to let him know when it was exactly on the end of the severed nerve; and having found it, drove the needle, searing through I cannot describe what tortures, into the grey filament of nerve itself. Then he began to inject some novocaine which would in a few minutes numb the nerve.

"How often do you have to repeat this process?" I asked him.

"I don't know," he replied. "I am not God."

I have described something of this episode in a novel called *The Dome of the Rock*, where I placed it in Abyssinia and made the sufferer, Nigel Carew, appear as the victim of scientific torture by an Italian Fascist Medical Officer, in an attempt to extract information from him. In this setting with all the elements of melodrama it is no doubt a touching scene. Yet is torture any less formidable when it is imposed, under the inescapable shield of Army discipline, on the Home Front? From the victim's point of view, it makes little difference, and pride and discipline may be as effective bars as any prison of the Ogpu or the Gestapo. At least an experience of this kind, cannot have a balancing effect on any legislator.

Rowley-Bristow was in favour of leaving the ankle alone for a time − but it would not leave me alone; and Oliver suggested a visit to another friend of his called Girdlestone; perhaps one of the greatest of orthopaedic surgeons. He had built up the Wingfield-

Morris Orthopaedic Hospital, at Oxford, with Nuffield's help; and he now ruled there as a very benevolent despot. He was square headed, grey haired, and with pale eyes that went through you like X-rays, seeming to ignore the flesh and see the bone. I visited him in his library, in a little red house just opposite the hospital at Headington. While waiting for him I noticed with pleasure his collection of books, and his love of W. H. Hudson's in particular — my favourite author, then — *The Purple Land, El Ombu, Green Mansions.* The reader of these books must, I felt sure, be a congenial spirit. And when he appeared, brisk and smiling, with a touch at once firm but tender upon that tormented nerve, he stood back against the fireplace, and putting his hand up to his forehead in thought, and shutting his eyes, said decisively: "You have a neuroma forming on the end of that severed nerve. That is why it has been getting worse instead of better all the time."

"What will you do for it?"

"I shall cut it off and bury the severed end in muscle."

I could almost have wept with relief. Plans were set in train for me to enter the hospital, by arrangement with the War Office as soon as possible.

I had one public engagement to fulfil before going in to hospital.

I had submitted, on behalf of the S.W. Norfolk Conservative Association, two resolutions to the Annual Conservative Conference, to be held in London at the Central Hall. The first urged the acceptance of the Beveridge Report and the second the adoption, in the interest of the countryside, of the Scott Report. In the end both were taken, and I had to move them both. There was some jockeying as to whose resolution should be taken on the all-important question of the Welfare State, to which the Tory Party would thus for the first time and for ever be committed. There were five resolutions on the agenda on the Beveridge Report. I canvassed support for mine in the House. The matter was clinched by Kenneth Pickthorne. "Much as I dislike you personally," he said, in his usual acid manner, "I prefer your resolution to the others."

But forthwith the axe was laid at the root of the tree, and Girdlestone, while I was under an anaesthetic, inserted his merciful knife and I found myself coming to, with a pleasant nurse smiling at me.

"Everyone is so kind," I murmured, and went off again. This was a bad time for me to be incarcerated in a ward. There was a call to the hospital from the Private Secretary at 10, Downing Street. The Prime Minister wanted to know how Mr. de Chair's operation had gone. And how long he was going to be incapacitated.

They told him, months. Fortunately there were plenty of the nimble footed about in the House of Commons; and I was not greatly missed.

One day, returning from the bath on crutches, I noticed hanging on the peg behind the door of my little ward an unfamiliar officer's tunic. Mike Wellman had left that morning, without his leg; and now I was to have another companion. What sort of man would he be? I took a closer look at his jacket. A small man, evidently. Among his ribbons over the breast pocket was a faded D.S.O. with the rosettes of two bars on it. What manner of fire-eater occupied this? He came in, wearing blue and white pyjamas; a small man, like a jockey, with dark hair and angular features. His arm was in a black sling. He had three fingers missing and had come here to have the nerves sutured. His name, he said, was Harding. John Harding. He had been in command of the Desert Rats and led them as far as Tripoli where he had the fingers blown off and a hole carved out of his leg. Two of his A.D.C.s, I learned later, had been killed beside him, at different times and the surviving one, Harry Legge-Bourke, said he was, "The bravest man on earth."

He was quiet and unassuming but inspired confidence.

Sitting, on the edge of his bed, with his legs in pyjamas, dangling over it, he told me about the Western Desert. He had been a Brigadier, General Staff, during the seige of Tobruk and when Alexander and Montgomery arrived to take command, they had relied much on him, "To put them in the picture."

"If you had to choose Alex or Monty for a big strategical operation," I asked him, "not tactical, but strategic," I emphasised, "which would you choose?"

"Monty every time," he answered promptly. And this was the more significant for he appeared to be personally just as well disposed to both Generals.

"I only had one operation order from Monty between Alamein and Tripoli."

We had a lot of time to talk, as soldiers do in hospital wards; and this was a small one for only two. It seemed to me that he was likely to be out of harness for a while and I tried to recruit him for politics. Victor Cazalet had been killed in an aircraft crash, (this was in 1943) and his seat at Chippenham was vacant. With difficulty I persuaded John Harding to let me forward his name to the Chairman of the Conservative Association.

"I will have to do my campaigning from this bed," he laughed.

I wrote accordingly, explaining that the party should not lose the opportunity of securing so splendid a candidate merely because he was in hospital for his wounds. The Chairman replied stiffly that it would not be possible to consider General Harding in the circumstances. They chose instead Mr. David Eccles. In due course John Harding, his nerves stitched up in time, returned to duty and after the war commanded in the Far East and on the Rhine before becoming Chief of the Imperial General Staff. The British Army thus owes to Sir David Eccles a debt of gratitude which it can never repay for his interest in politics. Although I thought then that Harding was an obvious future C.I.G.S. on the strength of his record and personality, I did not think that the Conservative Party showed much imagination in allowing him to slip through its fingers; and I wrote to the Chairman of the Party in vigorous terms. Nor did I think much of the system of which he complained, whereby the Army had reduced him to Colonel's rank and pay, while he was out of action on account of his wounds.

Oliver, bound for a meeting of scientists whom he was to address at Oxford, called to see me in hospital. He was accompanied by Nogs Kipping.

"Cheer up," he said, "you will soon be back with us. You will soon catch up."

But he spoke without conviction. The race is to the swift, and I could never catch up again.

It was a sad day for me when I gave up my association with Oliver; and, I think, for him, if his letters are to be believed. He wrote on November 8th in his own hand from the Ministry of Production, Great George Street.

My dear Somerset,

I can't let this day go by without telling you of the sad blank which I felt at the time of Parliamentary Questions today.

It is always satisfactory to be missed and I can assure you

that you have every cause to feel that satisfaction fully.

At the same time you are quite right to go and be unmuzzled for a bit at least.

You know how keenly I shall be interested in your career and if there is any way by which I can further it at any time you know that you can count on me to try and repay part of the debt I owe you.

As this is a letter of warm gratitude I will preach no sermons on the marriage of exuberance with eclecticism!

Thank you, dear Somerset, and drop in sometimes.

Yours ever,

OLIVER

He was a master of the two-edged compliment. He always introduced me as The Unknown Soldier. I had been his P.P.S. for two and a half years; but the remaining six months freedom of speech before the election was just not enough to carry my constituents with me in 1945, and I was to be defeated, after a recount, by only 53 votes. To Carlo it was a very sad blow for sitting there, now in declining health, in front of Narford, stripping the bark from a prostrate pine trunk, to make a flag-pole on which to run up the Union Jack when Victory Day should come, he had persuaded me to turn down the offer of a safe seat with a 17,000 majority near the house I had moved to. "You are our only hope," he said, lugubriously. Of course I could not let him down.

"You picked me out of the ruck at 23 and stood by me then," I said; and I did my very best, sitting on a shooting-stick with a microphone at ninety open air meetings. But it was a fierce and cynical election when it came, which tossed even Churchill, from his war winning, aside. And, as my opponent pointed out in a leaflet, one needed to be very robust physically to be able to represent such a widespread agricultural constituency in peacetime. Carlo died after an internal operation, six months later, and the last and least thing I could do for him was to get a great silver salver, massive as he deserved, subscribed for him by all the members of the Conservative Association, as its president.

I attended his funeral at the little church in his grounds beside the lake, where I had heard him read the lesson, that first Sunday long ago, about the bones. And when his coffin was lowered into his ancestral ground; and his two sons threw a handful of earth after him, I too, waiting till they were turned away, threw down upon him my tribute of earth. For it is right to do homage to great friends and great men. I wrote an obituary letter to *The Times*; which was quoted later by his vicar in that church: "He was an oak among pines and sycamores."

In gratitude to Girdlestone I dedicated the popular edition of *The Golden Carpet* to him.

'For Gathorne Girdlestone, patient and successful restorer of a Palmyra Ruin'.

And he wrote to me, affectionately, 'My dear P.R.' signing himself G.R.G. He was known to his staff by these initials.

His friends said, "We did not know you were an archaeologist," and he replied, "Nor did I. But I specialise in ruins. And there are many kinds of ruins. Not all are the effect of time — nor are they all ignoble in decay."

CHAPTER 4

I lay in the drawing-room of my mother's flat in London, with my leg in plaster of Paris: it had been carved expertly in time for Christmas, like the drumstick of a turkey, by Girdlestone at the Wingfield Morris Orthopaedic Hospital. Now it was Boxing Day, and my family remote from the invalid; why, I do not know, and where, I have forgotten. Possibly my nerves were thought to have been tightened up enough after two operations, like violin strings before a Concerto, and to drag the unresined bow of children's voices across them would have been discordant.

It was Boxing Day 1943, and I lay listening after the one o'clock news to the voice on the Home Service of a bored young guardee talking about the capture of Baghdad. It was the first of a new series — 'Now it can be told'. And I was telling it. That was the puzzling part. I had made the recording at the B.B.C. for this Boxing Day Broadcast before going back to hospital. But I scarcely recognised the voice. Barnes, the Director of Talks, had rehearsed me too often, ironing all the expression out of the voice. Now it was as lifeless as a man conditioned for a public confession in a police state. Could it really be that I sounded like this at all times? "We got to Rutbah don't you know. Jolly decent, and Fallujah, frightfully jolly. Baghdad, not a bad show, eh?" Listening to this sort of thing at any time would be bad enough but hearing oneself doing it was a surrealist nightmare, and I was annoyed because the announcer before the News forgot to say that it would follow, and owing to the shortness of the News, insulated it from the listening public by five bars from Bach. I was indeed touchy. And why not? I had been carved up once too often for my liking.

During the afternoon, lovely Eleanor Morris-Keating came round to see me, comforting me with her soft gazelle's eyes. I was beginning to paint — my father had just given me paint, brushes, and an easel to keep me happy in my infirmity over Christmas. I had started on a picture of little Helena of Abu Sinan from a photograph I had taken of her at Gethsemane. Eleanor thought it promising, or was tactful enough to say so. I should have painted her while I still knew her with her lovely red hair hanging to her shoulders, but I was not yet proficient enough to desecrate so much beauty. "What did you think of my talk?" She thought that wonderful too. Such charming insincerity at such a time was surely permissible.

The tired old Parliament — the longest since the Long Parliament — was drawing towards the end of its life, although we did not know it. It seemed as if the war might go on for ever. In 1942 there had been demands for the Second Front. In 1943 they told a story of Churchill and Stalin at Teheran. When Winston went up to bed, it was said, he found an infant girl propped up against the pillows with a label round her neck. 'I shall be ready for you by the time you land in Europe.'

I had come back to England from warring in the Levant; and while still, in and out of hospital, Parliamentary Private Secretary to Lyttelton at the Ministry of Production, had some preoccupations of my own in the House of Commons, being newly appointed to the Select Committee set up to consider the rebuilding of the Chamber blitzed by Hitler in 1941. I had pleaded in debate for the Select Committee to have a free hand, both as to design and in the siting of the Chamber — possibly overlooking the Terrace. Winston was set on restoring the old chamber he had known with all Pugin's fig leaves intact. Girdlestone was in the gallery, eyeing me between operations like a capon reserved for slaughter. I thought he looked bored and wanted to hear his patient speak. I spoke accordingly and could find nobody to divide the house with me, except Maxton and his I.L.P. It was a bad moment to challenge the leader of the Coalition on his pet subject, and Winston's motion was carried by the comfortable majority of 99.7%. Jimmy Maxton and I acted as tellers. I overheard Winston, enraged, after the division: "Silly young fool, Dudley de Chair," his mind straying back no doubt to his disagreements with my father who was Naval Secretary at the Admiralty to him in 1913. In half an hour I had dissipated all the goodwill of the war. I was not evenly balanced; and Girdlestone should not have allowed me near the legislature.

I also wrote to *The Times* pleading for a fresh approach; and in Northern Ireland viewed the Georgian architecture of the local Parliament with an appraising eye. From hospital I wrote to the

Secretary of the Select Committee saying that I could not attend the first meeting but would send an architect to take some measurements in the House of Commons for me. I received a reply from the Lord Chamberlain's Secretary: 'measuring was not allowed in the Palace of Westminster', which was a Royal Palace. I was incensed. How could members of a Select Committee on the rebuilding of the Chamber get on if they were to be impeded in their researches? Eddie Winterton, the Chairman of the Committee was sympathetic, indeed choleric with indignation, when I told him. Five members of the Committee agreed to meet in the Central Lobby with measuring rods, if need be, and tell the Lord Great Chamberlain to arrest us if he liked. I received an apologetic letter. It had all been the Secretary's mistake. Of course I could measure anything I liked. When the report of the Select Committee was finally debated, James Willoughby d'Eresby, son of the Lord Great Chamberlain, said he was sorry my application had been rejected. But I ought to have known that all requests to the Lord Chamberlain were automatically refused the first time. (Laughter)

The Select Committee quickly narrowed the field of choice as to style of architecture; and the site was pin-pointed by the terms of reference, which I had challenged in the division unsuccessfully. I pleaded for a competition among architects. This was pushed aside and the contract offered on a silver salver to Sir Giles Gilbert Scott, an expert in medieval restorations. I drew a charcoal sketch for my colleagues of a suggested interior for the new Chamber with large mullioned windows, and this influenced Scott a little; also my memorandum on making the voting lobbies resemble the long galleries of celebrated private houses like Haddon. To soothe me, no doubt, my memorandum and sketches were printed in the blue book of our deliberations. I had fought an unequal struggle but the result when we entered it in 1950 was not bad. Those of us who had dreaded a neo-neo-Gothic Chamber of Horrors were pleasantly surprised. But it was still the same size as it had been when I first entered the house in 1935. I had pleaded for a little more room; as there would only be seating accommodation on the floor of the House for half its members. I very nearly got an extra row of benches added each side; but it would have meant moving the Lady Members' Cloakroom elsewhere; and Eleanor Rathbone asked me for an assurance about this. I could not give any such assurance but said I hoped for the best. Without assurance on this all-important subject she shifted her weight, and my motion was lost by one vote — 6 votes to 7.

I was also now Chairman of a committee of Conservative Members set up on Dorman-Smith's recommendation to consider the future Constitution of Burma. The committee included Sir Stanley Reed upon whom I leant confidently. He had been editor of *The Times of India*, and was a wise old bird. There was Keeling, who had oil connections with Burma; Godfrey Nicholson, a very sound Tory; and Sidney Shepherd, who acted as Secretary. We interviewed a succession of Burmese Statesmen and Civil Servants then in exile from the Japanese. Also prominent business men, like Sir Kenneth Harper whose firms had operated in Burma. I left the drafting of the report to Stanley Reed. He remembered everything, including the Indian money lenders, who used to get such a hold on the Burmese rice growers.

We suggested an agricultural lending bank and much else. We advocated self-government within the British Commonwealth at the end of a period of direct rule by the Governor of 6 years. This period, Dorman Smith, the latest Governor, thought essential to restore the physical and political conditions of the country to normal after the Japanese occupation. During this period we advocated an advisory council of leading Burmese and a representative assembly towards the end of the period to which the proposed constitution would be submitted. Advance reports of our plan caused some stir in the Indian press and the Secretary of State, Amery, wrote to me accordingly.

Our plan was published by the Conservative Central Office as the 'Blueprint for Burma' and I secured time in the House to debate it. I opened the debate, to a good-natured murmur of applause in recognition of my persistency in this field; and began with a tribute to the 14th Army. "This is no forgotten army," I cried. "This is the shield behind which India has enjoyed the imperial prerogative of successful defence against aggression and behind which British power has advanced once more to the banks of the Irrawaddy." These words were taken up by the press; and we all hoped to see Burma a self-governing part of the Commonwealth. But the Indian press screeched at the idea of six years of direct rule in the interval.

I was elected vice-chairman of the Conservative Members Imperial Affairs Committee, in succession to Leonard Lyle; and continued to labour for Burma. But our labours were in vain, for the Socialist Party was elected in 1945 and the Burmese ruby was very quickly extracted from the Imperial Crown.

Power was handed readily to the new anti-Fascist People's Freedom League under Aung San and a delegation of this party and other Burmese factions was invited to London. Among them was a former Burmese Prime Minister U-Saw, who turned naturally to me, as Chairman of the Conservative Party Committee. After a reception he invited my wife and myself to come up to his suite at the Dorchester where he sat on the bed and talked volubly. His face had the hue of teak; and was very hard. He wore dark glasses.

"I have just been to a specialist in Harley Street," he said, "to have bits of glass taken out of my eye. You saw Aung San at the reception?"

We had seen Aung San, a youth of remarkably Neanderthal appearance.

"He had me followed and shot in Rangoon. The bullets hit the windscreen and some of the glass got in my eye."

I had noticed him looking intently at Aung San in consequence (the atmosphere at the Government Reception, where the two gentlemen appeared in the same room, had been somewhat strained) and it was not long afterwards that U-Saw's own henchmen, disguised in army uniform gatecrashed Aung San's Cabinet meeting and sprayed him and four of his colleagues with Sten gun bullets, whereof they died. But for the present U-Saw was confined to words.

"Let me tell you about Aung San," he said. "About this man whom the British Government fondly imagines it can persuade to accept Dominion Status. He was one of the 'Thirty Heroes' – Burmese who were trained by the Japanese in Japan. When the Japanese army arrived in Burma, Aung San was with them, in the uniform of a Japanese Major-General. That is the uniform he has been wearing in London. When the army arrived at a certain village, they said to Aung San 'the headman is a bad man'. He had two or three wives. So without any sort of trial and just to show his own power, Aung San had this unfortunate headman tied up to a tree in front of 4,000 people. Then he took the Japanese sword and ran it through the man's ribs. The man cried out and wrenched his head this way and that. Then Aung San handed the sword to another general, who began stabbing him, and so on till he died. Aung San has admitted, in the vernacular press, to this atrocity."

This atrocity was well known to Attlee and Cripps. According to Maung Maung Gee, a brother of U-Saw, who was a constituent of mine in Paddington for a time, they used it to threaten Aung San.

"They put Aung San in a room by himself at 10, Downing Street," said Maung Maung Gee, "to think it over. 'If you do not agree to Burma remaining inside the Commonwealth, we will have you tried for your atrocities as a War Criminal before the War Crimes Tribunal'." Aung San resisted this pressure. Moreover he lived long enough to proclaim the independence of Burma. All this seemed to me very muddy politics both in Rangoon and Whitehall, and there is little doubt that if the Conservatives had been returned to power in Britian in 1945, Burma would have been helped, like Ceylon, towards self-government within the Commonwealth. But after the pressure on Aung San had failed, we heard much of the sacred principles of self-determination. Undoubtedly Cripps was fooled, for he said to me during a reception for the Burmese delegates, "Don't you lobby them too much. You leave them to us and we believe they will stay in."

All this interest in the remoter parts of the world was very puzzling to my constituents in S.W. Norfolk, whose horizon was bounded by their own hedge rows. Nor had farmers been at all enthusiastic about my remark, on returning from the war, that they were all making 'fantastic profits'. This had been much featured in the press. A very charming woman from *News Review* came to interview me on the subject; and I limped up Whitehall with her, giving her my views. "It makes me squirm," I told her; and the report was headed 'Soldier Squirms'. The Minister of Agriculture, Rob Hudson, said to me thoughtfully, "That was a very courageous speech of yours." One of the few, probably, delivered to my constituents which they remembered. When the vote came, I was defeated by 53 votes, on a recount. Not bad in a General Election which swept away all Tory seats in Norfolk. Indeed there may have been many agricultural workers who remembered this speech about their employers also. Nevertheless I was out, and that was that. I could feel as cynical as I liked, and having refused the offer of a safe seat in Kent out of loyalty to my supporters in Norfolk, could now advise them to get a candidate living on the spot who would nurse the constituency back to life again. They chose a fen farmer, Denys Bullard, who was defeated by 250 in the 1950 election but managed to win the seat back again in 1951.

*   *   *

The first operation on my wounded ankle in 1943 marked a conspicuous break; far more than the wounding itself. For thereafter I was thrown out of my stride, and thown off my balance. I revealed in my speeches and behaviour the effect of shock from this abrupt manipulation of my nervous system. It fundamentally altered my faith in religion, and reduced my feelings to essentials. A great deal in my system seemed to be jettisoned as the price paid for freedom from the continuous pain which I had suffered for two years. Dr. Black, my army surgeon in Jerusalem had warned me that I would lose either my sense of proportion or my sense of humour. I settled for the sense of humour and lost my sense of proportion. I would have to be on guard to watch out for this. But the change came imperceptibly and unalterably. Comfort and love of beauty became insistent motives for action. Effort, which was for long painful, had to be cushioned. Reserves of tact and patience were quickly used up and I said cynical or bitter things with a neatness of phrase which unfortunately gave them currency. When I described the Tory Reform Committee in the House as the Young Comtemptibles, Oliver Lyttelton looked up from his desk with a fiendish smile. "That's lethal," he said. "Do you mind if I put it into circulation?" He had fought with the older variety. I was off to hospital again and did not care what he put into circulation. But the remark cut very deep among my contemporaries who, as one of them pointed out, had merely had the good sense to keep their heads down. But their healthy smiles and springy step were not always appreciated in the corridors of Westminster by the survivors of Passchendaele and the Somme. Nor were their political activities popular in high places. Three weeks before D-Day, they voted against the Government on the issue of equal pay for women, of all things. Winston, heavily, indeed unbearably preoccupied with the impending stroke against the Continent, was much upset. For a moment he seemed an old man, and his head nodded uncontrollably, but his mind was clear.

"We cannot go on like this," he said to us, in the Smoking

Room, after the vote. "Twenty votes and thirty votes. The House of Commons must show itself a solid platform." And then Peter Thorneycroft, Secretary and mainspring of the Reformers, came up to him and said, "I think the drinks are definitely on me today." But the Prime Minister was not amused, and left soon afterwards, still shaking his head, from fatigue, strain and annoyance.

Before my remark about the young contemptibles got around, they were very keen on my joining them. I was not enthusiastic, although I shared many of their reforming views. I pleaded divided loyalties in my role as P.P.S. to a member of the War Cabinet. So they put up the oldest of their number, Lord Winterton, to ask Oliver what objection he had to my joining the forty members in the Cave of Adullam. He said, "I don't object to Somerset joining anything, if he wants to, but if it is suggested that every young man under 40 is a genius and anyone over 40 is a silly old buffer, I don't think so much of young Tories."

Eddie Winterton, in the 70s was able to reassure him, but my continued reticence after that changed their attitude towards me. Peter Thorneycroft, searching for talent to lead the new contingent no longer said even jestingly, "You're my leader," (to which I had cocked a good-natured snook in reply).

Now came the first of the flying bombs, panting through the night with trails of fire. Some plopped down, off their course, around Godalming. Back in London, I found them coming in thick and fast. My wife and I were sleeping in a ground floor bedroom; and when we heard one cut out overhead and crash a few hundred yards away I shielded her with my body. But after that we thought it prudent to sleep in the basement, where we had almost a dormitory for the cook, and our ex-chauffeur and his wife, who came in from their flat in the mews at night. Rest meant everything to me, for the cure of my ankle, but it was difficult to sleep with these fiery horsemen of the Apocolypse, roaring over the roofs at night.

The House of Commons was now sitting at Church House, Westminster, and to pass the time while the flying bombs were about, I went up to the secretarial rooms and dictated a translation of the First Crusade from the Gesta Francorum, which I had been obliged to master long ago at Oxford. I sent off the sections as they were typed to Christopher Sandford, in Herefordshire, who prepared to publish the book, in his Golden Cockerel Press, with wood cuts by Clifford Webb. This brilliant artist was assistant Petroleum Officer for the North Eastern Region, up at Newcastle, and relished the diversion of depicting the fall of Antioch or the painful path of the Crusaders up the steep defiles of the anti-Lebanon. The translation was published, soon after the war, in a vellum binding, limited to 100 copies at 20 guineas, with 400 more in quarter vellum at 5 guineas. It was a pleasure, almost a vice, to be produced in such a rarified form, but gave me a reputation for literary inaccessibility which I deplored. Yet few authors would resist the temptation to have their work produced, at least in the first instance, in such editions if a publisher was prepared, as Christopher Sandford was, to finance the project. I certainly never contributed a penny, though there were no doubt some cynics who thought I could never have got my books published like this otherwise.

My mind was also seized with the project of acquiring Chilham Castle, of which I had seen the particulars in hospital. I secured, after some negotiation with the agents, an option on the whole estate at a low figure, soon to be kept low by the incessant fall of flying bombs in that part of Kent. £42,500 with 1,400 acres.

I told the agents for Chilham that they would have to sell the Island of Gigha at a fixed price which would enable me to buy the estate in Kent. They had six weeks, and set about it briskly. By good luck, they produced a millionaire, Colonel Horlick, who was looking for an island in the Western Isles; his search was not in any way delayed by the explosion of flying bombs around his factory at Slough. He came up to London to see me, a little man with drooping moustache, who had been an intelligence officer in Istanbul at the end of the First World War, which gave us much to talk about.

"I like to know why people are selling things," he said, and I explained about the option in Kent.

A large part of Chilham was occupied by the army but the main rooms downstairs and five bedrooms above, had been removed from the requisition on account of their architectural interest, so we were able to settle into them at weekends.

Self-portraiture in print can scarcely hope to rival that of the great artists. A picture, they say, can tell a story better than any number of words; and as we gaze into the forlorn and disillusioned self-portrait of an ageing Rembrandt, dying in poverty, we are seized with pity and admiration. Yet the portrait in words can add a fourth dimension to those at the disposal of the sculptor or the painter, for the writer can add depth in time. It should be possible, thus, in the written portrait, to watch the gradual change and decay of the sitter, which, on an immortal canvas, is only arrested at one moment of time. A series of portraits, like those of Philip IV by Velázquez, from the serious youth of 1628 in the Prado to the sombre melancholy of the portrait bust in the National Gallery, does convey a sense of growth through life. In a book we may notice the gradual hardening or softening of the character, but I must record now a hardening of outline for a few years at least. The impact of the war was such as to produce a marked sharpening of the expression and hardening of the outlook. Self-preservation becomes a marked characteristic. In the photograph taken of me on returning from the Middle East, there is a steely, almost ferocious glint in the eye; perhaps more than a hint of pain, and this portrait in uniform, used as an election poster with its hard look of impatience and marked expression of an unwillingness to suffer fools gladly or otherwise, was almost enough to frighten the electors. It looked, said one of my supporters, as if I were just about to rip off my tunic to fight somebody. This may not have been bad portraiture in a soldier home from the wars, but it was bad politics. Nevertheless I maintained, seated on my shooting-stick, at innumerable open air meetings in the summer election of 1945 a reasonably cheerful front. On the village green at Rougham, with old Freddie North sitting on the grass beside me, and King, broad shouldered at my back, the tougher element danced about in front of me with clenched fists. (They were southern Irishmen working on aerodromes and appeared accidentally on the register.)

"Why did you go off to foreign parts?" they yelled. "Why didn't you stay here? Now look at Mr. Dye. There's a man who doesn't go off to foreign parts during a war."

But it was a shock when the votes were counted to find that I was 53 votes short of a renewal of my mandate from the electors of S.W. Norfolk. They dispatched me, I think, more in sorrow than in anger; but Norfolk wanted a Labour Government and what Norfolk wants it usually gets. This is a consistent feature of election results in Norfolk; they reflect to a remarkable degree the national trend. It is a borderline area. I was therefore in the way of the clean sweep, and out I went.

CHAPTER 5

I had by now settled down at Chilham and my opponent Dye made full use of the fact, pushing through the letter boxes of every door three days before the poll, a leaflet headed: 'A MILLIONAIRE'S CASTLE or HOMES FOR THE MILLION?' The millionaire was of course my predecessor at Chilham, Sir Edmund Davis; but this was not clear in the leaflet, and the voters were left to suppose that I was the millionaire, and that in some obscure way my castle, which had been built for some centuries, was an alternative to the building of council houses in S.W. Norfolk.

Somehow nothing went right in that election. There was a young lunatic called Scarborough whom I had tried to help with his invention. Just after the successful sale of the Island of Gigha and therefore at a very propitious moment to touch me for a loan, a bespectacled youth turned up at the House of Commons to see me, with specifications of a combined dictaphone and type-writer. There was much talk of photo-electric cells and he could point to the fact that a Japanese patent for this process had been taken out at one time. He looked certainly like some mute, inglorious Einstein yet unsung, and spoke with absolute self-confidence and conviction. He did not seem in the least unbalanced, and I sent him on, with his plans and his request for the £100 required to make a model of his dictaphone-typewriter, to my solicitors in Lincoln's Inn Fields. He brushed the senior partner aside and sat himself comfortably in a chair, expounding technically. They rang me up. "He certainly seems the genius type," they said, "and no respector of persons." But the worst that could happen would be the loss of the £100, which at that particular moment did not seem disastrous. So a simple form of agreement was drawn up under which I advanced him the money to make his working model, and if the invention proved a success I would receive a share of the profits. Off he went with his £100, apparently sane but studious. No sooner had he got home to Norfolk than a torrent of abusive postcards, unstamped, for which I had to pay 4d on delivery, began to arrive through the post.

36 Lyn Road,
Downham Market,
Norfolk.

Sir, 5/12/44

I have written to Tweetie to say I want to end our agreement. The thought of being a partner with a Tory makes me feel sick. The Deputy Food Executive Officer here is one no doubt and he has played tricks with my rations — I have not yet had a Ration Book. I went to Liverpool in Sept. applied for a new Identity Card, etc. (I had lost all my 1943/4 documents) *but 4 weeks passed* with no action from anyone. I have since sent him a temporary Identity Card substitute form (I paid 1/- for it in Liverpool) and he hasn't the decency to acknowledge it. Not that I think you care a tinker's cuss whether I get my R.B. or not.

Anyway, if you don't like my statement of my intentions, you can lump it. If you insist on the £100 being returned, I shall tell you to go and fry your feet.

If this country had anything but a lot of grasping Tories in power I should not have had such a bad time of it — investing and never getting paid. You own Chilham Castle and probably throw a £100 away several times yearly on bottle parties or a trip to Paris.

What do I get out of the agreement? If you sue me I shan't complete the Patent to time, if there is no other way of getting rid of such an expensive hanger-on. I wish that Baghdad bullet had caught your skull.

J. Scarborough.

4d to pay 16th Dec. 1944

To Baron Streuben,
Turret 625,
Chilham Castle in the
County of Kent.

No regrets that the slot machine is empty.

36 Lyn Road,
Downham Market,
Norfolk.
15/12/44

Why should you have 3 addresses? Have you got more than one Ration Book? *What about mine?*

I have today written your Tweedledum & Tweedledee but I fear that their dullness of comprehension may cause them incorrectly to deliver my message obliges me to write direct.

Even you can hardly deny me the right to one twentieth of expected profits, and this figure will be £50,000,000. How would you like me to get so irritated that I refused you the slightest chance with other inventions? I shall anyway.

4d to pay   16th Dec. 1944
Mrs. de Chair,
Chilham Castle,
KENT.

De Chair's in his hammock?
And a thousand feet up high?
Slung atween the turrets
Of Chilham Castle, Kent?
Captain, art thou sleeping up above?

4d to pay   2nd July, 1945
Stingy Streuben,
Somerset de Chair (M.P. for another fortnight)
Narford Hall,
NARFORD.

You bribed the Commons police to threaten me if I went back to the House and thought that was why I didn't go back! It was because my feet were blistered and I was sick of the sight of it. You are the most scoundrelly little twerp who ever lied his way into Parliament and your bribery of the local police to threaten me with arrest will not work as it didn't the first time. You had better come here and sign a proper release from that agreement (with my parents as witnesses) or I will let the whole country know. You must be crackers thinking that people believe your "return the £100 and you shall be released" attitude is reasonable. You know I *can't* return it. You can't fool all, all of the time. Wake up, you twerp. I gave you many opportunities to act decently.

J. Scarborough

Ward Eleven,
Mental Asylum,
Thorpe,
NORWICH

Dear Sir,

Mother tells me you called to see the demonstration model on Saturday. It is no good you seeing it without me being there to explain. The best thing by far is for you to come here and discuss it. I have full perspective drawings, etc. etc. and can explain it in an hour, or less. I am able to go into the grounds, we could talk privately about it.

Yours faithfully,
J. Scarborough

These made entertaining reading though rather expensive at 4d a time. As the election approached, however, he grew more abusive and more threatening. He promised to turn up at my election meetings and wring my neck, etc. He wrote to my agent, King (all this on open unstamped postcards read by all) 'Don't you realise that you are working for a lunatic?' and so on. Unknown to me, the police intervened quietly, afraid of some violence, and led him off to a lunatic asylum. There the guardians tried to curb his literary zeal, and his postcards (of which the last one above is an example) became more moderate in tone, until he was released after the election. He then sent me specifications of a robot waiter who would pour out your whisky and stop when you said "when". It would have required very remarkable specifications to induce me to support this aspiring genius again, and I wondered ruefully how many of the missing 53 votes during the election could be accounted for by his damaging postcards. It was a sharp lesson to me about helping struggling inventors. I did not mind sending a similar sum to the driver of the ambulance who found me in the desert after my own had been destroyed, for that was a debt I could never repay. I had left the driver something in my Will in any case and had ascertained his name and address for the purpose. So when he wrote to say that he was in difficulties with payments to a building society and I had just completed another successful deal (this time the sale of Chilham Castle) it gave me a great deal of pleasure to be able to help him out in his own moment of need.

Hilaire Belloc writes: 'There is a lonely place in the woods by Chilham in the County of Kent, above the River Stour, where a man comes upon an irregular earthwork still plainly marked upon the brow of the bluff . . . That earthwork is the earthwork (I could prove it, but this is not the place) where the British stood against the charge of the Tenth Legion, and first heard, sounding on their bronze, the Arms of Caesar. Here the River was forded, here the little men of the South went up in formation: here the Barbarian broke and took his way, as the opposing General has recorded, through devious woodland paths, scattering in the pursuit! Here began the great history of England. Is it not an enormous business merely to stand in such a place. I think so.'

What must it be to live in such a place? I had always believed that there must be, deep in the heart of England, some perfect village, as yet unspoilt by the spread of industry; some village where the buildings of graceful periods in our architecture have produced a cluster of warm red roofed houses at the foot of some old castle; and where in that graceful backwater of our turbulent history known as the Jacobean period, some wealthy Squire had built a dignified manor in rose brick which should by now have had three hundred winters in which to weather. No doubt it would be surrounded by a park studded with lordly trees, where deer start out of the bracken beds. There would be woods of oak; and downs; and a river winding slowly through the valley.

I dreamt of such a place as I swatted flies in the deserts of Iraq, just as others, no doubt, were dreaming of their own desired abodes. In a measure I was fighting for such a place; for what was left of rural England. Every road must have an end, and there may be some satisfaction for those who followed the arid journeys of our fighting in the Levant, in learning that for one desert traveller at least there was peace and coolness in the end, this side of death.

What a long shadow a little bullet can cast. December of 1943 found me, long after the war had rolled away from the Levant, entering the Wingfield Morris Orthopaedic Hospital at Oxford for a second operation on those nerves of an ankle which had been severed abruptly, before Palmyra on the 21st June 1941. I had arrived, thus, footsore from much wandering, to a place of great kindness and consideration. I had been there six months previously for another operation, and knew the loving efficiency of the place. On that occasion, within a few hours of recovering from the anaesthetic, my bed had been wheeled along the concrete verandas to a Theatre which contained all the driftwood of the war, it seemed. Rows of beds, where men's legs were suspended from overhead appliances, beds with inverted shaving glasses above, so that the helpless cripples could look up from their pillows to shave, beds with adjustable rests for those who could sit up. And there we lay back as the curtain went up on a little stage, and on a gallant troop of actors who wanted so much to be cheerful, but whose voices quavered just a little as they looked down at the strained faces of men and women (for there were civilian cripples too). And when it was all over, and the actors had taken their bow, a Captain in the army, who had been blown up by a mine in the Palestine Rebellion six years before, and whose spine had just been operated upon, struggled up into a sitting position to move a vote of thanks to the performers. These had to run away from the stage to hide their tears.

Now, when I returned for my second operation in December, many who had been bedridden in July were walking about on crutches, or wheeling themselves in chairs. Some had been discharged altogether. But their places were taken by others; the rising tide of war brought in more driftwood every day and for the devoted staff of that hospital, as for others, there could be no rest.

I shared a ward with Dyer, a Pilot Officer in the Royal Air Force, who had caught the germ of infantile paralysis in Libya. He could sit up in bed and use his hands, but if he were to catch cold there was danger of his strength being too little for the working of his lungs. Every day and four times a day arrived a kind old body who applied a treatment which had proved efficacious when an Australian Nurse Kenny had used it on children in the bush. It consisted of applying hot ferments to the legs every four hours. And so great slabs of cotton wool would be dipped in boiling hot water, dashed through a mangle, and pressed firmly on Dyer's legs with the help of a V.A.D. Both the old body and the V.A.D. were volunteers from outside, since the overworked staff of the hospital could not cope with such elaborate experimental treatment in wartime. Every now and then the old body would detect, so she thought, some improvement in the muscular activity of one leg or the other; and at such moments the ward, with the frosted windows shut against the raw breath of winter, with its electric fire on and water from the mangle dripping into and over the edge of enamel bowls all over the floor, would be alive with joy. Then a day came when the V.A.D. fell ill and could not help with the Kenny treatment, so my wife was able to fill a gap and the treatment went on. Professor Seddon shook his smooth and dome-like head over all this mess and was unable, technically, to see why wet heat should be more efficacious than dry heat. Dyer spent a large part of the day lying on his face under an arch of wood inside which a number of electric lights glowed to provide a penetrating heat. Whether it was the wet heat or the dry heat or the faith of the old body or the patience of Dyer or just Time the great Healer, I don't know, but when I revisited the hospital some months later Dyer was wheeling himself about in a chair, and by now, if his hopes are fulfilled, he should be walking upright on the earth.

It was in these surroundings, on the morrow of the operation in December, as I lay reflecting how much more fortunate I was than all those around me, that the post arrived and I opened a sizeable buff envelope.

There is always some romance in opening a strange envelope. However wearied with correspondence we may have become, the sporting instinct and the promptings of curiosity always stir us a little. It may be a bill; or it may be a legacy. Hope and apprehension therefore clash and neutralise. If we recognise the handwriting we may experience elation or irritation. There are some people whose writing on a bulky envelope which obviously contains a dozen pages, rouses me to a rage before I have even opened it. This time it was a business envelope and being weary and in no hurry I fell to wondering whether it was worth opening at all. It might be a circular about the Co-operative Movement or a bulletin of The Primrose League. It contained, in fact, the particulars of a house, and as I glanced at the particulars with an eye hardened to cynicism by many a fruitless journey, by years of a barren quest, I experienced a certain tremor of excitement. Could it be possible that in this final trial I was to be gratified with my heart's desire? From the envelope I then extracted a photograph — after which I had very little doubt. There stood, above its graceful terraces of great clipped yew trees, a house of Jacobean brick, with stone mullioned windows, and tall chimney stacks. The sun was glinting on the leaded light window panes, and a great cedar of Lebanon cast a rich black shadow over the smooth upper lawn.

A map of the estate followed and, with an eye trained to conjure a landscape from the most arid of military maps, I quickly guessed the terrain. On the spur of a long ridge of Kentish weald was marked in Gothic script the legend 'Chilham Castle' and almost adjoining it, the words 'Old Keep'. It seemed as if the name of castle was a misnomer, applied to the Jacobean house and it retained the courtesy title by virtue of the surviving keep of a Norman castle. A short drive flanked with trees led to a village square, evidently the old baillie of the castle, judging from its position on top of the hill. To south and east of the house a series of terraces descended to a small lake, in which stood an island, and beyond this, water meadows stretched down to the banks of a broad river, the river Stour, six miles above Canterbury, through which it flows towards the sea. Beyond the river were marked the forest-crested downs, on the lower slopes of which were curious features marked by the surveyors of this Ordnance map. One was 'Julaberries grave' and near by a perfect circle labelled 'earthwork'. In the valley beside the browsing river was a water mill.

To south and west of the house spread a huge irregular area bounded by roads, within a ring fence, and described as a 'deer park'. Three or four avenues of trees appeared to radiate into the park from the house, leading in a westerly direction to where great woods belonging to the estate — Felborough Wood, Ridge Wood, Big Bourdane, Little Bourdane, Fagg's Wood, Six Beeches, Cutlers and Stanners Woods, — merged into the vast acreage of King's Wood belonging to the Crown.

This was quite enough and I lay back exhausted. The first lines of a poem formed themselves in my head:

More beautiful to me than any picture
Is the map of my estate.

I was too tired, and the beginning too Japanese for me to want to go on.

But it is from there that I had been writing, at odd intervals, ever since. I had reached the end of the road, and I must earn my Norman Keep.

At Chilham there was a lovely park running westward from the house to Felborough Wood, where a heronry, mentioned in King John's reign, was regularly reoccupied every year by the herons on St. Valentine's day. Beyond that was Godmersham Park, where Jane Austen had written her novels and the Trittons now lived amid considerable luxury and good taste. They were stimulating and charming neighbours who brought their guests to see Chilham — "A great possession," as Elsie Tritton described it to me, looking up with her shrewd, appraising dark eye, from the lower terrace. Their guests were often interesting; among them not infrequently Somerset Maugham. I was impressed by Maugham's respect for T. S. Eliot. "What is it about his verses that you particularly admire?" I asked Maugham.

"The undertones, the overtones, the whole god-damned thing," he replied, looking like some crustacean monster from a remote world. He told me that he had read forty books on religion for one chapter of *The Razor's Edge*.

We returned the calls to Godmersham with our own guests. Sometimes I would ride over while the rest of the party walked. Chilham stood high up on a commanding ridge. Godmersham, a rose-brick Georgian house, was cupped in a bowl of parkland. And behind us both stretched the 10,000 acres of King's Wood, where the wild deer still roamed and I could ride for hours in a Robin Hood's world of remote bridle paths, deep in woods of Spanish chestnut. It was at dinner with the Trittons that I discussed the future of Royalty with the Duchess of Kent. She had been to lunch with us on the occasion of the pageant which I ran at Chilham for the Boys' Clubs and Soldiers', Sailors' and Airmen's families, but the Lord Lieutenant and others had been there and the occasion had not lent itself to consistent conversation. Now I asked her whether she would not prefer a completely private life to the ceaseless banging of champagne bottles on the prows of ships. She answered, "No, I enjoy my life. I am very well looked after. I drive down here in a very comfortable car. I have people to look after me."

"I know," I said, "but is there any future in it? I am a historian in a way, and therefore study trends. I have noticed that this country has followed the continental trend in most ways but about 50 years later. A great many royal families went after the First World War and now after this one, look what has happened.

In Italy a referendum decides against the monarchy by a small margin."

"The situation in Italy was handled very badly," she replied sharply. "If only it had been handled the way it was in Greece — "

"Do not think I am trying to be difficult or disloyal," I protested. "I am only looking at this business impartially as a student of history. How long can it go on?"

"Who would want to get rid of us in this country?" she asked incredulously.

"Suppose," I said, "a Communist government. They might say 'we have nothing against you personally but we just don't approve of the institution'."

She shrugged her graceful shoulders and the conversation ceased.

No one would deny the immense popularity of the British Crown today; yet it depends a great deal for its success on the character of the monarch. It may survive for a long time on a succession of popular monarchs, and a long and eventful reign under a young queen should greatly strengthen its place in our tripartite constitution. Yet it remains something of a miracle, defying the laws of historical gravity.

CHAPTER 6   *Trerice Manor*

Then there was Trerice. I saw a small advertisement of this Cornish manor house in *Country Life* during the 1945 election. There was a delay of three weeks after polling day before the votes could be counted and it seemed an agreeable way of passing this anxious time, to journey down to Cornwall and inspect the house. There was probably no serious purpose behind the visit — I had barely settled into Chilham. Nevertheless, when my wife and I drove up the winding lane from Kestle Mill, up one hill and down one dale, and saw abruptly on our right the oldest house in England — or so it seemed — of ancient stone with outward curving gables, ending in grinning stone masks, carved by some Italian prisoner of war of Queen Elizabeth the First's time, I was unable to resist the temptation to acquire it all. This house had a great stone mullioned Tudor window containing 576 panes of glass, of which 210 were original Tudor glass, green and opaque. The place seemed to have been bypassed by the hurrying centuries. From it emerged and walked down the narrow garden path, an old man of great charm — Mr. Shepherd. We returned with him, up the garden path. His daughter had just married an American G.I. and Mr. Shepherd was unable to visualise the picture of him settling down in the English countryside. He planned abruptly to sell the house and spend the rest of his own days in Barbados. He made a mental calculation of what the house had cost him in 1924, with 16 acres; what he had spent on it, adding the electric circular saw and the cement flooring in the apple store; drew a line under the whole calculation and added up the result; £8,000. At this price, four prospective buyers, including ourselves, had arrived in the remotest part of Cornwall within 48 hours. He selected me deliberately for my interest in domestic architecture. And was there ever such a surprising house? He led us into the great hall, where the wide open Tudor hearth of about 1490 was over-built and dated 1572, with a fine plaster chimney piece flanked by supporting caryatid figures. One of these was a bearded man, the other of a woman –

79

possibly Sir John Arundel and his wife, for when the house was built, their initials J.A. (John Arundel) and K.A. (Katherine Arundel) appeared in the finely ribbed plaster ceiling which had replaced in 1572 the old raftered hall of the manor. At the same time a minstrels' gallery had been added with a row of miniature arches, looking down into the hall. A massive refectory table had been built immovably in the hall itself and was flooded with light from the immense Tudor window.

Admiral Arundel had been Admiral, Western Approaches, to Queen Elizabeth I, and, finding it necessary to spend his winters in Cornwall, had built himself this snug abode in a sheltered fold of the hills four miles from the Atlantic cliffs. Perhaps there would, as usual, be Victorian horrors in the recesses of the house, but Shepherd led us on, by a half stair opening from a corner of the great hall, to a vast apartment on the south side of the house. This was the drawing-room and I gasped at its ceiling – one of the few original barrel-shaped Tudor ceilings in moulded plaster still surviving. There is one in the only wing not destroyed by the fire at Lanhydrock, and a Jacobean one at Chastleton. Here there were angles to the curve, and five great pendants of modelled plaster work hanging along the centre. At the far end were the Norfolk arms in plaster – two deer supporting the shield and the motto – VIRTUTIS LAUS ACTIO. There was, unbelievably, a Tudor oriel window in mullioned stone, a semicircular embrasure in the centre of the outside wall; and beside it, tapped the leaves of a giant magnolia tree. Facing the window was another Tudor hearth, surmounted by an elaborately carved plaster overmantel. This had many shields upon it, including the swallows (hirondelles) of the Arundels and the Vivian lions. On each side were heroic figures – in what might have been Saxon robes. To top it all, the plasterer (he would have been called the playsterer) had begun the date in Roman letters: ANNO DOMINI MCCCCCLXX, and running out of space for the III had put the arabic numeral 3 instead, to complete the date 1573. All this was very authentic. Beyond the drawing-room ran a long passage also ceilinged in ribbed plaster, and half-way along it – culminating surprise – was a Plantaganet spiral stone stairway, in a separate turret, like the one at Cranborne Manor, surviving from the earlier building. Beyond the house on this side was a majestic Elizabethan stone barn, buttressed at the end like a cathedral. There was a columbiary in the grey stone wall, and pigeons fluttered up on to the ridge coping of the great barn, where they pirouetted about, cooing incessantly. There was a small garden with high stone walls, against which pear trees ripened. Also an orchard from which Shepherd and his congenial gardener, Dingle, had collected eight tons of apples in a good season.

With one swift glance select the best.* There could be no doubt about this — and whatever might be our new (and as we believed) permanent commitments at Chilham, there could be no doubt in my mind that Trerice would always hold its present value.** All my resources had been thrown into the acquisition of the Chilham estate; as had previously been the case with the Island of Gigha, and my wife was therefore persuaded to invest money temporarily in Trerice until I relieved her of all liability in the matter in 1949 at her request. Shepherd was delighted, and when Thelma and I saw with finality in the assembly room at Swaffham the last 50 votes being counted which tipped the scale to my Socialist opponent, she turned to me, squeezed my hand reassuringly and said, "We shall have a lot of fun with Trerice." We did, and perhaps, if we had been content to stay there, we should be there still, mellowing like the autumn pears upon the sunny walls beneath the great umbrella pine trees, but there was Chilham with its restless demands, and the urges, still felt like a severed hand after an amputation, of the political life. We advertised Trerice to be let furnished, and a frozen voice, from the north of Scotland, spoke on the long distance telephone agreeing to take Trerice for a year without even seeing it first. This was Elton, blue with cold and anxious to find a warmer climate for his wife before he returned to his trading connection in India. So we returned, a little sadly, and possibly not without premonition to Chilham, with its materialistic atmosphere and its false dignities. I was invited by the central Advisory Council for Adult Education in the Services to do a flying tour of the Middle East to lecture to our troops out there; and in the vacuum of my life created by the loss of my constituency in Norfolk, it seemed wise to my wife and me that I should accept and find diversion there. I was returning, inevitably to taste again of the waters of the Nile.

* From an Edwardian book on nursery etiquette, 'Do not fumble with the cakes. With one swift glance select the best.'
** A judgement which was fully upheld when the National Trust bought the house from me in 1953 with funds made available from the Woodward bequest, for £12,000.

CHAPTER 7

I have known the Sphinx when she was still half hidden by the desert; like a woman in the Orient, appropriately veiled. And that dates me, for since 1929 or so, the busy archaeologists have been burrowing between her paws, unearthing tombs and temples, until today she has few secrets from the prying eyes of the passer-by. There is little of her mystery left; and even the riddle is partly answered. I suppose I am a romantic, and cannot help watching a little wistfully the engulfing of the Middle East by the tidal wave of Westernism. Yet it retains its magic for those who keep to the byways; and mysticism is its motive force. Passing down a street in Suez the presence of this force was real to me for an instant, a towering black wall on my left like a dark face obscuring the sky — then the impression vanished. And there were only men bowing their heads, humbly to the ground, in the direction of the black Qaba at Mecca. They were still doing it, all over the Middle East, at stated times of day, when I left. It is not difficult to feel uplifted amid so much prayer.

I flew out to Cairo in December 1945. Treaty revision was in the air, and it was during that first realisation among Eastern peoples that the Churchill Government had crashed, and already the rattle of stones which precede the avalanche could be heard, heralding the crash of an Empire, with great blocks like India, Burma and Palestine falling away from the mountainside. And I felt that sense of melancholy which comes over a man whose family has inherited vast estates and a great position, but whom the incidence of taxation and social legislation has forced to relinquish the outlying parts, perhaps the very ones which, because of their remoteness from the family home, have the most happy childhood associations. For I was visiting lands where for more than half a century, an Englishman was venerated as lord and master, had ended his association with dignity in the victories of Iraq, Syria, Abyssinia, Eritrea and the Western Desert, and having survived all, was now being sold up under the contemptuous gaze of peoples who had once considered him little short of supernatural; and sold up, moreover, by men whose view of the estate seemed to be that, if they could not imitate the grandeur of former days, they could nevertheless convert the family place into maisonettes and administer the home farm on communal lines.

The approach to Egypt was instructive. Dawn over the Western Desert – a brown ribbed land. Then, sharp as a drawn line, the Nile Valley.

Cairo, from the air, was characterised by its cube-like houses; flat roofed. Like blocks of loaf sugar on the ground. A buff city, with a pale blue sky.

Cairo has a strident, definite personality: a personality of brass. The noise is tinny and incessant; tram bells clang, motor-car horns hoot, buses roar. Street vendors shout their wares. It is a continuous roar, like the inside of some factory designed solely for the making of noise. The characteristic garb is a single white, or dirty white gown, with a cloth skull-cap. But there are all sorts. The effendis wear grey suits with red fezes. Two men across the street, dressed like desert bedouin, with flowing black robes and white linen headdresses; carrying sticks. But one does not often see the Keffiyeh of Arabia – that linen head-covering bound on with a black or gold aqal.

Outwardly Cairo had changed very little since I was there during the war. Across the street from my hotel, under the name of the Pharmacie Mazloum Bey and the words 'Articles de Parfumerie', was a portrait of the Queen of England. In front of it, under a lime tree, a woman swathed in black with sandals on her feet carried an immense bundle of sacking on her head; she upset a basketful of brushes and knicknacks. Farouk was building a buff palace for himself at the foot of the Great Pyramid. It looked like a corn on the toe of a giant.

I lunched with the Killearns and afterwards had a very interesting talk with the Ambassador in which he discussed frankly the inside facts of the political situation there. To say the least, he did not think Nokrasy's the right government with whom to negotiate a revision of the treaty. He asked me to use the Embassy as my home whenever I was in Cairo and I stayed there both when they were in residence and when they were in the Fayum, where I also visited them.

I had not met Killearn before and had only met Lady Killearn once during the war when Bill Astor had brought her to hear me lecture to American soldiers at the Churchill Club in London on 'Britain's Position in the Middle East'. She had sat in the front row beside my wife, exclaiming, as she listened, "He has such fire!"

Brigadier Anderson, donnish and bespectacled, called for me to go to dinner with the C.-in-C., Paget. There were seemingly dozens of generals, with a sprinkling of brigadiers. Boy Long, a neighbour from Norfolk, now a Brigadier on Paget's staff, came up at once and his knowledge of what had happened in the recent General Election in Norfolk proved a helpful introduction to the Commander-in-Chief's martial entourage.

I sat on Paget's left and he opened up on Egypt and Palestine. He was very pro-Arab on Palestine. He thought we should continue to administer the mandate indefinitely, and considered Partition impossible from his security point of view; he thought that the Egyptian Treaty should be regarded as obsolete, in view of the new world organisation and the futility of local Canal defence. "We must," he said, "regard the Middle East as a whole." He was very keen on army education and welfare of troops. He had found men sleeping on floors — and had given them beds. The massacre of Jews in Tripolitania had taken him by surprise, but he had just moved a battalion there for fear of a massacre of the Italians. So they had come in handy.

On the train to Alexandria in the Pullman saloon next day, a Pasha next to me, Badrawi Pasha, offered coffee, and we got into conversation. He wanted to know why England would not allow Egypt to export her cotton to other European countries (which was not true). He also wanted to buy a family aeroplane. I recommended de Havilland and he was impressed by the speed of the Mosquito — and even more impressed by Jet Meteor 605 m.p.h. How much would it cost?

"Only built for fighter purposes at present."

"Yes, but 'à peu pres'?"

"About £50,000."

He invited me to lunch on Boxing Day at his home in Cairo and I reciprocated with an invitation to visit me when he came to England.

Badrawi got out to change trains, clasping my hand in his, and with many expressions of pleasurable anticipation for the 26th, when he hoped that I would bring anyone else I liked.

Egypt was looking lovely from the train, under a clear soft blue sky and with warm sunshine gilding the mud walled villages. There were feathery trees along the route as well as palms. Oxen and donkeys toiled in the green fields. We crossed a bridge over a wide sweep of the slate blue-brown Nile; a shale colour. A felucca with tall mast nestled in to the bank; and more of these lined the distant shore, where a black chimney stack and concrete buildings struck a more modern note. On my left a square brown house, flat-roofed, stood in a grove of palm trees.

An ox went round and round in a patient circle under an olive tree drawing water. We passed a village where children in clouts squatted in the dust, and a slave girl stared through the bars of a window at the passing train. The sunlight filled the fresh green growth of the flat black fields with emerald luminosity. A white wader, rather like a small heron, strutted along in the shade of a stately line of palms, and a black raven hovered over the moist ground. In the villages, dogs, goats, black water buffalo and donkeys wandered about. The soil was cultivated like the black fens of Norfolk. Not an inch was wasted.

At Alexandria I got a Chilean international lawyer whom I met at the Carlyle Club to come round to my hotel and expatiate on the clauses of the Egyptian Treaty. We marked up a map with the zones of permitted occupation after the war.

To arrive in the greenness of the British Embassy on return to Cairo was good and refreshing, after the desert of hotel life.

The only Oriental touches in my room were Chinese prints of the Great Wall which Killearn had no doubt brought with him from his days at the Peking Embassy, which are described by Daniel Varé in *Laughing Diplomat*. The scarlet telephone by my bed had old Arabic numerals in the dialling holes.

The Ambassador asked me at lunch to join him and Lady Killearn down in the Fayum and arranged for a car to drive me there. I swept past the Pyramids, through a great British military camp at Mena, and out on the desert road to the Fayum, which I reached in the dark. A buff archway beside the road led up an avenue of cactus to what was for all the world like a Californian hacienda – and no wonder, for it was built by American archaeologists excavating the Graeco-Roman ruins of Karanis behind it. Egyptian sentries stood about in the dark wearing their red tarbushes, with rifles slung over their shoulders.

Kom-Aushim was a pleasant change for the Killearns from the Embassy, and Lady Killearn was enjoying the peace of it while waiting for her baby. After dinner we sat talking and Killearn drew me out on the unity of the Empire, and I grew excited about the federal conception of it and the need for the Empire to speak with one voice if it were to survive as a great power. I was too wound up to sleep easily afterwards.

For the most part I had the Embassy in Cairo to myself. The Master of Balliol, the late Lord Lindsay of Birker, once wrote to me: 'You are not fundamentally a democrat', and I fear he is right. The solitary splendour of State apartments is too much to my taste. There could certainly not have been anything more soothing than to dine at the Embassy alone in the evening, waited on by the Egyptian servants, who brought course after course of delicious foods on silver plate before me, while full-length portraits of Edward VII and George V looked down and seemed almost to nod in approval; to sit after dinner in the small drawing-room with the shaded Chinese table lamps casting a pleasant glow on the olive-green satin curtains and the Oriental rugs spread on the fawn carpeting. Hassan, the doyen of dark servants, who remembered Lord Lloyd with affection, was standing by a tray of drinks as I passed through the hall, to show me where to find one when I went to bed. But alone I drank only the lemon juice. My contribution to the servants' fund that day may have made the tread of those silent-footed Egyptians more springy than usual. They certainly conferred an inestimable boon of peace on me under the strenuous conditions of the modern world.

When I went upstairs I stepped out of my bedroom on to the balcony. A half-moon shone down upon the garden. An Egyptian police guard wearing a red fez and a long dark cape, in the act of lighting a cigarette (his cupped hands illuminated by the flaring match), hurriedly dowsed it and moved silently off across the lawn to merge into the dark shadows of the giant acacia-like maw trees. In the still waters of the Nile the lights along the farther bank were reflected brilliantly. The distant palm trees merged in the night into an indistinct outline of darkness reflected in the water. It was cold in a thin silk dressing-gown; my stomach felt the balustrade through it, where I leant; and I stepped back into the warm bedroom through the swinging mosquito-proof doors, leaving the shutters down and french windows open.

The day had been mild and sunny and I had spent much of it tracking down two Regency Negro figures in gold brocade robes, holding lanterns, which I had noticed on my way in from Tura. An army car and captain drove me and, when we found them, took the Egyptian shopkeeper and his friend down a labyrinth of twisting narrow streets to his house in the very heart of old Cairo, to see the missing stands and lanterns. I had them in mind as a Christmas present for the Killearns. The man wanted too much for them, but one assumes in the East that quoted prices are only ranging shots in a long-drawn battle.

The figures were obviously antique, and probably Italian. But when I said they were old, the vendor's interpreter thought this was meant to be disparaging, and said, "Not old, he make them self."

"In that case," said I, "the value is considerably reduced."

"Oh, them very antique. He make them when he very young. He very old now."

I gave Lord Carlisle a lift in the army wagon, with driver and escort which G.H.Q. 2nd Echelon gave me to run down to Kom-Aushim. After a pleasant dinner, the Ambassador took us across the Fayum in his car to the new hotel by the lake, where we sat at a table watching about two couples dancing. The hotel was very empty. There are 80,000 bedouin there, and it used to be said that you could get a man 'stuck' for five piastres. He told us on the way back how the Minister of State (Oliver Lyttelton) came to be appointed in the Middle East. Wavell and the Service chiefs were asking for what amounted to a political C.-in-C. on their own level. They did not much like Killearn's idea that what was needed was someone from the War Cabinet. Which is what they got.

Sunday was spent colourfully – shooting duck in the Fayum where the Ambassador had a marsh of about 100 acres, with four or five butts of dried palm frond, in which we crouched while a few duck flighted in at first, and then left us alone. George Carlisle and I only shot one each. The Ambassador and Giles Bey – an English Colonel in the Egyptian police – got about fifteen apiece. One Egyptian boy, in a long white gown and a white cloth wrapped round his head, crouched inside the butt, groaning from time to time, making horrid nasal sounds, and indicating his wrist to show that he was in the grip of malaria. But the lure of twenty piastres for the day was presumably too much. The other boy, a grown man, with black moustache, walnut complexion and bloodshot eyes, drew his gown up to his hips and waded out to place my decoy duck, and then crouched down in the marshy ground about fifty yards behind the butt, where I urged him to make himself more grey and less white in garb so as not to frighten off the duck. At last he lay down, covered in some clout almost indistinguishable from the surrounding land. There were reeds all about, and palm trees fringed the area. Two mounted Egyptian police, in blue uniforms and red tarbushes, patrolled the area on white horses.

The morning was pleasantly bright and hot, and the drive into the Fayum was fascinating. The mud road was edged with a thin ribbon of railway line, scarcely eighteen inches wide, along which a man in traditional garb rode a donkey. We passed a camel loaded up with two flat tables. Everywhere in the villages of mud-walled or peeling plaster houses, men and women stood about, as if time were endless. (This was not their Sunday, which is on our Fridays.) Every now and then the smooth waters of a canal would plunge down a weir to some lower level of irrigation. The fields were growing clover, beans, maize, sugar-cane. The cultivation went on with camels, with water buffalo, with oxen; the same old wooden prong in the same old Egyptian earth. The land was owned mostly by the pashas and let out on tenancies of four or five acres to smallholders.

A man standing in the village street wore a brilliant gown of yellow-green. Women walked past, clad all in black, with black head-cloths, and gold crescents pricked up into their right nostrils. They belonged to one tribe.

Back at Kom-Aushim we explored the ruins of Karanis, I taking a guide with a fas, the local pickaxe-hoe. I found a large Roman coin encrusted with verdigris and left it to be cleaned by a Dr. Halter who lived near by.

I always return from ruins wondering how soon our own household utensils will be found in mounds of fragments as at Karanis and Hiroshima.

As we descended from the ruined Roman city, Kom-Aushim looked for all the world like a *Beau Geste* fort of the Foreign Legion in the desert. The Union Jack fluttered from the central tower. Five cream camels of the guard provided by the Sudan

Camel Corps were tethered to pegs beyond the enclosure. The black-faced Sudanese, wearing khaki tunics, breeches and puttees, stood at the slope arms position every time one entered the gate or left it.

After dinner I gave Carlisle a lift back to the Embassy in my army wagon, with its driver and escort smartly turned out, a credit generally to the Anglo-Egyptian alliance. There is no doubt that in addition to Killearn, the British Tommy was a strikingly impressive ambassador in Egypt; a modest conqueror.

When I passed through Cairo again on my way from Tripolitania to the Sudan I fell in with some old friends at Shepherds; Wavel Wakefield and his wife (Wavel, hot on the trail of post-war Civil Aviation) and Bill Allen, now press attaché at Ankara, married to a pretty and charming Russian who introduced me to some Turks as "un Homme fort Dangereux". We lunched together at Shepherds, and I was amused to see Bill acquiring the solidity of outline and poise of a happily married man. He told me how some Englishmen had defended Kars for the Turks in 1875.

I also ran into Altounyan unexpectedly at Shepherds, wearing a Colonel's uniform, on which his Passchendaele M.C. glowed happily, on my way through to Khartoum. His greeting was characteristic.

"You were absolutely right about my poems. You will be pleased to hear that All Souls have decided that they are It; and six of them are being set to music." Presumably there was no direct connection between these two pieces of information, but it called up a delightful picture of the Fellows of All Souls sitting round the fireside, tuning up their violins and cellos, while Altounyan's dark and mystic face peered half apologetically from behind his large round steel rimmed glasses, as he declaimed:

"My sorrow is a smooth and perfect thing
Carved of the silence that must now endure."

In the Canal Zone, Austrian prisoners of war were chipping stones to make gravel and path edging 'fur Schönheit'. Aircraft were parked on the desert aerodromes there like cars at a race meeting – rows of them. I reflected cynically that there had only been thirty-six altogether for the Syrian campaign in 1941. Two large Italian cruisers lay out on the great Bitter Lake. If the intelligence of the Arabs is in their eyes, they must have recognised in Britain a very great power. They had seen the German armies hurled off their doorstep at Alamein. And now our captives, wearing grey dungarees with a black stripe down the side and a black diamond patch on their backs, were cheerfully chipping stones in the barrack gardens of the British. I asked one where they were captured. Italy. One came from Salzburg, another from Steirmark. I asked them what it was like in the Canal Zone. 'Sehr heiss im Sommer.' But they seemed fairly contented. One said he had been there a year by December 1st, 1945. The desert mountains there, which edge the plain and hem it in to the south are the most barren feature in the world – the Jebel Attarca. Some say it has never been explored. Across the blue water I peered at the Sinai hills, somewhere in which American oil-seekers claimed to have broken into a shaft of King Solomon's mines.

On the way to Genifa I drove along the Canal bank and saw the grey three-funnelled *Empress of Aus alia* (war wear had removed two letters) steam majestically down the blue strip of water between stone banks and sand ridges. The decks were crowded, as if there were standing room only, with Australian Air Force boys homeward bound at long last from their gallant service in England and Europe. I waved from my stopped utility van, and they waved back. Then the Egyptian driver drove on furiously as ever, pointing out with relish the twisted and rusty hulks of bombed merchantmen on the banks where they had been dragged from the Canal after German attacks. I assumed that his glee was due to the fact that they had been sunk by the Germans – but it may have been due to the Canal being kept clear. I could not tell.

Driving to Ballah I picked up two young Black Watch soldiers who wanted a lift to Ismailia. They had just arrived from Germany and, although only lads, had been in the stiffest fighting on the Elbe. One, wounded at Uhlsen, said: "I was number one on the Piat and was told to get out across a ploughed field. Then we saw some people and we looked at them and they looked at us and we said, 'Crikey, they're Jerries'. They scuttled back to some buildings and opened up with a 20mm flak gun. The Corporal was just turning round when he got it in the hip. We got back to the wood and the officer said to dig in in front of it. Well, I was lying down trying to dig – of course I couldn't dig a slit – when another of these shells they use for aircraft hit me. Not all of it, you understand, only a fragment."

"Did it knock you out? Did you have to go into hospital?"

"Oh, yes."

"For how long?"

"About two months."

"It was only a flesh wound?"

"Yes," said he, and I explained the difficulties of more complicated injuries.

This one (from Aberdeen) had been in the Argylls then; the other, from South Wales, in the Gordons. He said:

"Someone told me it was the German women who would win the peace and it is – – well right. Lovely they are. And living well."

"We are told," I reminded him, "that the Germans are living on half our ration."

Both laughed. "So they say. But when you see them they've got everything. Lovely they are too. They've had people to work for 'em all the time, Poles and Russians. They used to lie on the beach – we was at a seaside resort – and complain because we made a noise disturbing them with our lorries going past in the afternoon."

"I hope you went on making a noise."

"I should think so. Why, one of these German women killed one of our paratroopers who had come down and broken his leg – killed him with a pitchfork. We put her up against a wall and shot her all right. Why, they murdered our chaps – our paratroopers. So when they was caught in their turn they was put in a barn and straw put all round and set fire to the – – place. When we was in a road outside one house the Sergeant told us to keep our heads down and kicked the gate open and walked up the path. One of these snipers shot him through the head. So then we got the flame-throwers on to the place and they came out with their hands up. But we stood 'em up and shot the lot. They are fighters – the Germans.

"All this of course was in the thick of the fighting. Now the German women make up to the men for cigarettes and chocolate – and are terrified of the Russians."

Aberdeen took up the tale.

"We were in Lubeck, and part of where we'd got to come

under the Russian zone. So we had to withdraw. The Germans were packing their suitcases within half an hour, trying to get into our zone. These Russians are awful. I've seen seventeen of 'em raping one girl."

"You have seen this yourself?" I pressed him.

"Yes."

"Was it dark or daylight?"

"Daylight. Seventeen of 'em rearpin' 'er. 'Save me, Tommy,' she called out."

"What did you do?" I asked.

"Well, what could I do? They're our great Allies, and it would start trouble if we began interfering. Besides, she was a German girl — when all said and done. And look what they did to our paratroopers. Besides, the Russians say it's only what the Germans did to all of their women, so what are you to do?"

"But they've no cause for to rape them," South Wales put in. "Besides, there's no need to."

Then they began talking about the American soldiers getting off with the English girls. "Got 'em all upside down they did."

"But," points out the other fairly, "what about us and the French girls? Weren't the French soldiers just as angry with their women for getting off with us? And can you blame them? It's the women's fault."

Well, this was the fine cutting edge of the British Army, and a milder-looking pair of boys you would travel far to find.

Aberdeen had his gold wound stripe on his battledress. Both had transferred to the Black Watch, to avoid going to Burma. And after a fortnight of Egypt, even out in the wilderness at Qassassin, they seemed delighted with it.

They thought Monty had got a bit swollen-headed towards the end, and had not cared much what happened to the men as long as they got on. They spoke of a division at Caen which fought for a mile and a half in an hour, and lost it, "The Jerries were just mowing them down with mortars." Aberdeen made a motion of his shoulders each way, to show how they toppled. And a gesture of mortars whizzing over, six at a time. But he was not in that fight.

A Great Power ceases to be a Great Power when its citizens become too tired to die on their feet. We did not seem to have reached that predicament.

After dropping the two youths in the dark at Ismailia, I had to go on miles to the wilds of El Ballah. As the Egyptian driver had to return to Ismailia anyway, and as I was due to pass through it in the morning on the way back to Tahag, I decided to stay at the United Services Club, but when I got there at eleven I found a dance in full swing: tipsy groups in a darkened bar kissing Waafs and bellowing Christmas Carols, "Noel — Noel"; the guest rooms all locked; and no sign of the keys as the soffragi who looked after them, being married, had gone off and no one knew of their whereabouts. So I was put into the absent soffragi's cubicle at the end of the corridor where two strips of thin palliasse, in cretonne covers, lay side by side over two-thirds of the width of the bed and admitted a fine draught from the floor. No sheet and two blankets. I spread out the towels that I could find and spent a somewhat restless night, with a reptile overhead in the eaves equally disturbed. But the place was beautifully situated on a lake, where yachts were moored. In the bright early sunshine a Vice-Admiral (Tennant) and two other naval officers arrived, as bright as new pins, and talked nautically on the veranda. They were asking for baths, and the soffragi dashed into my room, seized a towel on which I had wiped off the dust of three deserts, and rushed out with it to the Admiral.

"Is this towel clean?" I heard the Admiral ask dubiously.

"Yes, sah. Very clean towel, sah."

I breakfasted near them on the sunny terrace; then sped on to Tahag for the last of that hellish week in the wilderness of the Canal Zone.

To drive across the Delta is an education in itself. My driver was something of a character. He wore Western clothes, with a cloth cap and a jacket with his elbow sticking through a hole in the sleeve. His skin was dark, with a forbidding face and thick-set jaw. His eyes were a muddy grey. I thought him the most lugubrious fellow, until something happened which made him laugh all the way back to Cairo. He drove at sixty miles an hour all the way, honking on his horn continuously and mouthing horrible adjectives in Arabic at passing cars which would not yield to him quickly. His favourite gesture when obliged to slow up was to throw the hand gear lever of the Ford out of gear with a gesture of disgust. He had no liking for army encampments. "Me not fond stay here," was his pithy comment, with a deprecating wave of the hand as he surveyed the bare open desert round Qassassin.

"I am not very fond of it either," I had replied, but the difference, apparently, was that I was expected to stay the night there and he was not. He had shot off to Ismailia. Now he drove fast across the Delta, gesturing impotently at the jolting surface of the by-road from Zagazig to Behna, where we joined the main Cairo-Alexandria road. He tore through Egyptian towns and villages, past the shambling groups of men in white gowns and women in black, past the flocks of sheep. He drove across the Delta to the peril of the wayfarers, though many, who erred therein. Along the canals, the great barges with their raised prows and triangular sails were towed along the bank, at the end of long ropes, by men in white gowns, straining forward in line, against the pull of the rope across their breasts. Their faces were distorted with strain – they sloped forward in a line – five of them, reminding me of a frieze of slaves on the walls of a Pharaoh's tomb.

We passed endless water-wheels being turned by patient black buffaloes, which trudged blindfolded in a circle yoked to the spindle, sluicing the water up from the canal level to splash out and run into little channels between the fields. Usually a small boy sat in the shade of a tree, giving the animal an occasional whack.

At last we came to Abu Hommus where a street of dingy houses, with shuttered windows, and men smoking their long narghelas in the open doors of the cafés, crowded the scene. The driver began asking, "Fin Tahir el Masri Bey?" and many and confusing were the directions. We asked three or four times, before we left the canal road at a cluster of grey mud houses, and began threading our way along a hard mud track, beside a twisting canal, with fertile fields of new green corn, beans and clover, irrigated by the same patient buffalo, and spreading in all directions. A camel laden down with sugar cane lumbered past us. There were clusters of hovels here and there, where women wore silver bangles on their bare ankles. The little girls dashed about in pink slips of cotton. We came to a house by a level crossing over the railway line, where some better-dressed women directed us to go on, over the line, till the track ended, they said, in the Qasr el Masri.

We saw it soon after that, an imposing outline of roofs and buildings set about with palm and pine. The fellaheen were everywhere moving along the canal banks, looking up curiously at the khaki army car, which dashed along the narrow track in the last rays of the setting sun. This was going down, gold, just ahead of us; and we found ourselves abruptly in a clearing of hardened mud, in front of the guest-house of the Qasr. And there, standing in the wrought-iron gateway, was the Bey, in a long robe of fawn silky hide above his flowing garments of grey and white. On his head he wore a skull-cap of maroon red felt, neatly creased down the front, and from the back of it swung a silk tassel of midnight blue. His dark face, with its greying moustache, was wreathed in smiles. Another man (his cousin) in European clothes, and wearing the red Turkish fez, stepped forward first to welcome me as I jumped down from the car.

"Tahir Bey is so glad that you have come to visit him." We shook hands.

"It is I who am delighted," I replied, moving to meet my advancing host, who took my hand, with a light touch of his brown one, and bowing and smiling led me up the steps to his guest-house. The white marble steps led into a hall of brownly patterned tiles, much worn by the feet of visitors, and on our right was a long room, surrounded by settees and chairs covered in white, where guests were received. The Bey led me to the central settee at the far end, beneath a ceremonial carpet in red and blue on a fawn background, emblazoned with the royal arms of Iraq and the date, from the Hejira, 1339. For this had been presented to him by the Regent Abdul Illah, on the occasion of an official visit by Tahir Bey and Hamad Pasha, representing the Egyptian Bedouin, to mediate in a dispute between the Shammar and the Ubbaid before the war. The walls were of stippled beige, and the windows barred in ornamental iron, with shutters painted brown without. Deep pelmets of scalloped maroon and gold velvet shielded them. On the side wall, framed in ornate gilt under glass, was a large photograph of Tahir Bey as a young man (he was by now almost sixty), in his robes and cap; and beside it one of his sons, Kassim, in bedouin costume, astride a high-stepping white Arab pony, pacing along some thickly crowded street. His cousin, Salah el Masri, seated himself on a chair to the left. Now Kassim entered, also wearing a blue suit and red fez. He was a commanding figure, of heavy build, with dark eyes and black moustache. He spoke English slowly, and with more difficulty than his uncle.

"My father says he is happy because you are under his roof."

"And I am honoured and proud to be welcomed to his house."

"It is yours."

We talked of my journey from Ismailia and Tahag. They were astonished that I had come so far (a detour of 320 miles), but I told them that I had been determined not to miss the opportunity.

A young soffragi in a powder-blue gown striped with darker blue entered with a tray on which were four tiny cups of Turkish coffee, which we sipped and handed back empty to him, where he stood waiting with the tray.

I began to wonder what happened next, and asked whether my driver knew where to put my luggage. So I was shown my bedroom which was next door, where two large metal four-posters, in the French style of the Second Empire, were made up on each side of the room and hung with mosquito netting.

"This house," Kassim explained, "was built especially for our guests. Tomorrow you shall see our house." The luggage was already laid on chair and sofa. There was a dressing-table in the French provincial style, surmounted by a large oblong mirror against the wall, but no sign of a wash-stand. So I asked where I should wash my hands, and Kassim led me across the hall to a collection of wash-places where Oriental jostled Western methods of sanitation. I was wondering about a bath, but he showed me into a shower-bath, beneath which a shell shaped basin was fixed against the wall.

"There is cold water," he said, "but if you wish hot, it can be brought."

Not quite understanding what I would bath in, I said I was not particularly interested in having a bath, but would like to wash my hands. We went out to the basin where there were ordinary taps and a towel hanging.

"Machmoud," he shouted, and the soffragi was told to bring hot water, which came, eventually, in a finely spouted Oriental flagon. Kassim had left me by now and I indicated to the boy that I wanted him to pour the water into the basin; but this he would not do, waiting until I thrust forward my hands, holding the soap, for him to pour the water upon. In this way the warm water arrived, and the washing was completed.

I found Salah in the reception room and asked whether we could stroll round outside while it was still light. He assented readily and we went down the steps and round the side of the stables beside the Canal. The Masri family, he explained, had been on these lands for over four hundred years, and various relatives lived in the houses scattered about the place. I asked after the principal activities of the estate, and learnt that cotton-growing was one of its main interests, but the cotton crop was all harvested (in October). The breeding of horses was another, and out of the yard, led by a groom, came a superb white Arab mare, bridled in blue and red, set with cowrie shells. She fretted eagerly and was held for my inspection. I stroked her ears, and put my arm round her white neck.

Kassim had reappeared.

"Would you like to ride tomorrow?" he asked.

"I would indeed," I replied, "but alas, I have brought no riding clothes."

"We could perhaps find you a pair of riding-breeches to fit you. We will see."

Now he went into the back yard, where a line of plaster stables faced the square servants' building, which met the guest-house at an angle. Tahir Bey was standing there; and a boy holding aloft a flaring acetylene burner. We went inside a loose box where a brown mare was accompanied by a three-week-old foal, which trotted round and under her. I made friends with this mare also, and then the foal was let out into the yard, where it trotted about, puzzled, in fits and starts, its eye bright in the glare of the lamp.

"It is called Foas," (Victor), Kassim told me. "The mother is Mabrouka."

We went back into the guest-house, by a door in the corner of the yard, wiping our feet clean of dung and mud on a scraper mat.

Inside the hall once more I asked what time we dined.

"As you like," said Kassim. "Six o'clock, seven o'clock, eight o'clock, nine o'clock. As you like."

"But when do you usually dine?"

"As you like. This is your house."

"Well, what about eight o'clock?"

"As you like."

I asked Salah if I should change for dinner. "In England I should change, after driving," but I hoped he would advise me, as I was not familiar with Egyptian customs.

"Whatever you wish."

"Well, then, I think I might have a wash and change."

Whereupon with many farewells till dinner-time, I retired to my room and set about unpacking my suits.

I found Kassim and Salah still talking in the reception room — indeed, I had been able to hear them in there while I was changing, as there was a door in the wall, with a glass panel over it. Tahir Bey had disappeared, but soon came in again, and we began a conversation on the Anglo-Egyptian Treaty. Salah, with his wise and beaky face, bespectacled, occasionally rubbing his fez to and fro over his bushy iron grey hair in his excitement, did most of the interpreting. He was the medium for the Egyptian point of view. "From the King to the Mobs," he explained, "the Egyptians want to see the last of the British troops leave Egypt. Some semi-cowards may tell you that this is not so." Kassim said, more slowly, his words coming more weightily, where he sat with one knee up on the settee on the right of his father's chair, "The Atlantic Charter promised independence to all peoples. What we ask for is independence."

"And you do not take the view," I asked, "that the treaty is an affair between sovereign independent states?"

"Not while the British soldiers are here."

"Ask Tahir Bey," I said to Salah, "if he thinks that most of the Egyptians who are asking for a revision of the treaty realise that under Article 16, the revision article, it is provided that any revision shall contemplate the continuation of the Alliance, the use of bases and communications in time of war or emergency, and refers to our right to keep a garrison of ten thousand men and four hundred air crews in the Canal Zone?"

This took a long time to interpret, and was accompanied by a good deal of shifting about of Salah's fez. The reply came quick enough from Tahir Bey: "Not two per cent."

Then he went on. "Of course we want to remain allies, close allies, like England and France. But there are plenty of places where you can keep your troops — Palestine, Cyrenaica."

"Well," I said, "naturally I understand your point of view. I respect your sentiments. But may I put this to you? You must realise that in England we have had a change of Government, we have a Labour Government, many of whose supporters admire Russia. We might very well take the view that we have defeated Germany twice, rubbed Germany out, and that our principal anxieties are over. We are having continuous trouble in Palestine.

In Egypt the Egyptians want us to go. Supposing we took the point of view that if we could not have our defence bases, our base workshops and all the rest of it, where it suits us for our strategic requirements, we would rather pull out of the Middle East altogether, and leave Russia to fill the vacuum. How would that suit Egypt?"

A silence of stony horror filled the room; even the acetylene lamp hanging from the ceiling seemed to flutter.

"There is no need to move in a hurry," said Tahir Bey. "Besides, you could move to Sinai."

"But for how long? Do you mean that in exchange for all the rights which we enjoy under the treaty, Egypt would be prepared to give us sovereignty over the Sinai desert, and agree to a joint defence of the Canal? In short, that the Canal should become the Egyptian frontier?"

There was a good deal of conversation in Arabic over this, until Salah explained for Tahir Bey that he was insistent that we should preserve an intimate alliance, but Egypt felt that as soon as she could build up an army of 200,000 or 300,000 men, equipped of course and trained by us, they could very well hold the country until we could arrive. Sinai would be needed by Egypt eventually for emigration, as the population would increase rapidly. But we could keep troops there for, say, ten years.

I pointed out that after building all our workshops and establishments in the Canal area, it would scarcely be considered worth while setting them all up in the Sinai desert, unless we had it for a considerable time. Besides, there is no water there. I pretended to think that the British public would end by feeling that as we were not wanted in the Middle East we had better leave the place altogether, and if Russia wanted Azerbaijan and Turkey and perhaps to advance over Iraq and Transjordan to the frontiers of Egypt, no doubt they would prefer to deal with that situation on their own.

At these words the family was pensive. They did not conceal their horror of 'Bolshevism'. Kassim laughed heartily when I observed, "Egypt is a land fit for pashas to live in."

Finally the soffragi came in and announced dinner to be ready, and they showed me into the dining-room, which was on the other side of my bedroom. The walls were of stippled blue, and a modern oil painting of a duck hanging up adorned one wall.

I was placed at the head of the table (contrary to our custom in England), with my host on my right. In a large oval dish in front of me was curled a young roast lamb, its head severed from its body, leering uncomfortably at me with sightless eyes. From it, however, arose a succulent smell. I was somewhat baffled by the utensil problem as there was a knife and fork and spoon dumped beside my plate at every course, and the plates were piled one above the other, so that when one course was finished and the plate removed, the one underneath was ready.

The first course was of lentils and macaroni, which I gathered, from Tahir Bey's example, were eaten with the spoon. After a course of this, with a renewed helping by my smiling host, I became aware that they were waiting for me to be the first to dip into the roast lamb. I helped myself gingerly with a carving knife and fork propped against it, but Tahir Bey, smiling and saying, "As with Hassan Suhail, eh?" began to help himself to the tender portion with his hands, and so I followed suit. He handed me the animal's jaw, from which I picked some juicy fillets of meat, as he appeared to be doing the same. Salah told me a story of a man who asked what were the best parts to choose and was told, "The heart and the tongue." "And which to avoid?" "The heart and the tongue." "Now why do you tell me to choose the heart and the tongue," asked the man, "if you also tell me to avoid them?" "Because if the heart and the tongue are sound, they are the best parts of the body. But if the heart and the tongue are evil, they are the worst parts of the body."

I enjoyed that immensely. We went on eating and Tahir Bey occasionally heaped more meat upon my plate, and the soffragi brought more vegetables, till I began to feel uneasy as to my absorptive capacity after years of living on a wartime margin in England. Fortunately as this was a Mohammedan household, there was no alcohol and I could wash it all down with water.

There was a white table-cloth, and a vase of roses and other flowers — peonies, I think.

The practice, apparently, when not eating with fingers was to use one of the utensils, most often the spoon, for beans and the like, leaving the knife and fork resting up against the right-hand side of the plate.

When we had done justice to the lamb, I was staggered by the arrival of another meat course — fried liver and mashed potatoes.

This too we demolished. The proceeding for salt and pepper was to dip with your own knife into a glass dish containing each. Beside each person was a folded wedge of crisp dough which could be torn gradually to shreds and eaten as the meal wore on.

After the liver, we began on bowls of stewed fruits; apricots, raisins and the like. Then my attention was drawn to a bowl of caramel custard, and I did my best to sink some of that. Then fruit, dates and oranges. The oranges were cut into four sections each for an easy bite. One orange eaten, Tahir Bey's brown finger pointed authoritatively at another while his eyes twinkled; and so down went another orange.

The hospitality of the bedouin is overwhelming but deep and sincere, a significant part of their way of life.

Tahir Bey belched his appreciation of every course, and at last we staggered across to the basin, carrying our napkins, and the soffragi poured water from the bronze jug over our hands, for us to rinse them. We abandoned the napkins on a settee in the hall, and adjourned to the reception room once more, where sweet tea, without milk and flavoured with mint, was served to us in tiny handleless glasses.

Beside Tahir Bey was an earthenware funnel-shaped receptacle full of ash, which served the dual purpose of an ash-tray, for discarded cigarette ends and a spittoon. I think that my host must have been suffering from an unusual attack of catarrh.

All the time after dinner Tahir Bey passed a rosary of red coral through his left thumb and forefinger. There were fine tassels of gold on the coral rosary.

A photograph album was brought and he showed it to me with pride – pointing with a happy exclamation of "Tahir Bey" to himself in groups taken in Baghdad on the occasion of his visit to mediate between the Shammar and Ubbaid. Most of the pictures included the Regent, Abdul Illah, and I noticed that in all of them my friend Hassan Suhail, with gold aqal and keffiyah framing his black-bearded face, was well to the fore. In one or two Hussein Suhail, the younger brother, appeared recognisably. I went to my room to collect the American edition of *The Golden Carpet*, and showed them Hassan's signed portrait in it, and the pictures of us in the tents of Aqqa Quf. They were immensely intrigued.

We discussed the idea of a ride in the morning, and three different pairs of breeches were brought for me to try on when I got up. One of cream corduroy seemed English enough, and about my size. I learnt later from Kassim that they belonged to his wife, Aida, the daughter of a Pasha who was a general in the Egyptian army. But of her or any other female there was of course, in this Mohammedan household, no sign.

We talked about Palestine.

"Why do the Jews want to leave Europe now?" asked Tahir.

"When a dog has been whipped," I said, "he wants to run away; and no amount of calling or coaxing will persuade him that it is healthy to remain."

Tahir thought this really funny.

"My father is very amused. Like a dog — ft — and he's gone." They all laughed.

I said to Tahir Bey, "You must not let me keep you up later than usual. You must treat me just as if I were your own son."

And again Kassim said, "My father says he is happy because you are here."

And reminding his father that I had been in Ismailia two hundred miles away in the morning, he made it easy for me to retire. They all saw me to my room, to make sure I had all I required. They asked if I would like a brazier to warm the room, and the soffragi brought an earthenware brazier glowing with red-hot charcoal, and set it down in the middle of the floor. "He will take it away presently," said Salah, "to avoid suffocation." Then Tahir Bey went off to the main house, but I could hear Kassim and Salah still talking in the next room, and when I went across to the wash-basin to do my teeth they were only just moving through the entrance door to retire themselves.

When I returned from the basin the brazier had gone, and I climbed under the mosquito net with the intention of reading before I went off to sleep. But by accident I dowsed the lamp, and creeping about the room in the dark searched fumblingly in all my pockets and luggage for my electric flashlamp. I remembered having had it in my pocket during the drive. I must have left it in the seat of the car when I jumped out to greet my host. I noticed however through the glass panel over the door into the hall that the lamp out there was burning, so I went out and tried unsuccessfully to relight my own lamp from it. I called for Machmoud who came and did it for me. I also asked him for some water and a glass which he brought and he carried the round deal table which stood in the hall into my room and set the lamp on it.

I read Mark Twain's story of a French duel in the *Strand* magazine, then turned the wick of the lamp down to a blue smudge keeping it as a night light (in the absence of my torch) in case I wanted to turn it up again to read. I opened the shutters beyond the window bars — the window opened on to the garden of the main house which was in darkness. I tried to sleep, but a frenzied barking of dogs broke out, beginning near, then taken up across the low-lying ground of the Delta. The barking would die down in one place, only to flare up in another. Suddenly a shot rang out, then another. The dogs barked louder than ever. The mattress was laid on plain wooden boards, athwart the bed frame. At last I dozed off to sleep, and then the veganin took hold and I slept solidly.

I had asked to be awakened with tea at seven, and was startled to find on awaking that it was already eight-thirty. I got up hurriedly and went across to shave, calling to Machmoud, who emerged from the back regions, to bring me some hot water. Kassim also appeared in fez and a long tweed overcoat over a riding-gown and a pair of red half-wellington boots. He was carrying a riding-switch.

"I have been waiting for you to ride since seven o'clock," he said.

"What!" I exclaimed. "I hope you have not been waiting for me. I thought we arranged for me to be called at seven, have breakfast at eight and ride afterwards. But no one came to wake me."

"I know," he said, "I gave orders for you not to be disturbed."

"Well, if you give me a minute I will dress and we can ride before breakfast."

"As you like. Let us breakfast first."

Tahir Bey appeared in his robes and red skull-cap, just as I was finishing my shave in a place open to the main hall. The alternative was a basin near the Egyptian form of convenience at floor level, which seemed to require some adjustment, and inclined me to shave in the outer vestibule. I waved to him and said I would not be a minute. I had already had great difficulty indicating to Machmoud, who brought the warm water, that I wanted it poured into the basin, not over my hands. At first he thought that I meant that the basin was not clean and used most of the water in swilling it down.

However, my shave was at last accomplished.

Madame Kassim's breeches fitted me very well, and I had a pair of khaki stockings — no boots, of course, in my air travel luggage. Salah took me outside and over the canal bridge, to a square mud-walled yard, where a grey buffalo cow, with a bloody tail, looked round at us suspiciously. Under a lean-to shelter on one side of the yard, a man was raking up the manure and laying dust in its place. Inside a stall in a corner of the yard, under a domed dovecote of muddy clay, we found the buffalo's newly born calf. I asked what the buffaloes were used for mostly. "Pumping and ploughing. Everything."

"In England we have no water buffaloes."

"What! No buffaloes!" exclaimed Salah in astonishment. We went back to breakfast conscious, perhaps, of the gulf which still separates East and West.

Breakfast was another lesson in bedouin hospitality. There were half-boiled eggs, to be shelled and eaten by hand; then to my astonishment a plate of six fried eggs was laid before me, a compliment no doubt to the English predilection for eggs done in this way — but six (and a half-boiled one already gone down, down, down to the devil, like Simon Legree) . . . I attacked the fried eggs wildly, with the spoon. After England, where one fresh egg a month (if you were lucky) was the ration, the task of stowing away seven months' ration in as many minutes was formidable — but undoubtedly pleasant. Then my attention was drawn to a bowl of fresh whipped cream and a bowl of honey, and these two halcyon ingredients of a godlike meal, mingled on a sheet of the dough-like bread, were consumed with enthusiasm. Next, Tahir Bey laid before me a special feature of the house — dates (from which the stones had been extracted) preserved in a wine-like jam; they tasted delicious. Next we began on oranges and bananas. A single orange in no way satisfied the generous heart of my host, and once again he pointed smiling to the largest orange upon the dish, until this too had gone the way of all flesh that had been laid before me.

After all this a ride was almost essential and soon the pretty white Arab horses were champing in the forecourt, held by dark grooms in long clothing. My mare was called Salma, Kassim's Salmeen, and Salah's Aida. Kassim's was bridled in Syrian style of red and blue with cowrie shells, but the others were bitted with snaffles and had saddles somewhat after the English style. We whirled and wheeled about the compound, mounting, and jogged off between the high wall of the garden of the main house (over which they promised to show me on my return from the ride) and a smaller house, of rose brick with pointed and shuttered windows, where Salah said another relative was housed. A palm tree soared above it. We came quickly upon a cluster of mud huts where women, children and fellaheen moved about or squatted. Beside one, maize had been taken from the long leafy husks, and lay thick in a square heap surrounded by the fibrous tassled husks. Kassim spoke to some of the men who greeted him smiling. "Il hamdulillah Mabsut."

"Allah Mabsut."

We could hear the hoopoes, giving that melancholy cry of whit-whit as we rode along. Salah said the bird was called Hud-hud in Arabic. They are a familiar sight in Egypt, with their fan-like crests, and black and white wings, although rarely seen in England.

We came out upon a broad track between the irrigated fields, and I thought it a good place for a canter. Salah had omitted to warn me that my mare was classified as a racehorse (of which they breed a fair number), and as I let her into a canter the significance of his cry "Be careful, be careful" falling away behind me, as the wind rushed past and my mount gathered speed, was lost on me. Salma was off like a rocket. I felt the great speed between my knees, tautened the rein upon her arched and straining neck. I felt the need to tame her quickly if I was not to plunge into or over the canal which we were fast approaching. The bedouin, tilling the fields on either side, were looking up startled and smiling. A woman swathed in black, with silver bangles on her ankles (a sign of marriage), washed her bare feet in a ditch. I applied strong pressure to Salma's mouth and she slowed down to a canter, to a trot and to a walk, her white coat grey with sweat, and her nostrils blowing. I turned her round and cantered slowly back to Salah and Kassim.

"You are very clev-er, you are very clev-er," cried Kassim.

I do not know what he had expected. After that we rode on between the fields, along the dykes and canals. At intervals there were the vertical water-wheels, made of iron, which sluiced water, in gulps, into little irrigating streams between the fields. They were turned by a horizontal rotating bar, to which was harnessed a grey

buffalo, blindfolded.
"Why are they blindfolded?"
"To avoid giddiness."
"And how long do they do this for?"
"Two hours at a time. Then they rest. Two hours, maybe four."
"But they only work in daylight?"
"Yes, except when we are very busy."

There were a good many geese about, and most of the huts (which were hovels to live in, nothing more) had the shade of a palm tree or an olive tree.

I asked Salah what the shots in the night were. He answered, without looking round, "Those are the guards." But why or at what they were firing he did not explain.

As we rode along the embankment I asked Salah if many Mohammedans had more than one wife.

"Very few," he answered. "The Prophet allows four. But nowadays it is only the big sheiks, or kings like Ibn Saud, who have more than one wife. King Ibn Saud has a hundred concubines. But supposing my wife was never pregnant, and I had no son, in such circumstances I might take a second wife."

We crossed the railway line, where Kassim talked to some men working on it, and rode on, in a whole circle, till we came to the houses where I had left the main road to enter the estate. We rode back along the main track. A car passed us, coming from the house, full of merchants who had been to see about the purchase of the stored cotton crop.

"We pick the cotton in October."
"And you keep it here for any length of time?"
"For some time."

A train of camels laden with sugar-cane plodded towards us and we gave them a wide berth. Their heads twisted sideways, staring at us superciliously. Back at the house we dismounted and handed our horses over to the grooms. There seemed an amazing number of other people about in gowns of all colours and head-cloths and caps equally various. One of them took some photographs. On the left of the entrance to the guest-house was the estate office, where a picture of King Farouk was hung; another of a bronze statue of Mehemet Ali, a photograph of Tahir Bey astride a horse. And an embroidered inscription, framed, in Arabic on the wall above the desk, 'Blessed is the man who is patient.'

The desk was covered with a sheet of glass which held down a scattered assortment of photographs, a sort of family album.

We went through a side door into the garden of the principal residence, a fine high square building of cream plaster in the Georgian style, with a portico of Doric columns, approached on either side by a curving flight of stone steps. The windows were also set about with Greek columns, but those on the floor above, where the women remained, were firmly shuttered. For all I know their eyes may have been peeping down at us through the slits. Above the centre of the façade was an arch on which was painted a dummy clock, with Arabic numerals. I argued with Salah about this, as he thought they were Roman numbers, but they were not, and were indeed the same numerals as I saw later on an Arabic clock face in the hall of the Embassy and on the Arabic dial of the sealing-wax-red telephone in my room there. The '5' for instance, was clearly the Arabic '0'. In any case the clock was symbolical; the hands were painted on at ten to eleven. The influence was again European of the Empire of Napoleon III – and dated no doubt from the time of the building of the Suez Canal by de Lesseps and the visit of the Empress Eugenie, for whom the Khedive Ismail had a theatre built and an opera written to be performed in it – *Aida*. On entering the front door we were confronted by more Doric columns, and several settees and chairs. On the right of the door was an audience room, hung with an old-fashioned glass chandelier to hold candles in vase-like sconces, and painted in floral designs. The settees and chairs were French gilt, upholstered in needlework, but were covered with neat white covers, which Kassim partly removed to show me what was underneath.

On the walls were photographs from illustrated papers, of Queen Farida with one of her children, and of her sister Fawzia, who married Riza Shah. We sat down on the settees and chairs, and coffee was brought in by Machmoud. Suddenly a visitor from Alexandria was shown in. He too partook of coffee. He was dressed in a blue suit, and wore a fez. His name, I think, was Hamil. He was a Turk, wall-eyed, wearing glasses, and had lived twenty-five years in Alexandria, where he was apparently manager of a big building contractors' firm. He seemed rather over-awed by the situation; who they had told him I was, I do not know. Salah asked me if I had the postcard photographs of Chilham to show him. The Turk nearly fell off his chair — and I signed copies at Kassim's and Salah's request as mementoes for them of what was for me a very happy visit to the Qasr el Masri. Hamil was abashed at being included in a family group which I photographed on the steps, and I was reminded of the ceremony when a new Speaker is chosen by the House of Commons and has to be dragged by the elbows, 'Showing reluctance', to his new throne.

The garden was of mud, sub-divided into beds in which purple poinsettia and other flowers grew precariously. But the mango trees, palm trees, and the pine-like tree (with upspringing needles) gave plenty of shade.

There was not much of the house to be seen. The hall stretched across it, ending in high windows of brightly coloured Victorian stained glass. Another room on the left was bare, ready to be furnished for guests, while on the ground floor, next to the audience room, was a bedroom with a pair of the four-poster brass beds with which I was already familiar. There were glimpses of wash-places in little courtyards, but the staircase to the rooms above was shut off by a pair of doors, painted brown.

I returned to my own room to change out of the riding clothes; and reappeared a little later with a book which I inscribed 'to my friend Tahir Bey', who was now in the reception room next door. He was very pleased, and got Silah to write out the inscription in Arabic on the opposite page.

We sat in our accustomed places, talking, and waiting for lunch, which was supposed to be at noon ("as you like"), since I had to drive up to Cairo, and wanted to reach the Embassy by five.

It was already after twelve and I watched an endless procession of visitors going in and out of the room opposite, some in European clothes, some in bedouin garb. It was the reception room for the lesser fry.

After I had changed out of the riding-clothes I went across to the wash-place, and encountered one of them coming out, an unfortunate man, with blinded eyes, and pock-marked visage, wearing a round cloth headdress, and long red-and-white robes, who groped his way towards me, sensing my presence, and wondering why I offered him no greeting in Arabic. I mumbled something like "Good-morning", and went on washing my hands, while he stalked sightless and firm by me out into the hall and back to the secondary reception room.

Presently the postman came in, a dignified old man with a beard, and a long grey cloak, on which was a pattern of thin blue squares, thrown over his shoulder. He strolled up to us and handed Tahir Bey a letter, then strolled off into the room opposite with a roll of printed matter. Tahir opened the letter written in the beautiful Arabic script, and, after reading it, handed it to Salah. It was from some bedouin, who, he said, were visiting Tahir Bey to ask him to head a delegation of bedouin to receive King Ibn Saud of Arabia, due shortly in Egypt. Tahir Bey represented 2,000,000 bedouin – not, I gathered, officially.

We discussed the composition of the Egyptian senate and Parliament. It appeared that Tahir was elected by a constituency of about 70,000 people round Abu Hommus. Kassim said, "You must come and stay with us for a long time, for two or three months. Then you can learn Arabic and you will teach me English. You can bring your wife."

But I explained that if I ever hoped to get back into the House of Commons, I should not get elected by staying most of the time at Abu Hommus. They laughed heartily at this.

Every now and then Machmoud would come in and bend over Tahir's right ear (the one furthest from me) and whisper, then go out again. At about two o'clock he came in to say lunch was ready.

This time it was mutton followed by liver, and a procession of food which left me stunned and stupefied, before I finally went off with my napkin (as Kassim, Salah and the unhappy Turk had already gone) to wash my hands, followed by Tahir Bey.

My departure was already long delayed, so I led the way to my room, to arrange for the luggage to be removed (which the driver came and did) while we all stood around sipping coffee.

I wanted to tip the servants and had consulted Salah about this. But Tahir came dashing in and seized the notes from me and shoved them into one of my pockets, with much laughter and good nature.

Then I left in a blaze of courtesies, Tahir Bey leading me by the hand to the car. He said again that he was honoured to have welcomed me to his house, and I replied that I looked forward to his visiting me in England. With which expressions of mutual friendship and esteem, we parted, and my car lurched off down the track which bordered the canal.

We dashed along. At Damanhour the driver got involved and

had to ask the way out. He redoubled his speed to do so, and tore past an old woman in black, riding on a donkey which she had some difficulty in controlling at the same time as a large round wicker basket. She began to gesture wildly at the donkey, which went round in circles, as we dashed past, and over went the poor old dame into the road, basket and all. I looked round and wanted to stop, but the driver was already doubled up with mirth, and had put nearly two streets between us and the disaster before I could make him understand from my seat behind him what I wanted. He could not conceive of the necessity for stopping, and continued to laugh and chuckle fiendishly to himself, slapping the wheel in delight, all the way to Cairo. I must say that my last glimpse of the old lady had been of her picking up her fallen goods philosophically enough in the middle of the road, with the black donkey standing by.

Approaching Cairo we passed a depot of some kind flying the Stars and Stripes.

There was a blood-red sunset which silhouetted vividly the dome and minarets of a nearby mosque. The citadel, in the distance, caught the last rays and seemed to float fairylike above the desert and the city; a pair of graceful domes, and the high pencils of its minarets, beautifully proportioned — fawn in colour like a gazelle.

I thought of Napoleon coming here, after the battle of the Pyramids, teaching the Moslems to drink water with their meals (which they still do).

At the Embassy, I tipped the dusky driver, who by now was rather impressed with all my doings and said softly and slowly, as if he would not forget to put in a good word for me when his countrymen started massacring the British community: "Thank *you*, Mr. Somerset de Chair."

CHAPTER 8   *The Sudan*

The green baton blinds were down along the arcades of Kitchener's
Palace at Khartoum, and the sun slashed through into the dim
interior like sabres at Omdurman cutting into dark bodies which
quivered and lay still.

There the Blue and White Niles meet and the division in
midstream is dramatically apparent. They mingle to go down their
long, long course to Cairo, before flowing out in a maze of irrigation
in the Delta to the blue Mediterranean a thousand miles from
Khartoum.

At Assuan, after the Nile enters Egypt, the waters bank up
behind the great dam which controls the irrigation of the Nile
Valley and nourishes the life of millions of Egyptians between it
and the sea.

The Sudan was not part of the British Empire (though a
casual visitor might have been pardoned for thinking so). The
administrators were British, but they reported to the Foreign
Office, not the Colonial Office, and shared with some shadowy
colleagues in Egypt the name of Condominium. All the Egyptian
officials were put into lorries and firmly expelled in 1924 after
the British Governor-General, Sir Lee Stack, had been murdered
in Cairo, and the Condominium was suspended. Since the Anglo-
Egyptian Treaty of 1936 it was nominally in force again, but except
for half a dozen Egyptian officials in the irrigation department and
others, the Condominium was not apparent. The green flag of
Egypt with its white crescent and stars flew on a pole beside the
Union Jack above the Governor-General's Palace, and when I was
staying there the Egyptian Minister of Education, Dr. Abd el
Razzak Bey el Sanhouri, was an honoured guest, on an official visit,
accompanied by an astonishing number of Press photographers.

In the absence of the Governor-General, who was touring the
west of the Sudan, the Egyptian Minister was even, as a guest of
the Governor-General, able to receive in the drawing-room of the

111

Palace such an important figure as the religious leader, Sayed Sir Ali al Mirghani, who occupied in the Mahommedan Sudan roughly the status of the Archbishop of Canterbury in Britain. The status of the Archbishop of Westminster was held by the rival Mohammedan leader, Sayed Sir Abdel Rahman el Mahdi, a son of the very Mahdi who was responsible for the death of Gordon. Sir Abdel Rahman el Mahdi aimed at independence for the Sudan, without any connection with Egypt, and in the meantime preferred British administration to any attempt at Egypt's influence in the country. There was a picture in the Palace of the Duke of Windsor (then Prince of Wales), visiting the Sudan, seated with these religious dignitaries on his right and left respectively.

Sayed Sir Ali al Mirghani swept up the white marble steps in the glare of the sun, while I was talking to the Egyptian Minister on the shaded veranda. He was clad in a robe of grey and bore on his head a maroon-and-gold velvet cap, bound about with the green fillet of the Haji, of the man who has made the pilgrimage to Mecca. He was escorted by a Kadi, all in purple. Dr. Abd el Razzak Bey el Sanhouri introduced me to Sir Ali, a short, dark man of fifty years or thereabouts, and I then withdrew to leave them in conversation; a conversation between the leading Moslem dignitary of the Sudan and a Minister of the Egyptian Government, held without any British officials present, and one with which they both appeared to be highly satisfied when they emerged to pose before all the photographers on the steps of the absent Governor-General's Palace.

Sir Ali al Mirghani said, "I am no politician, I am a religious man." He had made no public statement about the future of the Sudan. But his followers had been supporting the move for union with Egypt.

There was curiously little panache about the Palace. Its affairs were run quietly by an efficient secretary Luce, whose wife was well famed there for her beauty and wrote plays for the West End stage; and by a single young A.D.C. in the Sudan Defence Force, called Captain Sherman. He spoke Arabic and attended to affairs of state without noticeable fuss.

The police on guard were turbanned in white, and clad in white tunics and shorts, with black cloth aiguillettes, and black puttees. Their faces were black as darkest Africa.

The Palace was full of ancient cannon, muskets and lances,

dating from Omdurman. It was built, appropriately, by Kitchener on the site of the one where Gordon was killed, and it bears the clear impress of Kitchener's interest in domestic architecture. It is of gleaming white, fronting on to the wide Blue Nile – a slate-blue river, changing, when the hot desert wind ruffles it, to shale brown. Two wings bend back, and all the windows are shuttered in green. Arcades of graceful pillared arches, like wide Roman arches, overlook the courtyard enclosed by the two wings, where there is a fountain which was being emptied with a bucket by a Sudani gardener, whose bare back glistened in the sun. He handed the bucket up to another clad in a loose cotton shift, while a third squatted on the bronze cannon, which glinted in the sun's rays. The temperature there rises even in January to 101 degrees in the shade, and wearing the thinnest tropical suit, and peering through smoked sunglasses, I could scarcely find the energy to put one foot in front of another.

A chaffinch chirped on the end of the only rolled-up sunblind, beneath which a white arch threw a flat pattern of sunlight on the black-and-white marble floor, partly overlaid by the glow of a russet Persian rug. Other birds hopped silently about under the chairs, hoping to avoid detection. On the card table, a large gleaming chromium vacuum flask containing iced water was surrounded by tapering glasses which had an inviting bulb above the stem for a measure of lime juice. Dark-skinned soffragis, in white turbans and gowns, belted in scarlet and gold, padded about in red slippers with upward pointing toes. They poured out cooling drinks.

On the fourth side of the courtyard, white steps descended to a well-watered lawn, which dries up and turns brown during the day. There are immense trees, shady sunt trees and very tall palm trees, with smooth grey stems surmounted by fronds that reminded me of the Hadenawa's hair (Kipling's Fuzzy Wuzzy). Through the chinks in the balustrade I could see the glow of ornage-red cannas with tall broad green leaves.

Sherman and I had our meals quietly in the dining-room, where Collier's portrait of Kitchener in his long grey coat stared at me with smouldering blue eyes. At the other end was a really remarkable oil painting, rather wistful, of Gordon, by Catherine Ouless. The memory of Gordon dominates Khartoum – there was a fine bronze statue of him riding his camel. He is shown wearing a fez — having been Governor of the Equatorial Province and later Governor-General of the Sudan under the Khedive Ismail between 1874 and 1879.

After Omdurman, Britain remained in occupation with the sleeping partnership of the Egyptians, as administrators of a foreign State.

Yet in few parts of the British Empire have I received an impression of equally beneficial administration.

In other ways the country was being overhauled. The former system of indirect rule through tribal chiefs, which tended to be rigid and fixed at an archaic stage of human progress, was being replaced by representative councils, partly elected, partly at first nominated. There were even some rural District Councils. But no one there dreamed that we should be leaving the country to its own device in 8 years.

I have seldom been more surprised by anything than by the difference in colour between the Blue and the White Nile, where they join to form the long Nile of history. They really are blue and white, and the division down the middle of the current was as clear as that between the cream sleeve of the tropical suit I was wearing, and the blue cuff of my shirt protruding beneath it.

I slept in the afternoon after a late lunch, bathed, and had tea on the balcony overlooking the Nile, where gay little painted sailing boats with dizzling white sails veered and luffed about in the river.

Lime juice and iced water in the drawing-room, with its Chippendale furniture, and floodlit ceiling, on my return — with a chapter of the *Iliad* — before Sherman came up to take me round to Mrs. Luce for drinks.

A young daughter called out, "Hello." Mrs. Luce got up to greet us, a slim figure in black, with dark hair and fine delicately cut features.

When I had an opportunity of talking to Mrs. Luce I said, "I want to hear more about this play of yours."

"I wanted to call it *Warwick*, but we are having an argument by cable. They want it to be called *The King Maker*. They say nobody will know what Warwick means — Rose Bingham and all that."

"We must talk more about all this."

"Are you free any other time?"

"I am lecturing to the Sudan Cultural Society tomorrow on the Suppression of Rashid Ali's revolt in 1941, and having tea with the Sudanese members first. But otherwise I am free."

"Then come over early for lunch."

The simple gold wedding ring on her left hand gleamed for an instant in the light of the windows, and we were gone.

A peculiar phenomenon occurs near the Nile there at this time of year. Every night clouds and clouds of harmless gnats clustered into the lighted rooms, and fell as thick as powder about the crevices of the bathroom door at the top of the stairs. I would open the door, hold my breath and dash through. The seething pile at the bottom of the door was perhaps an inch deep. If I trod in this inadvertently, forty or fifty thousand gnats were extinguished — a whole army corps. Their souls departed abruptly to Paradise. If I did not tread on them, they died a natural death in the night, and the patient soffragi, with dustpan and brush, crouched along the red-tiled balcony, sweeping the corpses up, to be thrown away. Every night on my landing alone four or five million gnats must have emerged into the light, and perished in the dark. How could they conceivably understand anything of the relations between men and women; but why should our souls be more immortal than theirs? Yet man struggles against the idea of total extinction.

I used to write in the mornings on the main veranda, where the sunblinds were down, and the sunlight threw a bright pattern of the balustrading in shadows on the marble. Through the inter-stices I could see the lawn, which was watered like a marsh so that the stems of two tall grey palm trees were reflected in it. The sparrows hopped about at my feet. Perhaps it was the corpses of the gnats which the soffragi's broom had overlooked that they were pecking at. There were several other insects dancing about in the sunlight; white specks against the deep green shadows of the big tree on the lawn.

My last and sunniest recollection of the Sudan was of cruising lazily up the Blue Nile on the Kaid's launch, which Brigadier Hardy Spicer (in the Kaid's absence) had put at the disposal of a visiting Brigadier Smythe, Colonel Balfin and myself. We photographed crocodiles.

After that and an address to the Clergy House (in the presence of the bishop) on 'Palestine in the time of Christ', which Smythe

116

also insisted on attending – and which much to my surprise, drew from the bishop, in a moving tribute, the startling assertion that it was the utterance of a real Christian – I boarded a silver-winged Lodestar aircraft, and flew down the Nile to Cairo. I felt rather like a gaudy dragon-fly flitting about Darkest Africa.

On the way down the Nile Valley we flew over thick clouds, and the sun, beating down on them, formed circular rainbows, in the middle of which the shadows of the aircraft would rush up from a dot on the ground far below, as the mist thickened, to a great winged image of ourselves, almost within arm's reach.

As we landed at Luxor, the pilot let down the slotted ailerons behind the silver wings to slow up the landing speed, and I could not help thinking that if some Divine Zoologist on high were studying us through a microscope, we would seem to be a single insect – this Lodestar, sticking out curious membranes from its wings as it landed. And of the varied personalities, of the Major-General (Percival) returning from a holiday on Lake Kiwi in the Congo, of myself eager to get home after much jolting, of the airmen moving down the valley from Wadi Halfa, of the pilot and navigator thinking their own thoughts in the front cabin – nothing would appear in the slide of the microscope. We were, for the moment, part of the insect. Later inspection at Almaza airfield might reveal the larvae hatching out of the side. But the whole behaviour of the thing would be very puzzling and might well qualify for a sentence or two in some celestial treatise on the Flora and Fauna of World I.

As I flew down the Nile Valley I pondered upon our position as a Great Power. At the Kitchener barracks in Khartoum I had been conscious of a certain scepticism among the soldiers serving there, so far from home, at the reasons I had given for the need to be strong in such parts of the world. There was a fan revolving noisily half-way down the room, and a knot of soldiers, who could not hear a word I was saying on account of its gyrations, talked idly to one another.

"You are nothing," I shouted at them. "By yourselves you are nothing," (for they were members of an English regiment), "without the Empire you are nothing but a little island off the north-west shoulder of Europe." And I shouted at them, louder still, so that they sat bolt upright under the whirling fan.

"If you believe in the British way of life, if you believe in the system of British justice under which no man can be taken out of his house and stood against a wall and shot without a fair trial, without all the processes of cross-question and evidence which are a characteristic feature of a British Court of Law; if you believe in the British institution of free speech under which any man may say what he likes about the government of the day, may write what articles he likes in the newspapers without fear of being arrested and imprisoned, why then you must be prepared to stand up in the world for these ideals and, if necessary, fight for them, as we have done. It is because I think Britain has used her power in the world wisely and in the interests of humanity that I believe the story of British imperialism is fully justified and one of which we can be really proud.

"But if you want to become a second-class Power, you can go the way of Spain and Portugal which once had great maritime overseas Empires and which today are nothing but chicken feed beneath the council tables of Europe.

"What would have happened to civilisation in 1940 if Britain had not been a great Power, with key bases in the Mediterranean, like Malta and Gibraltar, with treaty rights to use Alexandria and maintain troops in Egypt and Iraq, and with a great overseas Empire and resources overseas? The last barriers were down. Austria had gone; Czechoslovakia had gone; Poland had gone; Norway had gone; Holland had gone; Belgium had gone; France had gone. And nothing remained between Hitler and the domination of civilisation but the English Channel and the fact that on the further side of it was Great Britain as the citadel of a large overseas Empire, built up during the course of centuries. America was not yet at war. Russia was not yet at war. If Hitler could have subdued us he could have dealt with them piecemeal, separately, and at a later stage. It was only the fact that Britain was a Great Power that enabled civilisation to survive, and it is because I believe that Britain has a contribution to make to civilisation, to the new United Nations Organisation in the maintenance of peace in the world, that I believe Britain should remain a Great Power. And her connections in the Middle East are a key factor in maintaining that position."

CHAPTER 9   *Tripolitania*

There were bullet-holes still in the walls of the hangars at Castel
Benito, and many of them were roofless from Royal Air Force
bombing, when I landed in Tripolitania. There was a cold rain,
and we crouched in a truck which jolted us for an hour along a
tarmac road to Tripoli, citadel of a wrecked Empire. The city was
laid out, with wide ways and bronze fountains, as a show-piece of
Fascist imperialism.

A stately column, carved with the date A XVI, supported the
bronze wolf suckling Romulus and Remus, and beside it fluttered
the red, white and blue of the Union Jack.

The weather brightened to brilliant contrasts within twenty-
four hours and I was soon sitting under the shade of the palm
trees in the public garden which fringes the waterfront, reading the
Iliad and occasionally looking up through smoked sunglasses at the
innumerable wrecks which stood jaggedly about the blue waters
of the harbour. We had not cleared them away. Why should we,
until some conference in Moscow or London or Washington decided
what was to be the future of this brilliant land? Russia had put in
a claim, and was mortified, possibly, by the reaction: "I will not
have Russia treading across the throat of the British Empire,"
said Ernest Bevin. So we remained in occupation, and the British
Military Administration ran it on a care-and-maintenance basis. It
had been in our hands ever since the Desert Rats broke in on their
advance from Alamein to Tunis.

Now Tripolitania was a country in suspense, not knowing its
fate. The French, coming up from Lake Chad, during the war, had
remained in the Fezzan, which is the wilder southern part, and
which they continued to administer. The Arabs certainly did not
like the French, who had massacred 12,000 Arabs, admitted by
the French press, in suppressing trouble in North Africa at the
conclusion of the war. Even less did they like the Italians and,
being well armed, would probably fight if the country were

118

handed back to Italy. America would not, apparently, accept a mandate. On the other hand there was no paramount chief, as in the land of the Senussi further east in Cyrenaica. So once again Britain seemed the obvious power to rule.

Julius Caesar first brought imperium to these parts in 46 B.C.

When I was looking round the Old City with an officer on reconnaissance (for the old part, where the Jews had recently been massacred, was still out of bounds), I had a brief glimpse of a platoon of the 60th on patrol, a tight quick body of soldiers, marching three abreast, in tin helmets, down a cobbled incline, looking neither to the right nor to the left, and wheeling abruptly out of sight. They had passed in a flash, but in that instant I had a glimpse of one of Caesar's cohorts, bronze-helmeted, marching compactly through the crowded alleyways.

There was now a rising problem of unemployment. At first the country had been living on the hump of the Eighth Army. Now that had gone, and the British Military Administration, with no more than a caretaking responsibility, could not embark on large-scale schemes of reconstruction and rehabilitation. The Royal Navy came and looked sceptically at the wrecks in the harbour occasionally; and went away, taking notes of what might have to be done.

There was a white hospital ship, the *Tevere* lying on her side, where we had bombed her to death. Not all the anguish and misunderstanding is on one side in a war.

Tripoli was full of surprises. I met more brilliant people there than in any other town of comparable size. There was, first of all, a message for me on arrival at the Albergo del Mehari (the Inn of the Camels) to ring up the editor of the *Tripoli Times*, Mr. Stevens. "I think you know my father-in-law, Colonel Altounyan," he said.

"Indeed I do."

He and his wife wanted me to lunch next day.

Stevens had to return to the office after lunch, to complete the final number of the *Tripoli Times*.

"I am beginning to dread what will appear about me," I called after him. He smiled a slow smile, as he crossed the road, and Altounyan's daughter and I began to walk down to the harbour front and along to the del Mehari.

"I like a walk in the afternoons," she assured me.

"I am afraid it is all this talk about the book being like *The Seven Pillars* that annoys you," I told her. "It is a bit misleading. Of course I have never pretended to be another Lawrence. I am not an Arabist. Do not even speak the language. I merely happened to be pitched into the only campaign which occurred during this war in similar surroundings. It is the book, not the author, that they are comparing to Lawrence's work. What you overlook in *The Golden Carpet* are the literary merits which were inherent in the story itself and for which I was not responsible — the artistic wholeness of the campaign with its beginning on the Mediterranean shore and its climax in the City of the Caliphs. I merely happened to be there. But so far as the reader is concerned, he does not mind how the story was contrived so long as it is there, between the covers of a book."

"I suppose," she reflected, "it is because I was brought up in a family which admires Lawrence so much, that I was resentful."

"You are a writer yourself?" I asked.

"Yes, yes," she declared passionately. "I have not published anything yet, except silly little things in the paper here. But I know I can write really good stuff."

"No doubt," I conceded. "I do not suppose you would have such an inner conviction otherwise."

"I have sometimes thought of telling the story of my family background — the meeting of Armenian and English in our blood."

"That would be very interesting," I assured her. "Start now. Begin it against the background of the brown citadel of Aleppo."

I was reminded of her father, telling me how at Cambridge the undergraduates threw him in the pond, because he assured them that he was a great poet. "Let us see some of your poetry then," they demanded. But he had not yet written any and they threw the man who was later to write *Ornament of Honour*, published by the Oxford University Press, into the pond.

We sat down on a bench in the gardens, overlooking the harbour.

"What you need is a good subject," I told her. "I will suggest one. Does the name of Sarah Aaronsohn convey anything to you?"

She started, but made no comment beyond "I think so."

"She was a Jewish girl who with her brother was one of the first Zionists, I suppose, for they lived in Palestine under the Turks. There were about eighty thousand Jews there then, and they

decided to help Britain in defeating the Turks, so as to get a
Jewish National Home established in Palestine. Aaronsohn made
his way to Egypt, where he presented himself at G.H.Q. in Cairo
and offered to help us for nothing. They thought he must be mad
or crooked because nobody else had offered to work without
money. However, he convinced them and arrangements were made
for him and his sister to supply us with information behind the
Turkish lines. We used to send a submarine to that old ruined
Crusader castle, on the promontory at Athlit, and collect the
information. But one day the Turks got on to the track of this.
They arrested Sarah Aaronsohn, and tortured her. They put
boiled eggs under her armpits, a most painful torture, and crushed
the tips of her fingers in the door. She managed to get away to the
cloakroom where she had a revolver and shot herself. There is a
story for you. There is a book about it somewhere called *Sarah
Aaronsohn*. I remember a Russian in Haifa telling me about it."

"Sarah Aaronsohn," she mused. " 'S.A.' The person Lawrence
dedicated the poem to. 'I loved you so I drew these tides of men
into my hands and wrote my will across the sky in stars . . . ' "

"Yes, it fits. Do you think that is who S.A. was?"

"Nobody knows for certain. But I remember my father saying
something about it. He went down to Tel Aviv once, especially to
see a man by that name. One is inclined to think that everything
about Lawrence is in the book, but of course it is not, only a
small part of it."

We resumed our walk along the front.

"That would account for a lot," I reflected, "if he had been
really in love with this girl, whom he might well have met either
before the war, or during these arrangements with her brother.
And then she is taken by the Turks and tortured. It would account
for his bitterness. He refers to the motive force of his acts being
extinguished long before he reached Damascus; and his wanting
to bury himself away in the Air Force like that."

I have a picture in my mind's eye of that crumbling old
Crusader ruin, of yellowish stone and mortar, where an Arab
village clusters in the ruins and the dogs had rushed up and down
the walls snarling and barking at me as I had explored it in the
dark one night on the way from Sarafand to Haifa. The waters of
the Mediterranean rustled along the crescent beaches on either
side. On the south side of the promontory I had groped my way

into a great baronial hall. It was a romantic place, where one could imagine the Knights Templar walking to and fro in their armour on the terraces, which now were cluttered up with dung and filth, the droppings of dogs, donkeys, hens and goats. Perhaps from a submarine, on such a cloudy night, had slipped Lawrence to meet a girl shrouded in shawls. Was it fair to peer so far into the past? But who was S.A. if not Sarah Aaronsohn? Yes, it all fell into place.

Brigadier Blackley was the British Military Administrator and lived, appropriately enough, in the Villa Volpi, a palace built by the Corsair family of Karamanli who ruled Tripoli as a pirate state in the eighteenth and early nineteenth centuries. It was a beautiful building, with an ancient heraldic lion in stone standing in the forecourt.

Blackley dined in blue blazer and flannel bags – which I had not expected in one who had been a District Commissioner in the Sudan. Blackley reminded me of a rather scathing Oxford don, surrounded by his more favoured and brilliant scholars. And the whole atmosphere was of the pirate lair, with Blackley as the Corsair waiting for me to step inside.

Blackley hoped that one of these days some conference at Moscow or London or Washington would remember Tripolitania – and take some decision on the future of this land, which he certainly thought should become a British mandate, administered, however, on something more than the present care-and-maintenance basis, by – who knows? thought I – The Corsair of Villa Volpi.

Instead it became, under the eye of a United Nations Commission, part of an independent Kingdom of Libya, to be ruled by our friend, King Idris, who had been Emir of the Senussi. This outcome was not unfavourable to Britain – while it lasted.*

* Like everything else we gave up it did not last long. It subsequently came under the control of Colonel Gaddafi who gave shelter to plane hijackers and other elements hostile to the West.

CHAPTER 10   *The Mystery of Sarah Aaronsohn*

Back in England, I followed up the suggestion that the S.A. to
whom T. E. Lawrence dedicated his *Seven Pillars of Wisdom* might
be identified with the same Sarah Aaronsohn. Altounyan and his
English wife came to stay with me at Chilham. He seemed to
accept the fact that Lawrence had known Sarah Aaronsohn, but
suggested that before writing anything about it I should visit
Professor A. W. Lawrence, brother and literary executor of T. E.
Lawrence. I wrote to Professor Lawrence at Cambridge accordingly.
A. W. Lawrence replied:

Dear Mr. de Chair,
        Thanks for your note of the 28th. Ernest Altounyan has
been here and told me you had heard the story of T.E. and
Sara Aaronsohn. When this first reached me, about 10 years
ago, I could only say I had no information on the subject, but
I learnt during the war from a responsible Palestinian Jew,
who had known the A. family all his life, that it is most unlikely
that T.E. could have met Sara at all except in her childhood
and impossible that they could have met after she was 17 on
geographical grounds.
        I discovered the source of the story, by mere chance; it
was a money-making scheme that failed for lack of evidence —
an American publisher was interested for a while — and the
details are quite entertaining.
                                Yours sincerely,
                                A. W. Lawrence.

It seemed to me that Altounyan was beginning to have qualms
about revealing what he knew of the matter, but I wrote to
Professor Lawrence again and received the following card.

123

OXFORD 13.2.47

Thank you for your letter. I shall look forward to meeting you in Cambridge on the 19th or 20th.

A.W.L.

Accordingly, I rang up Professor Lawrence on arrival at Cambridge and he offered to come round to the University Arms, where I was staying, in order to have tea. I was sitting in the lounge when he arrived and I had no difficulty in identifying him, when he came through the door, by his resemblance to T. E. Lawrence; very much the same nose and cast of countenance. He was wearing an academic gown over tweed jacket and flannel trousers.

"I am glad you have decided to take an interest in the matter," he said, "because I think there has been far too much talk about it already, and the sooner something definite is said the better. Personally I do not think there is anything in the idea because I do not think he could have met her before the war, except perhaps as a child, and I don't think he could have met her after that."

He now produced from his coat pocket a flimsy piece of paper folded four ways on which he had scribbled down, while still fresh in his memory, the substance of a conversation he had had with Shertok.* The writing was so obscure and the names so weird that he found some difficulty making sense of it. But he handed this to me at the end of our conversation so that I could have fair copies of it made, "Because," he said, "in any case I ought, I suppose, to deposit a copy of it somewhere."

Then he read from the memo: "Some German Jews called Oppenheimer went to America about 1937 and met Alexander Aaronsohn, a member of a Jewish family which had settled in Syria in Turkish times. They attempted to publish a book containing a story that T.E. had been in love with Sara, Alexander's sister, and that his journey to Damascus during the war was mainly undertaken to visit her; they at first described her as his bride but subsequently explained that they had used the wrong English word and meant fiancée. This book had not been published but references to the story have appeared in print. It is almost inconceivable that it can be true, according to Moshe Shertok, Political Secretary of the Jewish Agency, who is Palestinian born and knew the Aaronsohn family before the war; Reuven Zaslani, his

---

*Later Foreign Secretary in the Israeli Government.

assistant, who too is Palestinian but younger, shares his disbelief —
I have not checked all details with him.

"Shertok states that Sara was married when almost a child to
a rich elderly Jew of Constantinople who had become interested
in Palestine sentimentally and been set on the notion of taking a
wife from the Holy Land. He went there and made an offer to
the Aaronsohns who regarded him as a prize because of his money,
in spite of his character. The marriage was unhappy. Sara lived
with him at Constantinople till after Turkey entered the war,
when she returned to Palestine and joined an organisation which
worked for the Allies. Two men, Aeshalom Feinberg and Josif
Lishansky, were rivals for its leadership and for the person of
Sara. They were adventurers in both senses of the word. The pair
of them made a trip into Sinai from which only Lishansky
returned; he said they had been engaged by a patrol in a running
fight in which Feinberg was killed, but it was rumoured that
Lishansky had bumped off his rival. Anyway, he became the
leader of the organisation and lived with Sara in the old Fast
Hotel at Jerusalem. Sara was put to death by the Turks on
discovery of her activities, and ultimately they hanged Lishansky.

"Shertok believes that Sara's marriage took place several years
before the war and consequently that T.E. could not have known
her. If he had met her previously, she would have been only a
child, and afterwards she was continually at Constantinople which
he visited only in December 1910. Alexander's record does not
inspire confidence. Among other things, he seems to have posed
as his dead brother Aaron and so secured a foreword from Allenby
to a book of reminiscences he never wrote; its synopsis, which he
sent to R.S.,* contains no word about T.E. An alleged statement
by Oppenheimer's lawyer has been reported to me, that another
sister, now living in Palestine, claimed to have documentary proof
in Sara's diary and letters from T.E. to Sara but would not show
them; I have not enquired into the matter as I gather that her
word would not be taken in Palestine as proof of anything."

When Lawrence had come to the end of the memo and folded
it up again I asked: "Where does the brother Aaron Aaronsohn
come into all this?"

"Aaron Aaronsohn," he said, "was one of these water people —

*Raymond Savage, my own literary agent at one time

what do you call them, hydrographers? – and was employed by the Turks to find water for them in the Sinai desert. He went down there and managed to fall off his camel and break his collarbone, whereupon he asked to be sent to a specialist in Berlin, and there managed to persuade the authorities in Berlin that he was a good person to send over to America. On the way to America the ship was stopped by a British warship and Aaron Aaronsohn was found in his cabin completely surrounded by subversive literature which was almost piled up to the ceiling, so he was taken off by the British Navy and brought into the Orkneys where he asked for a message to be sent to Lord Eustace Percy at the Foreign office to say 'Mr. Aaron Aaronsohn has arrived in the Orkneys.' The reply came back quick enough: 'Send him down at once.' And he was then sent out by us to the Middle East to find water on the other side. He had all the plans of his surveys with him in an aeroplane just after the war which crashed in Calais harbour, and the French police sat on the quay and watched him drown."

"Do you mean they let him drown deliberately to suppress his information?"

"I don't know," Lawrence replied, "but they seemed very indifferent to rescuing the party. Anyway, that was the end of Aaron Aaronsohn."

"Of course you may know who the S.A. of the dedication refers to," I suggested.

"I think I do," Lawrence's brother told me. "I think it is a composite figure which he had in his mind, representing partly his dead self, partly Syria as a whole and partly Dahoum – especially Dahoum."

He saw that I was puzzled and did not know to what or whom Dahoum referred, and said that Dahoum was a young Arab boy whom T.E. had brought over to England before the war to educate, and tried to bring up as a representative type of the awakening Oriental. "He used to sign himself Sheik Akmed. He was originally a donkey driver at Carcemish and eventually became a photographer. There was another boy at the dig whom T.E. brought over to have educated as well. Dahoum died in an epidemic up at Carcemish in 1917."

I could understand the attraction of having the young Arab mind educated, because I had done something of the kind myself, in the case of Helena of Abu Sinan.

"Do you seriously suggest, however," I asked, "that Lawrence could have been sufficiently interested in Sheik Akmed to have dedicated the poem to him?"

Professor Lawrence was silent for a moment before replying, and there was a far-away look in his eyes when he did reply: "Yes, I think so."

"I confess that it seems improbable to me," I said. "Had this business he referred to anything to do with his experience with the Turks at Deraa?"

Lawrence was thoughtful before replying. "Perhaps so in a way. Also he had completely lost confidence in himself. It was partly having all his bodyguard killed doing a job which he felt to be dishonest. I agree at all events," A. W. Lawrence conceded, "that something now ought to be said about it if only to allay further speculation. I cannot very well do it as I am an interested party, but I think you would be the right person to do so. I don't think there is enough in it to make a book, what I had in mind was something in the nature of a paper in the Royal Central Asian Society's Journal. I expect you would like time to think the matter over and have a talk with me again later about it." I agreed that this would be desirable and we thereupon parted.

A. W. Lawrence wrote to Newcombe later and received the reply that so far as he was aware T. E. Lawrence made no trips in the submarine to Palestine while he was working in M.I. at Cairo before 1917.

In the circumstances it seemed to me that an accurate record, which this is, of our conversation would clear up the fable more effectively than any article I might contribute to the Royal Central Asian Society's Journal.

I was still a profoundly religious man, and at Chilham I stood by the Judas Tree in blossom, a gnarled old tree which had grown against the Jacobean wall since the terrace was built, giving off young shoots of a purple-pink flower. And I philosophised:

By the Judas Tree in blossom I paused and said
Oh God, I await the unfoldment of Thy plan;
And a rain of blows descended on my head.

I felt sorely treated by the election and other disappointments;

although there were not lacking consoling voices. Oliver Lyttelton, for whom I had worked when Minister of Production, wrote:

... But I do beg of you not to be discouraged or to feel inclined to throw over the political career which was opening to you with so much promise of immediate office if we had been returned.

There had been a letter from Gavin Astor, waiting for me when my aircraft touched down, after a lecture tour I had given to troops in the Near East, asking me to a meeting in Maidstone to help the launching of the Kentish appeal for the National Association of Boys' Clubs. I attended and rashly offered to hold a pageant at Chilham. I had no idea what I was in for. I received a lot of help and also a lot of hindrance. E. P. Smith, a fellow M.P., who was also a playwright under the name of Edward Percy, entered into the spirit of the thing and we sought out Edie Craig. She was Ellen Terry's daughter and lived in a little black and white house at Small Hythe, where she preserved a memorial theatre to Ellen Terry in a barn. She agreed to produce the pageant for the cost of re-thatching the barn, which in those days was £100. All others who sought to run expenses accounts I beat upon the head. I was Chairman of the Pageant Committee. I also had to write the pageant. It began with Caesar and ended with Montgomery (impersonated by his War Office double, who had fooled the Germans at Gibraltar). E.P. was helpful. He and Edie had done a pageant before. All dialogue, he explained, must be confined to one point where there is a narrator, and amplified. He and I dressed up as Chaucer and an ostler — Oh very correct our costumes; Edie Craig saw to that. There were seven yards of scarlet cloth in my ostler's hood. We did a cross-talk act. It was a nightmare getting ten or a dozen villages to act ten or a dozen episodes. But they did it; and the long loft over the still disused cow byre abandoned by the army, was turned into a dressmaking establishment under Edie's eye, to dress 600 performers. For some we had to hire costumes — Georgian Preventive men and Kentish Militia of Napoleon's time. The neighbours joined in warily at first. Bobby and Elsie Tritton came magnificently attired as Edward Knight and his wife. Prudy Loudon as Jane Austen. Ken Hardy, Chairman of the Kent County

Council, whose family had owned Chilham where he himself had been born, acted the part of Sir Dudley Digges who built it, and a youth from Wye College played the part of a young and then unknown architect called Jones — Inigo Jones. Wye College, under the antiquarian eye of Michael Nightingale, an agricultural student there, provided this episode. The race provided for in Sir Dudley Digge's Will to ascertain which was the fleetest maid of the parish was won by the head gardener's beautiful daughter Rosemary Verral amid general acclaim. She was chaired off by beribboned villagers.

I said, "It is lucky for you that there is nothing in Sir Dudley Digge's Will about the winner being embraced by the squire."

"Oh, I should have liked that," she laughed.

The programmes took some printing and designing, with a portrait of Henry VIII, who owned the Keep for about 3 years, on the cover. They were sold by beautiful medieval maidens wearing wimples and yielded £400.

There was a great coming and going of performers through the main gates of the castle; and they were provided with performers' passes. There were impressive figures popping in and out — mitred clergy, barons in armour; King Henry II and Eleanour of Aquitaine, Richard Coeur de Lion as a young prince; Henry VIII of course, almost to life, and Ann Boleyn, unbelievably lovely, portrayed by Barbara Sconce. I protested that Henry had been married to Jane Seymour when he owned Chilham, but Edie brushed this aside. "No sex appeal. We must have Ann Boleyn." Edie was a marvel, with her twinkling grey eyes and infectious laugh, capable at need of vigorous censures. She stared at my script, "The mime proceeds," she laughed. "What does that mean?"

"That's your affair," I told her, — we got on like semi-detached houses afire. She summoned up pipe and tabor. She did the impossible and out of the bare bones of my script produced a pageant as light as a soufflé.

At the gates an impressive figure in episcopal robes sought admission on the opening day.

"Your performer's pass?" they demanded.

"I haven't got a performer's pass," replied the dignitary.

"Well, how do you expect to get in without a performer's pass?"

"I thought I would be able to pay for a ticket."

"Oh you want to buy a ticket?"

"Yes. A two guinea ticket."

It was Dr. Fisher, the archbishop of Canterbury, dropping in after some ecclesiastical ceremony at which he had appeared in full canonicals.

The Duchess of Kent attended the first of the four performances and we made in all a clear profit of £2,600 in two afternoons for the Boys' Clubs and Soldiers', Sailors' and Airmen's Families Association.

At this time I was courting my second wife, Carmen, and had arranged to meet her in King's Wood on her 20th birthday. And what a glorious day it was — one of those perfect English days in high summer long to be remembered. The groom had the mare saddled and bridled in the stable yard, and I jumped into the saddle and cantered out of the yard — the iron shoes of the mare clattering across the stones: and galloped up into the park under the great walnut trees. Up on the ridge of the park, where the bracken closed in towards the house, I slowed to a walk and stopped to admire the view. Turning round, I saw the distant spire of the Cathedral. This was the first glimpse of it which had gladdened the footsore pilgrims of Chaucer's day, coming down from the Pilgrim's Way and the great woods. From here the grey stone tower of the Norman keep and the mellow red of the Jacobean brick house standing above its majestic terraces, always presented the most spectacular picture.

Below me, where I leaned forward on my mare, patting her neck, an avenue of Spanish chestnuts dating, some said, from Roman times, ran along the lower slope of the park ridge, to meet a beech avenue a mile away, where a heronry, dating from King John's time, made the Title Deeds rustle of Magna Carta. I was walking up that long avenue one day with Norah Lindsey, who had come to see about the possibility of improving the layout of the gardens, and Hamilton Kerr, who had been in the House of Commons with me. Both of whom were staying for the weekend. We came upon some charcoal burners at the bottom of the heronry avenue: they were piling wood into large round iron charcoal drums the height of a man. "Il ne manquait que ça," Norah had remarked.

1 could now see two of the gardeners working in the lower herbaceous border, against the Jacobean brick wall of one of the

terraces: getting all tidy for the Pageant. Spinner, the young carpenter, was busy in the far corner of the lower lawn, between the furthest pair of yew trees, erecting a little wooden pavilion, where Chaucer and I (as the ostler) would read or recite the narrative of the Pageant into a microphone. I whisked the mare round.

I cantered up through the oaks and bracken towards the great woods. Further up the park I passed a pile of warped metal, still preserved by my orders amid the bracken fronds. It was the remains of a German flying bomb — the V.1 which had crashed there, making such a resounding noise that the windows of the Great House had rattled.

I knew where I was to meet Carmen, at the head of the track which wound up between my land and the Godmersham Estate, belonging to the Trittons. They, too, had a house of extraordinary beauty: but whereas the personality of Chilham was very masculine, assertive and rather sinister, Godmersham had a feminine charm. It was Georgian at its best, with white wooden sash windows in the rosiest of brick; and all cupped like a jewel in the hollow of a park which was the exact complement of ours, which rose to a ridge. The two properties were indeed complementary to each other in every way. Sometimes we were amused by their displays of wealth: they had bought the house from impoverished aristocrats who had covered the Georgian façade in some previous generation with white stucco. The removal of this had only been partially successful and the Trittons had accordingly had all the bricks on that side taken out, turned round, and put back again to expose their more authentic Georgian surfaces. Their adaption of the house inside had evidently left something to be desired also, so when it was nearly completed they had moved the south front out a yard into the garden, to allow for more corridor space inside; and every chair was a museum piece. It made us feel at Chilham as if we were naked savages squatting amid hides and stones.

So now I was quite content to sit my horse under the shade of the wonderful elms which fringed Elsie's park and gaze my fill on her domain with its symmetrical house, so like a little red doll's house at this distance, surrounded by well trimmed gardens. At this time she was reduced to six or seven gardeners, who moved with robot-like precision about the swimming pool borders or the well painted greenhouses, making my four seem to struggle like apes or Neanderthal man.

The flies danced about the mare's head and eyes, and she rubbed them constantly against her forelegs and stamped her hind legs, and swished her tail. I was wearing an open necked army bush shirt, with my cavalry army breeches and brown field boots; a habit carried over from my army days. I even wore spurs, because Oletha, the mare, was very idle about riding away from home. I carried my army riding stick, a knotted swagger-cane, covered in leather. I had also brought with me a ciné camera, intending to take some pictures of Carmen. Oletha was by now in such a lather of sweat, indeed it was as if she had been soaped, the white lather emerging between the saddle and her flanks, that I decided to tether her and wait for Carmen dismounted. It was probably vanity that had kept me sitting astride my horse, hoping to cut an impressive figure when she approached. But I had scarcely lain down on some moss in the shade, leaving Oletha under some elders, when I heard an extraordinary thing. At least it surprised me – a pure singing voice, as if some opera star, playing the part of Brunhilde, were riding through the woods. It was a woman's voice of wonderful clarity, holding a long high note of tremendous exaltation, and it was accompanied by the clinking of a bit and the footfall of a horse slipping on the rough surface of the track. It did not occur to me that this could be Carmen, and I waited in some curiosity to see the approaching rider. It was Carmen, nevertheless, riding a rather shaggy chestnut horse. She was wearing an open necked shirt of yellow checks, and a pair of trousers – probably her father's – which turned out on closer inspection, to be of a small brown and black check pattern. Her face was sweating and shining, but her lips were made up with a very dark carmine colour, and her hair hung loosely about her shoulders.

"Was that you singing?" I asked.

"Yes, who else?"

"But you sound like an opera star."

"I know. I was trained to go into the opera. Madame Zenada said I had a wonderful register."

"Well, why don't you go on training to be an opera singer?"

She shrugged her shoulders, and I helped her off her horse as she swung her trousered legs round to slip off the saddle. Her old nag had his ears pricked and was staring at Oletha a few yards away in the elders. She had her head turned round with equal curiosity. We tethered them together, where after a little preliminary neck biting, they rubbed noses and began to doze in the shade or munch the leaves and bracken fronds.

"Do sing some more," I begged Carmen.

"No, I can't sing to order," she said, "or not while anybody is listening."

"That won't go well in the Metropolitan Opera House," I laughed.

She made an impatient gesture — how could anybody be so stupid, it suggested. But the curious thing is that I never did hear her sing another note, and later on, after she had trouble with her chest she said her singing voice had gone altogether — so I am left with that one sustained octave of pure sound soaring above the woods and parks of Godmersham and Chilham in high summer, while the flies cruised about in the shade. She was an extraordinary girl.

"I have brought you a birthday present," I told her, after I had given her a birthday kiss. It was the limited edition, bound in vellum of one of my books *The First Crusade*. I had inscribed it 'to Carmen — sweet and twenty', both of which attributes were exact.

Carmen had brought some tea in a thermos flask so that we would have a sort of celebration — rather pathetic, I thought, visualising all the champagne bottles lying on their sides in the cellar. On my way back I met Black, the woodman, walking home to his cottage. His family had been woodmen on the estate for four hundred years. He had no son of his own, which seemed a tragedy, for it meant the dying out of all that lore. He could tell the age of a tree at a glance: and fell it within an inch of an intended mark. He was a bit of a rascal: an old cavalryman, like myself. But that was a bond between us. He patted Oletha's head absentmindedly and held her bridle automatically, while he talked about the felling of some mature oak in Cutlers Wood, a mile and a half away. Black was no more enthusiastic about felling trees than I was; but we would ride through the woods carefully — at least I would ride while he walked and mark them selectively, so as not to disturb the amenities. He recognised that the estate needed the money in these times. So after a short talk,

I spurred the mare and galloped back across the rise facing the library windows, towards the stables down below the Norman keep. It had been an unforgettable afternoon for me. What I had in fact discussed with Black was the heronry. "It seems very quiet" — I had just ridden down through it: "except for a little clucking in some of the nests." They were all high up in high beech trees. "And I could not see any herons circling above the trees." I think I had a permanent superstition that if the herons left the property, some disaster would follow. I worried every time a tree crashed in a gale in case it should frighten them away.

"You don't need to worry," Black explained. "The older birds go down to the rivers and the marshes about now. As soon as the last of the fledglings can fly, they will all be gone. But they will be back next year on St. Valentine's Day."

"Really!" I exclaimed delighted. "On February 14th? Can you be sure?"

"They're always supposed to be back by then," Black smiled. "Do you want me for anything more, Sir?" He had let go his hold of the bridle, which had been jumping about in his hand on account of the flies fretting Oletha; and walked off up the great chestnut avenue. He was a man of over sixty, with clear blue eyes, sparse grey hair, and a weathered but rather rosy complexion. Very English. Indeed, he was like one of the ash trees — grey and springy; and sensitive to the weather. Perhaps in England the ash had come before the oak. It was a more subtle wood than the hard unyielding material of which Nelson's ships were built: and might in the end last longer.

I dismounted in the stable yard, where the chauffeur was washing down the car: and handed the mare over to him. "She's in a fair sweat," he observed.

"Yes, I galloped her up the avenue. But it's a hot day, too."

"It sure is," he wiped his brow. He was in shirt sleeves.

I walked up to the house between the dark growth of yew and laurel, which gives this approach from the stables a rather forbidding appearance. The dungeons of the old keep were reached on this side through a long tunnel, of which the entrance showed up in the bank as a dark archway. Sixteen skeletons had been found in there, in a crouching position: yet curiously enough it was not the old Norman building above it which seemed haunted so much as the more modern house beside it, built in 1616. Indeed I wondered as I walked round to the front door if the house could possibly be exercising a curious spell over us all, driving us on to some unpremeditated disaster.

I remembered dancing the polka on the night of the Victory Celebrations upon the square, lit up with strings of coloured lights for the purpose: while a band played from a hay wain. I had danced this polka in spite of the damage I knew it would cause my ankle, with the doctor's wife, a witch-like old creature who had pointed up at the castle and cackled, "La belle dame sans merci." This was Doctor Fennell's wife. Was this a good description of it — a heartless beauty? Time would show.

I decided to turn aside and entered the dark deserted building of the Norman keep. The spiral stone staircase smelled of mildew. I went into the rooms on each floor and opened the windows. In a small bedroom half-way up, a narrow slit of a window looked down upon the more modern house, and another window overlooked a narrow courtyard inside the high curtain wall of the keep. Beneath this window a shallow stone tray with a hole through to the outside, was, in fact, a medieval convenience. Outside, a narrow passage inside the walls led to an arrow-slit. On the upper floor was another small room with a narrow window, topped with a rounded scroll of stone outside, dating from King John's days: this was the most authentic part of Chilham. Here King John had held his historic meeting with Archbishop Langton. But in Georgian times an octagonal panelled drawing-room had been provided in the central part of the octagonal keep; with large rounded wooden windows overlooking the park. I climbed up the spiral staircase to the leaded roof. Here some young women in the eighteenth century had marked out the imprints of their square-toed shoes in the leads by pricking the outlines, and dating them 1788, and so on. The water tanks of the castle were up here on a level with the rooks cawing in the elm tops: and the water hissed and gurgled into the tanks. I walked over to the parapet and looked down at the stone flagged path. From up here I was granted a lovely view of the terraces, with their orderly clipped yew trees, the orchard below and the lake. The water meadows and the line of willow marking the river where the kingfishers would be darting their blue fire along the banks: and beyond, the beech trees hiding the road and the railway cutting; then the low slope of the Downs, with its coarse yellow grass, and along their summit the chalk track, which I called the Silver Mile, in front of the woods, where I was wont to gallop. To my right stretched the park, my eyes following the tops of the great chestnut avenue of the beeches of the heronry and the blueness of unending woods beyond.

I see now what a lot Chilham had to offer in the denuded conditions of the post-war world. At least it had a keeper, a woodman and a carpenter: which, added to the garden and farm staffs, most people would now regard as a princely retinue. But they were always reminding me of the bygone days of the Copper King, Sir Edmund Davis, who kept four woodmen, three keepers, a whole building-staff (of which Spinner, the joiner, was the only survivor), twelve gardeners, and so on. I was made to feel that the estate had gone to pot. It was the same in the village. The V.J. celebrations had been compared with the Coronation when the Copper King had roasted a whole ox for their edification. Yet I might have been warned by the fact that they spoke of him in the same breath as a man of no breeding, who merely threw money about. There is no pleasing English villages. Nevertheless I was very satisfied with Chilham as it was and felt a sort of despairing rage at the pit opening before my feet. This was a domestic matter which was in fact to lead to the break-up of my first marriage and my marriage to Carmen.

Having dated from Sir Edmund Davis's time was a sort of levee that used to be conducted in the back part of the house behind the hall. Leading members of the estate, the heads of the departments as I suppose they would have regarded themselves, would gather there for a sort of audience before doing any real work on the place at all. Everybody wanted authority to do something or other.

Spinner and Black were the first to be shown through to the back passage by Troke, the old butler who had survived from Sir Edmund Davis's time and had indeed found him lying dead in his bath. I always suspected Troke of being an old lag. I imagined that he had something on Sir Edmund Davis. He tended to be very shifty eyed and always had dandruff on his collar.

Spinner, on the other hand, was a bright young man, not more than thirty, with very blond hair, but expert at his job, as the joiner and carpenter. He wore a pair of blue overalls and carried a folding brass-hinged and brass-tipped ruler. Black, the woodman, wore an old tweed jacket, out at elbows, and held a cloth cap in his hand. His large square head, with his sparse grey hairs and ruddy face, looked surprised.

"It is about the old mill," Spinner began. "I've had a look at the main supporting beams, as you asked, Sir, and one of them is rotted nearly through. The other can be cleaned up and supported. But they're very long. Black and I have just measured them: twenty-eight feet."

"Have we got one on the estate that will do?" I turned to Black.

"I know you're keen to have a beam out of Chilham oak," Black said, uneasily, looking away through the windows which overlooked the courtyard, with a glimpse of the park beyond. "But it takes a very straight tree to get a clear beam the size young Spinner wants."

"It will have to be eighteen inches square before roughing at the least," Spinner put it.

"Well, Black, out with it. You know every tree on the place. You know just the tree and don't want to fell it. Is that it?"

Black looked more uncomfortable than ever. "They're your trees, of course, Sir. But the way I look at it is this. The value will always be in oak. It's not like beech, which reaches maturity in a hundred years or so, and begins to go back. There are trees in the heronry avenue which could come down now; if it wasn't for the look of them. But the oaks in Cutlers Wood will stand another two hundred years if you like. And you could order a baulk of timber from the merchants, just as good, exactly the dimensions Spinner needs. Do you really need to fell one of the Chilham oaks? It will take such a good one for this job."

"Where is it?"

"In Cutlers Wood. You may not have noticed it, because the underwood there is pretty high: about seven years' growth. It's one of the group on the rise overlooking old Cutler's Farm."

I said we would go and see it.

"Tell Troke, I will see Verral at once, and then I will meet you at the Garage Yard." Troke reappeared with the head gardener: a worried man with a bulging forehead. Verral's eyes seemed permanently sunk into his skull in despair.

"It's the raspberry canes, Sir," he wailed, as if the last trump had sounded.

"What of them, Verral?"

"We must get some new ones now, if they are to be any use this year; they ought to have been set in March." He was wringing his hands in grief.

"By all means get them without delay then."

"Yes, Sir. But we haven't got them yet, Sir, we must order them, Sir."

"Well, order them, Verral."

"Have I got your authority to order them Sir?"

"Indeed you have."

"But it will mean my going into Ashford, by bus, today, to order them, unless we are to wait over the weekend and the post."

"By all means go in by bus."

"Oh, thank you, Sir." He ducked and twisted about, scampering away to order the precious raspberry canes.

Troke grinned, so that his false teeth gleamed. "He's been worrying himself into his grave for you to get back — just to order his blessed raspberries."

"Nevertheless, Troke," I admonished him, "they sweat for duty, not for mead," which was more than could be said of Troke — but the quotation was lost on him.

The chauffeur/groom had left in the New Year, after wearing a plum coloured chauffeur's uniform for six months, which Thelma and I had had made for him. We thought it rather smart when he drove us in the Rolls to the Trittons in it: but I suspected that the chaffing he got from Spinner and Troke was too much for his cockney sense of humour: and in any case there were not enough horses to keep him happy in the dual role of chauffeur and groom. We planned, therefore, to replace Troke when it could be done fittingly, by a chauffeur/valet, who could look after my clothes properly, instead of spilling dandruff on them, and clean the car also when required.

Jeans had been up to see me after breakfast and said that the gypsies were camping as usual in the woods on the Downs and poaching all the nesting pheasants (not that there were many).

So I rode Oletha down to the bridge: along the Ashford road for a short distance: and turned left over the narrow railway bridge, which brought me again to my own land on the chalk. I followed some thin scrub and furze bushes growing in the long faded yellow couch grass, the growth of years, shot through with spears of fresher green, and came upon the gypsy encampment — where the high woods descended in a spur towards the valley. There were two old wooden caravans, painted gaudily in colours of green, yellow and red. These were still the days of horse-drawn caravans. They were rounded and wide at the top, and steps led up to a door in the back. The shafts were resting on the ground and a couple of shaggy nags, not unlike the one Carmen had ridden on her birthday, were tethered to thorn bushes near by. Washing was spread out on the twigs in the sun: and a number of incredibly dirty children in grey wisps of cotton darted about. Two young mothers, with copper-coloured skin and shining black hair coiled about their heads in plaits, like snakes basking in the sun, scowled up at me, as I reined in my bay mare.

"We aint't doing no 'arm, Mister," said one of them.

"Maybe not," I said, noncommittally. "Where are your men-folk?"

"Minding their own business," said the other.

"You had better tell them that these Downs are private property."

"We know that, Mister, we ain't doin' no 'arm."

"I don't mind casual picknickers, but I am afraid I have had to make a rule about people camping," I said, eyeing a circle of bronze pheasant feathers round the blackened ashes of an old fire. The older woman followed the line of my gaze. "That wasn't us, Mister. Honest to God: they was there wen we come."

"Anyway, I shall be up here with my keeper and others tomorrow morning," I said firmly, "and I shall expect to find your caravan gone."

The younger girl rushed up to the mare, brandishing her fist, and screeched, "I'll put the gypsy curse on you, Mister. You'll be cursed. We ain't doin' no 'arm to you;" and she grasped a passing child and hid it behind her blue skirts.

"I'm sorry," I said, as I rode off. "But I can't make exceptions."

"You'll be cursed," she screamed. And so, perhaps, I was.

These weird people certainly seem to convey a sense of menace of an occult kind. I remember the palmist— 'I see dark tragedy for you: for all'. Was it possible that Carmen was in league with them: that secretly her gypsy blood wandered to these places when the moon was full? These Downs were old in history. It was here, possibly, in these very woods that the outposts of

Cassevelaunus, retreating guardedly before Caesar's landing on the coast a few days earlier, had watched the 10th Legion marching up the valley: and with sudden shouts, hurled their darts upon the bronze shields of the Roman soldiers. I rode round the circular earthwork, a hundred yards in diameter, still clearly marked upon the shoulder of the Downs, and tried to reconstruct the scene. Nearby was a long barrow, still known as Julaberries Grave, and thought by archaeologists to mean the burial place of Julius Caesar's casualties, possibly named after one of his tribunes, Julius Laberius. It was the beginning of England, as we know it. From that day all followed as the night – the jurisprudence, the hot baths, the central heating: the anagrams unearthed on the mosaic floors of Roman villas. Even, some said, the foundation of the keep at Chilham. This now came into view across the valley; a grey smudge between the great cedar trees on the lawn: and beside it the rosy pile of the house, and the streaks of terraces below: edged with the giant clipped yew trees. I could see the patches of orange colour on the upper terrace, where Thelma and her mother were probably still sitting in deck-chairs. Yes, there was the gleam of a Sunday newspaper, turned over in the morning sunshine.

I got out my handkerchief and waved it, slowly, above my head: then put Oletha into a gallop along the Silver Mile.

I rode for a mile through the upper beeches, gripping the pommel as Oletha struggled up the steep slopes between the great roots, and came out on a bramble-fringed field of plough-land beyond. This was my boundary, my frontier, and I was not greatly interested beyond it. So I let Oletha take me slithering downwards, along a sunken lane, through the million greenness of the beech trees, in May, to the chalk track: and, dismounting, took the reins over Oletha's head and let her chew the cool grass, while I sat looking across at the house. The chairs were now definitely empty; and I expected that this meant Thelma and her mother were on their way up to join me.

As I was sitting there, in the spring sun, while Oletha cooled down, I noticed a tiny oak seedling not more than three inches high, in the grass. And I tried to project my mind into its slender strength, and freshly curled leaves. I thought: 'If this young oak could speak would he not say – "Even the grass is twice as tall as me, and when I see the barley growing grey – ".'

Mrs. Arbuthnot was now widowed and not particulary excited by the prospect of spending another fifteen or twenty years on earth. She had no doubts about the future. She would join her husband after no more than a pause, as if she had got left behind at some wayside railway station, while he had gone ahead to the terminus. He would be fretting about for her at the barrier: watching every train till she arrived — she had no doubt.

Petrol rationing was still in force at this time just after the war, but I had discovered from Bullock, who was an engineer, from whom I was buying a yacht, that a car would run almost equally well on paraffin if it was first heated up, so a day or two later, I went in search of Spinner. I found him in the workshops, where the long saw benches, for the cutting of great baulks of timber of byegone days, were still serviceable. Spinner and Black were, in fact, guiding the enormous trunk of the oak tree felled in Cutlers Wood for the Mill beam, on to the long metal surfaced bench. A timber haulier had been engaged to drag it down, crushing in its wake a million bluebells and primroses, and transported it to the workshops. These were at the bottom of the hill, near the village hall: and housed also the deep well pumps which supplied the castle. These were run on paraffin and it was in search of this fluid that I wanted to see Spinner.

"Ah, there she is," I exclaimed as soon as I saw the enormous tree trunk. "How large it looks in here."

"They always do," said Black mournfully.

Its base was sawn through, laboriously by cross-cut saws, wielded by Black and an unwilling Jeans: till the cut reached the bite taken out of it first by Black with an axe on the side where the tree was to fall. What a crash that had been, tearing through the branches of smaller trees. The chestnut underwood around its base had first been cut by Black over a radius of forty yards. The giant had fallen with a roar and shuddered on the ground, leaving a groove, a yard wide, long visible. Now it lay like the trunk of Gulliver's body, while the mortals climbed about it on the long benches. They were chaining it about with chains, and levering it with iron crowbars, to bring it into line with the hungry fanged saw: whose sharp teeth gleamed in the half dark of the saw sheds. Spinner had filed each tooth with his files, till they had a metallic glint. The surfaces of the saw were greased so that it could cut swiftly and smoothly into the flesh of the tree, first flaying off its bark, with long steady cuts, right along its length. The upper branches, where they forked away from the main stem, had been cut off and left to later dissection on the ground.

"Spinner," I said, "I want some paraffin. I have been told by one called Bullock, a resourceful man and an engineer, that once a car is warmed up and running, if you fill the tank with paraffin, it will go on running, so long as you don't stop. Anyway, I intend to try!"

"Not in the Rolls, surely?"

"Yes. It can't do it much harm once in a while. I want to get down to the yacht, which has arrived at Southampton, or thereabouts. It's a journey of 150 miles. So I propose to start the car on a gallon of petrol before I leave tomorrow, and come down to you here about 3 o'clock, where you will be ready with funnels and drums to pour in fifteen gallons of paraffin. Have you got it?"

"Oh, yes. We have fifty gallons at a time for the pumps and the sawmill: the tanks have only just been filled."

Black was leaning against the ancient bark of the oak, and looking at me thoughtfully out of his pale blue eyes. Perhaps he was just staring into space and thinking of beer — it was a preoccupation of his, and many a time could he be seen, sloping his old cavalry shoulders through the darkened doorway of the village pub.

His eye remained undimmed and his hand never faltered with the axe.

"Now let us see what you are going to do with the tree."

"Is she in position?" Spinner asked Black, who walked out into the sunlight and lined up the trunk with an aiming mark beyond the saw.

"She's true. Let her spin."

Spinner moved a lever and the big blade — the biggest in the workshops — began to hum; and gradually to increase speed to a whine. Another lever brought the hooks up between the metal benches, and spiked the belly of the tree: then slowly began drawing it towards the eager saw: which let out a screech as it bit into the hard wood. The tree shivered and seemed to hesitate on its rack: but relentlessly the power of engines dragged it on, away from the light, towards those whirling and gnashing teeth flashing in the gloom. Onward slid the tree and the humped arc of the blade was almost swallowed up and hidden in the body of the oak; only its grinding top, now labouring round, biting ever more slowly into the bark and wood. Smoke began to pour out of the wound: and Black held up his hand: Spinner swung the lever and the trunk stopped advancing: the blade had now cut into one side of the tree about two yards. Black gave the order to stop the saw, while he clambered up on the bench to examine the cut. He hammered a wedge into the cut, where the saw had already passed, so as to keep the cut open and allow the saw more freedom at the sides. Then the operation began again: and I left them, amid a cloud of sawdust and flying bark, to complete the stripping and taming of the giant.

I had told Carmen about the paraffin, as I didn't want to have to stop the engine of the car: and she was waiting for me at an inn where she had gone by bus, with her grip, at the point where the Ashford and Chilham roads converged in the direction of Southampton. To a casual observer she would have given the impression, standing outside the locked doors of the pub, of cadging a lift. She made a great joke of pulling her skirt up nearly to her thigh, as I approached, and exposing one of the smartest pairs of legs in the south of England: and jerking her thumb in a westerly direction.

"Is that how you usually get driven about the countryside?" I laughed, as I pulled up, leaving the engine running in the meantime.

"I don't like buses much," she said.

"With that technique I should think you could get to John o'Groat's in motor cars. What happens when you get inside them, that's what I wonder!"

"Ah!" she said. But she was very young and was still protected by a look of lingering innocence. Two years later we were married, and I had moved to Blickling. Chilham was sold at auction in 1949 for £94,000. The 4 farm tenants were given special terms to buy their farms, which fetched about £8,000 each with some 200 acres on the average. (One of the farms, Hurst Farm, bought by the farm tenant for £8,000, a lovely Tudor house on the river with 230 acres, was resold in 1973 for £230,000). The castle and some 400 acres, including the park, was bought by Viscount Masserene and Ferrard, who has lived there ever since.

CHAPTER 11 *The Greatest of These . . .*

Shortly before leaving for the Middle East, I had been asked to address the Faversham National Farmer's Union, and invited Kenneth Pipe, the *Daily Express* Agricultural Correspondent, to spend the night at Chilham for the meeting. He sat in the front row as I said of Lord Beaverbrook: "He may be a ganster and a back stairs intriguer, but you cannot deny that this gay old Empire Crusader has done more than anyone else to make the citizen of this country aware of his responsibilities to the Empire." Kenneth Pipe left out the bit about the gangster and the back stairs intriguer and flourished 'the gay old Empire crusader'. Beaverbrook was delighted and wrote to me, 'This is the first kind word that has been said about me since the election. Come and have dinner.' I was just off on the trip to the Middle East but I replied that I should be delighted to dine with him when I got back. Faber's sent him an advance copy of my forthcoming book *A Mind on the March* and he replied:

I am very glad to have the opportunity of reading it. For in my view the author writes brilliantly and has much of value to say.

It is my view indeed that he has an important future to play in the country's affairs.

Shortly after my return I dined with him as arranged. He was in much better health than when I had seen him before the war. He produced champagne while we dined together. He was at pains to convince me that he had not been responsible for the fatal broadcast with which Winston had opened the 1945 election.

"I first heard it from that radio sitting in this room." He declared, pointing to the instrument as if it were a viper, "To whom was the speech shown first? To the people to whom it should have been shown; to the Chairman of the Party and the

144

Chief Whip."

Brendan Bracken arrived with a new member, Marlowe. And I turned roundly on Brendan. "You more than anyone are responsible for our defeat. You and the Beaver here." Beaverbrook chuckled and rubbed his hands with glee, enormously enjoying this sort of thing. But Brendan's red hair flamed and his eyes flashed behind his square horn-rimmed spectacles.

"You don't seem to see – " he began.

"He's not in a seeing mood," laughed the Beaver.

"The Capitalist pond is shrinking," I went on, "and as it shrinks it gives off stronger odours. One of the reasons we lost the election was that half the Tories were directors of companies, and as they were working for the war effort, they began getting up in the House to defend their own companies, thinking no doubt that they were doing so in the national interest, but the public did not like it."

There was something about Brendan with his *Financial Times* and his companies and the direct personal influence he had exercised over appointments, which had given him the nickname of the Patronage Secretary, that provoked me thus to overstate the case. But I was not, as the Beaver said, in a seeing mood. Brendan was gloomy to the point of wishful thinking about the prospects for our economy after the Socialist victory.

"The country will be flat on its back by next July," (1946) he said.

"The only place the country will be flat on its back," I retorted, "will be at Margate or Blackpool."

It was not long after this that I published the *Teetotalitarian State*, in which a triumvirate consisting of Lord Bonaparte, Bendem Backem and Mr. Safe Ash-can (the Chairman of the Preservative Party) dining at the Tarleton Club concocted a plan to lose the general election for fear of the dire consequences to the Party of governing in the conditions likely to prevail immediately after the war; and all the incredible mistakes that we made were duly advanced for satirical purposes, as part of a deep laid plot. What the Beaver thought of it I do not know, but Brendan was not amused. Ralph Asheton stopped me one day, and said, "You know, we did not really try to lose the general election."

"I had not supposed that you did," I replied. "I merely thought it the most kindly interpretation to put on it!" Is it

146

surprising that I have never been the blue-eyed boy of the Preservative Central Office?

The Boys Clubs were very pleased with their £1,300.00 half share of the profits of the Pageant and to my surprise and some embarrassment, elected me Chairman of the Kentish branch. I felt increasingly unfitted for such a role; but I attended many of their affairs, especially at their new training centre at Chartham, near by. I handed over the job to Miles Killearn, when he became tenant of Chilham in a year's time.

I was also made a governor of Wye College; and in order to get celebrations they made me Chairman of the Centenary celebrations Committee. These were impressive. The Archbishop of Canterbury preached a sermon in the church; and there was a ceremony in a marquee at which the Chancellor, Lord Athlone, appeared in robes of black and gold; almost the first time I had seen him since he pressed buns upon me at Government House in Cape Town on my way out to Australia at the age of twelve. Ted Hardy* was there in striped trousers, frock coat and top hat. Reflecting that this was an Agricultural occasion I had come in a tweed suit, over which an academic gown was thrown – we all wore them that afternoon – and my tweediness among so many top hats was conspicuous.

The success of the Pageant – a field notorious for the losing of money – led other charitable organisations to turn towards me for help. I had recently joined the United Nations Association and was now co-opted to its National Appeal Committee and in turn to its National Executive Committee. The Appeal Committee was an impressive body on paper; but like most committees of this kind the work was confined to a devoted band. Among these however must be numbered Mrs. Attlee, who was a very regular attender and Mrs. Philip Noel-Baker. Their presence did nothing to counter-act a certain leftish tendency in this non-party organisation; but on the subject of the appeal for funds all parties were agreed. Mrs. Attlee proposed at the second meeting I attended that I should be elected Chairman of the Committee. This involved much more work than I had contemplated devoting to the organisation, but as I was out of Parliament I had little else to do. So I accepted and although I found money very hard to raise, we succeeded in bringing

*Chairman of the Kent County Council

in £36,000 in three years. Most members of the Committee, like Mrs. Attlee and Lord Salisbury, had only intended originally to be on the Committee for a year at the most, and I very much appreciated their continued support. By the end of three years we were able to appoint a professional organiser of sufficient calibre (Miss Nancy Scott) to take over the work of raising money without a Committee.

My work on the National Appeal Committee brought me a good deal into contact with the Attlees, and I came to have a deep respect and indeed affection for both of them. Mrs. Attlee, with her beauty, charm, dignity and practical mind, yet with a fundamentally feminine, unassertive personality seemed to me in many ways the ideal wife for a Prime Minister. One could dance with her at an International Ball and joke about clothes rationing without ever doubting her serious devotion to public affairs. I was first summoned to No. 10 to discuss with Mrs. Attlee the list of guests to be invited to the meeting which she had agreed to hold there to launch the appeal. Attlee joined us and took a surprisingly detailed interest in the names to be omitted. Some of these surprised me. The atmosphere was not very different from what one would expect when any host and hostess were considering the names of guests for a private reception.

Afterwards Attlee took me down to the Cabinet Room and gestured to a seat beside him. So we sat down to discuss further details of the meeting.

Attlee was a devout supporter of the Charter of the United Nations and consistently spoke, as Prime Minister in support of our appeal. On one occasion he addressed a large rally at Chilham, where I took the chair. It rained and he spoke at the tops of umbrellas. I invited the leading personalities in the neighbourhood to meet him and Mrs. Attlee for tea. They stayed on for an auction (by Gillie Potter) in aid of the cause; in spite of the driving rain. It was held under the spreading boughs of a cedar tree, but I feared that I should have a Prime Minister's death from pneumonia on my hands. He stood in a raincoat with collar turned up, and the rain dripping down the back of his neck. Mrs. Attlee bought a bottle of Bols for £14 but she wrote afterwards to say that it had fallen out of the car when they got home and was broken in the gutter. It was not always easy to get Tory speakers of equal calibre and sometimes, as at Arundel, I had to appear with Attlee and some distinguished Liberal like Lord Reading, as the third party speaker. Eden spoke twice for the appeal at Rallies which we organised, at Sutton Place under the chairmanship of the Duke of Sutherland and at Warwick under the chairmanship of Lord Warwick. Eden had just returned from a guelling tour of the Commonwealth before the Warwick meeting and in the heat of the afternoon fainted twice in my arms, during his speech. This caused far more comment in the press than anything he said or had intended to say. An unkind wit in the party said that the speech had been prepared for him in the Conservative Central Office research department but that owing to a typist's mistake, he came upon a blank page and fainted. Recovering himself he turned over the page and went on till, lo, there was another blank page, and this time he collapsed altogether. It was an irony that my 'Anthony Eden' hat was thrust upon his own head, to shield it from the sun. At such meetings there is invariably a carafe of water and glass upon the table. On this one occasion, there was none. The fainting statesman gasped 'water'; the St. John Ambulance dashed at him with brandy, and he spluttered 'water'. Warwick hurriedly called upon me to move the vote of thanks, which I did with record brevity and we withdrew to the castle and revived the deputy leader of the Tory party with a cup of tea.

My only dealings with the film industry came about through our need to have a propaganda film made for the Appeal. I can only say that it struck me as the most ill-organised and wasteful economy I have ever encountered. Had it not been for Sir David Cunynghame, a neighbour in Norfolk, who was Korda's distribution director, the film would never have been completed. He pressed buttons and things occurred. I had to sit at a desk in a studio library of embarrassing sumptuousness and make the appeal at the end of the film, after the no less horrifying spectacle of the atom bomb and Nagasaki. I am not good at this sort of thing and unwisely refused to be made-up. Consequently I shone at all angles, like a wet sausage. Fortunately I had been able to persuade Captain Anthony Kimmins, a noted broadcaster, to voice the script narrative which I had written for the film and this was pleasing. I persuaded the Rank Organisation to show the film in all their cinemas; and it was duly shown in 550 cinemas. After all this I was glad enough to be able to wind up the Appeal Committee and hand over the task of raising money from a reluctant public to the competent but less sensitive Miss Scott, who came to us fresh from raising half a million for the King George's Fund for Sailors.

The most pleasant assignment I had for the United Nations Association was to speak with Lady Violet Bonham-Carter and Hector McNiel at a rally at Welbeck Abbey under the Chairmanship of the Duke of Portland. The Duke was tremendously impressed by Lady Violet's oratory. "A chip off the old block," he whispered to me, thinking of Asquith. We all stayed with the Duke and his charming wife and daughters at the new house he had built for use in the modern world, while the big house was handed over to the War Office as a training college for young officers. Nevertheless the Duke showed us over it and we were amused by the railway line used in pre-war days to carry the food from the kitchens to the dining-room.

When the daughters were asked why they showed no inclination to marry they replied that they had such wonderful parents and such a lovely home, that they doubted if they could ever be as happy anywhere else. The younger daughter did marry later an Italian nobleman, but on a visit to her parents in Scotland fell victim to poliomyolitis and died. I had seen her only a short time before, sitting with her Italian husband sipping drinks on the piazza at Capri. It was difficult to believe her dead. The elder sister Lady Anne Cavendish-Britol has never married, although she struck me as representing all that makes English country women most attractive.

One of our last actions as a Committee was to issue a letter to men of supposed substance, appealing for support. It was signed by Mrs. Attlee, Lord Salisbury, Jimmy de Rothchild and myself (as Chairman). It only brought in about £1,000. These thousand pounds were hard to come by. I ran a concert at the Albert Hall, with Sir Malcolm Sargent conducting and Miss Eileen Joyce as the pianist (we had to pay her £150 – Sir Malcolm did it for nothing). We counted ourselves lucky to make a profit of over £1,000 on that.

I had since the wounding and operations, to realise increasingly my physical limitations, the limits placed above all on my physical endurance and stamina in work. Although I returned for a while to Parliament, the physical frame in which I worked, invisible to others, gradually affected the portraiture proceeding within it.

More and more I was driven to find expression in literary pursuits and, at first, while my creative energy was weakened or numbed by the shock of the operations, on non-creative, pedestrian work, I realised instinctively the need to mark time, and devoted myself to three historical works — a translation of the Gesta Francorum, (*The First Crusade*); *Napoleon's Memoirs* rescued virtually from obscurity; and a new presentation of *Caesar's Commentaries*. These were my main output between 1943 and 1953. They were all published in the first instance by the Golden Cockerel Press in very sumptuous limited editions (at their expense). At about this time (1946) I was startled to receive a request from the National Portrait Gallery for my portrait to be done at a photographic studio which they indicated. This portrait was used by Faber's on the back of the dust jacket of their edition of *Napoleon's Memoirs*. I began to wonder if I was better known than I supposed.

My time at Chilham was drawing to a close. The lease of Blickling was negotiated at length, a carefully thought out affair, to last if I desired, at least 21 years; and to provide in its clauses, as far as possible, the answer to the economic revolution.

I was still without a seat in Parliament and had advised the executive in S.W. Norfolk after the election in 1945 to get a candidate living on the spot. Now that I was returning to Norfolk and to Blickling, I regretted this, but, of course, another candidate had been chosen. I was fortunate, however, in being selected for a good seat in London containing in almost equal proportions, refined boarding houses overlooking Hyde Park and brothels overlooking Paddington Station all of whom believed in private enterprise. It was in parts a tough area, where the film of *The Blue Lamp* about the London police force was taken. I campaigned energetically on the corner of Star Street and Edgware Road; and above the din of the comrades demanding my blood, a polite Jew darted up to the hustings and called up to me, "Did you sell your castle?"

"Yes," I replied in a key of equal suavity.

"Did you sell it well?"

"Yes," I assured him and, well satisfied, he darted back into the throng.

Before being adopted I had undertaken to do a lecture tour of the Far East for the Central Advisory Council for higher education in the services and so the morning after I had been adopted by the

Conservatives of South Paddington I boarded a Constellation Aircraft and proceeded to put 8,000 miles between myself and my prospective constituents. I was accompanied for part of the way by my wife, who had of course, to pay for her own passage and expenses, while I travelled at the expense of a grateful (Socialist) Government. My wife took advantage of an invitation to India from Singapore, and travel to Bophal, while I went on to Hong Kong, and toured Malaya.

CHAPTER 12   *Singapore*

I took occasion to visit the Far East in much the same spirit as some people who have been denied the advantages of a school education, attend night classes after their day's work, in order to catch up with other people. It is difficult for anybody claiming a voice in affairs today to speak, without at least a brief acquaintance, about an area which is becoming increasingly important in the struggle for world mastery between the Russian and American Way of Life.

If the aim of Russian strategy is to Communise Asia as the fortress from which to make an assault upon the rest of the world, then it is well to have been over the terrain.

Three things have convulsed the Far East: the rise of Asiatic nationalism; the disintegration of European prestige in the Far East under the impact of Japanese militarism; and the export of Communism to the area.

Three things make the area especially important: the need for bases from which to get to grips with Russia in a war; the collapse of our previous strategic bases in Palestine, Egypt, India, and Burma; and the dollar-earning capacity of Malayan tin and rubber.

It was at the suggestion of the Special Commissioner in South-East Asia, Lord Killearn who had been so hospitable to me in Egypt, that I visited the Far East. He drew my attention to its increasing significance not, he thought, properly realised in Britain, and he urged me to hop on to a plane, which I did. I had for some time been toying with an invitation from the Central Advisory Council to lecture again to British garrisons overseas; and they were quite willing to send me to the ones in the Far East. I had therefore, as it were, to work my passage; but that in itself provided interesting contacts and opened up useful fields of enquiry.

It was amusing, after last seeing the Killearns at the British Embassy in Cairo, to find them ensconced in scarcely less regal state, in a palace lent to them by the Sultan of Johore, somewhat to the dismay of the Foreign Office, who felt that for such blessings it was better for our proconsuls to be indebted to H.M. Government. As usual Miles Killearn brought to his post a characteristic gusto and shrewdness, and no introduction to the Far East could have been more stimulating.

I visited the Far East — as I had visited the Middle East — during the term of office in England of the Socialist Government elected in 1945.

At Singapore there was a lean Colonel Gadd in khaki linen shorts and jacket to meet me: likewise an A.D.C. of the Killearns, Johnny Kerr.* We tottered, dazed by the change of climate and air pressure, into a tent with its side flaps rolled up, and listened to Colonel Gadd expounding the programme for my tour of Singapore, Malaya and Hong Kong. John Kerr was there to escort us to the Special Commissioner's residence, in Johore. We knew all about this — one of the Sultan's palaces — but had not realised that it was three-quarters of an hour's drive, across the Causeway from Singapore city. There was a desultory baggage inspection by Malay customs officials, but the Union Jack cast a very dense shade indeed and our bags were not opened at all. Colonel Gadd saw us to the car in which we were to go to Bukit Serene, and we arranged to foregather at his office on the morrow.

I had never before visited Malaya, and my impression of it through literature and war reports was of an uncomfortable climate. Certainly such an abrupt arrival was not calculated to ease the transition. Yet I was surprised by the reasonableness of the climate: and there is little change in it, no alternating summer and winter, for it is on the Equator. This day was sunny with a lot of cloud about; I was soon to find that the sun shone very little, the sky being nearly every day overcast with an oppressive layer of grey, felt-like clouds.

The city had all the evidences of British administrative architecture, but encrusted and overlaid with Chinese influence. It was the Chinese influence which surprised me most — streets of Chinese shops, impressive villas and terraced gardens built by Chinese rubber magnates. I was thinking all the time of this city as it must have been when the Japanese marched in.

Outside Singapore city, the road ran past a high ramshackle

*Lord John Kerr, subsequently head of the book department of Sotheby's in London.

corrugated-iron rubber factory. The smell was pungent in the extreme, the smell of burning rubber; and its title, in English and Chinese characters, proclaimed it as the Lam Kwong Rubber Factory. I wondered what it must be like inside that iron building in the heat of the day. The road passed prosperous European villas, one of which was labelled 'Residence of the A.O.C.' Another was pointed out as the residence of General Ritchie who was now British C.-in-C. in the Far East. The island was certainly flat. Soon the rubber trees began, plantations of slender grey trees, with feathery leaves, reminiscent of Australian eucalyptus trees. The trees extended in endless rows, with little earthenware cups fastened to the trunk at a point where the bark was cut in a groin-like formation, to let the white latex drip out. It dripped in the cool hours of the morning, and was collected from the cups by ten o'clock.

The mangrove swamps began and suddenly we were confronted with a majestic inclined ramp of earth, rearing up on our left. It had been built by English and Australian prisoners of war, as a triumphal hill for the Japanese, who had set on its summit a great monument to hail their conquest of Singapore. (One can understand their self-satisfaction. We had boasted so long that it was an impregnable fortress.) This monument was the first thing we had made the Japanese pull down, when we returned. But I found that prestige, whether it be Japanese or British, is easier to pull down quickly than to build up quickly in the Orient. If one had succeeded in enshrining an English cricket ball in some pagoda and persuaded the local inhabitants to worship it with great reverence, and then some Yamashita had come along and hit it out of the ground for six, one could understand that merely reinstating the red-leather-faced object on its pedestal might not secure it the same reverence as before. And so it seemed to be, all over the Far East.

The question of prestige grew to be the paramount one, as my impressions on the Far East clarified. We were, it seemed, since our return, very much on trial in the eyes of 500,000,000 Asiatics. Not merely the humiliation of our defeat at the hands of the Japanese, but the jettisoning of power in India, the abrupt abdication in Burma, even the embarrassments we were experiencing in Egypt, Iraq and Palestine, added question marks to our stability in the Further East. How could the Orientals of Malaya be expected to understand that we were digging in again at Singapore, when the imperial edifices of Delhi, built at so much care and cost by Lutyens and Herbert Baker, were being handed over to Indian politicians?

"Consolidation on a new basis," was Ernest Bevin's definition of the Labour Government's Empire policy. But no Minister paused to explain to the wary millions of Asia what and how we proposed to consolidate.

In Malaya a new constitution had been evolved, after embarrassing negotiations. On the morrow of our victory Sir Harold MacMichael had arrived with a new constitution in his pocket, and a rapid visit to each of the Sultans in turn had secured their signatures. For undoubtedly they feared the stigma of collaboration with the Japanese, and fully expected to be tried as war ciminals if they refused to sign. As the succeeding months went by, and they realised that they were not going to be proceeded against, they began to take heart in council and protest openly against a retrogressive constitution. They were glad enough to accept a Federal constitution which left them rulers of their own states and changed the British Residents into British Advisers, while providing for a Federal Council, representative of the States governments with some representatives of the business communities, and recial groups and some officials nominated by the British High Commissioner.

The achievement of this new constitution was principally the work of the new Governor-General, Malcolm MacDonald, whose quiet yet assured manner no doubt helped to allay any suspicion of imperial grandeur which may have occurred to those who saw Killearn.

The Causeway stretched ahead of us, a solid grey granite roadway with sloping sides, some eight or ten feet above the water level. The Straits of Johore stretched away to right and left, a ruffled grey. The Causeway was not over a quarter of a mile long. Why, one wondered, had such a feeble effort been make to demolish it? Why no more than sixty or seventy feet blown up, a gap now bridged and easily recognisable, over which we were soon passing at the far end? Admitted that the Japanese assault on the island was made in boats; but with the Causeway intact, a steady stream of reinforcement and material was able soon after the landing to pour over. The Johore side of the strait was dominated by a lofty pagoda-like building of Government offices; an imaginative piece of British architecture, harmonising well with the East. It reared up, its square central tower as dominant as the keep of a medieval fortress; but with its tilted gables giving it a touch of China. The foreshore was fringed with palm trees.

As soon as possible after dinner we got away to bed; for in spite of a certain febrile momentum carried over from the journey, we were shaken to jelly and tired.

Now I lay down to sleep; but the atmosphere was sticky, and only a sheet was possible to bear. Out of the dark came a violent noise — *knock, knock, knock.* Pause. Then — *knock, knock.* It was a monstrous bird in the trees outside, *knock, knock, knock* or *toc, toc, toc, toc, toc, toc, toc.* This was incredible. Nobody could sleep through this. *Toc, toc.* I began unwisely to speculate on the number the noisy fellow would rap out next time. Three? Four? Pause. *Toc, toc, toc, toc, toc.* Tricked again. This was the song of the coffin bird. The Chinese, who are inveterate gamblers, gamble with each other on the number of notes the coffin bird will sound next. It went on all night, and at last I fell into a kind of stupefied doze; I could not describe it as sleep.

Here was something new in my experience. I began genuinely to wonder whether this noise drove Europeans mad after a few nights, and accounted for some of the exhaustion in the Malayan campaign. But I learned that people soon get used to it, and indeed I did myself become accustomed to it, and came to regard its harsh, knocking noise as a friendly accompaniment when I went to sleep. Yet there was something ominous about it; a persistent hammering as of nails being driven into a coffin, which went far to justify the bird's name. I thought of writing a book about the insistent advance of Japanese arms, down the length of the Peninsula, under the title of 'The Song of the Coffin Bird'.

I was already feeling acute pain across the back of the legs from sciatica and groaned when Killearn's secretary, Major Alexander appeared next morning to announce the arrival of a Major Cameron who had come to escort me to G.H.Q. in Singapore. I was to deliver a lecture to the British Military Hospital on the future of the British Empire. I was by no means prepared for this, and began, in the intervals of making conversation with Major Cameron, to marshal my thoughts on this subject. There was no use in deceiving oneself. The Empire was undergoing profound changes. The sun was setting over large areas of it. Was it the beginning of disintegration or was it possible to see a great future for it? In the first place it was necessary to realise the change that had come over the balance of power since the First World War. At that time Russia, preoccupied with her internal revolution, had returned into isolation with her five-year plan and her second five-year plan. America, after helping to win the war and set up the League of Nations, withdrew into isolation when the U.S. Senate refused to ratify Wilson's arrangements. So Britain was left with France, as the dominant world power. Now this was all changed. America and Russia were on the march. We were merely picnicking with the victors among the ruins of Berlin.

Secondly there were the actual changes in the fabric of Empire. Burma had gone altogether, and the future of India was at best uncertain, and all was undershot with the red glow of carnage. More people had been killed in a year of transfer of power from British to Indian hands, than in the whole course of British history in India. Certainly India could no longer be relied upon as a source of manpower and material in the same way as before. The Middle East, which had proved a stable base in the Second World War, was now a deteriorating asset. Our relations with Egypt were strained and we were committed to withdrawal. Our position in the Sudan was to some extent compromised by the trend of the Egyptian negotiations. Nobody, at that time, knew the fate of the former Italian colonies. Palestine was in flames. Iraq indignantly repudiated even the mildest new treaty with Britain. All this had happened under the auspices of 'We, Ernest Bevin', (as he was described at the front of my passport) who retained, nevertheless, the affection of the British people, for his robust denunciations of Russia.

We might eventually make up, in organisation and development of what was left of the self-governing and dependent Empire for what we had lost in numbers and prestige. But the fact of the matter was that our whole second line of Imperial defence across the Middle East, India and Burma, had collapsed, and we were obliged to regroup along the Equator, from West Africa through Kenya, where we were building up a big ordnance base to Ceylon, and on to Malaya. So Malaya became a nodal point of Imperial defence. I would at least tell them that.

The hospital, when I got there, was much like all tropical hospitals: a large cream building, with wide verandas.

By the time I returned to Bukit Serene, the sciatica was acute and I retired to bed, feverishly nursing hot-water bottles to my side, under a blanket, in heat which was already oppressive. It was the only way to relieve the pain. At six o'clock the local doctor arrived; a man of jerky mannerisms and somewhat barbed comments on all subjects which soon became a familiar sign to me, indicating that the person in question had been under the Japanese, and was trying mistakenly to get even with people now who wished him only well. This jerkiness and astringency was so marked a characteristic that one former inmate of Changi said to me in Seremban: "We have been in gaol. Don't you recognise the mark of the beast?" And indeed I could. One came across it again and again, a condition calling for measureless sympathy and understanding – but the sort of condition, alas, which only a lover can heal. It is a state of mind comparable in many ways to shell-shock cases. It is characterised by a sense of persecution mania, and this is scarcely to be wondered at. It is aggressive, for there is in it a feeling that no one else has suffered so much; there is perhaps an element of shame, for how can a man live through a degrading experience for months and years, without feeling a sense of shame? Is not his whole soul outraged, in all those finer feelings which have in normal life lifted him above the beast? And I found another thing. The European community in the Far East was divided sharply into those who had been 'inside' under the Japs and those who, for whatever reason, had got away. It would not be true to say that the former were not on speaking terms with the latter; but a great gulf separated them.

This doctor had been employed by the Japs, when they occupied his hospital, and since his work was humanitarian he had carried it on. He knew a lot about sciatica in Singapore. "Acidity must be eliminated."

It was arranged that I should fly to Hong Kong on the following Saturday by flying boat, but when it became apparent that my host and hostess could not themselves get back from Ceylon till Friday evening, my departure was postponed to Tuesday, when I could fly by Dakota instead, going, I was happy to learn, by way of Bangkok.

I was amused to notice that the War Office, in a sensible attempt to eradicate from Oriental minds any impression of martial weakness, had stocked the Far East with all the toughest-

159

looking generals they could find, Kerr, Bouncer Cox, (the G.O.C. Singapore), Neil Ritchie, (C.-in-C. Far East), and General Erskine (G.O.C. Hong Kong). A formidable quadriumvirate, any one of whom would have been an ornament to a rugger scrum. General Cox's verdict on the fall of Singapore was: "If the fight had been continued Singapore would have been in ruins when we returned but British prestige would still have been standing; whereas, we found Singapore still standing but British prestige in ruins."

I was taken by Major Cameron to the Malaya Broadcasting Station to record a speech on the Empire. Some of the engineers were Malays and the recording did not go easily, for technical reasons. First the microphone would not work. Then I had to go to another room; this time some sentences got left off the record in the middle. We clustered round a machine listening to it. My voice came back high and brittle — "When you are holding a line right around the world, something is likely to crack somewhere, and it is unfortunate that the crack came in our defences at Malaya and the Far East. But the line held further back. India was saved. Australia was saved." The rest was silence. So I had to begin all over again. In the afternoon I had to lecture to troops and then return to Bukit in time to meet the Killearns, who were due at last from Ceylon; then came back to Radio Malay for a brains trust on which I had been asked to sit.

It was easy to see, as I approached Bukit Serene, that the Killearns were back, for the Foreign Office flag fluttered from the flagpole on the terrace. They were in their rooms upstairs, but appeared in the fading light on our veranda soon after. Jacqueline advanced with that feline alertness which characterised her, affection darting from her, like sparks from a cat's fur. Miles lumbered behind like a benevolent Labrador.

"But, my *dear*," (from Jacqueline), "how wonderful to think you are actually *here*. And such a *bore* our not being here to meet you."

"Finally threatened to have an aeroplane sent all the way from Singapore to fetch us," Miles chuckled. His hair still lay across his forehead. He appeared as youthful and exuberant as ever, his brown eyes intent and intelligent.

Jacqueline was a woman of more than ordinary attractions, with a considerable reservoir of charm, of which the tap could be turned on or off with disconcerting abruptness, according to the particular objective which she had in mind and according to whether or not this objective had been obtained. She was small and neat; a considerable asset in a woman, enabling her to look up at men with that helpless look of awe and appeal which they find so gratifying. Her eyes had the darkness and vividness which one would expect from a woman of Italian parentage on one side. She was a woman with a long-term clarity of view as to her motives, which rarely failed to bring her the desired results.

Certainly the dinner party which the Killearns gave at Bukit Serene on their return from Ceylon was representative. The Duchess of Grafton, who happened to be passing through Singapore by air to Australia, was whisked off her Constellation almost at the airport; while Miss Hanbury, the attractive new commandant of the W.A.A.F., arrived on a tour of Air Force establishments in the Far East, made an interesting addition to the board. There was a Chinese Consul-General recently from Shanghai, who thought that the Russians must be stiffening the Chinese Communists because they showed none of the traditional Chinese capacity for compromise. I found myself sitting beside Mrs. Murray-Aynsley, the wife of the English Chief Justice in Singapore. She was a woman of fifty or fifty-five years of age, with black hair and heavily lidded eyes. She was a Russian, which accounted possibly for a slightly Oriental appearance. Yet it had come as a surprise to her, when the Japanese officer marching her and other British civilians from Singapore to Changi had asked her whether she were Japanese and offered her a lift; which she had declined.

Mrs. Murray-Aynsley was a soft-spoken woman and told me about that dreadful day when they were told to collect their hand-luggage — only what they themselves could carry — and assemble for the march of eighteen miles to the gaol at Changi. She spoke with a kind of weary wistfulness of it all; as of a nightmare which nags at the memory. Along the hard macadam road, past the rubber plantations, up hill and down hill — for there are hills on the way to Changi — and finally the horror of that great black, forbidding concrete building, over the portcullis of which is emblazoned the Royal Arms and the legend 'H.M. PRISON — 1936'. The walls loomed up, perpendicular, concrete, black or grey, the inner edifice like a long gallery under a sloping black roof, surrounded by high slippery walls. Once inside . . . Yet these women, separated by this time from their menfolk, had enough strength and spirit, when they filed into that grim courtyard, to sing "There'll Always Be An England, While There's a Country Lane" — to the astonishment of the Japanese guards who scuttled hither and thither trying to find out what this surprising outburst was all about. The Englishmen, if they met their fate with fortitude, could only admire this final proof that their wives were, in truth, better halves of themselves.

And once inside, all sorts of little torments began. The Japanese would let it be known that a consignment of letters had arrived and were being sorted out or censored. After the tantalising thought of letters from loved ones overseas had been allowed to tickle the anticipation of the prisoners for days, possibly weeks, the letters might be brought out into the courtyard and burned in a pile; "For security reasons."

Although Mrs. Murray-Aynsley and her husband were in the same gaol, it was many months before they were able to meet.

The real horror of the gaol was the congestion. Two to three thousand Europeans were crowded into quarters normally designed to imprison five or six hundred convicts. The cells were what one would expect in one of H.M. prisons designed for the efficient accommodation of Chinese and Malay convicts. There was a concrete slab bed in the middle of the floor and a convenience at floor level with flushing arrangement, in a corner of the cell. The light came from a wired grill about four feet long by eighteen inches deep, set high in the wall. The doors were of iron bars, admitting of no privacy. The feeding was communal, and all, presumably, took turn in laying the food out. There was not much of it: a bowl of soup at one meal, a bowl of rice at another — that sort of thing.

The prisoners were expected to bow to the Japanese guards. "What happened," I asked one of the victims whom I met later at Seremban (he who spoke of the Mark of the Beast), "what happened if you refused to bow?" "You didn't do it twice," he replied laconically. Yet there were some who persisted in kicking against the pricks for a while — and theirs is the saddest story of all, for it is the story of the crushing of courage and pride, two of the finest flowers in human character. I recall a Brigadier Duke, for whose troops I lectured in Johore — a typical fighting brigadier, stocky, tough, fierce, with a bar to his D.S.O. earned, one presumes, for great gallantry. He tried to refuse to kowtow, until his face was raw with weals across the skin, and his cheek bones were raw. And even he decided in the end to make peace with the most odious of captors. What wonder that weaker men have been driven to yield? Those who survived best seem to have been those who regarded the whole thing as a children's charade in which they were unexpectedly called upon to play a part — and one which they played with inner condescension and outward good humour. But to attain to such heights of philosophical detachment, in the face of probable death and possible torture, is more than can be expected of many.

The principal guest at the Killearns' dinner party was rightly, Dato Ohn, the Mentri Besar, or Prime Minister of Johore. His brown skin and acquiline features reminded one rather of Indian than of Malay blood. He wore also a pandit's cap, similar to that worn by Pandit Nehru, comparable to our army side-cap; but of dark maroon, embroidered silk. He was dressed in Malayan garb, with the long sarong, tucked about his waist, also of maroon silk. We sat together, after dinner, on a settee at the end of the veranda, hoping for a little coolness to come up from the Straits of Johore below us. A moderate man, this, or believed to be; he had played a prominent part in getting the extremists to adopt the new constitution. He explained the difficulties which he had overcome and his hopes for a settled future. Miles played up to him a lot, treating him as the great man of Malaya, and Dato Ohn, surrounded by so many distinguished European guests, preened himself quietly like a self-confident peacock. I noticed Air Commandant Hanbury's eyes fastened on us from time to time. She knew that I had been adopted, against the competition of some friends of hers, to stand for South Paddington, only a week previously, and was evidently amused to see me so far away from London W.2 deep in conversation with a Malayan Prime Minister.

Dato Ohn was, nevertheless, dismissed by the Sultan in 1949 on the grounds that he devoted too much time to affairs outside Johore.

On another evening, we assembled in the dusk upon the shore not far from Singapore harbour, and here, at a Chinese waterfront café, we were introduced to a Chinese fishing family: Mr. and Mrs. Lim Beng Teck with their daughter and son-in-law, who owned a number of the fish traps offshore. With them was a Chinese, called Cheah Kim Bee, who had his own tale of the Japanese occupation.

The party was joined by some journalists, one of them a cameraman from the *Straits Times*. By now Killearn was with us, and we all got into a launch, which seemed very full of people, mostly Chinese. As we came alongside the tall pile of a kelong, which rose out of the water, more Chinese, above us, lowered a rope. For amusement I swarmed up this; to the delighted exclamations of the Chinese. The rest of the party followed more sedately up a rope ladder.

Darkness was now falling swiftly, and we moved about the planked deck of the kelong by the light of an acetylene lantern which swung from the eaves of the thatched roof. A precarious gangplank led from this to the wide square basin, surrounded by piles, driven into the sand, where the fishing-net was spread out below a swinging light. The net was hauled up, where its meshes sparkled in the lamplight by ropes wound on long poles. A primitive wooden winch at one end, wound by two men, turned these, and the wet and glistening rope began to curl round the long poles. The net, when it came up, contained a multitude of fish of every shape, size and colour. There were great numbers of little inconmerah, like sardines about two and a half inches long. Miles said they contained more vitamins than anything else and had contributed substantially to the diet of South-East Asia under his dispensation. Some of the fish were of jewelled beauty, like the pucho — a jade-and-red coloured fish nine inches long.

There was a flat gold fish barred with stripes of lapis lazuli which reminded me of Tutankhamun's headdress. This was babi, the pigfish.

One of the most profitable fishes was like a large version of an English mackerel but green in colour — and appropriately called perang, the knife fish. There were large and graceful angel fish with their high triangular fins, and broad bands of grey and green colour. The Chinese called it, prosaically enough, the basin fish — bona.

Great numbers of sumpin icon were also caught, with brilliant yellow stripes across their dark brown surfaces at right angles to the head.

Among other creatures of the deep was a small writhing octopus, known to the Chinese as the sotong-kreta or motor car fish. It hung up on a hook, where it continued to draw up and let down its tentacles in a most disconcerting way. A great sorting of fish began; all the small inconmerah being cast into great trays, and the individual varieties laid out for our inspection.

While all this was going on, dinner was being prepared in a wooden galley in one corner of the thatched space. It was spread out on a table about eighteen inches high, and we sat upon rugs and cushions on the flooring, to eat it. Bottled beer was served with it, and Mr. Kim Bee told us the story of his own experiences under the Japanese occupation.

"I am a solicitor, by profession," said Mr. Kim Bee, "but when the Japanese came, I did not want to be mixed up with them, and so I took to working with our friend here," — at which our host grinned and bowed. "I used to live on one of these kelongs, until the Double Tenth. You remember what happened on that day. Some submarines got in here and torpedoed a lot of Japanese ships. The Kempetai were enraged and began hunting for spies. They knew about my living the life of a fisherman and they thought it impossible that a man could want to live for months on end on a kelong, as I did."

Mr. Kim Bee was a stocky young Chinese of some thirty years. He had an aggressive, resolute face, with heavy dark eyebrows; and might have been thought by the Japanese to be in some way formidable.

"So they rounded me up," he went on. "They rounded everybody up. And I was taken to Syme Road, where they tortured me for months."

"What sort of torture?" I asked quietly.

He showed the skin of his arm, bare to the elbow, where he wore a tennis shirt. "They burnt my arm with cigarette ends and demanded to know if I had given the information about the ships in harbour on the Double Tenth. I didn't know anything. I told them so, but they didn't believe me. So they went on questioning me for hours. The minor officials were getting into trouble themselves and one of the chief men of the Kempetai came down to demand results. I was taken up to see him at all hours. He had some shoes with spikes sticking through the soles, and used one of them to slap me across the face, so that it tore my skin. Then he would go off to rest for two or three hours and I would be kept there, till he came back to continue the interrogation; possibly at three o'clock in the morning."

I was deeply sorry for Mr. Kim Bee, but could not restrain a suspicion that he was making the most of his story.

"Did they interrogate a lot of people like this?" I asked.
"Yes. After the Double Tenth, they were wild, and arrested all sorts of people. The Bishop of Singapore had the worst treatment. They had left him out at first, but they suspected him of being in communication with the British."

There was no evidence, from Mr. Kim Bee's experience, that the Japanese tortured people for the sake of inflicting pain. Far worse things could have been done, if that had been their object. It seemed almost as if they accepted the use of physical pressure as a matter of course – the minimum which seemed necessary in any given circumstance to secure the admissions they required. They used torture as a tactical weapon and regarded it as no more uncivilised than the indiscriminate bombing of civilian populations by the British or Americans. It is in the cold-blooded selection of the victims that the Anglo-Saxon mentality senses the inhumanity of the Japanese crime. But who can doubt that if the Axis powers had won the war, a man like 'Bomber' Harris would have been singled out as a war criminal on the grounds of indiscriminate slaughter and maiming of thousands of haphazard victims? It is necessary to realise that there are two ways of looking at these things. The more one hears of the Japanese treatment of prisoners, the more incomprehensible their attitude seems to us. One woman records that in the intervals of being tortured her Japanese guard would speak most kindly to her, telling her all about his own family and personal troubles, till the time came to look at his watch, when he would say, "I am dreadfully sorry, it is time for the next torture." One is driven to the conclusion that they would usually have preferred to avoid the use of torture; but to them the end automatically justified the means; they regretted what they considered the stupidity of their victim in failing to understand the importance of co-operating in the co-prosperity sphere of East Asia. They felt, themselves, the paramount need to survive and they did not quail at the prospect of looking their victim in the eye, rather than through the convenient aperture of a bomb-sight which was about to deliver an atom bomb that would scorch the flesh and rot the hair, when not actually killing them, of a hundred thousand people in a few seconds. Is it not the brutal fact that war makes criminals of us all? That we are all war criminals?

From now until we met again in Karachi, on the way home, my wife and I were to travel our separate ways; she to Bhopal and I to Hong Kong.

I found myself allotted the rear seat on the port side, with a narrow gangway separating me from the air hostess. The passengers included, she assured me, the son of a former Governor of New South Wales; and she even pointed him out — a well-tailored young man up at the front. I was startled for a moment, as it seemed surprising that a single Dakota, skimming over the palm trees towards the open sea, should contain two offspring of such parentage. He was in fact a young man called Beattie, a friend of Alan Lennox-Boyd, and he had not only taken my seat but expropriated the car sent to meet me on arrival in Hong Kong. It is an interesting pastime, in an aircraft, to try to place one's fellow passengers. There is the Chinese business man in European clothes, not yet perhaps quite used to air travel. There was one couple who bore the indelible stamp of Englishmen: the wife in rough tweeds, almost with a dog at her heels; then her busband, tall, slim, elegant, with the slightly bald head and light blue eyes, his clothes so obviously the product of Savile Row. It surprised me, therefore, to learn from the air hostess that they were the Portuguese Ambassador to China and his wife. She could not have been mistaken, as she was herself a Portuguese citizen from Macao. She admitted, later in the journey, to a Chinese mother, which accounted for the somewhat Oriental cast of her countenance. But her name was Fernandez and her father had been a trader in wines and spirits on the Portuguese island of Macao. The Japanese had not molested her in Macao, but the business had got into the hands of creditors since her father's death, and her ambition was to earn enough money as an air hostess to pay off the debts and run the business herself. She lived in Hong Kong, or more precisely in Kowloon, and had four or five days off, after every fortnight of flying.

Bangkok was in fact a squalid town, but after the hygienic streets of Singapore, where a daily dose of D.D.T. removes even the flies from circulation, the very squalor of Bangkok gave it a whiff of the East which was more convincing than anything I had seen in Malaya. Here there were even orange-robed Poongyis travelling on the rickety trams and people chattering in the streets, as if time were unimportant. I was anxious to see something of the city in what was left of the daylight. A driver who spoke English took me without hesitation to one of the wonders of the world – the Temple of the Reclining Buddha. Here, within walls of precious ornamentation, where slender pinnacles arise in symmetrical composition, was raised a temple of fiery gables, incandescent in the afternoon sun; tongues of gold curled up, iridescent against the deep blue of the sky. These tip-tilted gables with their dragons' tongues leaping flame-like from every tip and corner, and seeming to burst into flame along the edges, entranced me; and I wandered about the almost deserted courtyards, with here and there a line of gold-leafed Buddhas under an arcade, till I was arrested by a majestic figure in stone, duplicated on either side of a gateway. In appearance the formidable giant bore a marked resemblance to the late Lord Baldwin. But the flowing robes and long curved sword were not in keeping with that enigmatic figure. The headgear was more appropriate – a top hat in stone. And it appeared that these statues, erected some hundred years ago, were meant to depict Marco Polo who, being a Westerner, was presumed to have worn a top hat.

An occasional priest in yellow – an almost orange yellow – robe, with bare brown feet, padded silently across the stone-flagged courtyards towards some inner shrine. And presently I heard the rhythmic melancholy chant of the monks and entered an inner temple, where they knelt upon the floor, bowing their shaven heads to the ground before a large golden image of the Buddha; chanting as they abased themselves – "Om, om mane padme om," or the Siamese equivalent of it.

Yet the greatest pleasure was still in store for me; the reclining Buddha itself. This mighty image is housed in a separate building, and an appeal from the curator of the temple, in various languages, urged the passer-by to contribute to the collecting-box, for the preservation of this remarkable edifice.

On entering the portals, I found myself in a very dim light, where there was a considerable amount of wooden scaffolding. It seemed to be built up beside an object which I can only liken to a submarine in dry dock — a long black thing, rising almost to the roof of this considerably lofty building. As my eyes grew accustomed to the half-light, I was suddenly aware that the vast smooth black surface confronting me was part of the Buddha's stomach, and that a hand the size of a motor car was reclining on his hip. I walked up a sloping ramp inside the scaffolding, and found myself face to face with the Buddha's head: a head as large as a room full of strange thoughts; and this in turn was propped upon a hand and crooked elbow far below me in the dimness of the scaffolding. A native craftsman was working on the repairing of one half-closed eye, much as a man works upon the painting of a ship's side, swinging on a boatswain's chair. I had seen the Colossi of Memnon near Luxor, and they are impressive because of their large aloofness, in the middle of the plain. But here was something almost frightening in the reclining Buddha's vastness, above and below me; very reminiscent, indeed, of the pictures in *Gulliver's Travels* of Lilliputians climbing with ladders all over a recumbent giant. I descended and walked all round the effigy, pressed between its towering, recumbent bulk and the perpendicular wall of the building, until I came to its feet. The soles of its feet, the size of large billiard tables, were of ebony, it seemed, inlaid with mother-of-pearl. If it is desired to convey to mortals a sense of majesty and power in the presence of gods, or of their prophets among men, then the technique of confronting us with outsize images is assuredly the most effective; and I thought, as I went away, across the courtyards, still warm in the afternoon sunlight, that I should like to detach myself from the velocity of Western affairs and settle down peacefully as the curator of the Temple of the reclining Buddha; where the gables flicker like salutary flame against a sky of perpetually sunny afternoon blueness. No wonder men have sought sanctuary in such abodes from the fierce exactions of human passion. Yet for me the seismic alternations of grief and bliss, rather than the steady blaze of an eternal contentment.

I was reluctant to detach myself from the last rays of that Siamese sun and drive past the forbidding colonnades of the War Office of Siam, or Thailand as it is now called.

It is surprising what a lot one can see in a few hours in a city like Bangkok, with the knowledge that the opportunity may never return. My driver wanted me to see some Anak dancers, but it transpired later that they had all been summoned, in the best Oriental tradition, to perform unexpectedly that evening before the new Prime Minister (who was shortly afterwards deposed by a *coup d'état*).

However, I was fortunate in my introductions, which brought me to a family, living in a wooden house, propped upon stilts, in a darkened muddy lane behind the façade of the main streets. The family consisted of an attractive young woman and two brothers. Their father had been killed in the first, brief fighting with the Japanese Army when Siam was invaded; and their uncle was a general in the Defence Ministry. The uncle's photograph revealed him as a massive man of indolent appearance; but the portrait of the father was remarkable; and I remember his eyes staring out of that large photograph at me with their calm intensity, whenever I hear people say that the Siamese did not put up much of a fight against the Japanese. Perhaps not, but this lean spare colonel, with the neatly fitting uniform and the short-cropped hair, was killed fighting them. The daughter was a devout Buddhist. She showed me her little room, of cedar wood, where a newspaper photograph of the Buddha's image was framed over the bedhead, and a curious admixture of Siamese and American feminism pervaded the atmosphere. She was full of laughter.

I had to return to my hotel, for a few hours' sleep before the bus departed to the airport. As so often happens at casual halts, the passengers had to double up, and I found myself sharing a room with a Eurasian commercial traveller bound for Hong Kong. He was already asleep, and as soon as I had lain down on the hard mattress of my own bed – mattresses in hot climates are deliberately hard for coolness – and slowed down the revolving fan above me, I too slept easily, lulled by the talking of street vendors across the road, who showed no disposition to go to bed at all.

Most of the passengers looked rather tired at 6 a.m. when we boarded the plane. After getting up so early it was aggravating to learn that there was no sign of the Australian pilot.

Eventually he appeared at the edge of the runway, being supported by two men, with a firm grip on each of his upper arms. His toes trailed across the tarmac. He had obviously spent the night on the tiles. I was in no position to talk, as I had visited a house of considerable pleasure, where a lively girl, in the intervals of sipping a drink, took me up to a room of the wide-verandaed wooden building from time to time. Somewhat to the amusement of my driver and the host, she began simpering and giggling in the way Siamese girls do when they are falling in love. She certainly gave full value for money; and that was before I went on to the dance place where I met the Siamese colonel's daughter, who finally took me back to her house. Consequently I had not slept much, when I arose at 5 a.m. to get to the airport. But then I was not expected to pilot the plane.

However, the Australian pilot soon found the controls once he was seated, and off we flew.

CHAPTER 14

To skim into Kaitak aerodrome, squeezed between the hills on the mainland opposite Victoria Island, emphasised the need for the much discussed large-scale airport in the leased territories further inland. Hong Kong itself is held in perpetual sovereignty by the British, but the hinterland known as the New Territories is merely leased from China under a treaty of 99 years signed in 1899. The sun sweltered down on Kaitak airport. I trudged across the blinding, baked earth to where an aluminium aircraft glittered in the sun, with the words 'Hong Kong Airways' in large blue letters. A Chinese mechanic working under the wing grinned at me. After the customs formalities, during which the officials did not hesitate to feel the pockets of the more formidable-looking Chinese passengers for arms, we went out into the sunshine where a bus was waiting to take the passengers to the Peninsula Hotel at Kowloon.

"Never trust a vain man," said Rhodes, and I suppose it was some lingering form of vanity that made me expect — after travelling 8,000 miles at the War Office's request, and after my expected arrival at Kaitak had been signalled for 2.45 p.m. from Singapore to G.H.Q. Hong Kong, and as my aircraft had duly arrived at 2.45 — to be met at the airport with some indication, at least, of where I was going and what I was to do. I stared hopefully at various arriving motor cars, but none of them seemed to want me, so I climbed, inevitably, into the Cathay Pacific bus, and travelled in no very amiable humour to the Peninsula Hotel.

I eventually reached the Kowloon ferry and ran after a disappearing coolie, anxious to see my baggage safely stowed. A vast crowd of Chinese surged down the ramp and up the ramp past me. Others, some of them European, passed by another gangway overhead on to the upper deck. Having seen my baggage and coolie safely placed aboard (as one might in England see one's luggage into the guard's van), my intention was then to detach myself from the coolies, of whom there seemed to be a great number all round me, and mount some handy companionway to the first-class passengers' deck. Already the ship was steering away from the wharf with gleeful cries from Chinese boys upon it. In vain I looked for a ladder or stairs to the upper deck. No communication, it appeared, was allowed between the upper and the lower stratas of this society, and I was constrained to take my colour films amid the admiring glances of a hundred jet-black eyes in high-boned Chinese faces. A proud junk careered past, her brown sail hoist athwart the mast in an engaging, piratical manner, and a Chinese seaman was holding the tiller upon the high poop at the stern. The sunlight sparkling on the waters of the harbour silhouetted another junk, with its broad-topped, ribbed and curving sail. It was all very different from anything I had ever seen before and all reassuringly Chinese. Hong Kong lay along the further shore at the foot of the Peak, and it would have seemed at any other time a goodly town; but in my exacerbated frame of mind it reared up like a Chinese puzzle. The deck planks above the coolies and myself had been nailed down!

At the Victoria jetty, I was just able to squeeze ashore with my coolie and baggage and find a taxi by the kerb of the water-front. "Just ask for Flagstaff House," someone had said, and I asked for it. The Chinese driver said, "Flagstaff House?" dubiously and I said vigorously, "Yes, Flagstaff House," implying that it was as much as his life was worth not to drive me there at once. Anxious to oblige, he drove round Hong Kong in circles for a while.

"Ask policemen," I said, indicating one in blue serge uniform with a Chinese face and flat-crowned uniform cap. But the policeman spoke no word of English, and was bent on keeping pedestrians to their correct crossings. So we drove on. Occasionally the driver put his head out of the window to shout at some fellow driver or pedestrian who returned doubtful answers. It seemed to me that this was the end. I could have stepped out and lain down in the gutter foaming at the mouth. Caesar and even Hitler would have had an epileptic fit long before this. Suddenly the driver began to drive up a steep hill (the Peak); but no flagstaff was visible, so he drove down again.

"Government House," I suggested, and he actually knew that one. So we climbed up the hill again, and asked the English army sentry at the gate where Flagstaff House was. He gave us precise but intricate directions. I felt the need to put a bit into the driver's mouth and a bridle upon his head, by the time we entered a narrow drive where a sentry came to the salute, and the taxi finally drew up before a large white building with green shutters and a pleasantly pillared portico. Here I bribed the driver to leave me, and he drove off, while I rang the bell. A Chinese servant in white coat appeared and showed me into the A.D.C.'s office. This young man — Bobby Darwin, as I came to know him — gazed at me as if I were an apparition. I may indeed have looked like one by this time. "How did you get here?" he asked, awed. The story takes time to tell, and I did not feel equal to its intricacies then.

"As signalled, by air at two-forty-five," I replied.

"But I rang up the B.O.A.C. and the R.A.F. and they said they knew nothing about your arrival yet."

"I came by Cathay Pacific."

"What, all the way round by Bangkok! That isn't fair. You had better meet the General's wife — Mrs. Erskine — she's next door."

When I walked into the drawing-room Mrs. Erskine said, "I hear you arrived by an unknown aeroplane."

"Not unknown to me," I said, and the conversation thereafter was a little stiff.

In due course I came down to dinner, and found my host — a spruce general in white dinner jacket, with a black cummerbund — waiting to offer me drinks. He was a highly polished individual, who was well aware of his own capabilities, and possessed of that self-assurance which comes easily to men whose looks make them much admired by women: a feeling that there is always a welcome for them in the world. He made half-amused apologies for the breakdown of the army arrangements — with a twinkle in his eye which suggested that he was really delighted by it all; as one might be when some favourite spaniel jumps with wet feet all over some rather unwelcome guest whom one feels obliged for duty's sake to entertain. He reminded me of wartime colonels who regarded politicians as their natural enemies; or at best of brigadiers who regarded them as the obvious butt for their wit. This General Erskine was no fool; and I came to regard him as one of the shrewdest military thinkers I had come across in the Orient. He was the first to say of war with Russia, "I am afraid it is no longer a question of if but when."

General Erskine invited me to accompany him on the morrow

to two Chinese houses: lunch with Mr. T. W. Kwok, styled the Special Commissioner for Kwangsi and Kwantung — in reality T. V. Sung's representative in Hong Kong — and dinner with Mrs. Eu Tong Sin, who lived in a grey granite castle in Hong Kong built by her late husband in imitation of Balmoral Castle; but not quite so much in harmony with the surrounding countryside.

T. W. Kwok was an aggressive personality. He was a Chinese — (I learned in Hong Kong that it is not polite to speak of a Chinaman) — a Chinese gentleman, supercharged by an American education; rather like a magnified version of that Americanised Englishman, Mr. Bossom. Mr. Kwok offered us cocktails and there were a lot of us. I talked to Mr. Kwok directly, for he seemed truculent and it appeared to me that in a competition of subtleties with this high-powered Oriental I should be blown away by the exhaust. "What is all this nonsense I read in the papers," I asked him, "about Hong Kong being in the Canton district of China for income tax purposes?" It seemed for a moment as if Mr. Kwok was torpedoed. He said lamely, "I am afraid *The Times* reporter got mistaken," and hurried us in to lunch.

The lunch appeared mostly on a revolving tray in the middle of the round table, and we helped ourselves to delicacies. There was shark's-fin soup, upon which descended a cataract of champagne.

I was due at 2.30 to lecture to the Buffs, on the other side of the island, on the future of the British Empire, if any; wherefore it was essential for me to leave Mr. Kwok at two o'clock in the General's car; and the General, and Col. Murray of the Iniskillins, stood by me in my retreat and left with me. "It looks," said Mr Kwok, "as if the British Army were pulling out again." Full marks, I thought, for Mr. Kwok's American university.

I lectured to the Buffs, some of whom knew of my existence in Kent, and learned from me for the first time, apparently, why they had to garrison places like Hong Kong. At least nobody had bothered to tell them before; and once again I realised that an army marches on its mind and can march further and faster if its brain wheels are oiled and cared for.

The streets of Hong Kong are very gay, for it is the habit of the Chinese shopkeepers to paint their names in gay Chinese characters, in brilliant colours, usually red or yellow, down the sides of the innumerable pillars which form the arcaded streets and support their dwellings above. A Chinese dashes across the road, carrying a bundle of long bamboo poles, and leans these up against the wall. Coolies still trotted with their gaily painted rickshaws. They wore blue-painted, flat-brimmed straw hats, bearing a number in white — comparable to the number of a taxi. But the increasing number of taxi cabs seemed to be driving the coolies out of business.

*   *   *

In the Far East, as in the Middle East, one is forced to ask oneself why it is thought desirable to imitate the West. Certainly Euston carried the cult of the West to extraordinary lengths. This grey granite castle in the upper levels of Hong Kong was sheltered behind a wall which would do justice to a prison. The front door opened and a marble floor extended before us. At the far end was a wooden horse in medieval trappings bearing a rider in the finest armour. Unfortunately the horse's tail had fallen out at some time and been replaced by a palm frond. To the right of the horse, across the glistening marble, were the doors of an electric lift, which showed in an arc of illuminated figures the progress of the lift, as in a department store, from the first to the fifth floors. We shot up a couple of floors, to a large reception room. Here, amid French furniture, supplied from London, and amid a liberal grouping of nude marble Aphrodites, larger than life, stood our hostess and friends. She was a good-looking woman in the forties, wearing a long black Chinese satin dress. She was accompanied by her son, a young man with heavy-lidded eyes in a dinner jacket, now, since his father's death, the heir to ten houses in Malaya — for Madame Eu's husband (and she had been his last wife) began life as a coolie in Penang and had built up an immense fortune in tin and rubber. Beside Madame Eu was a handsome young man, with a dark, clipped moustache, also wearing a dinner jacket. This was General Yi, of whom I had heard Erskine speak.

Yi had at one time been A.D.C. to General Chiang Kai-shek, but had deserted the Generalissimo and sought refuge in Hong Kong. This was too much for the Generalissimo, who had sent his secret police to arrest General Yi in the lounge of the Peninsula Hotel, in Kowloon. This was more than the British administration could stomach, and it was explained to Chiang that this was going too far. Face was saved by General Yi travelling of his own free will to Canton with a cheque-book which he evidently used effectively, for he reappeared without harm in Hong Kong. He spoke to me of the need for a third party in China to overcome the deadlock between the Nationalists and Communists.

Another guest was a venerable Chinese, eighty-nine years old, who wore the traditional garb — a pagoda-like cap, and a flowing maroon robe of silk down to his slippers. His white hair protruded from his cap, and he wore a white pointed beard. His name was Sir Shuston Chow, and he was a prominent Chinese member of the Governor's Executive Council.

"In all my eighty-nine years," he said, "I have never known the situation in China so dark. I used to work as a boy on the Pekin-Mukden railway — now it is in the hands of the Communists; and it looks as if even Mukden may fall." He thought that the Communists under Mao Tse-tung would inevitably reach as far south as the Yangtze, and hoped at best that China would be divided along that line. No one whom I met during this visit seemed to realise that within eighteen months the Communist Armies would be at the gates of Hong Kong.

The other guests were a Chinese doctor Li-Shui-Fan and his wife. We sat down to a round table, in a Victorian dining-room with yellow oak panelling embossed with heraldic devices. But the food was Chinese; delicious shark-fin soup — the shark-skin flesh shredded into slivers of gelatine-like meat — noodles. I sat on Madame Eu's left, General Erskine on her right, and she instructed me in the handling of the ivory chopsticks. The secret appeared to be to hold the lower chopstick rigid between the middle and fourth fingers of the right hand and manipulate the upper chopstick between the fore-finger and thumb, against it. In this way it is not too difficult to grip the succulent little squares of flesh and other delicacies. Madame Eu kept revolving the central tray towards me, to suggest some fresh surprise, and in this way ten courses went down on top of Mr. Kwok's consignment.

I asked Madame Eu to tell me her experiences under the Japanese. These were instructive. The Japanese arrived ceremoniously at her front door in the person of generals and begged for an audience, which she granted. Knowing her to be one of the richest Chinese residents they treated her with respect; but she found their frequent visits exhausting and obtained from the Japanese commandant a permit to visit the Portuguese island of

Macao. Thither she accordingly went with her five children; and from Macao without further ado she boarded a boat bound for French Indo-China and remained there for the duration without molestation.

In Hong Kong, as in Singapore, I had to give a press conference and a broadcast.

The Hong Kong broadcasting station was run by a fair-haired young man called Hardy in a couple of rooms at the top of the Gloucester Hotel. He edited the script, went along to the recording-room to fix the recording machinery, darted back to the studio to give me some instructions, and then took me along to hear the record run, not off wax but from a long spool of sound track film.

He thought I was a bit fierce on the Chinese and modified some of my observations for fear of precipitating more Kowloon incidents. The gist of my broadcast this time was that the British Lion has had cubs, like Australia, Canada, South Africa and New Zealand, and that people who make the mistake of thinking the Old Lion is done for suddenly find themselves set upon by a whole pack of lion cubs.

I returned in the evening to give the live talk. Hardy placed me at the microphone and then went down to his suite to have a bath. A part-time announcer looked in, wearing a dinner jacket, to read the news and announce my talk, which I delivered staring at the back of a deserted grand piano in the studio. But this amateur set-up for broadcasting on the fringe of China's millions did not prevent Hardy insisting on my accepting a fee for the broadcast, even if it were only forty dollars, which was forty dollars more than the heavily subsidised Radio Malaya chose to pay. Hong Kong Radio estimated that fifty per cent of its listeners were British; whereas Radio Malaya catered for an eighty per cent English-speaking Asiatic audience. It seemed to me that the whole business of broadcasting from Hong Kong could be more heavily financed and used for more continuous and effective propaganda to the mainland of China than was possible for Hardy hopping in and out of his bath on the floor below.

After delivering the broadcast I went down to Hardy's room in the hotel, where I met his wife and had a gin and lime, before going on to dinner at Government House, where I found that my host and hostess, with Edmund Blunden and other guests, had just been at the receiving end of my talk. The Governor seemed pleased enough with the sentiments I had just expressed.

Edmund Blunden was on leave from his university in Japan, and I was naturally delighted to have an opportunity of making his acquaintance. His quiet, bird-like character seemed eminently suited to a poet. I enjoyed a busman's holiday, in listening to a lecture by him at Government House on "The Universe of Shakespeare, Milton, Hardy and other poets." His interpretation of Shakespeare's universe was superb — and quite squeezed out that of the others. There was a considerable audience in the ballroom to hear him — and I was somewhat unnerved by the comment of my hostess, Mrs. Erskine, on the way back to Flagstaff House, "What an interesting lecture! But who is Edmund Blunden and why were there all those people there to hear him?"

What hope, thought I, is there for the rest of us? No wonder she had been startled on my arrival by such headlines in the Hong Kong press as 'Somerset de Chair in the Colony'.

Lady Grantham, was a tough little American woman, very deaf, but full of spirit. Her sister, whom I had met at the dinner at Government House, was one of the people who had cause to feel most bitterly about the Jap occupation; for her husband was taken out of the camp one day by the Japs and shot. She attributed this to weakness on the part of the Hong Kong Colonial Secretary, who had been a new arrival just before the surrender and did not know the position as well as longer residents, but who insisted, nevertheless, on exercising the rights of seniority to represent the British prisoners in all negotiations with the Japanese. She thought that he showed undue weakness in propitiating them and saved his own skin at the expense of others. The European colonies throughout the Far East were riven with these sorts of rancours as a result of the dreadful happenings of the occupation, and a casual interloper would be unwise to express any opinion on the merits of the cases; beyond saying that all must have lived under unbearable strain and that it can never have been easy to know what was the right thing to do.

It is surprising how invigorating a fresh point of view can be to long-established residents in a place like Hong Kong. I was invited to attend a Rotary Club lunch in Kowloon at the Peninsula Hotel, and I chose the occasion to rebut the suggestions put about in the Chinese press that Chinese residents in Hong Kong were liable for Chinese income tax.

"I should have been very surprised," I told the Rotarians, "when I was visiting the Channel Islands which, like Hong Kong, were overrun by the enemy and were occupied by them, to learn that the Channel Islands came into the Cherbourg district for income tax purposes – or that Gibraltar came into the Malaga district of Spain for income tax purposes." And I pointed out further that some very distinguished gentlemen had made the mistake of misunderstanding the British Empire. These had included Napoleon Bonaparte, Kaiser Wilhelm II, Adolf Hitler, Signor Mussolini and, if they liked, General Tojo. I hoped that nobody in this part of the world was making a similar mistake about our attitude on Hong Kong.

I was anxious while in Hong Kong to see something of the mainland.

The New Territories are simply a piece of China roped off from the rest of the mainland for the landward protection of Hong Kong. The old road to Canton runs across them, and what is known locally as 'the oldest bridge in China' spans a small stream, in three graceful semicircular arches, built of old brown stone. Mrs. Churcher, an artist, took me to see this, and we nearly trod on a large brown snake which wriggled away from us at the foot of the overgrown steps approaching the bridge. The bridge was not more than three feet wide and can never have been more than a footbridge on the old track road to Canton.

Further inland we were passed by girls of the Hakka tribe, scurrying along in their black coats and trousers, with wide flat-brimmed round black hats, and carrying poles across their shoulders on the ends of which were immense bundles of fodder. These girls are proverbially shy and run away from a camera; this cannot be said of most of the Chinese. I stopped a Chinese family tilling their acres amid these flat grey plains, bordered by ranges of inhospitable hills. The father wore an old European felt hat, with his otherwise Chinese garb; the mother was a sturdy type and a young son carried the baby in a sling on his back. We passed Chinese women paddling about in some ponds, searching for something under the water. At a small Chinese village I bought a coolie's wicker hat, high-peaked, sweeping out in a wide brim, like the roof of a pagoda. It cost two Hong Kong dollars (14p).

At one point where the vast swampy plain, designed to take the new aerodrome, opened out on our right we saw two Chinese peasants herding a drove of tame duck along the road, a battalion of duck, pushed and guided by the two men with long bamboo poles. Eventually we came to the walled city of Kam Tin, its old brown walls rising from a dry moat. A drawbridge crossed the moat from an area of beaten yellow clay, where a single tree spread enough shade to provide a gathering place for some of the Chinese villagers, who sat about on crude benches under it. I sat there and sketched the old town, with its square corner towers and arrow slits. There was only one entrance; that by way of the drawbridge. On each side of this, and over the lintel, were pasted fading strips of orange paper bearing Chinese characters. "The Chinese paste them up for the New Year," Mrs. Churcher told me. "They would have been vermilion then, but have faded to orange in the interval."

She sketched studies of children's heads; but they were difficult to pose, jumping about her, all round her, in front and behind, in ecstasies of excitement all the time, snatching at her block to see how their faces were being drawn.

I went into the walled city, pausing under the entrance, with its heavy and weathered gates of ancient oak, down a narrow central street scarcely two arm's-breadths wide, where the old folk of the village sat in the doorways smoking, and the girls darted inside the darkened rooms. Cross streets, just wide enough to walk down, dissected the village at intervals. And the whole colony was rigidly enclosed by the walls and the moat, which was usually full of water. In this fashion most Chinese communities had sought shelter from brigands for generations of China's unsettled history.

On the way back Mrs. Churcher spoke of the difficulties which many of her acquaintances had experienced in dealing with husbands who had been victims of the Japanese. The wives (those who had been evacuated in time) were usually invited to attend a course on the problem of psychological rehabilitation. But one friend of hers had found it simply impossible to lift her husband out of his prolonged fits of morbid depression. In the end she had implored him to have an affair with some other woman in the desperate hope that this new interest and excitement might lift him out of the slough of despondency into which he seemed permanently to have collapsed. That wife was certainly a very devoted and courageous woman.

We stopped in the afternoon sun, on the way back to the ferry, at a ruined summerhouse down by a small cove, and watched a huge junk crowded with passengers from the mainland speed along the coast. Suddenly it anchored and skiffs from behind the adjoining headland rowed rapidly out to it, took off two loads of passengers, and deposited them on the shore. No sooner were they in the skiffs than the junk had weighed anchor and was speeding towards Victoria Island and the official anchorage. Little wonder that it was difficult to check the flow of immigrants from China, or stem the habitual smuggling of the China coast.

CHAPTER 15

Lieutenant Dowson, a shy and apologetic young man, detailed to look after me, drove me in a jeep to Clearwater Bay to fill in the time before lecturing to troops at Sham-Shi-Po on the mainland. Here was the smugglers' cove of all China coast fiction. From a considerable height we looked down on a large brown-sailed junk entering the bay, tacking slowly from side to side to reach the little jetty, where a jumble of Chinese wooden houses lined the waterfront. I watched the admirable seamanship of the Chinese captain, manoeuvring his bulky craft in the narrow space of the calm bay where the water was opalescent between ranges of hills. The junk slanted slowly across the ruffling water and then gybed to go about, its single tall sail swinging round. The cries of the Chinese seamen were borne clearly up to me in the still afternoon sunlight. We sat on the grass lawn of a wrecked and deserted European villa on the slopes above the bay. There were half a dozen such houses — white villas, blasted into ruins, first by the original landing of the Japs, later by the Anglo-American return assault at the end of the war, and after that by systematic looting and destruction by the local residents. By contrast the little Chinese village down by the water's edge seemed undamaged. A jetty ran out into the water, and Chinese were running up and down it with bales of merchandise. The junk tacked nearer and nearer to the jetty, and the cries became more distinct.

I had to leave before the junk came alongside the jetty. I lectured to an outpost troop of the Irish Fusiliers on *How Parliament Works*. "I spent ten years there and never found out," I told them. Perhaps the easiest lecture of all.

In the intervals of work, I used to go shopping in Hong Kong, where silk pyjamas and all manner of exotic things could be had at a very low price. A general sense of weariness and frustration was assailing me; and I was thus naturally refreshed to see, emerging from a shop in the Gloucester Arcade, the most unusual if not one of the most beautiful women I have ever seen. My first impression was of the New Look, which had scarcely, otherwise, reached Hong Kong. My next impression was of a beautiful, provocative, young face, with alert grey eyes; and my final impression, which was what startled me most of all, was of a luxuriant head of grey hair, rinsed blue, and coiffured like a modern Madame de Pompadour. The contrast between that vivid young face and the prematurely grey hair intrigued me at once. I followed her incredulously into a shop.

I returned to Flagstaff House, where I found my hostess and Mrs. Talbot, the good-looking wife of a British Naval Officer, playing with their respective children on the lawn. "Who," I asked, "would be a woman with a very young face and very grey hair?"

"Ah ha!" they exclaimed joyfully. "You have seen our Mrs. Owens. She was captured by the Japs," they said significantly. "She could tell you an interesting story, no doubt."

No doubt, I thought.

"I would have invited her in to drinks to meet you if I had known you wanted to meet her," Mrs. Erskine added.

"Is it too late to start now?" I suggested.

"All right," said my hostess teasingly, "I will tell her that you have seen her in a shop and want to meet her." But Mrs. Erskine was in fact more diplomatic and came back to say that Mrs. Owens would ring me up in the morning to suggest a meeting some time during the day to tell me about her experiences.

"If you succeed in entertaining Mrs. Owens to lunch," said Mrs. Talbot sweetly, "you will be the envy of *every* officer in Hong Kong."

General Erskine, when he returned, added a little information about Mr. Owens. "He is an American who sells drugs to the Chinese — represents Park Davis in Hong Kong and South China. He wears a red bow tie with his dinner jacket."

I was a little late arriving at the Gloucester Hotel because I had a request to repeat my lecture to the naval hospital on the other side of the island. So Mrs. Owens was coming down the stairs from the restaurant — which was the Grips — not knowing, after all, what sort of a person she was going to meet. An elderly gentleman with a beard, compiling facts and statistics about the Japanese occupation, perhaps?

I saw her, suddenly, in a wide-brimmed crimson hat, turned up

184

fetchingly at the front and her famous grey hair curled up under it. She wore a black silk dress, hobble-skirted in the fashion prevailing in Paris, almost to her ankles, and she had the smallest American high-heeled shoes.

We went upstairs to the restaurant, and to a table for two. I was conscious of admiring and curious glances.

"First of all I must tell you what I already know. You came to Hong Kong, when you were eight years old with your parents, from Sydney. Your name was Allison Fisher,* your hair was a natural blonde and after you grew up and married Mr. Owens, you were both arrested by the Japanese. After your baby was born you were repatriated to America. There, after your second baby was born, your hair turned white — am I right?" She nodded. "Now, you are the Belle of Hong Kong. Am I right?"

She laughed. "You know everything. What more is there to tell you?" But over the coffee and liqueurs she told me her story.

"We had a house in Kowloon," she said, "not the one we have now. Our old one has been blitzed since. We heard some aeroplanes and Reggie went to the window of our bedroom. At first we thought of course, they must be British planes practising. But then we suddenly remembered there weren't any British bombers. These were Jap planes, heading in for the airport at Kaitak. So we got in a panic. I ran for my cosmetics and all the vitamin pills — that's all I had time to grab — and we went down to the Peninsula Hotel. Everybody else had the same idea, and we lived there for days, sleeping in the corridors, everywhere. When the Japs landed at Clearwater Bay we crossed over to the island. And then the fighting began on the island. We were at the American Club, down by the waterfront, when the surrender flag went up on the flagstaff at Government House. We could see it from the window but we just couldn't believe it. Then the Japs came in and rounded us up. They marched us down to an old brothel in the Chinese quarter — a low hotel, called the Taicoon. Do you know," she broke off, "I've never thought to visit it since. Would you like me to show it to you? We could walk down there after lunch. I should like to see it again after all these years."

"How did they treat you when they marched you down?"

"The Jap sentry hit me across the tummy. Then somebody

*Her father, Howard Fisher, was a brother of Geoffrey Fisher, Archbishop of Canterbury.

told him not to, as I was going to have a baby. So he hit me again."

"Deliberately?"

"Oh, yes. Another mouth less to feed, I suppose."

"But otherwise did they molest you? Did they know you were going to have a baby?"

"At the time it was only my word against theirs. But that was a little later, in the camp at Stanley. At first we were kept in the Taicoon."

It seemed easier to reconstruct the story on the spot and so we left the Grips and walked through the town, to the more exclusively Chinese quarter. At first she could not find the place. But when we passed the fish market she said, "It must be somewhere near here because I used to watch the Chinese and Third Nationals fighting each other for food. We could see them scrambling over each other's bodies to get at the fish. Life wasn't so bad for the British and Americans. At least you got enough to keep you alive. It was the Portuguese and others who had such a hard time to live – although of course they weren't prisoners."

We found the hotel at last, a few paces beyond the fish market where the Chinese vendors were chattering amiably with their customers. The Taicoon Hotel was a mean building, squeezed between Chinese shops. Inside, the Chinese receptionist looked up, startled by the apparition of two Europeans entering the little hallway. On our left was a rack with dozens of cards bearing Chinese characters; presumably the names of residents. Mrs. Owens ignored the man at the desk and walked with the assurance of a woman who had cause to remember every detail of the building, up the dark flight of stairs to the first floor. Here we found ourselves in a narrow passage, with rooms partitioned off by thin boarding to a height of about six feet, above which was wire netting to the ceiling. The woodwork was painted a pale, dingy green.

"This was our room," she said, fingering the numberplate on the door. "Twenty-six. There was a hole in the wall through which the Japs used to watch us."

She went on down the passage to a turning which took us out on to a balcony, overlooking the street. A Chinese servant came towards us puzzled, but she ignored him, as if she had been a ghost (as indeed she was, in a sense). She pointed down into the street.

"That is where the Sikh sentries used to stand on guard over us. There was always one standing there, with a rifle."

"Sikh sentries?" I echoed incredulously. "What were they doing? I thought they were on our side."

"They went over to the Japs at once. Some of the worst things were done by the Sikhs."

This was an uncomfortable sidelight on the British Empire.

As we walked back down the passage it occurred to me that our presence in the hotel might be misunderstood by the Chinese.

"And what," I asked, as we reached the top of the stairs, "what do those Chinese characters on the red glass lights at the end of the corridor mean?"

"Ladies and gents, I expect."

I must say Mrs. Owens was very stimulating company. She looked back on it all so lightly, as if it had been an entertaining experience. Yet her shoulders looked so very small to have borne such a burden of terror and anxiety as must have been hers with that face and that form.

It is always gratifying to escort a woman whose beauty attracts universal attention: and I was happy to encounter Brigadier Dowse, my fellow guest at Flagstaff House, as we retraced our steps to the European part of the town. Mrs. Owens took me on to the American Club for an orange squash. We went up in the lift, to a lounge where some American women were playing bridge. There was a lending library and we sat in a corner of it, sipping the cooling drinks. She took me to a window and pointed out the sloping tiled roof of Government House, with its unmistakable tower. From a flagstaff now fluttered the Union Jack.

"It was on that pole, from this window, that I watched the white flag go up," she said. "We couldn't believe it."

And yet it had been true, and I tried to reconstruct the frame of mind in which those American women had seen that signal of surrender go up over the Governor's residence; wondered when the Japanese troops would march in — and what would happen then.

This was to be my last day in Hong Kong, so I was free of further lectures. My time was my own, and as Mrs. Owens was going home for tea in Kowloon and as I wanted her opinion on some Chinese pyjamas which I had selected at a shop in Kowloon, we took a taxi down to the ferry.

How different the ferry seemed from my previous impressions

of it when forced to travel upon it for military purposes. This quaint craft, peopled by smiling coolies and happy Chinese or cheerful Europeans, going about their lawful occasions, brought us to Kowloon in a flash.

The Indian vendor in the silk shop agreed to the price Mrs. Owens prescribed, as if he were a cobra lulled by a snake charmer. Then we refreshed ourselves with a cup of tea in the lounge of the Peninsula Hotel. How different it all seemed from that first cup of tea, the day I arrived.

At length we taxied on to Mrs. Owens' house, an attractive white building, set back in a little garden, in Waterloo Road, near a convent, and with a view of the nearest hills of the New Territories. In these hills a few days previously, a British officer going for a stroll had been killed by bandits. Later on, she and her husband moved to a modern apartment on the Peak.

Mr. Owens was back early from the office and greeted me warmly. He was a short dark man of pronounced features with a black moustache and a head of bushy black hair which, after going grey in the prison camp, had been restored to its natural colour, he told me, by taking Park Davis vitamin pills. I told him that I had got some wonderful material from his wife for a book and suggested that as I was due to leave first thing in the morning they should join me for dinner at the Ritz.

We met again at about eleven and drove along the coast for a few miles, till we came to the Ritz. Here we found an atmosphere of shaded pink light and overhanging grey satin, with a number of the wealthier European and Chinese residents dancing, or sitting at the dining tables. There was a bar in the corner, and the manager, Mr. Ho, whose acquaintance I had already taken the trouble to make, greeted Owens as an old friend. We ordered drinks, and I lay before Mr. Owens the only thing I had with me, a bundle of typed translations of my press conference from the Chinese vernacular press. Leaving him to study these I took the floor with Mrs. Owens in my arms.

I recognised various people in the restaurant, including young Eu Tong Sin, who bowed with perceptible affability.

The Ritz closed at two and I secured a taxi, in which they dropped me off at Flagstaff House at 2.30.

"If your plane doesn't get off in the morning, Somerset," laughed Reggie, "come back to us."

The Commander-in-Chief himself arose at 6 a.m., wrapped about in a bath robe, to see Brigadier Dowse and me off at the front door. No doubt to make sure we were really leaving. We left with the A.D.C. in the staff car which was to take us down to one of his two fast and shining white launches, and thence to the flying boat base at Kaitak airport.

"Goodbye and a pleasant voyage," he said firmly. I felt as did Brigadier Dowse, that I had somewhat outstayed my welcome at Flagstaff House.

Bobby Darwin came with us on the launch, and stood till the last upon the landing-stage, while the engines of the B.O.A.C. Sunderland flying boat roared, and we taxied off in a cloud of spray.

Dowse and I were seated opposite each other, at a little table, and we watched the great wave of water spring up under the portside float of the aeroplane and then sweep in a green and translucent arc obscuring the view. When we were airborne the wave subsided. Ships swung by, just below us, and soon we were through the cloud gap at the end of the harbour, heading for the wide Pacific Ocean and the island of Singapore, 1,400 miles away. At the adjoining table sat a robust individual with grizzled hair, called Findlater. He represented among other things in the Far East a well-known brand of gin which bears his name. He was eager to get home, and settled down happily into his seat.

Thus we journeyed for an hour or more, until the pilot put his head through the door and said, "I am afraid we shall have to turn back to Hong Kong on account of engine trouble."

Various were the reactions to this announcement. For we had already travelled 150 miles. We should not, the pilot assured us, have to stay in Hong Kong for more than a couple of hours, to put matters to rights.

Behold us, an hour and a half later, mingled with a great number of Chinese travellers in the canteen of the Civil Airway terminus on Kaitak airport.

"Good old B.O.A.C.," laughed the Chinese page-boy as he saw us trooping back.

I telephoned Mrs. Owens. Was she amused? She had an assignment at the hospital, and would call in there on her way to join me in a cup of coffee at the airport. Car after car rolled up, full of Chinese passengers. But not Mrs. Owens. Suddenly she was among us, a little breathless, in a grey-brown tweed coat and skirt, her grey hair uncovered, a little ruffled by the harbour breeze. She had been to the R.A.F. in search of me, and only after drawing blank there, realised that I was travelling on a civilian airplane. We drank coffee, and then went out into the sun, wandering a little way off to a bollard on the jetty, upon which she sat against a background of mountains. Near by was an aluminium Dakota, labelled 'Hong Kong Airways'. I suppose all this is very unimportant, but I enjoyed it; and so, I believe, did Mrs. Owens. The rest of the passengers seemed to feel that it was almost worth flying back to Hong Kong to get a glimpse of such a vision; and there was nothing but good cheer as I clambered aboard the tender, when the engine was ready, and Allison waved goodbye to me for the last time, beside the colourful Red Ensign which furled and unfurled itself in the breeze upon the pontoon. I had a last glimpse of her, turning on her neat size 4 fawn suede American shoes, to mount the gangway steps, and a final wave of her hand.

Those who have to pay for their own passage, and have chosen to travel by air, usually do so because they want to get to the other end quicker than they can by boat; so most of the passengers were happy. And I, who had an overriding reason for wanting to get back to England, reflected that it was all for the best.

Presently little cartons of fruit and biscuits were brought round, as well as the latest magazines and newspapers. But if I thought about any weighty matters as I flew away from Hong Kong, it was only fitfully. We cannot be serious all the time.

After about another hour and a half's flying, the pilot put his head through the door and said, "Sorry chaps. Afraid we shall have to go back to Hong Kong. Got to fix the aerial this time." I began to wonder what was taking *him* back.

Brigadier Dowse, who had a high, rather bald and massive forehead, and looked like some German Chief of Staff, had enough sense of humour to enjoy this development. But Findlater who, I had reason to believe was working for M.I.6 began to give off sparks visibly. It seemed to me that his grizzled hair crackled like a wireless aerial on a ship in an arctic storm. This was B.O.A.C. 1948 vintage.

It certainly did not take the mechanics long to fix the aerial, once we had touched down again in Hong Kong. By now the approach over the streets of Kowloon and the aerodrome hangars, to skim down on to the water, was becoming quite familiar.

Once more we took the air. But this time, they explained, so much of the daylight had been used up that we should have to go to Bangkok. Findlater pointed out that he did not want to go to Bangkok. He wanted to go to Singapore, and had even booked a passage for that reason. Everything, they assured him, comes to him who waits, even in the British Overseas Airways Corporation. And after all, Bangkok is a pleasant place. Certainly I thought so. Findlater was seized by a silence of will-power, comparable only to rigor mortis. Some people really do have to move quickly, and he may have been one of them. At least we were heading away from Hong Kong, if only to prove that the Sunderland was not tethered permanently to the jetty there.

Lunch was served. Chicken drumsticks and lettuce, if I remember. We studied the silky pattern of the ocean far below us, studded with brown islands. And so we arrived in due course at Hong Kong. Yes. After an hour and a half that obliging pilot put his head through the door and said, "Sorry, chaps. Got to go back to Hong Kong. Engine still giving trouble. Carburettor."

"And what," they said to me, "have you put into the carburettor?"

We returned to Hong Kong this time, they said, for the night, Saturday night. They would ring us up in the morning to let us know what time the plane would start — and in the meantime B.O.A.C. would give us each twelve Hong Kong dollars (15/-) to pay for our board and lodging for the night.

This time I telephoned Reggie Owens at his office. "As you surmised," I said, "the plane did not get off — or not for long."

"It never does," he said. "Come back to us, dump your kit with the Chinese boys at the house, and join me for lunch at the American Club."

After three forays or sweeps over the Pacific, it seemed difficult to realise that they had deposited me in the early hours of this same morning at Flagstaff House. Neither Dowse nor I felt that we had the face to turn up again at the General's, so while he found a room at the Peninsula Hotel, I left my bags at the Owens' house, where I was greeted like an old friend by the Chinese boys and the Amah.

Reggie Owens and I lunched at the American Club, and then went to the races where Allison joined us, in a hat which consisted of a single spray of artificial flowers, arching her dazzling grey hair. Nobody looked much at the horses.

Next morning the B.O.A.C. people rang up and asked me to report at the airport at 9.30. As I went off from the house in Waterloo Road, Reggie Owens told the Chinese boy to put the coffee on again. "He'll be back," he said; and sure enough the engine was duly pronounced unfit for further flight that day. "Tomorrow," said the B.O.A.C. "we will get you off, even if it means sending you in another plane."

So we spent a lazy morning and after lunch set out, by way of the ferry, and across the island, to see Stanley Camp, where my host and hostess had been interned. Standing by a bus stop was Ian Morrison, (subsequently killed, as a War Correspondent in Korea) *The Times* Far Eastern Correspondent, also the author of *Malayan Postscript* (about the fighting in Singapore). We stopped and gave him a lift — he was also bound for Port Stanley. His pale blue eyes, which had last rested on me in Singapore in company with the Killearns, twinkled with some inward amusement. He seemed to be wondering if I had known this creature before — surely not in Sydney before she was eight? — and come all this way with a very different purpose from that of enlightening the garrison troops on the partition of Palestine or the future of the British Empire.

As we drove out to Stanley, Owens expatiated more on the life of the European inmates of that concentration camp. "There was a good deal of romance going on, one way and another. People got segregated from their families, and didn't know if they would ever see them again. The cemetery was the usual rendezvous. The Japanese sentries used to get furious. One of them found a couple making love under a tent in the middle of the compound and whipped the tent off them with his bayonet. Another curious feature of the camp was the way people got cured of alcoholic poisoning and stomach ulcers, during their stay on the promontory. It was a healthy spot in that way."

Allison added that her mother had diabetes when she went in and came out completely cured.

All this was rather shocking to me — and it was not until we drove down to the narrow neck of land, which joined the headland or promontory of Port Stanley to the rest of the island, that I was able to visualise the scene. Here a notice board at a barbed-wire barrier bore the words 'Stanley Camp'. The barbed wire was now pushed aside. Beyond this entrance the promontory widened out in bluffs and screes, covered with light undergrowth or heathland — very reminiscent of a headland in Scotland, surrounded by the sea. On the southern slopes were three or four large modern buildings, with cream-washed walls. We dismounted at the rear of one of them, where the warders' quarters had been. Here a black iron railing gave access to a ground-floor kitchen. "This is where we lived," Owens explained. "They gave us two rooms (a kitchen and living-room) in the warders' quarters, on account of Allison having a baby. We used to get our meals from the communal kitchen, but we were able to feed by ourselves. You know, Allison always managed to look smart — even if it was just a bit of old curtain that she got hold of and cut up to make a dress."

Yes, I could believe that Allison contrived to remain smart, even in a Japanese camp. And I supposed that it was her cheerful and undaunted spirit that had brought her through a unique ordeal — for in due course she was taken into the camp hospital and there her baby, Madeleyn was born: the first American citizen to be born in the power of the Japs. Allison's father and mother as British subjects remained in the camp, when the Owens were repatriated to America.

On Sundays, dancing went on in a different part of the Grips — and we danced there, after drinks at Repulse Bay with a naval officer whose wife had died under the Japs; and he showed the same febrile, half-crazed symptoms as most of the survivors. He chattered of the days when he and my brother had charged round the island in destroyers, gambolling like porpoises in sunlit waters before the war with Japan.

Afterwards we had drinks with an army officer's family. In the darkness the officer and I sat on a parapet where the waters of the China Sea lisped below us, and he confided in me his adoration of Mrs. Owens, whom he hoped to marry one day. He tagged along with us for the rest of the evening — I assumed wrongly that this must be the great love of Allison's life, until I asked her if it were wise; and she nearly fell over backwards laughing. She had been happily unaware of his sentiments. We dined at the Repulse Bay Hotel, and went back to Hong Kong for a last dance.

Time was running short. I had a feeling that I would at last

The Author with Helena of Abu Sinan at the Russian
Orthodox Church, Gethsemane, 1941

After it was all over

The Rt. Hon. Oliver Lyttelton, D.S.O., M.P. Minister of Production with Captain Somerset de Chair, M.P. and Brigadier Morrow at Chobham Tank Research establishment, 1944. The secret was the Cromwell tank

Mrs Thelma de Chair, the Author's first wife. She subsequently married Sir Jocelyn Lucas, Bt., M.P. Portrait by John Merton

Chilham Castle

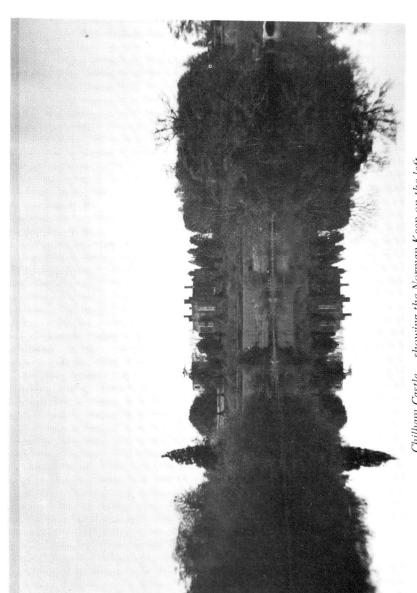

Chilham Castle – showing the Norman Keep on the left

Admiral Sir Dudley de Chair, K.C.B., K.C.M.G., M.V.O. (the Author's father) with his son, grandson Peter, and daughter-in-law, at Chilham, 1946

The Author's sons, Rodney and Peter de Chair at Chilham, 1946

Tahir el Masri Bey in front of his house at Abu Hommus

The Author with Salah and Kassim at the Qasr el Masri, December 1945

Qasr el Masri

The last of the British Pharaohs – H.E. Lord Killearn at the British Embassy, Cairo, December 1945

Some of the sons of King Ibn Saud with the Saudi Arabian Ambassador to Egypt and Lord Killearn

On the Blue Nile

'We photographed crocodiles'

*Gordon's statue at Khartoum, 1946 (since toppled and removed,
along with the Union Jack)*

The Governor General's Palace, Khartoum, designed by Lord Kitchener

In Kitchener's Palace, Khartoum

Fountain at Tripoli

H.R.H. Princess Marina, Duchess of Kent

Pageantry at Chilham Castle. The Author dressed as an ostler of Chaucer's time, with his first wife Thelma, receiving H.R.H. the Duchess of Kent, and the Lord Lieutenant of Kent, Lord Cornwallis, 4th July, 1946

Barbara Sconce as Anne Boleyn in front of the Keep, Chilham Castle pageant   The Times *photograph*

Thelma with the Georgian ram's-headed stone urns, moved from Necton in Norfolk to Chilham

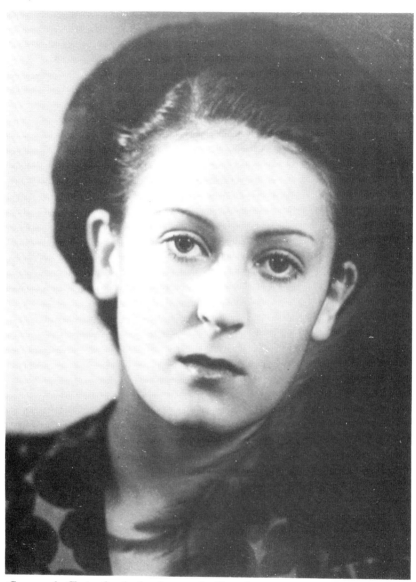

Carmen de Chair, the Author's second wife, subsequently Mrs Bedrich Kaufler

Blickling from across the lake, showing the north front and the Peter the Great room

Peter Dudley Somerset de Chair (1939-62) at Blickling, 1949 – the south front

Blickling from the east showing the lake

Sir Harold Nicolson, Mr Humphrey Hare and Lady Melchett at Blickling,
August 1952

Peter and Rodney de Chair, 1949

'In the still afternoon of my life I took to oil painting.' The angel from Leonardo's Madonna of the Rocks. *Copy by the Author, done at the National Gallery, 1951/52*

Harebell *skippered by Captain Trevor Lean, R.N. moored alongside*
H.M.S. Vanguard, *1954*

Aboard Harebell – Gwen Harding, Carmen, and Trevor Hampton

With Carmen aboard Harebell

Dame Pat Hornsby-Smith, P.C., M.P., Wing Commander John Walker, Commander Selwyn Harrison, R.N., and Carmen on Harebell

Allison Owens, née Fisher; niece of the Archbishop of Canterbury Dr. Geoffrey Fisher

Toni Leong – found in the Keklokse monastery, disguised as a boy!

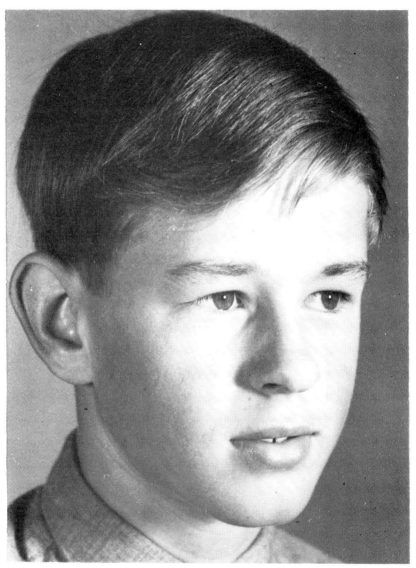

Rory de Chair

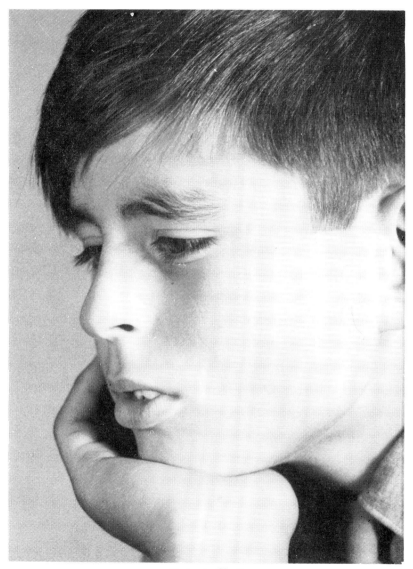

Carlo de Chair

St. Osyth Priory, from a painting by Julian Barrow, 1984

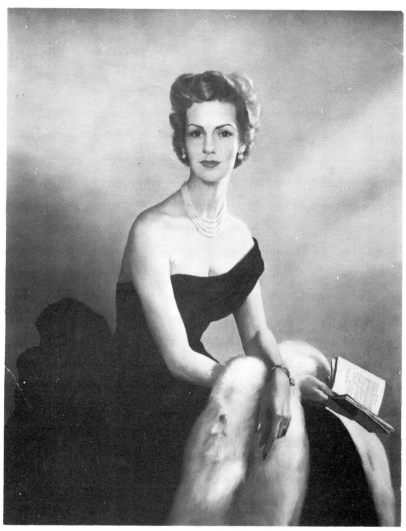

*Portrait of Tessa de Chair, the Author's third wife, by Anna Zinkeisen –
exhibited the Royal Academy, 1959, Glasgow Fine Arts, 1959, and at
Zinkeisen exhibitions, London and Woodbridge*

*Teresa de Chair and Sir Toby Clarke, Bt. after their marriage
in the church of St. Peter and St. Paul, St. Osyth, July 1984*

'Then there was Trerice . . . '

*Tessa and the Author setting out from St. Osyth for a fancy
dress ball. The painting of the Gatehouse is by Tristram Hillier, R.A.*

Teresa and Gillian Rumsey at the farm in New York, August 1972

Helena de Chair at the farm in New York, August 1984

St. Osyth Priory c. *A.D. 1475, with the Georgian wing in the foreground housing* Whistlejacket.

Painting by Felix Kelly

Whistlejacket *by George Stubbs, A.R.A. lent to the Stubbs exhibition at the Tate Gallery, 1984. We had to lower the floor nine inches to fit him in at St. Osyth*

Lady Juliet de Chair, the Author's fourth wife

Teresa de Chair on her wedding day at St. Osyth. 28 July, 1984
Photo by Alan Davidson

be airborne in the morning. I even wrote a doggerel rhyme for Reggie's benefit on the delay of my aircraft:

> The Chinese traded time for space
> But I have traded time for grace
> And Allison is like a State
> Invaded just a little late.
> Divided for a single hour
> The Kwo-min-tang is back in power.

Since then the Kwo-min-tang has not been doing too well.

The more one studies human behaviour in general and one's own actions in particular the more clear it becomes that we are not single personalities but multiple personalities; that our decisions are not the decisions of a single will but majority decisions in the Cabinet meeting of our minds. An alternative of decisive and momentous consequences presents itself to us. Whether we decide for one or the other at once or only after agonising deliberation; is it not a majority decision only that prevails? As if the twenty of us seated around the Cabinet table of the mind advance each his or her separate reasons and arguments. When the discussion is ended the Prime Minister, who is our will — often a distracted being — puts the issue to the vote. Perhaps twelve are in favour of one course and eight for the other. The will of the majority prevails. But do the eight accept Rousseau's dictum that even though he finds himself in a minority, he recognises that the majority must be right? By no means. The defeated eight set about lobbying in the outer corners of the mind — and even if they are driven underground for the time being are all the more active and insidious on that account. The victorious twelve, on the other hand, having for the moment gained their point, probably sit back. Apathy overlays their initial resolve. Thus one day, unexpectedly, the same two alternatives reappear in a slightly different guise on the agenda of the mind and the minority have by this time suborned or coerced a couple of waverers and, behold, the will accepts a new and contrary decision.

I see myself sometimes presiding in the Cabinet of my mind. I try to be fair — to give all my personalities a hearing. I have a special weakness for my good self; who, although ageing and somewhat decrepit, is still Lord President of the Council and is much respected. Then there is my Chancellor of the Exchequer, who has an irritating way of viewing everything from the financial angle and bringing the argument back to mundane realities. There is of course the Minister for Foreign Affairs – a dashing fellow and far too glamorous. He leads me into deep waters. And there is the Attorney General who gives his view from a detached and maddeningly fair standpoint. When they have all said their say, I decide whatever it may be – to go abroad or to move house. But whatever I decide, be sure there will be a powerful discontented minority watching out for every opportunity to say "There, what did I tell you?" and exercising their pressure in the most obscure but effective ways.

So here I am far from England on the night train from Johore Bahru to Kuala Lumpur; and half my mind is complaining bitterly of the heat, the discomfort and the needless toil. The *Strathnaver* has just docked at Singapore with the wives of officials all over Malaya; so there is no sleeping compartment available for the weary traveller who has already travelled 1,400 miles that day. No, he has a bunk in a range of sleeping berths, one up, one down, along a single coach. There are no curtains and no privacy – the men, mostly officers, lie down on the hard palliasses; some strip off their boots, some their clothes; some change from a grip into pyjamas. The train jogs through the Malayan jungle. I find the heat with the windows closed unbearable, and open one beside me. Soon the compartment is full of malarial mosquitoes, and sleep is very difficult. At half-past six in the morning the train draws into Kuala Lumpur. It transpires (later) that the army transport detailed to meet me has broken down, and I am left, as usual, to find my way about.

The officers of the K.O.Y.L.I. at Taiping were very hospitable and threw some light on the mentality of the Japanese. One Jap who had been a particularly unpleasant individual, the Colonel told me, and whose blood everybody was after, for torturing and beheading Englishmen, remained in Taiping after the Japanese collapse, and presented himself to the British Army with every expectation, apparently, of being treated with ceremony as an important Japanese official. It was beyond his comprehension that he almost headed the list of war criminals and was tried and executed accordingly; going to his death no doubt with a puzzled sense of grievance.

To lecture in the noonday heat of Taiping for an hour after travelling continuously for three days absorbs a considerable amount of energy. The sweat trickled down my face all the time and I dabbed at it with a tight-rolled ball of handkerchief, gesticulating, as I always do, with my free hand towards the map of the world.

"Give me an india-rubber," I began, and advancing to the map tried to rub out the bright red patch of Burma. "That's gone, for a start," I told them, and much more beside, but as fairly as I could. They were clearly interested when I came on to the new importance of Malaya in the defence of the Empire. "That," I told them, "is why you have to sit in places like Taiping, listening to people like me, instead of going into some pub in the Old Kent Road at home."

'Now why,' their expressions clearly indicated, 'hasn't some bastard explained all this to us before? Perhaps, if somebody had put it that way, we should not have felt so browned off up here all this time.'

I suppose that in any voyage there must be a worst moment, the blackest patch; and in this journey it was undoubtedly Ipoh. I was then so far from the beginning of my labours that I could feel the effects of exhaustion without being near enough to the end to feel the exhilaration of completion. It seemed as if there were no end; and here I was in the very middle of Malaya, lecturing to a lot of sweltering soldiers in shorts, and nothing else, gathered, probably against their will, to hear me lecture in a wooden hut, where a fan made my voice inaudible and where to lecture without one made the heat intolerable; and to listen to me moreover on a subject I knew nothing about, 'How Parliament Works'; as if I were a Gilbert Campion. But that was not the matter; after ten years in Parliament a man could lecture on anything for an hour, without pausing for breath. In the afternoon I lectured to a group of delinquents in a barbed-wire detention camp on 'The partition of Palestine'. "You will find quite an intelligent audience," the Commandant told me.

No, it was not the detention camp. It was the railway station hotel at Ipoh, under the arcade of which lines of newly arrived Gurkhas sat, seemingly all day, on their kitbags, waiting for transport to collect them. There was a long lounge in the arcade, and the bedrooms opened off these. And off the bedrooms opened a winding staircase, leading down to a murky basement, in which was discovered a subterranean bathroom. Occasionally trains came and went; north and south along the great central railway of

Malaya. And I lay under the mosquito-proof netting, hung high above the bed like a square cylinder, and watched the three broad blades of the electric fan turn slowly round and round, high up in the ceiling; and I wondered, as I lay there, with my clothing off, waiting for the night train, what it must have been like to be a Japanese general lying in this hotel, having advanced so far down the peninsula of Malaya and having reached Ipoh – would I be bothered to go on? And I felt certain that I should have decided "no". Ipoh was the end.

At Seremban I was to stay with the British Adviser, Mr. Gordon-Hall, till recently the British Resident, in the charming white colonial house formerly known as the Residency, presumably now known as the Advisory.

Seremban was altogether pleasant; set high amid rolling hills, with mountains in the distance. The whole place was laid out like a park or botanical gardens, with the European residences screened behind feathery trees. The Residency was a spacious building with white pillars and, inside, a mellowness of old polished panelling not found elsewhere in Malaya.

My host was a wizened little man of quiet authority and long experience of Malaya. There were two other guests, men who had shared with him the rigours of Japanese imprisonment. One was returning to England shortly after thirty-seven years in the Service. It was he who said of his imprisonment, "Can you not detect the mark of the beast upon me?"

They were having tea when I arrived and Gordon-Hall explained the luxury of the furnishings: "This house was requisitioned by the Japanese Governor and the Japs went round all the houses in Seremban. If they saw anything attractive they said 'Take it up to the Residency'; thus was the collection assembled. After the occupation we expected people to come up and ask for bits of furniture back again, but no one has claimed any, and here it is. That is the way the Japanese governed."

They talked of Changi gaol where they had been imprisoned. The Mark of the Beast said: "After a while the Japs allowed husbands and wives to meet in a compound at the back of the prison. You had to present a ticket, like going into the cinema. Later they extended the privilege to fiancées as well. So everyone in the camp, even people of about eighty, managed to find a fiancée. I know one husband who preferred not to avail himself of the opportunity of meeting his wife."

After tea my host took me for a stroll in the twilight along the neat tarmacadam roads which wound about the park-like slopes above Seremban. Every now and then we would pass a group of young Malays: men and girls who would call greetings cheerfully to Mr. Gordon-Hall, which he would answer with becoming informality. There was no doubt that he enjoyed the respect and even the affection of these people; and I began to see a new imperialism growing up, in the spirit of Imperial partnership, altogether different from the martial prestige associated with the great Empire-builders like Curzon, Cromer and Killearn. Malcome MacDonald, (on holiday in Canada, bird-watching), whom I had known as a junior minister in the House of Commons, with his mild manners, slightly protuberant teeth, and calm self-assurance, was possibly the new representative of a different but not necessarily less significant concept of Empire. Everywhere in Malaya I found evidences of respect for his administration; and the fact that there were no sentries clicking heels at his approach had not apparently lowered his prestige in the eyes of the Malayan or Chinese communities.

My host spoke of his new position as Adviser. "Dato Ohn is playing a clever game. We know he is at the back of it. He circulated all the governments advising them not to consult the new Advisers. So nobody asks me for advice. Of course the day may come when I have to tender my Advice with a capital A, backed by all the authority of the British Army in Malaya; but short of that they seem keen to establish the principle that they function independently of us."

The post office in Seremban was a pleasant little white plaster building standing beside some ornamental water, and thither I repaired to send my cables. I also did some shopping in a drowsy street where all the vendors seemed to be Indians.

On Sunday my host drove me and his friends down to Port Dickson where he had a seaside residence. On the bonnet of the neat black Humber saloon car, fluttered side by side the Union Jack and the emblazoned yellow flag of Negri Sembilan. We drove through miles of rubber plantations. "The price of synthetic rubber began to compete with the raw stuff," my host told me, "but they have made a discovery called bud-grafting which has increased the yield of trees three times. You see these little earthenware cups, stuck to the trees, where the bark is cut. They normally collect latex, about a third of the cup full. With bud-grafted trees the cup is full. Very early in the morning they go around these plantations and make a fresh cut, about an eighth of an inch, in the bark. The latex bleeds down into the cut until the day begins to get hot around about ten o'clock in the morning. Then the women come round and collect the latex from the cups."

Here and there we passed tin workings, primitive overhead water shoots, with a thatched workman's hut perched up on a little bamboo or wicker bridge. Yet the sober fact was that the rubber and tin output of Malaya earned more dollars (£192,000,000 worth in 1948) for the hard-pressed British Empire than all the exports of the United Kingdom's industries put together. Once again the significance of Malaya in the post-war world was inescapable.

The Resident's (or Adviser's) bungalow on the coast had an attractive garden, with a garden-house on a little promontory. Some friends dropped in, and two of us changed in the bungalow and walked along the blistering sand to find a congenial part of the beach from which to bathe.

As we drove back through Port Dickson, we passed the police post, and this prompted Gordon-Hall to remark, "This is where our friend Gammans (a fellow M.P. in the House of Commons) started his career — as District Commissioner for Port Dickson." (So my next greeting to Gammans was "I have just come from Port Dickson.")

Back at the Residency at Seremban I tried to sketch the view from the balcony of my room. The mountains were hazy with purple, overlaid with green vegetation on the lower slopes. There were heavy-headed trees dotted against the veldt-like middle distance. Palm trees lined a road, and in the foreground the lawn of rubbery grass was laid out with a stone-flagged path and flower-beds around a square central pool. A long stone balustrade flanked the further edge of the lawn, and thereby enclosed the gardens. The heat up here in the hills was a little less oppressive, but the fan still stirred a sultry atmosphere; and I wondered what it must be like to live for thirty-two years in the Government service out here and at the end of it all to find the Government you were working for unable to protect you from the claws of the Japanese. In the last resort the old Roman Empire was the one most calculated to survive. War on all the frontiers till the day it died and no half-measures. It collapsed in the end, but only after 500 years, and then it survived in Byzantium for a long while. Its influence on all Europe was colossal; and I sometimes wonder whether we in England are not in the position of the decaying Roman Republic which preceded the rule of the Caesars. The Senate and the Roman people were admirable in their time, but it was left to Julius Caesar to establish an enduring system.

My journey from Seremban to Tampin was not a happy one. The army car punctured opposite some Malay huts just when the tropical rain began to descend. The jack did not fit, and when a passing car-load of Chinese with babies had supplied the deficiency, it transpired that the wheel brace did not fit either. Eventually a Public Works Department lorry was stopped, and at last in drenching rain the wheel was changed. I went over to the Malay huts, where an evening meal was being cooked beneath the palm-thatched roof, on an open hearth, and asked for water to wash my hands. A bucket and soap were produced and I got off some of the grime. Two Malay families lived in this simple line of thatched rooms; the women wearing their long gowns of purple or grey, wrapped sluttishly about them, the children standing around to stare open-mouthed. I arrived late at the camp in Tampin, where, however, I was able to have a hot bath, and where a room was provided for me in a hut. The conversation at dinner was remarkable in so far as there were present a Canadian officer, an Australian officer, a Rhodesian officer and English officers all serving in the same unit, and I was delighted to find the Rhodesian (who was in command), the Australian and the Canadian all in full agreement that the time was overdue for a binding Federal Organisation of the Empire.

"What are you waiting for?" urged the Canadian.

I laughed. "I was always under the impression that it was the Canadians who would not enter such an organisation. Mr. MacKenzie King – "

"Oh, MacKenzie King," the Canadian brushed such reasons aside.

I slept happily, having found at Tampin in the heart of the Malayan jungle, the hard core of Empire Unity. Next morning, after the customary lecture, I hurried on towards Singapore, and as I wanted to reach Singapore before dinner, I arranged for a picnic lunch. My host at Seremban had advised me, for interest, to take the coast road by way of Malacca. I stopped with my driver by the roadside to eat my lunch, seeking some shade — for the sun was shining — beside some palm trees, where a Malay Kampong lined the road. Here I found that the ground was swampy and the drainage of the thatched houses primitive in the extreme — running into open ditches. The driver would not eat the meat sandwiches, being a Mahommedan, but he consumed all those filled with tomatoes. However, not unnaturally he wanted more, and I was consequently delayed at the ferry in Malacca where I had to go in search of the driver in a Malay eating-house if I was not to miss the first crossing. I bought some bananas from a stall by the ferry. The driver, a dark and sturdy Gurkha, emerged with his rice on a chipatty and consumed the rest of it on the way over the broad river.

There was something of an atmosphere about the town, sprawled on two sides of a broad river, not to be found elsewhere in Malaya. It spoke of eighteenth-century traders. From here, presumably, had come the Malacca cane. But there was no time to explore, and I urged the driver on towards the south. At about tea-time, I passed below the green roofs of Bukit Serene, perched on its hill above the Straits of Johore, but did not stop. I drove over the Causeway and into Singapore, where I had a long search, owing to the ignorance of the Gurkha driver as to the lay-out of the city, before I found the Sea View Hotel on the waterfront a mile or so outside Singapore.

Here I was hoping to run into Allison Owens again, stopping off on her way to visit a sister in Australia; but there was only a cable from Hong Kong at Bukit Serene, waiting for me: 'Alas, duty calls. It would have been fun. Allison.'

There were reproachful telephone messages from Bukit Serene asking why I had not come there direct. I had imagined that in the throes of packing up for their return to England they would have preferred to be spared a guest; but thus pressed I made my way there.

Next day I lunched with Brigadier Duke, commanding Johore District, who took the chair at my lecture in the afternoon. It was he who had the bar to the D.S.O., and whose red and stocky face had been slapped by the Japanese guards till the bones showed through the flesh. And I felt, as I studied his tough and martial countenance, now healed of these inflictions, that I was no nearer an understanding of what had really happened to British subjects in Japanese hands, than when I had first arrived. I had listened to a lot of stories, tried to piece their accounts together; tried to put myself in their frame of mind confronted with such appalling circumstances; tried, even, to grasp the mentality of the Japanese; but in the last resort the whole thing escaped me — as if it were a surrealist nightmare which had happened to someone else, and which I could not begin to share or understand. No doubt the inner story will be revealed in time, by some writer gifted with 'the double-power to go and to write'; and perhaps then it will all seem clear and explicable.

I lectured in the afternoon in barracks on a hill — and it seemed to me that I had been lecturing to the same soldiers in the same building all the time; that I had never really moved around Malaya at all. My journey was nearing its end. But there was one story in store for me — the story of Toni Leong.

I met her that night at a farewell party given for the Killearns by Tunco Makota, son of the Sultan of Johore. Killearn was asked to make a farewell speech, which he did most effectively; and then insisted on my making one too. "Tell them about the strategic significance of Malaya," he whispered. I did as I was bid. Among the Chinese guests were Mr. Leong, dressed in a European grey suit, and his lovely wife, who wore a black sheath dress, slit from the knee downwards. I was introduced to her and danced a little, in the course of which I invited her and her husband to join me at the Sea View Hotel the night before I was due to fly home. Her eyes were certainly arresting, being of that jet black, large pupils set in a brown iris, which is more often found in Orientals than in Europeans. Her face was Chinese of a peach freshness, although her hair was black. And she spoke English with a saucy Americanism which was altogether charming.

"I was seventeen," Toni Leong explained, "when the Japanese arrived, and was just engaged to my husband, who had a job in Singapore. (I was living with my family in Penang.) When the Japanese came he was naturally worried about me, as the telephones were cut off for a few days. But there is a monastery on the slopes of Penang, the Keklokse Temple; and my family took me up there, disguised as a boy. I lived in the monastery under the care of the priests; I was very full of spirits then."

"As you are now, it seems."

"I was even more full of them, then, and of course I could not sit still like a monk, so I was always playing games, and running around like a mad thing. The old monks used to love it, standing there with their hands tucked into their wide sleeves, shaking with inward mirth watching me up to my pranks. Then one day the Japs came along to take a party for forced labour. I was chosen with a lot of boys, and we were marched out to a place where we were expected to strip and get down to work. Of course I could not strip. That is how they found out I was a girl."

"What did they do then?"

"They were very angry. But they couldn't do anything. It was quite a relief not to have to go on pretending to be a boy. It had been quite embarrassing at times, expecially when the Japanese caught my husband and me — we had got married by this time — in bed together."

Here, then, was yet another piece of the mosaic — the story of a Chinese girl living in the guise of a boy in a monastery on the slopes of Penang till the Japanese asked her to strip. She seemed to have found the whole business a splendid joke and here she was at the end of it all, the least despondent of the lot. She hoped that her husband's business — wholesale linen merchants — would take them in due course to America. Perhaps they would visit England. I hoped that they would. She was woman of unpredictable whims and considerable personality; an ornament to any community.

In the morning I was within a stone's throw of the aerodrome. It was a Sunday and Colonel Gadd was there in sports coat and flannels, to say goodbye. "I like," he said with a twinkle in his eye, "to see lecturers off myself, to make sure they really have gone . . . . "

So began the homeward flight, pausing at Rangoon, where it seemed to me, who had once set such high hopes on the future of Burma within the Commonwealth, that as an independent republic the place resembled nothing so much as a clock running down, with nobody there who knew how to wind it up again. I made a pilgrimage to the Shwe Dagon Pagoda, a majestic spire of beaten gold, around the base of which clustered a multitude of lesser shrines in fretted wood or mother-of-pearl. The Burmese strolled about in their gay coloured robes. Some knelt continuously in prayer. I asked the guide whether he was happy now that Burma was independent. He shrugged his shoulders philosophically.

"British not Buddhists. Japanese Shinto." That seemed to end the matter. And in the Press I read the question asked in Parliament as to why English was still being used in Government publications, and Thakin Nu's answer that this was only a temporary expedient.

Thence to Calcutta, where women came down to the Ganges to fill large brass jars with water; Karachi; where my wife rejoined me from Bhopal; Bahrein at the head of the Persian Gulf, where I began instinctively to feel at home again; and then in one hop, across the great deserts of Iraq and Transjordan (which I had once crossed so much more laboriously at ground level, the other way), to land in Egypt. For a moment, when we found Cairo obliterated by a khamsin and were crash-landed in a storm on the Great Bitter Lake after failing to put down on the Nile, it seemed as if our journeys were to end abruptly; but the pilot made a landing which surprised himself and we slept in an R.A.F. camp at Dev-ar-Suar in tents on the sand. The passengers met in a canteen for breakfast, where tea was dished out of the communal urn and buttered bread had to be dipped by all in the marmalade bowl. Such was the emergency accommodation provided for world travellers by the B.O.A.C.

Thence to a houseboat on the Nile at Cairo. It was labelled, incongruously in such surroundings 'The Puritain'. My wife pointed it out. "That is what I am," she declared, "and proud of it." I could claim no identity of outlook. Then a short flight over the Mediterranean to Augusta in Sicily, where Communist slogans and photographs of Stalin plastered the walls for the coming elections; and finally high over the clouds of France, to land peacefully on Poole Harbour.

CHAPTER 17

There is no doubt that this was the moment for an ambitious
young man to have taken stock of his position. I was on the eve of
a break-through on the political front. Although out of Parliament
I had been readopted in competition with Leslie Hore-Belisha
and Jack Profumo, among sixty others, for the safe Tory seat of
South Paddington. I was on the executive of the United Nations
Association and Chairman of its National Appeal Committee
which included such august personages as the Prime Minister's
wife, Mrs Attlee and Lord Salisbury. I had just appeared on a film
in aid of the appeal, which was shown in cinemas throughout the
country, demanding of governments throughout the world that
they must see reason before being overwhelmed by an atomic
explosion. Even my father, who saw it at his local cinema in
Kensington, said he thought I had never been more convincing.

On the other hand the girl with whom I was passionately in
love had been pregnant since April; nor could this be considered
accidental. Sooner or later the position would have to be regularised,
but this was before the idea of a man in public life, having had a
child by his private secretary, and living with her in a separate
establishment, had spread to the Royal Family. In 1949 it was so
novel as to be shocking and Parliament had not yet enacted that
the subsequent marriage of the parents legitimised the child. Torn
between the fires of passion, excitement at the arrival of a new
child and the temptations of political success, I played for time.

Something however had to be done about the approaching
event, and the first thing seemed to be to change Carmen's surname
by deed poll. This was necessary so that she could live peacefully
under a new name by which she was not already known, and
under which she could draw the essential ration card and obtain
prenatal care from the Welfare State. It would have been little
protection to call herself Mrs. Appleton, while having to deposit
her ration card with the local grocer as Miss Bowen, or present her

identity card under that name at the clinic. Her name was duly changed from Carmen Bowen to Carmen Appleton, and we set about renting a small house in a fairly fashionable part of London. Anybody who has tried to rent a house in Belgravia while telling the truth about the unmarried girl he is living with who is about to have a baby will understand the wisdom of presenting her as his own wife. Yet this would have been impossible in a capital city where my own wife was by now a well-known member of the London County Council, who appeared not infrequently with me in photographs of social occasions. So I appeared before the house agents as Mr. Appleton, and thus began, for me, the complications of leading a double life. We were soon sent to a couple called Ellis who wanted to let their house in Caroline Terrace, furnished. Ellis could be overheard whispering to his wife at the bottom of the stairs, "It ought to be possible to cash in on the baby," by which is meant I take it, in legal circles, that young couples in our circumstances were not likely to grumble over the rent, or over-excessive claims for delapidations.

Asked for a reference I obtained a glowing one from that well-known author and former M.P. Somerset de Chair at Chilham Castle, a fair riposte I felt, for 'cashing in on the baby.' We soon engaged a couple of servants. All this was greatly facilitated by the sale in July of the Chilham Estate, which even after paying off the mortgage of £30,000, the land agents' accumulated deficit, bank overdrafts and repaying Thelma anything she had lent to the project, still left me with about £40,000 in capital profit untaxed.

Of course Mrs. Ellis was very impressed by our going to stay with Somerset de Chair at Blickling, which we did before Rodney and Peter arrived for holidays and navigation of the Bure. The oil painting of the house which I had completed when Rodney was sailing the dinghy on the lake was duly framed and hung at 10 Caroline Terrace, but I took the precaution of overpainting in green water-colours the initials S. de C in the corner.

I now settled down at Caroline Terrace to write *The Story of a Lifetime*, based on an extraordinary dream or vision which Carmen had recounted to me, in which she had been vividly associated with Jesus in hiding in a hill-village outside Jerusalem after the Crucifixion, which in her dream he had survived and to which he had been spirited away from the tomb by his friends. I continued this with her on the Island of Skye, where we stayed at a remote farmhouse, run as a guest-house called, if I remember rightly, Ullinish Lodge and gazed at the far Cuillins. There I wrote the chapter of the massacre of the innocents at Bethlehem and described how the narrator, as a cavalry officer in the Roman army at Tiberias, has received intelligence of the planned massacre and arriving in time, had used his authority to escort Mary, Joseph and the child out of the burning hill village under the eyes of Herod's local Militia. This book, like *The Golden Carpet, The Silver Crescent, The First Crusade, Napoleon's Memoirs* and *Caesar's Commentaries* was published by the Golden Cockerel Press in a limited edition. It was the only publication to which I had contributed part of the cost and the reason for this was that I did not want the book reviewed or promoted in any way. Only 100 copies were printed, and these were bound in white alum-tanned sheepskin. The woodcuts, exact illustration of the episodes I would have chosen, were done without guidance or prompting by Clifford Webb who had illustrated my translation of *The First Crusade* and *Caesar's Commentaries*. Even in such a limited edition, however, it required a lot of courage for Christopher Sandford to publish it, and for the printers to set it up. It is a book which is bound to shock many and for those who like to compare *The Golden Carpet* with Lawrence's *Revolt in the Desert, The Story of a Lifetime* could be compared with *The Mint* which also remained in a secret edition for many years. There is no real vanity in saying this, because *The Mint* turned out to be a thoroughly bad book, whereas *The Story of a Lifetime* is in my own opinion, at least, the best piece of writing I have ever done and I am prepared to let it be judged impartially in time, but not yet. The cost of production was £1,900 (in 1951) and the G.C.P. bore £800 of this on the understanding that they could have the proceeds of the first forty copies at the wholesale price of £20 to pay for these. The published price was 28 guineas per copy, approximately £30 and they soon sold the requisite number of copies. I retained the rest and kept about forty. I gave copies occasionally to people for special reasons — to Anna Zinkensien when she painted my portrait; to Christopher Sandford's son, Jeremy, as a wedding present. He never bothered to write a letter of thanks, although his father was the publisher, but he went on to achieve a certain fame through his television play on the housing problem called *Kathy Come Home*. I also gave one to my god-daughter, Roxana Lampson, on her coming of age; as I had given her the special editions of *The Golden Carpet* and *Silver Crescent* as christening presents.

Nothing is harder for an author than to take his reputation seriously. One minute he is overpraised to such an extent as to be ridiculous in spite of which very few copies of his books may be sold. Then television arrives to take the importance out of fame — since any newscaster's face becomes as familiar as the Prime Minister's — and in any case people's memories are short. So that within a few years your name and work is quickly forgotten. Sometimes you get a surprising reminder of forgotten praise. My god-daughter's grandfather Sir Aldo Castellani, had sent me his own autobiography *Men, Microbes and Monarchs*. In toasting the health of the bride and bridegroom at his granddaughter Bunty's wedding reception in Chelsea Town Hall, I said it was difficult from reading the book to know in which of these three fields he had the widest acquaintance. I had thought it appropriate to bring him a copy of my latest novel, *Bring Back the Gods*, and was startled when he wrote 'No wonder you are described as one of the three or four best writers in the world.' And no wonder, I thought, that he has been such a successful physician to so many exiled monarchs, with a bedside manner like that. Yet an author cannot help wondering at times whether he is getting through to the public at all, and whether there is any harm in his writing being so often described as caviare to the general. There may be a smaller sale for caviare than for fish and chips, yet there is no particular merit in the fact that the latter is a best-seller. One comes back again and again to the spectacle of Rembrandt painting unknown and unrecognised masterpieces in absolute poverty, after his decline in popularity from the days of the Night Watch, to the dubiety of his life with Hendrika Stoffels. Did he sometimes wonder why his contemporaries paid so little heed to his masterly brush strokes? And who had ever heard of Jan Vermeer till three centuries after his death, his luminous canvases began to attract universal acclaim? I have dwelt a little bit on this in relation to *The Story of a Lifetime* because I sometimes wonder what it is that makes me go on writing at all. It certainly is not any hope of financial gain. In the two years when I was writing *Bring Back the Gods* all I got from the royalties was an advance of £150, while I made a tax-free capital gain of £48,000 on gravel extraction on my estate from McAlpine and Son during the same period. Every minute I spend with a pen in my hand writing a book instead of signing cheques could be said to be conducive to my financial ruin; nor does it add anything to one's social position to be known as an author. It is in fact social death – bracketing one with gossip columnists or hired hacks. My father used to say that he could not go into one of his clubs for six months after one of my novels appeared. It is not as an author but as the owner of interesting houses and a collector of works of art or a beautiful wife, or a yacht at the Coronation Review, that people seem to seek one out. Yet some strange compulsion – perhaps akin to the urge towards the confessional – forces me to put on record facts about my life which I have previously only hinted at, such as the strange goings-on at No. 10 Caroline Terrace.

During the autumn and winter of 1949 I left Carmen alone there as little as possible; but I had to carry on the work of nursing my constituency in South Paddington on the other side of the park, and speak on behalf of the United Nations Association. It was after I had appeared in newsreels, speaking as the Tory representative on a platform at Arundel Castle, with Attlee, who was the P.M. and Lord Reading the Liberal speaker, that we were invited by our landlords to dine quietly at a restaurant one evening. Mrs. Ellis asked me casually whether I knew the Duchess of Norfolk, next to whom I had been sitting on the platform. I saw no harm in admitting that I had met her, though it seemed to me that Robert Appleton was getting about rather more than I had intended. We thought the interrogation had passed off all right, and all might have been well if Mrs. Ellis's mother had not by ill chance happened to live in my constituency of South Paddington. Mrs. Ellis, having moved out of her own home, not unnaturally went to stay with her mother and was staggered on emerging from the lift one day to be confronted by a life-size poster of my face and the words 'Somerset de Chair is right for South Paddington'. Next time we met she commented on the extraordinary likeness between me and my cousin (with whom she knew I had been to stay at Blickling). I agreed that the likeness was indeed remarkable and was often commented on. But Mrs. Ellis was not so easily put off this time and lost no opportunity of pointing out to the candidate's wife that her house was let to a cousin of her husband's called Appleton who bore a truly remarkable likeness to him.

On top of this the woman telephonist at the Royal Thames

Yacht Club, where I was supposed to be residing when in London, turned out to be a member of the same Christian Science Church as my wife. She quickly decided (whether any money passed I do not know) that her loyalty to a fellow member of the First Church of Christ Scientists of Boston, Massachusetts, easily outweighed her duty to the members of the Royal Thames Yacht Club who paid her salary and relied on her discretion. I could not at first understand why this telephonist, whom I recognised, was to be seen haunting Caroline Terrace and noting down the number of my Rolls Royce parked before the door of No. 10. Now I can almost hear the reader snorting, if not from indignation, at least from incredulity, that anyone in public life trying to get away with it to this extent should have been so casual in taking precautions. Why no other car (I could not afford one) or at least switched number plates? The answer must surely be that I did not care enough about the public life. The care of my future wife and child seemed at least as important to me at this time. Yet the election was approaching at the very moment when Carmen was nearing her confinement, and the conflicting pressures were enough to drive me mad. We dined alone at a restaurant in the King's Road on January 4th 1950, having made all arrangements with the good-looking gynaecologist (who fell at once in love with Carmen and, as I learnt later, urged her to elope with him to South Africa), and with a nursing home in Wilbraham Place. Carmen experienced periodical labour during dinner and I then drove her to Wilbraham Place and tottered back to bed at Caroline Terrace, where I was telephoned in the early hours of January 5th by the matron to say that Mrs. Appleton had been delivered of a fine baby boy.

There is no doubt that there is something about love-children which makes them particularly adored by their parents. To bring into the world a being from the union of yourselves in the teeth of all the conventions and obstacles placed in the way of such an event, seems to ensure a particularly close bond between parents and child. Although I am devoted to my children born after marriage I have the feeling that they are more armoured from birth and that those who have had to contend with the sort of problems Carmen and I experienced need and receive a special kind of loyalty and support from their parents, which may be denied to them by society.

To tackle a General Election on the morrow of becoming a father while leading a double life might be said to tax the stoutest nerves. Yet I was called upon to face this within a month because of the Dissolution of Parliament in January 1950. What I did not know was that my beloved wife, alerted by Mrs. Ellis and the telephonist at the Club, had now engaged private detectives to follow me throughout the election, so that when I staggered back to Caroline Terrace after an exhausting series of meetings north of the Park, my movements were duly noted down. How could my constituents, who were cheering their heads off throughout the election, fail to believe that I had gone through the whole performance with my tongue in my cheek, when Thelma immediately after my victory received the dossier built up by her sleuths and, enraged by the discovery that I had acquired another son, whammed in the divorce papers? So let me make this clear to those aggrieved Paddingtonians. I may have deceived them as to my private life (and which of them could afford to cast the first stone?) but on the charge of having been elected under false pretences knowing that I was going to be divorced as soon as it was over, I am wholly innocent. Can as much be said for the wife who, shortly after the election, told the Chairman of my Conservative Association on the platform at a large rally of our supporters, that she was about to divorce me, without telling me?

CHAPTER 18   *The 1950 Parliament*

In the General Election of February 1950 I was returned for South Paddington to Parliament with a majority of 6,810 votes.

It was, I gathered, a very different Parliament from the one that met in 1945, which I had missed. Then the Socialists were shouting "We are the masters now" and singing "The Red Flag". Aneurin Bevan had been graciously pleased to confide in the public that with so large a Socialist majority it had not been necessary to resort to revolutionary measures. They could afford to guide socialism through the parliamentary machine. Of the revolution there had been no doubt. Its impact had been severe enough to take the leading families out of politics for the duration of a parliament in order to sort out their own affairs. But the instinct of the nation had been sound. "One pace to the left, quick march." And stand at ease. Now it was "Attention" and soon to be "About turn, quick march."

But Tories were in full force – only six seats from a majority. As the votes were counted, during a feverish night and day, there was a moment when it looked like a Tory win – the moment in fact at lunch-time when the wireless announced the election of Somerset de Chair for South Paddington. We were then level-pegging. But as the afternoon wore on, the Socialist lead returned, and reached 6. Attlee emerged from a worried Cabinet at Downing Street and said, "We carry on."

The House was still sitting in the Lords' Chamber, while the Commons was rebuilding, after the blitz. I found a place on the second bench, behind the Shadow Cabinet, for I had last been sitting behind them on the P.P.S. bench, when Oliver Lyttelton was Minister of Production. Winston, looking moodily round the serried rows of his new supporters and those who had held the bridgehead for four years, said, "I am glad you are back, but you will find it difficult to catch up, with all this – "

The B.B.C. asked me at once to prepare a broadcast on the

forthcoming debate on Foreign Affairs, for German listeners in the Overseas Service. The issue had been sharpened down to German participation in Western Defence. Eden was very apprehensive of French reaction to this, but Winston had already spoken in favour of it. Patrick Buchan-Hepburn, the Chief Whip, unkindly nicknamed the ageing peacock, stopped me as we moved towards the Division Lobbies. "For goodness' sake have a talk to Anthony, before you deliver the broadcast."

I was not at all keen to do so, and seeing Churchill's stocky figure looming behind him, said, "I should prefer to discuss it with the leader of the party."

Patrick shrugged his shoulders in defeat, "Oh, very well."

Winston bent and cupped an ear, as I walked beside him and explained that I should like his advice on the text.

"I should like to see it now," he said. "Have you a copy?"

"I can fetch it. Where shall I send it to you?"

"I shall be on the bench after the division."

I collected the script after voting and joined the press of Tories, milling about the left hand side of the Speaker's Throne, and passing to and fro along the front bench; or going up to the nearest of the three bewigged clerks at the table to hand in questions. I found myself standing next to Walter Elliott, who was waiting for the Whips to appear and announce the result of the division.

"I want to get this to Winston," I said, feeling somewhat apprehensive at thus publicly approaching the Great Man.

"Did he ask for it?"

"Yes."

"Then go ahead. There he is."

Winston was sitting opposite the despatch box, in his black jacket, striped trousers and pearl-buttoned boots. He wore a bow tie, and his fists rested squarely on his parted knees, while he waited for the result of the division. Every division was an excitement then — as likely as not the government would be defeated. I trod on as few ministerial corns as possible, passing between the Shadow Cabinet and the clerk's table; and reached Winston, who looked up, beaming, took the buff envelope, and held it up, with a breezy, "O.K." which somewhat startled me. I then went on, down the green coconut matting, to the bar of the House, and found a seat on a big cross bench of padded red leather.

Next morning there was a message from his secretary. Mr.

Churchill wanted me to speak not of a German Army, but of a German Contribution. I agreed to the change and went off to Bush House, where a German Professor rehearsed me, and I was taken down to a recording studio and 'put it on wax' as they said there. Subsequently I listened to it going out. I had not done the translation, and my wife thought the phrases rather impressive 'uberschwemtwerden'. "But then," she said, "I have not had your opportunities for practising German."

This was a long way away from the happy days we had spent together in Vienna, studying the language under Frau Mitrofanof. There was an inescapable brittleness in our relations. She had taken a house in Halkin Place, overlooking Belgrave Square, and we had fought the election from there. But it was no permanent home. The editor of the *Tatler* rang me up, and said he understood that we were giving a party. I said, "I don't think I should call it a party. Just a few friends coming in for a drink. Do you mind my asking who told you?" He refused to be drawn.

"We should like to send a photographer. Do you mind?"

It was not long since the *Tatler* had devoted its front page to a picture of my wife and me with our two sons. All looked extremely savage and uncomfortable upon the bridge over the moat at Blickling. My Aunt Beatrix White was also in the photograph but, screened behind her dark glasses, appeared inscrutable. There had been a time when I had thought it would be rather gratifying to appear in the glossy magazines but I found that they left me cold and now did not think these pictures of a united family very timely.

"I will talk to Mrs. de Chair about it and let you know."

I could not imagine which of the guests would have done this, but there seemed no harm in letting a photographer in; and a certain amount of harm in refusing. I noticed, when the photographs appeared: 'A cocktail party in Halkin Place': that Lady Hammond-Graeme featured prominently in them. I had asked her because she had run a ball at the Dorchester for the National Appeal of the United Nations Association, of which I was chairman. This apparently much publicised cocktail party struck an incongruous note when a few weeks later the buzz went round that my wife was divorcing me. My constituency executive was particularly incensed. Had they not all appeared a month before on my platform? I felt completely overwhelmed. No doubt I had exposed myself to the procedure which my wife was now adopting – but if I had ever considered the prospect of a divorce seriously, it had been of a dignified parting at some remote and convenient date.

When she had said to me, only a few days before, "If we should get divorced, I should like to continue my work on the London County Council," I had replied, "Of course." It had never occurred to me that her membership of the L.C.C., which had been undertaken in the first instance with the object of strengthening my own parliamentary condidature for the same constituency, would prove the stumbling block to my continuing as the Member of Parliament for South Paddington. Nor that it could all happen on the very morrow of the election. Had she gone through the whole election with her tongue in her cheek? It seemed incredible. And when a man in a black suit, put his head incongruously down the hatch of my yacht and said, "My name is Tansy of Withers & Co. and I am representing your wife," I could scarcely believe my ears.

I said, "What is worrying you?" and hurriedly produced one of my future wife's friends, who was also on board and her 7-year-old daughter. But he was not satisfied and sat about all day, like a black crow, on a bollard at the end of the quay, to count and identify the party when we emerged from the yacht.

Whenever a realignment of interests and the play of passions has grown so strong, that divorce proceedings are started, there is, along with the violent shock caused to the divorced party, an inevitable sense of relief that an impossible situation is being brought thus abruptly to an end — and that everything can now be open as the day, where hitherto it had to be as obscure as the night. Along with this sense of relief, akin to the lancing of an abscess, came endless regrets and uncertainties at the dissolving of a long and largely happy association, stretching back to one's youth. The wife, in this case, had reached her decision on information laboriously secured, after prolonged and agonising deliberation. But when she acted, it was deliberately, having brought herself gradually to the decision. For me it was a violent blow; which gave me no time for reflection; and felled me, moreover, on the threshold of my resumed political career.

The members of the South Paddington Conservative Executive were not the sort of people who could afford to compromise with moral laxity. In vain the wife of the Chairman, Lady Marion Philipps, pleaded for time before the member so carefully chosen and so loudly hailed by them was thrown aside. She spoke with the robustness and length of view, which only twelve generations of public distinction can impart, and in Paddington her plea fell on deaf ears. Here people kept their ears so close to the ground that these were full of dirt and heard nothing. After I had addressed them, telling them exactly what had happened and not, in my innocence, aware that truth can be a very strong drug, which should only be administered in small doses, the answer was prompt. "Announce that you will not stand again; or we will announce that we are choosing a new candidate." When I suggested that it might be better for me to apply for the Chiltern Hundreds at once and leave them to fight a bye-election, they threw up their hands in horror. No, I must do my duty, for which I had been elected — but only for as long as it suited them. Thus pressed, harassed and hounded, I told *The Times* Lobby Correspondent, Mason, that I would not be standing at the next election.

Having only just got me back into the House, my friends were aghast. I could never survive a second set-back like this. Alan Lennox-Boyd, pleaded with me to let him see my wife and urge her, at least to agree to a three year separation. But I felt that matters had gone so far that it was best to let the Gordian Knot be cut.

Winston beckoned me over in the Smoking Room.

"Why are you giving up your seat?" he asked.

"Well, you know," I said, "divorce."

"What is the charge, adultery?" his voice boomed.

"Yes," I answered him.

"Are you going to marry the other party?"

"Yes."

"Is she a Conservative?"

"Yes."

"Well, you should not have given up your seat. The beloved member can usually get away with it in his own constituency. He makes the speeches. He answers the letters. But when he comes to try for a seat somewhere else. Ah," he waved his cigar deprecatingly, "then they are looking for somebody without any handicap. Why did you not come and consult me before giving up your seat?"

"I scarcely thought I could bother you about my own affairs."

"You should have done so."

"And there are other difficulties. My wife not merely represents the same seat on the L.C.C., she is a member of the executive committee in my constituency as of right, accordingly."

His aquamarine eyes bulged.

"You don't attend the local committee do you?"

"Not yet having reached the rarer altitude of your position, I do sometimes attend the local committee," I admitted.

It was, as I saw it, a complete stymie. But I felt somewhat deranged. My more phlegmatic friends like Bobby Perkins shrugged the matter off lightly. "Take a Parliament out," said Bobby, "that's all."

This was for me a very painful period. It was a fiercely balanced Parliament in which every man's vote was needed and demanded. To pass through the lobbies, twelve or fourteen times in a night during the passage of the finance bill under the scrutiny of hundreds of eyes, whose curiosity was clearly awakened by one's predicament, was an uncomfortable ordeal. There were speeches to be made; and at the darkest moment of all, I was called in a debate on Foreign Affairs, immediately after Ernest Bevin, the Foreign Secretary. This was an opportunity for the performance of a lifetime, and I simply had not the sparkle, vivacity, and energy of mind to rise to the occasion. There were audible groans from the members of my own side waiting to catch the Speaker's eye themselves. I spoke of the difficulty of restoring British prestige in the East and supported Bevin in his recognition of the Communist Government of China. More groans from my own benches. I was glad to sit down; and turned increasingly in this Parliament to the central correspondence column of *The Times*, as my chosen platform for expressing my views on the topics of the hour. These were usually carefully planned and written missives.

I wrote a long letter on the Schuman Plan to which I was heartily opposed, as was *The Times*. I received a message from the Editor. He would very much like to print it, but in its present form it would take up more than the whole column. Could I cut it to three-quarters of a column? I did.

*   *   *

In the literary field, the success of *Napoleon's Memoirs* had naturally led me to apply the same technique to *Caesar's Commentaries*, and this new book I wished to dedicate to Churchill.

218

"I should like to see the proofs first," he said. And these, in due course, I sent him. He took a lively interest in the book. I came into contact with Churchill much more in the 1950 Parliament than before, because of his interest in this edition of Caesar. He beckoned me out of the Chamber as he was leaving the Front Bench after some exchanges on the Egyptian situation and we passed through the swing doors into the Noe Lobby.

"I have been reading your book with pleasure and profit," he told me "and I am proud to accept your dedication. I am deeply impressed by what I have read so far. It will certainly be a great achievement if you can rescue Caesar from the classroom where he languished for so long."

Winston drew himself up to the fullest extent as if he were conscious of the dictator's competition.

"I do not think, however, that I should write a Foreword to the book as people might think that we had been arranging an exchange of compliments, but that will not prevent me sending you a note on the subject which you could use later on when the book comes out. I have been looking up what I wrote about these matters in my *History of the English Speaking Peoples* which I hope to publish one day if I live long enough, and I see that I agree with what you say about our man Casabianca (Cassivelaunus). Justice has by no means been done to him yet."

Of the Golden Cockerel Press, he said, "They certainly produce a very beautiful edition and the proofs are wonderfully got up." Winston stopped half-way down the lobby and confronting me said: "There are one or two words which I thought could be improved. There was one place, for example, where I thought the word 'repulsed' would be better rendered by 'overcome'."

"I wish in that case you would be kind enough to let me know them," I suggested, "so that I can have them incorporated."

"Certainly," he replied, "I will let you know; I will send you back the proofs but I should like to have them back myself so that I can have them bound up for my collection."

Author's Note:
I made a point after my talks with Churchill of writing them down straight away — either in memos, if they were short exchanges, or in letters to my father if there were more to report. I felt that everything Churchill said and in the circumstances in which he said it, would be of growing interest as the years went by.

I explained that I would of course, in any case, be sending him a copy of the limited edition when it came out but he appeared to attach importance to the corrected proofs.

The conversation was resumed in the Smoking Room.

"I am going to send you my manuscript of the *History of the English Speaking Peoples* but I am having a little difficulty because I believe it is the only copy I possess."

I expressed some alarm at receiving his only copy of the *History of the English Speaking Peoples*. "It would be like looking after the Magna Carta," I said.

"The book," he explained, "begins from the earliest time — from the dawn of history. Do you know that England was joined to the Continent then? Two thousand years after the great Pyramid was built, you could drive a wagon from England to France. Of course, the cliffs of Dover were always there but once the waters broke through the isthmus, it wore away very quickly and cut the Channel deep. I sent the Chapter on the Middle Ages once to a Medieval expert who said that it was the first time he had ever understood the Wars of the Roses. I am not very happy over the part about the Tudors; Henry VII, Henry VIII and Queen Elizabeth. If I live long enough I intend to light up the Tudors a bit but the war between the Cavaliers and Roundheads is all right; then, of course, when I get on to Marlborough and his times, I am on familiar ground. I am satisfied with the period about Napoleon too."

"This must," I observed, "be a monumental work. What is its length?"

"A million words," he said sombrely.

This led him to his *War Memoirs*. "I have just sent off the fifth volume today." He turned to attract the attention of a passing waiter and had to bellow, "Waiter!" to attract the man's attention. "A whisky and soda," he ordered. Then he ordered one for Norman Hulbert, myself and Hugh Molson. Hugh said he had to leave but accepted Winston's cigar ash on his tea plate and remained in order to hear his account of the *History of the English Speaking Peoples*.

A discussion between Winston and myself on the Gallic Wars followed and I referred to Labienus having gone over to Caesar. I pronounced it in the modern style. Winston said, "I call him Labieenus."

"That," said Hugh, "is the difference between the generations," indicating Winston and myself with either hand.

We then passed to the subject of the Crusades. Winston said he had seen a film of the Third Crusade at Chartwell, with a floozie in the middle of the film as Berengaria. "In the film," he said, "she was married at Acre instead of Cyprus."

Not to be outdone, I told Winston the story of how Richard Coeur de Lion and Berengaria came to be married in Cyprus, how they were proceeding across the Mediterranean in separate ships to satisfy propriety, when the convoy in which Berengaria was sailing was smitten by a violent storm and 120 of the ships sunk; how her ship put into the harbour of Limasol where she was badly received by the ruler of the island Isaac Commenus, and had to return to her ship. Richard, when he arrived, was so incensed that he landed his army, conquered the island and was married on the spot to Berengaria whom he crowned Queen of England and Cyprus.

I leant across the table to Winston. "It was on this occasion that Richard Coeur de Lion spoke the only English words which were ever recorded. Speaking of Isaac Commenus, he said, "Ha, de debil he speke like a fole Breton" (he speaks like a fool from Brittanny).

In the meantime, Winston was getting the drinks. "If I put up one finger, I get one whisky and soda; if I put up two fingers," (he made the 'V' sign) "I get two whiskies and soda; if I put up three fingers, I get three whiskies and soda." And although it was somewhat early in the afternoon, I felt that I could not resist the opportunity of receiving a drink from the successor to Cassivelaunus and Oliver Cromwell, so I accepted the offer.

I listened to what he had to say about his *Memoirs*.

"What is the title of the volume you have just sent off today?" I asked.

"I do not know yet," he replied, "I thought of 'Closing the Ring'."

"What about the 'Twilight of Hitler', the Götterdämmerung motive, you know; the twilight of the Gods? He was very keen on the Wagnarian motive."

"I think 'Closing the Ring' is better. It explains exactly what was happening." But he seemed a little unhappy about it.

"The 'Hinge of Fate' I thought perfect," he went on.

"How many volumes will there be altogether?" I asked.

"Six," he said. "The last one I have called 'Triumph and Tragedy'. After our triumph, we got booted out — not," he added hurriedly, "that that was a tragedy, but we threw away our chances. I would have gone with Truman to meet Stalin in the front line when we had our troops there in Germany. All this withdrawal from Germany before the Russians . . . .

"I had never paid much attention to Truman before he became President, I would pass him and say: 'Good-day, Senator.' But Truman is all right. I am not saying anything against Truman."

I suggested that Truman must certainly have plenty of guts to have sacked MacArthur in all the circumstances.

"Oh, yes," said Winston, "he has guts." But I could see that Winston felt that after Roosevelt, Truman lacked what Napoleon called the sacred spark.

Sir Ralph Glyn happened to pass and Winston caught hold of him to ask why he had voted against the party over the issue of the American Admiral and Glyn explained that it was because he did not approve of Winston's idea of an American Commander in the Mediterranean in view of our commitments in the Middle East. Somebody else referred to Mountbatten being in the House during Bevan's speech.

"I thought he would get the Mediterranean Command but I don't think he will now," said Winston. He had made the case for a British Admiral in the Atlantic and an American Admiral in the Mediterranean. He thought the Government had been wrong to pay any attention to their present Chiefs of Staff.

"Slessor takes Bevan in to White's Club when he might have left that to somebody else. They are all eager to please the Socialist administrators. Fraser is past it: I know Fraser, I like him: he is a goose but an amiable goose."

I recalled the fact that I had run into Glyn coming out of the film of *Captain Hornblower*. Actually, Glyn had said to Carmen and myself on that occasion that in spite of the film, he felt that we ought not to vote against the American Admiral in the Atlantic.

Winston said, "I remember when I was crossing the Atlantic during the war, I read a copy of Hornblower which Oliver Lyttelton had given me. I enjoyed it immensely and I sent a cable 'Tell Oliver Hornblower Lovely'. The Egyptians picked this up and said, 'What is this Hornblower Lovely? — This must be a new code word!' "

222

The conversation ranged over very wide topics, as it does in the Smoking Room and I asked him if he thought that the danger of war had receded in view of the preparations being made under the Atlantic Pact.

"No, I don't," he said, "you have got to look at it from the other fellow's point of view. You say, in these affairs, the first year doesn't matter so much, but the second year — Ah, it is getting more difficult. The finest Russian troops," he said, "are the political troops, they are the troops who correspond to you in the Life Guards and the Blues. I inspected them at Yalta — very smart, very spick and span. When I inspect a unit, I always look at each man carefully and try to look him between the eyes. Some people pass down a line of men talking to somebody on their right," — Winston turned his head over his shoulder — "that is very wrong. Apparently, my attention to them created a very great effect, so I was told afterwards."

"What do the political troops correspond to?" I asked. "The S.S. under the Nazis?"

"No, the Swiss Guard," Winston replied.

Of course, there was talk about Bevan's speech to which we had just listened.

"I admire the way he speaks without a note," Winston conceded. "If I had to begin my political life all over again, I should never have more than three or four points on the back of an envelope. Arthur Balfour would never have more than three or four points jotted down and perhaps a sub-heading or two, to answer a whole debate: but he always paused for the right word" — here Winston imitated A.J.B. gazing heavenward for inspiration — "and the whole House would be on tenterhooks trying to help him get it, and sighing with relief when he got it. I think a fully rounded and impromptu sentence is the best. My best phrases have often been impromptu."

Hugh Molson suggested that when Winston had referred to Bevan as a squalid scoundrel, or words to that effect, the word 'squalid' had been used after careful thought.

"Yes, it was," said Winston, "I will not deny it: I will not take it back."

I asked him if he thought an election imminent now.

"Yes, I do and, *entre nous*, I am not going to America now for the Pennsylvania speech. In any case it would be difficult for me now while this controversy with MacArthur is going on." He waved his hand with the cigar in it from side to side, which seemed to drop ash on both parties in America: and sipped his whisky and soda.

On the subject of some recent resignations from the Socialist Cabinet he said, "You will remember what the people of Paris used to say when the leaders of the Revolution were changed. 'They're turning over the dung-heap again'."

When we were talking about the naval battle in the Hornblower film, (which Winston said he was having sent down to Chartwell that weekend,) I commented on the amount of stuff falling on the deck from above; masts, spars, rigging and sails, which was very convincingly portrayed in the film.

"Yes," he said, "it makes you think when you consider Nelson walking up and down his deck with all his gold braid and epaulettes on, being shot at every time. This island was not built on milksops." He spat the last word and his face became suffused with colour.

"Has a film ever been made of Caesar?" Winston asked. I said I thought not.

"Well," he said, "if you and I get thrown out of office, we had better think about making one!"

The Chief Whip, Buchan-Hepburn came along to discuss some points with him. Winston made room for him to pull up a chair. "Come and beat your old father about," he said, and they fell to discussing technicalities.

Then Walter Monckton's name appeared on the ticker-tape, which showed that he had risen to make his maiden speech and we all got up to go along to hear it. As we moved off, Winston laid a hand on my arm and said, "I want to have a talk with you some-time," and after Monckton's speech, he beamed at me benevolently as he walked out of the Chamber again.

I had a certain amount of correspondence with Churchill at this time when I sent him the proofs of the Commentaries and he replied from Chartwell.

I am reading them as fast as I can in these difficult times. I am deeply impressed by what I have read so far. It would be a great achievement to rescue Caesar from the class-room. I am much honoured by your dedication.

As he had asked about a handy life of Caesar and I had recommended Buchan's, I sent him my own copy of Buchan's but he had already contacted Mr. Wilson of Bumpus, the high priest of the book trade, and wrote accordingly:

> I have already got hold of CAESAR, so I return your copy to you herewith. I look forward to reading Napoleon, which from a quick glance, looks most interesting.
> I so much enjoyed your masterly JULIUS CAESAR.

I was startled by the detailed interest he was taking in Caesar; it was as if he had always focused Napoleon, but had come late in life to an intimate acquaintance with Caesar. He had clearly read the proofs very thoroughly, for he wrote again:

> As I have spent so much of my life reading proofs I cannot help marking points as they occur to me. I send you a few suggestions on your account of JULIUS CAESAR. It is beautifully printed. May I keep the proof sheets you have sent me?

Among other suggestions he referred to the introduction:

> I do not like the last four lines, particularly the use of the word 'bounder' . . Napoleon was not an aristocrat but a country gentleman. Have we not seen the charming little house in Corsica which belonged to his family? He was certainly never a bounder, nor did he ever become an aristocrat; he became a sovereign. These four lines would harm the whole introduction.

Referring to 'the immortal gods' on page 23 he asked:

> Are you sure 'immortal' is in the original? It is not necessary to the sentence nowadays — rather a cliché.

I explained that Caesar had used the phrase Deos Immortales . . 'I presume', I wrote in reply, 'that we must allow Caesar his own clichés.' But I compromised on Napoleon's boundarism after recounting Winston's objections to Oliver Lyttelton at the round table over luncheon in the Members' Dining Room. "I had intended," I explained, "to say that Caesar was an aristocrat turned bounder; Napoleon a bounder turned aristocrat."

"The great figures of history, my dear Somerset," laughed Oliver, "are finding it increasingly difficult to fit themselves into your epigrams."

Shortly after this Churchill stopped me in the lobby of the House.

"You should certainly take out the word bounder. You cannot call Napoleon a bounder." Winston, surrounded by members of his Shadow Cabinet, paused and confronted me, raising his hand, rather like a policeman on point duty: "The great night of time descends," (his hand fell slowly like a curtain) "but the glow of the emperor's personality remains. And those who were his friends are gilded by it and those who were his foes are clouded." His aquamarine eyes glittered as he spoke; and he looked intently into my eyes. "You could certainly alter that. You can lift out the introduction without altering the rest."

I told him; "The publishers are quite willing to re-set the pages for your sake, but they are damned if they will do it for me. So they want me to acknowledge the fact that you have read the proofs. They are naturally tickled by that. And want me to say that I have incorporated your suggestions."

"You are welcome to do that. They are not much. But you certainly ought to alter perseverance."

"It shall be done," I said.

He began to move on.

"It is a great work. But you can't call him a bounder."

"No," I said, "I see it in a different light since getting your letter. That is why I am anxious to change it. Thank you Mr. Churchill."

He passed on, rounding a corner with a muttered, "My Napoleon phase is over, but there are all his admirers . . . . "

Another day he made a place for me to sit beside him in the Aye Lobby while we were waiting to vote; and I thanked him for his proof suggestions.

"Were they all right?" he asked. "I sent them to you; not the publishers."

"I am in something of a difficulty," I explained, "as you have kept my copy of the page proofs and the only other set is with the printers in Edinburgh: but they have a reader who is a classical scholar, and he is very helpful."

Winston seemed somewhat dissatisfied with this and I did, in fact, check all his points myself later and write to him on the controversial ones. In the meantime, I told him I was cutting out the reference to Napoleon as a bounder. "I do not know if you got my letter about it?"

"I am sure you are right," he said. "I still say that he was a country gentleman — his mother? — "

" — was a Ramolino," I pointed out.

"Yes, well, she was all right. Napoleon may have been a violent man. You might say he was a murderer — "

"The Duc d'Enghien?"

"Yes."

"Maybe. But he worried about having him killed till the end of his life. I always think that is what distinguishes Napoleon from Hitler with his mass murders."

Winston shrugged his massive shoulders, "Ah, when you go into the wholesale business!"

We got up and moved towards the green turnstiles, where he pointed to his name and said, "Churchill," as if the clerk did not know.

When I could get away from the House, I spent most of my time aboard the yacht, and visited the quiet ruins of Netley Abbey near by. I found a conscious peace and consolation in this deserted spot, where the monks had passed their lives in seclusion so many centuries ago. The stone walls of the refectory rose out of the grass in drowsy sunshine. Here and there an archway or the remnants of stone windows, showed the shape of the former abbey, once so full of life; of choristers; and the singing of matins. Now the butterflies settled in the hot sunshine on the cistern heads, and an occasional tourist peered at inscriptions under glass. This is what it all came down to in time. Why fret? The Commons House of Parliament could get on very well without me — and one day there would be grass on its floor, and butterflies settling on the exposed foundations. Perhaps the walls, which I had helped to redesign, would still stand up, with the blue sky showing through the bleak stone window frames. And young tourists from Nigeria and Central Africa would peer at inscriptions under glass. 'Here Winston Churchill stood' (where the dandelions are gold in the sun) 'to make his famous speech upon The Battle of Britain.'

I stayed twice during this summer at Sutton, with the Sutherlands; who had, perhaps, more sympathy with my predicament than some.

Sutton* is the English country house with a vengeance. Built by Sir Richard Weston, whose son was beheaded with Ann Boleyn, Hollywood could do no better, if indeed as well, and if I were to describe a Whitsun weekend there in the middle of the twentieth century, few social historians of the future, I feel certain, would believe a word of it. They would have to accept the private polo ground, completed in 1950 at a cost of £90,000, for there was a spectacular opening tournament between various county polo teams, much photographed at the time. This ground, which resembles so much a medieval jousting ground, surrounded by green trees and bounded by the meandering stream of the Wey, makes a pleasant place for a canter. I was taken for a ride round it by the Duchess: and as we cantered polo ponies round the ground, she asked me a number of questions. There are not many country places in England today where you can stroll out into the stable yard and find two grooms holding the bridles of horses when you have the whim to go for a ride. I had not brought any breeches with me and had to borrow Bill Ednam's jodhpurs. The last time I had seen him was in a punt on the Thames, at Boveney with Tommy and Elizabeth Clyde who rented the adjoining cottage to me at Boveney, while Tommy and I were stationed at Windsor at the beginning of the Second World War. Bill was now married to a very charming Argentine bride who was a student of Napoleon. When I arrived for the first time at Sutton, some of the house party were playing Canasta at two tables in the hall. This is the central part of the house, and the hall occupies its whole height. The Duchess got up to greet me with the unexpected comment: "I don't know why we have asked you to stay," and proceeded to introduce me to the guests. Clare Sutherland's sister, Vera, was more tactful and said that they were all drawing lots to sit next to me as she had heard (obviously from Lady Ednam) that I had written a wonderful book on Napoleon. The book actually had been written by Napoleon which accounts for its excellence, but as I had edited it, I accepted the tribute without a blush. Very good looking these two sisters with their pert, retroussé noses.

*Sutton Place near Guildford, subsequently bought from the Duke of Sutherland by Jean Paul Getty.

When the word went round next day that Vera was in the swimming pool, there was a marked drift in that direction to inspect some of the additional surfaces thus exposed.

We sat down 24 to dinner each side of a long oak refectory table; and were waited on by at least four men — a major-domo in a blue suit; a mere butler, and two footmen, though not in livery — that went out, I think about the time I was leaving Oxford in 1932. Certainly there were footmen in livery then and probably in many houses up till 1939; but I have not seen one since the war.

The card tables were set up in the drawing-room, a pleasant apartment done up and furnished in Clare's impeccable taste. There was a large picture in the hall painted by Romney of the Leveson-Gower children, dancing a ring-a-roses, with the Muse of Poetry in attendance. On a previous occasion when I had organised a National rally of the United Nations Association at Sutton addressed by Anthony Eden, the Duke had drawn my attention to this picture. He had been offered £120,000 for it.*

What was so unusual about Sutton was the combination of such wealth in the 1950s with a family of ancient lineage and a historic home. Clare was wearing the famous Sutherland diamonds — a necklace of stones which had belonged to Marie Antoinette. The second row had been converted into clip, brooches and bracelet which were subsequently stolen by a thief who got into a cottage on the estate where the Sutherlands were living during the winter, and removed the baubles from her dressing-table while they were playing Canasta downstairs. Fortunately, the necklace was in situ — round the owner's neck. So only the made-up pieces were lost. Even those were valued for insurance at a conservative estimate around £60,000. It would, I reflected, take a long time for any Chancellor of the Exchequer to knock out a family with these reserves.

Meanwhile, they entertained in a way which enabled one to reconstruct the life of the Edwardian era perfectly, with a dash of dry Martini and a dip in the swimming pool added. Towels and bathing costumes for all were ready in the rustic pavilion beside the pool, and under a trellised shelter, cocktails were prepared.

After a game of tennis on the hard court inside a veritable hangar with a glass roof, a dip in the pool was very welcome.

*It was eventually sold in the 1970s for £160,000

Towards lunch-time on Sunday a number of visitors began to arrive, headed by the Duke of Alba, not long previously Spanish Ambassador to the Court of St. James. Lord Barnby, sunbathing in a pair of bathing shorts, arose with dignity and greeted the ex-Ambassador with a becoming bow of his somewhat stringy polo-playing frame. Alba was accompanied by his daughter and son-in-law, the Duke and Duchess of Montoros. Their wedding had been from all accounts, a sensational event in Spain and I was surprised to find them such an unassuming couple. I sat next to her at lunch and questioned her about Franco's regime. She gave me very interesting replies but she was more interested in her little son, aged 18 months, left behind in Spain. She was a true Spanish mother. With Alba, I discussed a picture belonging to me of Philip IV at the age of 18 in black and gold armour. I wondered if it would have been by Pantoja, but he said that the date 1628 would not have fitted. The Spaniards returned to London after lunch. The numbers at nearly every meal were bewildering – twenty was not unusual. At dinner, I sat on the Duchess of Sutherland's left and she said, when the silver-gilt plates were set down, and I examined mine with some curiosity, "Do you always wave your plate about like that? You really are a barbarian. I don't know why I thought you attractive. You ought to cut your eyebrows."

Her sister, Vera, was very sympathetic. I was passing through the uncomfortable domestic crisis of the divorce and had just been asked by a troubled Executive Committee not to contest my seat in Parliament again. Vera was happily unaware of this and thinking that some sort of distraction would be good for me, such as big-game hunting, said brightly: "Why don't you go into Parliament?" In all the circumstances, this advice to a harassed M.P. took a lot of beating but so charming was she, that it was impossible to do anything but agree.

I have perhaps been guilty here of confusing or telescoping two different weekends but the impression was one of ceaseless entertainment, in the most luxurious surroundings.

I also spent some time alone at Blickling; where my Aunt Beatrix White* came to help me entertain a few friends. She had

---

*Mrs. Geoffrey White. She was my father's sister, and previously married to a Mr. Studley. Her only son Derek Studley-Herbert was married to Lady Seafield and lived in Banffshire at this time.

a robust idea of family loyalty. For her, blood was infinitely thicker than water. She would ring me up in London where I was living amid the painters and builders at 92 Eaton Place, which I was handing over completely, under various legal arrangements, to Thelma.

"I want you to dine with me at the Berkeley, darling," Beatrix said one day.

I took her there, and she began to choke on the vol-au-vent. She went very red and gasped for air and retired to the ladies cloakroom. Bernard and Barbara Rickatson-Hatt happened to come in for dinner at another table; and I urged Barbara to go to my aunt's rescue. She emerged with her presently, none the better. "Brandy," gasped Beatrix. It arrived in a large balloon glass, but its fierceness, at other times no doubt welcome, only made her choke the more.

She managed to whisper, "Ring up Geoffrey."

I went to the telephone box; and spoke to her husband.

"My God," he said, "she is always choking. She has a small epiglottis."

"Well, she wants you here."

Geoffrey arrived, more Edwardian than ever, with pockets seemingly all over his neat jacket; and the brim of his Homberg hat curled very tightly up. He sat himself down beside her, with his hat on his knees and said, "Can't you get it down, old thing?"

She looked daggers at him out of a very red face.

"Doctor," she coughed.

Geoffrey and I went to the telephone. He cut a very distinguished figure with his slightly wavy silver hair neatly brushed, his grey moustache, and monocle.

"Mrs. White is choking at the Berkeley," he told the general practitioner over the telephone.

"Take her to St. George's Hospital," was the advice.

We returned and told her. The Chairman of the South Paddington Conservative Association, sitting with some young friend at an adjoining table, gazed on the scene with self-conscious amusement.

"You must come to the St. George's Hospital," Geoffrey said.

Beatrix got up, clutching her glass of brandy.

"You can't take that away with you," he said.

She nodded vigorously, holding her throat. "Yes I can. The

head waiter says I can bring the glass back tomorrow."

Geoffrey looked heavenwards and went out into the night. I got them into my car and to the St. George's Hospital. Beatrix in her long evening dress ascended the steps of the Welfare State majestically, still clasping the balloon glass, in which the amber brandy lurched precariously. The out-patients seated on a bench, looked up incredulously. I found a doctor and explained the intricacies of the situation. He took Beatrix behind a screen from which amazing sounds emerged, as he pressed an electric lamp down her throat.

"Don't you bother to wait," Geoffrey said.

I said 'good-night'; but waited outside in the car to give them a lift back to their flat in Park Street. The electric light had done the trick, pushing the Berkeley vol-au-vent down into the dark. It was an uncomfortable ending to our evening out; but if Beatrix had wanted to demonstrate publicly her solidarity with her nephew she could not have done it more thoroughly. As usual, I was left to pay the bill.

It was a relief when the summer session of Parliament came to an end; and I made preparations to put to sea.

I was travelling one day by train to Southampton, when I found a colleague of mine from the House of Commons on the seat opposite. We got into conversation, more about architecture than politics, for his own home had been built long ago by the same architect or master builder who had designed the one I lived in. I had recently come across the accounts of the building and thought these might interest him. But while I talked, thus, of Jacobean brickwork, my attention was occupied with another occupant of the railway carriage. In the corner seat, looking out of the window with a remote expression, was one of the most beautiful women I had ever seen. She was fair haired and her short nose and clear grey eyes were very perfect. She wore a dove-grey travelling suit, and neat high-heeled shoes. In my somewhat unstable frame of mind, I felt that any man worth his salt ought to follow her, if need be, to the ends of the earth, and I was beginning to wonder what I should do if she did not also alight at Southampton. In the meantime, I gave up the desultory conversation on domestic architecture; and took what opportunities I could from the protective screen of the *Evening Standard*, of studying this flawless goddess. I had not been so impressed since I had met Hedy Lamarr in Vienna when she was 27. There were other people in the carriage also. Three a side. My colleague in the House had now relapsed, himself, behind the pages of a magazine; and quite frankly, I regretted his presence, which would, I felt, embarrass me in making the acquaintance of the girl in the corner. As we neared Southampton, I felt the opportunity of doing so rapidly diminishing; and if I was not already head over heels in love with this strange beauty, I was very near it. No word had been spoken by her throughout the journey; but some preserving instinct now made me lean forward and say to my colleague, "You don't by any chance happen to know who the woman in the corner is?"

"Oh? My wife? Haven't you met?" He performed the introduction and she gave me a cursory smile; acknowledged the introduction and resumed her contemplation of the passing countryside. I got out at Southampton without further hesitation.

"Do you live near here?" she asked, as I got my bag down off the rack.

"No. But I have a yacht in the Hamble River."

I had never seen her before but, as so often happens it seemed as if I could never enter the House of Commons after that without being aware of her. But I could do nothing whatever about it — except to admire her excellent taste in clothes. I heard of her, from time to time, flitting down the Rue de la Paix. She would come into the Central Lobby of the House, wearing a hat on the side of her head like a sky-blue sponge; or sit patiently up in the gallery, in that exacting Parliament, waiting to drive her husband home; and looking down, a little bored and wan, upon the Commons, from the shade of a wide brimmed straw hat, edged with midnight blue. Or I would pass her, again with a slight bow, which she may or may not have acknowledged, as she sat on one of the side benches against the stone outside the Members' Lobby, pulling on her dark blue leather gloves and smoothing down her dark blue dress. It was no Parliament for so beautiful a young woman to have a husband locked up in. Ascot week went by with many a sigh while there were votes to be taken. Once I spoke to her as she was sweeping down Westminster Hall on her husband's arm, wearing an apricot dust coat and cap to match. The dust coat trailed out behind her above the great square flagstones, so far below the mighty rafters. Here Charles I had been condemned to death and Warren Hastings had stood his trial. And like a wraith too, she was gone.

I was also able to pursue my hobby of visiting interesting houses; and had even begun, during the long all night sittings in the last Parliament, to write a book on the way they were surviving the social revolution. It was to be called 'How are the Mighty Fallen on their Feet'. Some owners were more co-operative than others. Lord Salisbury was very co-operative and I was anxious to include a study of his home in Dorset, Cranborne Manor.

I saw it first on a day in July; and came upon it about four o'clock in the afternoon. Cranborne seemed to me almost unreal. It is hidden from the village, from which it is approached by a simple wooden gate and a short drive which meets a grassed avenue from the south, at the entrance to the forecourt. Two charming summer houses, topped by low pyramid roofs of russet tiles, guard an arch all overgrown with roses, and this simple entrance, like the gateway to a forbidden city in China, makes the house beyond seem more aloof.

The old brick walls inside the courtyard were ablaze with white roses in full bloom. Here all is trim and tended by gardeners with white moustaches. Through a small arched gateway in a corner of the hall near the house one caught a glimpse of tidy lawns and long herbaceous borders, bursting with ordered colour. It is Sunday afternoon and a great stillness hangs over the place; as if it were enchanted. The central front of the house is very old; with arrow slits in a buttress, all part of King John's hunting lodge. But a porch of crumbling stone, three arches of Renaissance design, has been added in 1612 or thereabouts.

When I rang the doorbell, a pleasant caretaker appeared with his hand bandaged up, and it was immediately apparent that Lord Cranborne had forgotten, in spite of two reminders, to notify him of my arrival. He used his discretion, however, in the manner of good servants and admitted me to the house. He apologised for the delay in answering the bell, which had been due to the fact that he and his wife were using the vacuum cleaner on the Jacobean stairs. The good lady peered sceptically at us through blue-tinted spectacles, and went off to the kitchen in the basement to prepare some tea for us under the porch.

Tea was soon produced by the kindly housekeeper and we sat in the pleasant heat of an English summer afternoon under the front porch where wicker chairs and a garden table are kept for such a purpose; and drank deeply of the scene before us. A friendly white bull terrier came across and begged for the cakes and biscuits which my wife promptly surrendered to it. Above and beyond the archway, rose the grassed avenue, with its towering beeches. The avenue was more suggestive than anything here of the past, vanishing out of sight in the direction of Cranborne Chase. So easily peopled with men riding; hooded falcons on their wrists; King John.

Meanwhile, the rear wheel of the car began to subside in front of our eyes. Perhaps the heat had been too much for it on the long run from Cornwall. Why not? The one on the other side had subsided after the long run down to Cornwall. In any other setting, after a similar experience, this would have seemed insupportable. But not here. Nothing could disturb the serenity of this English garden; not even the gentle, expiring sigh of a new Dunlop tyre. Being a motor car of elaborate design the interior hydraulic jacking system never worked; and an alternative jack borrowed from the local garage in Norfolk seemed equally unmanageable. The caretaker and I fiddled with it unsuccessfully; and he went in search of the chauffeur, while we finished our tea. The chauffeur spun into the courtyard on a bicycle bearing a jack from Lord Salisbury's car. He was a gaunt fellow, who seemed, I may be wrong, to belong to the old coaching days. There was a touch of the ostler about him; but he knew all about motor cars and was happy to lift this particular one off the ground; while I photographed the house.

The beech trees shaded the croquet lawns; and rounding the north-west corner of the house, I came upon a lower garden where a broad grass path led from some imposing wrought iron gates to the famous Renaissance north portico with its fantastic masks. For one shattering moment, it seemed to me that these were life-like representations of Lord Woolton at different stages of his career — the small one at the near end, on taking his seat in the House of Lords; the others of him as Minister of Food, Minister of Recon- struction and as Chairman of the Conservative Party. There was one in the middle which could easily have been done from the life at the Llandudno Conference. It was a relief, upon more sober reflection, to realise that these had all been carved in the seventeenth century. A wicker *chaise-longue* was made up as a bed under the porch and it was evident that somebody had been sleeping there al fresco. Looking past the array of faces on the portico, I was confronted by the church tower, rising behind the garden wall; and these roaring ribald masks, bellowing at the old church tower, seemed to emphasise in a curious way, the juxtaposition of Church and State in our affairs. Just why the squire should still have the patronage of the living in so many parishes, is a little difficult to understand.

The inside of the house had almost as much charm as the outside. In the hall is the hunting saddle used by Queen Elizabeth, padded in green cloth and providing a pair of unequal horns at the saddle bow through which the Queen could crook her leg. Perhaps it was upon this very saddle that she harangued her troops at Tilbury before the Armada; at least she must have galloped on it across Cranborne Chase.

From the further end of the great hall, a doorway opens on to the foot of the Jacobean staircase with unusually slender balusters; the dark oak treads, rising to a half landing. Here a small boudoir leads to the drawing-room. On the window ledge of the boudoir quantities of rose petals were heaped on a sheet of newspaper, to be made into pot-pourri; and it seemed to me that in all my wanderings in country houses, nothing could have been more representative of the life of the English country house, than this unrehearsed preparation of fading rose petals, to store up the scent of summer in wide Chinese bowls during the dark winter which lies ahead. There were family photographs standing about.

I felt like an intruder but Robert had said to me; "You will have to wander about wherever you like as the caretaker is a new one who has only been there a short time." The bedrooms opened northwards off a long passage and were labelled, curiously, in Gothic script, possibly during some army occupation, as 'Queen Elizabeth's Room', 'King John's Room', etc. A large double room facing north and west was close carpeted in pale grey with a large double bed of attractive and unusually delicate brasswork. There was an ewer and basin in transparent glass, on the wash-stand; and a central heating radiator below the north window from which a bird's-eye view could be obtained of the sunken garden far below, with the broad grass walk, bordered with flowers leading up from the wrought iron gate. Beside the bed were Bibles and books of Common Prayer; as well as Searle's *Invasion of Russia in 1812*. The dressing-room, next door, had a four-poster with original Elizabethan hangings of pomegranates and other fruit embroidered on them. It confronted an alarming effigy in stripped wood, of a Pope's head and shoulders, with bony life-like hands, one of which was uplifted in an attitude of admonition. Robert Cranborne told me later that it had been acquired by some uncle of his during his travels in Italy, and installed in this position. Opening off the south side of the landing was a spiral stone staircase which interested me. These spiral stone staircases like one at Trerice are rare in Tudor houses because they were usually replaced altogether by wider and more graceful staircases, like the other one at Cranborne, in the Jacobean period.

There is a sublime sense of unostentatious waste, in a fine house, lovingly cared for, drowsing away in eternal sunshine, until the distant owner can come there to relax from his cares, and draw upon those hidden springs of tranquillity which lie in a secluded English house and garden. To the connoisseur of domestic architecture in search of perfection the Cecils might well reply, "You want the best houses. We have them."

All this summer there was a mounting crisis over the situation at Abadan. At a reception given by the Speaker in the autumn of 1950, just after Herbert Morrison had succeeded Bevin as Foreign Secretary, I said to him, "I hope you realise that the Persian Majlis is going to nationalise the oil industry."

"Oh, they wouldn't do a thing like that," said Morrison, looking jauntily out of his knave's eye, "and even if they did, we would demand compensation and it would be so much they could not afford to pay it."

Here was a man until now wholly preoccupied with the Festival of Britain on the South Bank. For him the Skylon was the limit. He spoke of the Persians as if he were dealing with the Southern Railway Company. I turned to Attlee and urged him to start moving warships and other evidence of determination into the Persian Gulf.

"The danger there," he said, "is that you may start a war with Russia." This was precisely the danger which haunted his government during the coming months.

I began asking Herbert Morrison very searching questions on the floor of the House about British rights in Abadan; and at first Morrison began replying with great courtesy.

"I am very grateful to the Hon. Member for drawing my attention to these matters." He had been warned, I imagine, that

I was supposed to know something about the Middle East. But after Dr. Mossadeq came to power and Dr. Makki began to exert the pressure which gradually ousted us from Abadan, Morrison's temper became visibly shorter. Hector McNeil stopped me and said one day, "You're going for the wrong man. Herbert's heart is in the right place. You should go and see him. He wanted to send the troops into Abadan; but we had to explain to him that it would look very bad at U.N.O."

It had, in fact, seemed at first as if Morrison's answers to me implied that he was prepared to use force if necessary to protect British property in the Persian Gulf; to keep the oil installations going. Then he restricted himself to protecting British lives, and after the violent riot in Khuzistan I suggested that the time had arrived to send the troops in. Abadan must, in my view, be held at all costs. British prestige throughout the Middle East would suffer an irritrievable blow if we ran; and the balance of power in the Persian Gulf be dangerously tipped in Russia's favour. He now began to get angry with me, saying that suggestions like mine were likely to do more harm than good. But although our own front bench were strangely silent, fearing the charge of warmongering when an election might be near, the Tory back benches were soon alight with indignation. In return Morrison accused us publicly of semi-hysteria. The public felt as we did. But with everything set to land troops at Abadan the fear of widening the conflict and bringing Russia in decided the Cabinet; and Britain humiliatingly withdrew. The Persians would not even allow the British gunboat alongside the jetty at Abadan to take off the departing technicians and their families. Promptly the Egyptians boarded the *Empire Rose* in the Gulf of Aquaba; and in heated exchanges across the House, I warned Morrison that he must expect such incidents to multiply throughout the Middle East since his deplorably weak handling of the Persian situation. Presently, King Abdullah of Jordan was murdered, the best friend of Britain in the Levant. And so it went on.

In the meantime I had begun, in public speeches, to urge the necessity for a Middle East Defence Organisation, comparable to N.A.T.O. under the United Nations Charter. *The Times* headed a short paragraph of my speech to the U.N.A. at Norwich 'MIDDLE EAST DEFENCE PACT SUGGESTED'. Then I wrote a letter to *The Times* on the subject, which they headed 'A MIDDLE EAST

DEFENCE PACT'. This was followed by a lively correspondence in which the positions of Greece and Turkey were prominently featured. The Turks especially were sore at their exclusion from the Atlantic community. So I tried to sum it all up in a letter to which *The Times* gave its leading position, 'THE DEFENCE OF THE MIDDLE EAST. NEED FOR AN AMERICAN GUARANTEE'.

The London *Evening News* carried a leading article on this letter, underlining the warning I had given. My letter was sent over by the American Embassy in London to the State Department, and had, I understand, some effect. The United States came round to the view it expressed, and within a remarkably short time the idea of setting up a Middle East Defence Organisation was adopted by the British and American Governments; while in the meantime Turkey and Greece were absorbed into the Atlantic Pact. I had never previously had such an immediate impact on policy, and was conscious in the discussions of the Conservative Party upstairs, that my views were being listened to for the first time and with a majority in support of them. It seemed particularly ironical that at any moment, when matters of so grave a nature were being weighed, I should have to quit the scene for reasons totally unconnected with world affairs.

When Parliament was about to rise early in August 1951 it was by no means certain whether I should ever address it again, and my new wife, Carmen, sitting in the gallery in the hope of hearing me speak on the Middle East, fainted. She was expecting a baby, and the Radio Doctor, Charles Hill, was quickly fetched by Colonel Wigg (a Socialist, opposed to me over Persia) and Carmen had her head thrust between her knees, to the astonishment of some passers-by who may have wondered why the Radio Doctor was practising ju-jitsu on this dark and beautiful young woman at the head of the Members' stairs.

We shook the dust of Westminster off our feet; and drove down to Touraine, where I was keen to show Carmen the château I had so much loved when I was a boy.

Antoine Menier's instructions were that we were to be shown Chenonçeaux 'from kitchens to attics' but it was clear that we would have to leave the kitchens and attics to a second day. There were some Gothic chests standing against the walls, which were hung with a set of almost priceless Gothic tapestries; all introduced by Hubert Menier's father. The lower part of the chapel opened out of this room, which had a fine over-mantel of the period. Between the buttress occupied by the chapel and the one containing the bathroom referred to above, was a little balcony. From here we could look down at the racing waters of the river, where fish played about in the clear depths. Hubert said, "During the First War, when I was a little boy, I had an uncle who used to pot the fish from here with a rifle when he was home on leave." Below the bathroom was a small alcove lined with silk embroideries done by Catherine de Medici with silk which she obtained from silkworms reared in the gardens by herself.

The two rooms on the other side of the entrance corridor looked west, downstream. In one of them was a much admired picture, though not perhaps of great artistic merit, by Van Loo of the three Mailly Nestle sisters, one of whom owned the château at the time of the French Revolution. They were the Comtesse de Mailly, the Comtesse de Vintimille, and the Duchesse de Châteauroux, and they were depicted without any noticeable adornments as the Three Graces. It would seem as if M. Van Loo must have had an enjoyable time working on these three very attractive subjects.

During the First World War, it had been a hospital, and during the second, it was only occupied by the Germans for two days, after which the troops were removed on orders from Hitler; who was sensitive to beautiful architecture when not actually having it bombed. The only damage done to Chenonçeaux had been caused by Allied shelling, during the liberation, when the house was regarded, with true Anglo-Saxon perception, as a bridge. Fortunately, the nearest shell exploded in the river, but it blew out all the chapel windows and damaged a large number of slates on the roof.

By this time, it seemed to me that the white moustache and shoulders of the elderly Regisseur M. Beaugais were drooping a bit, and Hubert invited us to come over to the home farm for a glass of wine. We accepted without undue demur. Getting into our cars, on the now happily deserted platform between the two drawbridges, we drove past the line of outbuildings, and on towards an enclosed space of farm buildings. There was no farmyard here, but a grassy area surrounded by pleasant white buildings, over which honeysuckle was growing, and inside which there were high, cool rooms for preparing or storing wine. In one of these, we found a tray of sandwiches and a bottle of Chenonçeaux wine on a table, before an empty hearth, and were received by a regal lady in a sweeping emerald green dust-coat who wore a neat straw hat shaped like an old-fashioned beehive. Not that there appeared to be anything old-fashioned about her. On the contrary, very Parisienne. She was Hubert's mother, Madame Georges Menier, widow of the late owner. She had just arrived in a fast American car from the Atlantic coast, and greeted us with aplomb, launching forth into reminiscences of her visits to English country houses in the past. She spoke affectionately of 'Sybil Rocksavage' at Houghton and seemed happily unaware that there was a new generation of that name. It was Madame Georges who had last used the bathroom above the alcove containing Marie de Medici's hand-woven silk tapestries.

It was Madame Georges who had run the house with charm and calm as a hospital; it was Madame Georges, with her light blue eyes and fair hair, who gossiped now on a sofa with Carmen, while Beaugais stood, drooping gradually towards a chair and explained with Hubert about the production of wine upon the estate. This bottle was of the most recent vintage. (We sampled some of the best a few days later at the cottage of M. Beaugais, when bidding him goodbye.)

I asked Madame Georges whether she would permit me to present her with a book of my poems, which I had brought in the car for some such purpose. She expressed approval and I dived down the steps, dodging under the honeysuckle and seized the book. In it I wrote 'For Madame Georges Menier, in honour of a poem in stone.'

"Where are my specs?" she said, hunting around for them. (A phrase she had picked up, she explained, from her English governess in youth.) Putting them on, she read my inscription and nodded towards the château. "That is already very eloquent. I shall enjoy reading them." I had some qualms afterwards as to whether, removed from the vicinity of the château, the phrase 'a poem in stone' would be thought to apply to Madame Georges.

It was very pleasant sitting there, with M. Beaugais (by now invited by Hubert to take a seat) and the head gardener's wife in a black dress, waiting on us; sipping the new Chenonçeaux wine in the coolness of the high room with the cretonne covered sofa and the wicker chairs; so close to the château which pays no rates (a concession in France to houses opened to the public). The bees hummed at the door in the honeysuckle, and as we left, with many invitations to Madame Georges to visit us in Norfolk, she plucked a spray of honeysuckle beside the door and presented it to my wife; possibly also with a view to keeping the doorway clear of the overhanging sprays. So we said goodbye on the rough grass where the car was parked, and where a few chickens scattered as we turned it about. Madame Georges in her swinging emerald dust-coat, with the rings of *entente cordiale* vintage glittering on her fingers, stood erect in the shady doorway beside the honey-suckle with its orange trumpets, under her beehive hat, and waved goodbye, for all the world like a sister of my Aunt Beatrix White; and calling up most powerfully that self-confident Edwardian cosmopolitan society, during which she had presided as chatelaine over the most beautiful house in Europe.

CHAPTER 20

As my mind goes back to August 1949 at Blickling, I am reminded of L. P. Hartley's book about a hot summer in Norfolk called *The Go-Between*. There is in the boy's recording of his visit to a Norfolk country house a recollection of cracked earth and the prickly sensation of having to wear tweed knickerbockers in the summer. Perhaps we did not have such a good summer in 1949, but the days spent with me at Blickling by my elder sons, Rodney and Peter before the divorce, commenced with a dry spell. The public tramped through the gardens and staterooms on Thursday and Sunday afternoons, so it was natural for us to invent some diversion that would keep us out of the house.

One of the sailing dinghies from the *Harebell* was being kept on the lake at Blickling for some reason. How it got transported there from the Hamble river, I cannot imagine — probably by rail for the very purpose of navigating the Bure. I know that I was painting a picture of the house from the east showing the formal gardens in front of the long side of the house with its gables and rose brick. A tremendous house in the grandest manner of the Jacobean period. It had been built by Lord Chief Justice Hobart, employing Robert Lyminge who had just completed Hatfield.

Beyond the house to the north-west, part of the lake was revealed and as I painted this in, the dinghy with Rodney aboard appeared under its little white sail. So I sketched it in; and that is how I remember particularly that the boat was there.

It may have been me, or Rodney just about to become a naval cadet, or Peter still at his preparatory school, who suggested that we try to take the boat from Blickling down the river to Wroxham Broad. For a summer diversion it was a capital idea, and we soon got the boat transported to the nearest point on the river. The Bure near Blickling is only a few feet wide and flows between water meadows, where Harold of England had once walked by the Beck Meadow as the Earl of East Anglia, and dreamt of kingly power. There are said by archaeologists to be the remains of his house under the turf.

Black and white cows came down to stand in the shallows, swishing their tails continuously to disturb the flies. The cows stared at us unbelievingly. The first stretch of the river brought us with leisurely stages to Horstead Mill, which I painted on another occasion.* It was a tall white wooden building, standing squarely across the river; and here, for the first time we realised that we were in for what Rodney called 'portages'.

Dragging a fourteen foot dinghy up the bank of a mill pond, across the grass and down a steep incline to the lower bank of the river beyond the mill, was more strenuous than I had anticipated. So we sat down on the grass and ate our picnic tea, while gazing at the reflection of the great mill in the still black waters in front of it.

At this time my first wife's resources and my own were not divided and we could be said to enjoy a comfortable existence. But in those days a head housemaid received only £1.50 per week; and a butler about £2.50. 30 years later wages had multiplied by 18 times, while food had risen by only 4 times; so naturally their standard of living had improved a lot.

The picnic tea had no doubt been prepared by Mrs. Pallister, the cook with the aid of the kitchen maid, and taken along the underground passage which led to the serving room and the dining-room, by old Sydney, who had been hall boy, odd-job man and under-butler at Blickling for the past forty-seven years. There it would have been handed over to Smith, my butler, valet and chauffeur. Smith was a slightly alarming man of steely-blue eyes, who had been chauffeur-valet to Victor Cazalet at Fairlawn for twenty-two years, and it was pretty generally accepted that P. G. Wodehouse who stayed there a lot, had derived the inspiration for Jeeves and the young master from watching Smith and Victor Cazalet in combination. Smith had accompanied us to the embankment in the car — a cumbrous Sedanca de Ville, Rolls of the Phantom III series. He had placed the picnic basket, with its neatly made up parcels in greaseproof paper and thermos flasks under the thwarts to keep them shaded and promised to collect us at the first night's halt — where the river passed under

*The picture now belongs to Rory

a certain bridge on the road, and there at the appointed time he was. We moored the boat securely to the buttresses under the bridge and drove back to the house, soon after the last member of the visiting public had left the gardens and the low iron gates at the beginning of the drive had been closed on them.

Thelma was not with us. Apart from the fact that she was attending a class of some kind in Boston, Massachucetts connected with the Christian Science Church to which, since meeting my mother seventeen years earlier, she had become such an ardent convert, she had by now obtained from Mrs. Pallister evidence for what we called in Parliament then, a prima-facie case for breach of privilege. I had a reputation- in the House of Commons for doing the right thing at the wrong time and I had only just been elected to represent South Paddington in February. It would have been more appropriate to have been living at Blickling during the ten years I represented S.W. Norfolk in Parliament; but unfortunately its owner, Philip Lothian wanted it himself then and it was not until he was appointed Ambassador to the U.S.A. in 1939 that he thought of leasing it to me. Adolf Hitler spoilt all that and it was not until after his death and the bequest of the five thousand acre estate to the National Trust that they offered it to me in 1947. By that time I had settled down at Chilham Castle in Kent and we had also acquired Trerice in Cornwall. It was not until August 1949 that I managed to dispose of Chilham to Lord Massarene (Jock Skeffington as he then was) and not until 1953 after my divorce that I was able to sell Trerice to the National Trust. So for a while with those three Stately Homes and an ocean-going yacht I felt somewhat stretched.

'Pas devant les enfants' would have been a good slogan for Thelma to adopt, if she could have kept it up. For the time being, having tapped my telephone extension and then got Mrs. Pallister to sit up all night in the attics over my room, she was what you might call building up her case. It was clearly the last summer holiday the boys could spend with me in ignorance of the break, but at this time they were probably quite unaware of any trouble. This is surely the tragedy of the twentieth century – the children no longer always come first. I think the undermining of the great fortunes by death duties and other insecurities had something to do with it. People in my parents' generation had a sense of obligation not only to their children, but to their estates and the continuity of their family settlements. All this had begun to disintegrate by the First World War. Now it was difficult for any couple who got on each other's nerves to see why they should not form new alliances elsewhere. These in turn lead to impossible pressures outside marriage. It was R. L. Stevenson (not Bernard Shaw) who first said that marriage must be something more than a friendship recognised by the police. It is certainly recognition by the police and all the established pillars of society which makes a remarriage desirable. My wise old father, the Admiral, came to see me at 92 Eaton Place during the divorce and begged me not to marry the other party — Carmen. "Do not tie the knot," he begged.

"I don't see how she could come and live at Blickling with me if not," I replied.

"No," he agreed, "she could not do that." So I got divorced and remarried from the *Harebell* on the enchanting island of Alderney, but that did not take place until the following August 1950. This month was given up to the boys and the navigation of the Bure. Naturally Carmen was not there at the same time.

Next day Smith returned us to the bridge and we resumed our rowing. There was scarcely room between the rushy banks to sail and in any case there was no breeze. 'Not so much breeze as on a summer's day robs not one light seed from the feathered grass.' We rowed in shirt sleeves, two of us taking turns at the oars, while the third held the arm of the tiller.

It was a white clinker-built boat, painted that summer, with a royal blue boot-top.

I asked Peter how soon he was going to Eton. He said, "Old Boyce is trying to gear me up for common entrance already. I am meant to start in the autumn half next year."

Ped, as we called him, was fair haired and had a very ruddy complexion at that time. His health was perfectly normal. In fact he was a very promising boy. Rodney, whose hair had been flaxen as a child, had gradually darkened to a brownish colour more like his mother. He was a neat, compact self-disciplined youth, well placed in the Navy. He took control of the navigation. I have a photograph taken on this summer cruise, of the two boys sitting in the stern of the dinghy, with the ends of bulrushes in their mouths like cigars. They are playing at being grown-ups — little knowing all the horrors and tragedy ahead. It would have been better perhaps, if that little craft could have sailed on through

Wroxham Broad, down the Bure to the open sea and on and on till we were overwhelmed by tempests and drowned out of hand, or one of us at least. But that is the way of life — we glide along by easy stages on the peaceful headwaters of some trickling stream and all is glossy and serene. The sun beats down as we refresh ourselves from bottles of lemonade, and there is no hint, no hint at all, of disaster. But Shakespeare has said all this better — 'Like wanton boys on bladders.'

Sometime in the afternoon we found ourselves passing the meadows below an interesting little Tudor house. This called for a break and some exploration. We tied up and walked across the stretch of long dried grass, burnt as yellow as corn, by the heat, to the old building. It was deserted. Yet it was of great interest. The brickwork was of that pleasing old two-inch thickness used for easy handling by the Tudors. The gables were triangular but had slender brick finials capped with crumbling stone. There were no curtains in the windows and the glass, glinting and black, revealed a blank interior. Some of the panes of glass were broken and the small garden was overgrown with weeds and old plants growing as high as a man against the walls, abandoned hollyhocks; sun flowers and delphiniums.

"It would make an attractive little house if restored," I suggested.

"Come the revolution," said Ped, "we could move into it from Blickling. It isn't far."

On our return we looked up the house in James Stratton's enormous leather-bound volumes of Tudor architecture. It was Little Hautbois Hall. Pronounced by the *cognoscenti* 'Little Hubbis'. This is one of the tricks of English parlance so dreaded by foreigners and arrivists. Not to know that a place is called Hubbis when it is spelt Hautbois dubs you as beyond the pale. Yet surely the French origin of this name, pronounced in the French way, would be a lot more agreeable, and romantic. Why not simply call it Tallboys (the name I gave to a family and a house in my novel *The Teetotalitarian State*)? At least we felt we had stumbled from the river bank on an exciting discovery which added something to the labours of the afternoon. By the time we reached the next change of level in the river it began to dawn on us that there could be any number of portages. In the end there were five before we debouched onto Wroxham Broad itself.

This and the surrounding six thousand acres belonged to a friend of mine, Betty Trafford, who was a woman of great wit, character and charm. She lived in the rather sprawling grandeur of Wroxham Hall, a Victorian house in yellow brick, which her son Edward, a ruthless landowner, as soon as he got possession, pulled down or converted for agricultural storage. He prevailed on his trustees to transform a small Georgian house on the shore of Wroxham Broad for his own use. This sort of crabwise move from the big house to a more manageable unit on the estate was going on all over England. We had seen the same thing at Welbeck.

The social revolution had moved a long way since the heyday of the Edwardian period, but as time passed it became apparent that the so-called ruling class were digging in along certain carefully prepared reserve positions. There might still be a Socialist Government, but its majority was reduced in 1950 to six and the Tories were in full cry. The tendency might be for the owners of big houses to cut them down to size (as at Bowwood); or move into smaller buildings as at Arundel, but the process was crystallising around a fairly gracious way of living. Most of the great houses now opened their doors to the public, and therefore, the outward difference between living in a house of our own and leasing one from the National Trust seemed almost academic.

Lord Lothian had himself been responsible for the system of preserving private country houses through the National Trust and had bequeathed Blickling with its estate and the wonderful contents, including the Gainsboroughs of his ancestors Lord and Lady Buckinghamshire; the Peter the Great tapestry given to Buckinghamshire when ambassador to St. Petersburg by Catherine the Great, and some wonderful furniture.

As I had already arranged a tenancy with Lord Lothian, the National Trust felt entitled to hand it all over to me at the same rent. The system worked very well for seven years, and it provided a partial answer to some of the problems created by the Revolution. In the first place death duties could never again be levied on the estate. The Trust agreed to maintain the gardens but began making obscure economies and adjustments which somewhat undermined the pleasure of living in a country house. They reduced the number of gardeners to six, pulling down all the hothouses, on the grounds that these would be too expensive to repair. The result was that although my lease provided that I could buy garden produce from them at wholesale rates, the more exotic fruits such as peaches and grapes were no longer brought in upon fig leaves, led by the gardeners, and had to be bought elsewhere. On one occasion when I was giving lunch to Lord Esher, who was treasurer of the Trust, I asked Sydney if the strawberries he was handing round came from the garden. He said that Willy, the head gardener had told him none were available, so these had come from the grocer in Aylsham. That night the grapevine reported that Mrs. Willy had bottled 20 lbs of strawberries for her own use. It was this sort of divided control which decided me in the end to move. I had no control over the gardens, and could not order the planting of a tulip or a rhododendron without a visit from Lord Rosse who was chairman of the Trust's Garden Committee. In short it was living in the grand manner by committee.

My friends, like Julian Amery, might call me the last of the grandees, but I was a constitutional grandee, if so, with no real authority, except inside the house. Even here there was a sort of condominium. The Trust did all the repairs and redecoration. After I left they had to pull the house apart as the structure had eroded over the centuries and with the help of various grants spent around £250,000 on repairs. For years it was cocooned in scaffolding. The Trust also contributed the wages of two indoor servants in consideration of the fact that they got the proceeds from the public showing. This was actually run by me and the money collected by my staff and handed over to the Trust, who entered it all in a balance sheet every six months. They also paid half the rates, and at first a quarter of the central heating. As this involved two and a half tons of anthracite stoked in an industrial hopper (and even then arrived cold at the drawing-room after going round such a large house) I persuaded the Trust to pay half. Even one and a quarter tons of anthracite a week is a lot. When I wanted some additional modernisation, such as a Trianco boiler for the domestic hot water or a water softener, the Trust would pay for those and charge me 10% interest on the installation.

The only serious bone of contention was over the continued sprawl of Nissen huts, left over from the R.A.F. occupation during the war. When I signed the lease and left on a lecture tour of the Far East to troops overseas in February 1948, these huts were empty and should have been pulled down overnight. But the Trust applied to the Ministry of Works to do the work and, in the interval of waiting, squatters moved in and were still hanging out their washing within view of some windows of the house when I left seven years later. A whole encampment of them in the park faced the eighteenth century orangery. I felt that had I been the owner when the Air Force left, the huts would have been removed and the situation never have arisen. The Trust tried in a feeble way over the years to get the huts vacated but even when some became empty and could be pulled down, the Trust could never prevail on the occupants, who were illegal squatters, to concentrate in one area.

I have mentioned all this because the National Trust system has replaced the direct landlord owner-occupier in a great many famous homes; and has proved a partial answer to the pressures of the time. Very few private owners could today face the burdens at Blickling unaided. Even inside the house with its 80 rooms, the cost of paying all the staff and household bills at this time (when Thelma abruptly withdrew her own contribution at a week's notice), in addition to the rent, rates, electricity and fuel which I had been doing, taxed my ingenuity a bit. No doubt Thelma in an aggrieved frame of mind hoped to pull the rug from under me; but I managed to stand firm. I had to let Smith go and rely on old Sydney as butler, with the head housemaid's brother, Leslie as his assistant in the dining-room. I remembered Lothian telling me that when he first arrived at Blickling (on a motor bike) to take over his inheritance and found Sydney stooping around with his long arms hanging down like a gorilla's, he decided that "it was no use trying to be pompous here." Mrs. Pallister, the sixty-year-old cook, inevitably departed with her dossier to cook for Thelma in London, and the kitchen maid took over as cook. The dusting and polishing of the house was done by Doris Skinner for whom with her husband I had had a house done up in the gabled wing of outhouses approaching the house. Her brother Leslie and his wife lived in the next one and assisted her. Doris's home was actually connected to the basement corridor near the pantry by an underground passage. There was an under-housemaid called Enid whose father was one of the estate builders, and she shared a room in the house with the young cook, in what had formerly been called the still-room. There was the usual quota of daily women to help with scrubbing floors, etc. Later on, after Carmen and I were married, there was a young nanny, who also had a bedroom on the ground floor next to the nurseries. Apart from the cooks who changed fairly often, this was the sort of set-up which enabled the house to survive into the second half of the twentieth century. One of the gardeners, Peart, came in every morning to empty the whisky decanter on the overnight tray in the Garden Room and provide suitable flower displays in the main living-rooms. In the lease the Trust had tried to stipulate that they would only provide flowers for the State rooms on the first floor open to the public, but I pointed out that nobody would agree to live in a country house without being able to draw on the garden for decorating the principal living-rooms. And they accepted this.

Perhaps these arrangements should have seemed adequate; but the desire to own a comparable home of one's own grew with the years. In spite of all the difficulties connected with my divorce at Chilham when Carmen had turned up to help me with the famous pageant there, I sometimes regretted having sold that spectacular abode. Yet in spite of its commanding position, overlooking the forest-crested Downs, it did not compare in perfection with Blickling. For me that was the Taj Mahal of England.

CHAPTER 21   *Winston Churchill*

Parliament reassembled only to be dissolved; and I felt somewhat
melancholy for the first time in fifteen years, to have no seat even
to contest at a General Election. I turned my mind to literature,
and Cass Canfield of Harpers, from New York, lunched with me
in London. I was trying to interest him in a popular edition of my
new translation of *Caesar's Commentaries*. But we talked mostly
of the election. I told him that I feared Attlee would try to revive
some of the prestige lost by the withdrawal from Abadan by
announcing that Britain had developed the atom bomb and was
about to explode it in the Australian desert.

"I hope you have warned Churchill about that," he exclaimed.

"I have not done so, but perhaps it would be a good idea," I
agreed.

Winston, it appeared, was convinced that we were without this
weapon and frequently took Attlee to task for his neglect. I had
watched the faces of Attlee, Shinwell and Morrison in response,
and was quite clear in my own mind, apart from reports in the
French and American press, that they must have developed the
weapon. I wrote to Churchill accordingly.

No reply of any kind was received to this, until he arrived at
10, Downing Street when my secretary received a quick apology
from his. Evidently they had discovered that the cupboard was not
as bare as they had supposed. The mystery was that £100,000,000
had been spent without Parliament knowing a thing about it.

The Golden Cockerel Press published *Caesar* just in time for
Christmas 1951, and sold the 25 guinea edition out almost overnight. I naturally sent Churchill one of this special edition, as
the book was dedicated to him and a wire arrived unexpectedly
from him on January 4th despatched on his way to America in
mid-Atlantic. This arrived simultaneously with the birth of a new
son, to my second wife, the dark-eyed Carmen, at Blickling. And
the woman gynaecologist, Dr. Townsley, lifting the receiver

251

beside the bed, as she thought there was some call for her, took down the telegram, which somewhat startled her in the midst of her preoccupations:

I AM MOST GRATEFUL TO YOU FOR THE SPLENDID COPY OF YOUR BOOK WHICH I SHALL ALWAYS TREASURE.

WINSTON.

I did not expect, however, to see much more of him now that I was out of Parliament and he had the added preoccupations of Prime Minister. I was somewhat startled, therefore, when the telephone bell rang at Blickling and I answered it myself. "This is Ten Downing Street." And then, "This is Mr. Churchill's Private Secretary. Mr. Churchill would like to have a talk with you some time. When would be most convenient?"

"Let us face it," I said, "I am doing nothing and Mr. Churchill is Prime Minister. Whenever suits him."

"He wondered whether you would care to lunch with him and Mrs. Churchill at 10 Downing Street instead of Chequers."

"Naturally," I said, "that would be very pleasant. Is my wife expected as well?"

I got into some difficulty over this, as Carmen was sure that the invitation had been to me alone. So I tried to ring 10 Downing Street back; but did not know the number; and was switched through to a department of the Home Office, who deal with the sort of cranks who say they are lunching with the Prime Minister and want to know if they should bring their wives. Fortunately the private secretary rang back shortly to say Carmen was expected.

It meant an early start.

In the hall we passed the Chancellor of the Exchequer, Rab Butler, somewhat startled, who turned to gauge Carmen, who was proceeding to the lift.

In the drawing-room of the flat (where last I had seen Mr. and Mrs. Attlee) we were greeted by Mrs. Churchill, radiant and young-looking in spite of her grey hair, and I introduced Carmen. She in turn introduced Mrs. Romily, a sister of Mrs. Churchill's and they asked where we were living. Astonished to hear that it was Blickling, of which Mrs. Churchill was aware, from Gilbert Russel's tenancy.

"Very uncomfortable then."

I explained that Lothian had done it up before the war with the help of his sister Minna and Nancy Astor. And all had gone into mothballs for the duration.

Winston came in wearing his short black coat, waistcoat and striped trousers, looking more youthful if anything than in the last Parliament. He was grumpy apart from smiles of greeting and slumped in his chair, brooding, I imagine, on the recent Cabinet. He was brought a tomato juice cocktail.

Carmen said later, "His eyes were almost touching the back of his head." But very soon the shutter lifted from his gaze and he looked out of his translucent aquamarine blue eyes alertly again.

"They live at Blickling," Mrs. Churchill told him, "a wonderful Elizabethan house."

"What Shire is that?" asked Winston, cupping his hand behind his right ear.

"Norfolk," I said.

We went along passages, green carpeted, and down an occasional step, to a small dining-room, and were seated, with Mrs. Churchill and myself on one side, the sister at the end, Winston facing me and Carmen next to him on his right, opposite Mrs. Churchill.

Going along the corridor Winston brought up the rear. I told him that I had seen Rab Butler departing.

"We have been left such a terrible legacy," Winston explained. "Higher bus fares and soon higher railway fares. By boards over whom we have no control."

"Can't you alter that?"

"Not in time to prevent this trouble."

At lunch the conversation was sustained pretty evenly. Winston was evidently in the mood to participate good-naturedly without monopolising. His pre-lunch deafness seemed to disappear miraculously.

Mrs. Romily asked me which three periods in history I thought the greatest. I said, "Pericles' Athens. Julius Caesar's Rome and — it's difficult with present company but — the Britain of 1940."

"How lovely," she and Mrs. Churchill exclaimed together.

But Winston said, "No. From Caesar you jump to Napoleon — there was the great figure." We began discussing the murder of the Duc d'Enghien again and he explained to his wife, who wanted to know why he murdered him, "He had him seized just over the border and shot."

"Was he court-martialled?" she asked.

"Yes. He was court-martialled during the night and shot."

"Why?"

"He was the head of a conspiracy for the Bourbons. He was a nephew, wasn't he, of Louis Seize?"

"Was he a young man?" asked Mrs. Churchill.

"Youngish, I think,"* I told her. "But Napoleon worried about having him shot till the end of his days. And there, I have always thought is the big difference between him and Hitler who, as you, Prime Minister, once said to me 'went in for the wholesale business'."

"Ah!" said Winston. "You cannot start talking about those two in the same breath. That drivelling Corporal."

"I tried to explain the difference in the introduction to *Napoleon's Memoirs* like this: 'What Napoleon Bonaparte failed to achieve Adolph Hitler need not have attempted.' "

Winston's eyes gleamed approvingly and he began explaining to Mrs. Churchill how I had put everything Napoleon had said together to read like an autobiography (which was not quite the case). Then he said, "He also wrote another book — about the war and the capture of Syria, that place, Palmyra."

"You were in the Guards Brigade?"

"Blues and Lifeguards. Really there were two books — *The Golden Carpet* about the capture of Baghdad and the other about Syria. You have them both; and I have a favour to ask of you Prime Minister. Wavell autographed my copy and I have always wanted to get your signature above his — so that we can get the chain of command."

"With pleasure," he said.

Mrs. Churchill had seen the Krak des Chevaliers and asked about Palmyra, but I had to explain that I was shot before I got there.

"You were wounded?"

"Yes."

Meanwhile there was champagne in the glasses and a salmon soufflé.

"Do we want mustard with this?" asked Winston stabbing at it.

"No!" cried his wife. "It's salmon."

*He was in fact 32

"Oh, I see." Then he asked how *Caesar* had sold. "I could not put it down. And a lovely edition. How much did you charge for the edition you sent me?"

"The edition you had was 25 guineas."

"And how many copies — five hundred?"

"No — only 75 and 250 at 12 guineas. The same book in a buckram binding. The 25-guinea edition is sold out. But of the others about half."

"It ought to appear in a more popular form."

I explained that I could not deal with another publisher till the private edition was sold out or after two years.

Winston asked how Napoleon had sold and I began to say, "Very well," thinking of the excellent reception by the critics and the fact that the limited edition had been over-subscribed and followed by the 2-guinea one. But I checked myself, realising that to a man who habitually sells 300,000 copies of each volume, my figures would seem trifling. "They sold about 1,500 copies of the cheap edition."

"That would only just about pay expenses," was Winston's shrewd comment.

"It was also published in America," I added lamely, hoping that the bigness of the American continent and people would cover my retreat.

"Are you a great Latin scholar?" he asked.

"No. But I had to study it at Oxford and I translated the First Crusade. Caesar's Latin is very easy."

"Latin is very easy?" he asked incredulously.

"No. Caesar's Latin."

"Oh, I see. But it is not a new translation."

"No," I explained. "It has been done over so often that you cannot screw much more out of the Latin. All you can do is to improve the English and remove the archaisms and change to the modern place names and use the first person."

"That is a stroke of genius," said Winston. "It brings the whole thing to life, and the use of the modern place names — " he explained to his wife — "he has used the names of places like Marseilles whenever a town still exists on the same spot, otherwise he has used the Latin."

Winston turned to Carmen, "Have you read these great books?"

She put her hand up in front of her face conspiratorially and said behind the back of it, "No!" with a laugh.

Winston said, on the subject of Latin scholarship, "Did you ever read what I said about learning Latin?"

"Yes," I said, delightedly, "mensa!" and thus encouraged, he told me how he had been asked to decline 'A table'.

Winston's eyes glanced at the small polished mahogany table around which the five of us were seated.

"I was asked how I would say 'O table' and I replied: 'But I would not say O table.' "

"Which book does that come in?" I asked.

"*My Early Life*," he replied.

"Have you thought yet of doing your memoirs — apart, I mean, from the bits that have come out?"

"No," he said, "but there are only a few gaps. There is the gap from about 1910 to the World War — the Liberal Government and all that. Then a few more years after the war. I don't intend to do anything about it."

(I returned to this subject after lunch, when he was reading me extracts from his *History of the English Speaking Peoples*. I felt it important to press him on this point. "Naturally," I said, "in editing *Caesar* and *Napoleon*, I have given a good deal of thought to the ingredients that go to make up personality, and in your case it is your conversation. There must be a great many of your contemporaries and of people much older than you alive now, who could remember what you have said. And the problem of your biography ought to be taken in hand now."

He brushed the idea aside, with what seemed almost unnatural gruffness, gesturing it away with the long, smouldering cigar between the fingers of his left hand, while the other hand held the proofs. "No. I have had more than my share."

I gave up the struggle with the comment, "Well, somebody will want to do something about it one day." I was thinking, of course, of the official biography — not of the numerous free-lance studies.*)

By now there was champagne in the glasses and the salmon balls, very soft, were followed by chicken and ginger pudding in glasses. Then brandy for Winston and myself. Towards the end of lunch, Winston leaned across and topped up my glass of brandy.

The whole episode seemed rather like the sort of thing you

*The task was eventually allotted to his son Randolph Churchill and after him to Dr. Martin Gilbert, who made a masterly job of it.

dream. A tiny table in a small room, with Carmen and Winston sitting side by side, and me and Mrs. Winston, no doubt looking equally incongruous to Carmen from the other side, while a sister of the great man's wife, of whom neither of us had ever heard, appeared between us, looking rather like her.

And surely the most remarkable thing about this man was that he appeared to be bathing mentally in the translucent depths of history; a little out of his depth over Athens – sunning himself in the glow of Caesar and Napoleon with apparently effortless concentration; while his several ministers who had just left the building were biting textiles or bricks and mortar over other lunches.

Eleven Conservative M.P.s from Lancashire had put down a motion, demanding the lifting of purchase tax on textiles as an emergency measure, and there was an outcry from the City about Excess Profits Levy, while the slashing of the food subsidies was stirring up the trade union movement. It was in the middle of all this stormy weather that Winston retired to the Dawn of History.

Then he began to expatiate on Caesar's character as it emerges from my book. "I was impressed by his great clemency. He ruled these tribes in Gaul – and they learnt to know his clemency. He treated rich and poor alike." Winston's eyes filled with tears as he spoke. "Then he went to Britain – but he did not get much out of that."

"I thought he conquered Britain," protested Mrs. Churchill.

"Oh no," exclaimed Winston and I together. "That is just the point," and Winston explained: "he did not get very far. He came twice and each time he had to go away again."

I told Mrs. Churchill how Cassivelaunas kept 4,000 charioteers in being to harass his advance. "He treated Caesar as Kutusov treated Napoleon."

And then we were back with Napoleon and Coulaincourt driving with him in a sledge across Europe.

"And he had to beat the news," Winston said, "or he would have had trouble. How long did these books take you?"

"Four years over *Caesar*, seven over *Napoleon*."

"Who was the young man at St. Helena who wrote about Napoleon?"

"Gourgaud."

"He admired Napoleon very much," Winston said, "and was

hurt by something Napoleon said. What was it Napoleon said? 'What more can I do for him? I can't sleep with him'."

I tried to explain how Napoleon dictated his memoirs to the different members of his staff: Gourgaud, Montholon, Bertrand, and Las Cases. How they brought out the bits in separate chunks.

"What are you working on now?" Winston asked.

"I have been trying to adapt the *Iliad* for the stage. And intend to put it on at Blickling for the Blind Institute."

"I find this very interesting," said Winston. "There is a great deal to be said for the Trojans. You ought to pursue the matter commercially as well. What about that young couple I like so much, who have been doing *Caesar and Cleopatra*?"

"Vivian Leigh and Laurence Olivier?"

"That's it."

"Well," I suggested, "next time you see them you might put in a good word for me and the *Iliad*."

"I don't think much of the T.V. and the cinema and the wireless," Winston dismissed them all with an expansive Victorian gesture, "but it is a great way of bringing these historical events to the people."

I suggested that history could always be vivid in its spectacular episodes. "Time makes very little difference — the great phases of history can be made to seem more recent than yesterday's newspaper."

I asked him, "Have you ever considered the possibility that the evolution of man reached its peak in the Renaissance — Leonardo, Michelangelo and Shakespeare — and that we are on the way back to the ape?"

"No, I don't think that. All that has happened is that more people have been invited to the table and therefore there is less opportunity for outstanding talent. The pyramid has been broadened at the base and flattened. But that does not mean that it is turned upside down. Now they have found other universes. Oh yes, others besides this."

"Inhabited by human beings?" asked Mrs. Churchill.

He smiled inscrutably as much as to say: 'Who knows?' and oscillated his champagne glass.

Now there was brandy and he began to light a cigar of enormous length.

"I have been made to reduce the number of my cigars," he

said, lighting it.

"But not the length," I observed.

Mrs. Romily helped him with a match.

"A thousand matches leap from their scabbards to light your cigars," she laughed.

"No, I have reduced the number and increased the length," he chuckled.

We discussed the invasion of Britain — and I made a case for the Dauphin's invasion.

"Do you mean?" exclaimed the sister, astonished, "that when we speak of nobody having set foot on English soil in a 1,000 years we are all wrong?"

"He ravaged Kent, Sussex and a large part of Middlesex."

"Do you hear that, Winston?" she appealed to him, and I repeated the claim.

"It came to nothing because King John died," I said. "The Barons had invited the Dauphin over to claim the throne, because they said King John was violating Magna Carta."

"There are friendly invasions which do not count, like 1688," Winston said, "where no blood was shed."

"I think some blood was shed all right by the Dauphin," I said. "However, perhaps you are right."

"You allow William the Conqueror as an invasion?" the sister said.

"Oh yes," I conceded, "I allow that."

"An invasion from Mars," said Winston, "that is the only thing that could unite this planet. It would even unite us and the Russians."

"Exactly," I chimed in. "Does not all history teach us that the enemy of today is the ally of tomorrow, and vice versa? We fought the French, then they fought with us. Now we have the Germans. The Russians were with us in the last war and now — it is so much of a pattern that one ought almost to work on it as a formula."

The last part I was saying to Mrs. R. — while Winston turned to my wife, Carmen, who though not ordinarily a feminist, deplored the failure of women to make use of their opportunities in Parliament.

"What have they produced?" she asked.

"I will stick to Priscilla,"* chuckled Winston.

*Lady Tweedsmuir

Mrs. Churchill thought of Madame Curie, "But," she said, "if you mention her to Lord Cherwell he foams at the mouth. He says that her husband invented it all and she was just clever enough to take it on. He admits that she was a good picker. First she picked the finest scientist of her day, Curie – then she picked the best of the next one, Juliot, for her daughter."

Carmen was protesting quite hotly that Madame Curie was clever enough after all and Winston was looking up sideways at her, studying her face and sizing her up.

"That angers you. I can see that it does," he teased her.

"There is a lot to be said for Cleopatra," I put in.

"Oh yes," he agreed with a chuckle, "there is a lot to be said for Cleopatra." And I elaborated.

"Of course we have Shaw and all that. But no one has done justice to Cleopatra in her villa on the other side of the Tiber during the last year of Caesar's dictatorship."

"Did she come to Rome?" asked Mrs. Churchill astonished.

"Oh yes. And she seems to have handled Caesar very well. She had a son of his."

"Caesarion," said Winston. "He died – where?"

"I can't remember."

On the subject of my choice of Pericles' Athens as a peak period Winston said, "I have never mastered that business – Athens in her glory." But of Caesar he said, "He led a dissolute life, and I mean dissolute in the extreme sense – somebody said of him 'husband to every woman and wife to every man', and then this greatness emerges at the end of it all."

"What age was he when he was murdered?" Mrs. Churchill asked.

"Fifty-seven or fifty-six according to dates," I said.

"The same age as Napoleon," Winston observed.

"Do you think it would have made any difference to his greatness if he had not been assassinated? If he had gone on?" Mrs. Churchill asked.

"Oh yes," I said. "It highlighted the whole of his achievement."

And Winston agreed saying: "If he had lived, he would merely have gone on administering." And this he said with resignation, as from one who has himself stood upon the summit of a mountain and hitched the knapsack higher on his back for the long climb home to base.

Winston asked Carmen what I did now and she told him of my painting. Mrs. Churchill underlined this for he did not seem to hear. "He paints as well."

I told him how I had been at the National Gallery in a canvas jacket copying the angel in Leonardo's Madonna of the Rocks.

And he leant forward eagerly. "Oh yes, I agree that there is a great deal to be learnt by copying."

Winston sat back, looking at me, with the expression of one who remembers an event long past and I guessed what was coming. He spoke to his wife. "When I was First Lord of the Admiralty his father was my Naval Secretary. That must have been in 1912 or 13. He came to me after Beatty."

"I thought it was 1911, the year I was born."

"No. It must have been 1913. Troubridge was there when I took over, and I brought in Beatty. I always like to tell this story. They told me of rear Admirals being appointed to this and that. And one of them would not accept a command in the Atlantic. 'We advise you to drop him' they said. Well, we knew all about the American wife with money. But I remembered a gunboat in the river at Omdurman firing a bottle of champagne from one of its guns. It fell into shallow water but I was able to retrieve it, and very glad I was of it. That was the last time I had seen David Beatty – and so I appointed him as my Naval Secretary."

I told him that my father was still keeping very well.

"Where is he now?"

"At the moment he is in Barbados."

Mrs. Churchill asked if he lived there permanently.

"No, he is staying with relations of my mother's."

"How old is your mother?"

"I really don't know. But I can tell you this. They were married in about 1902 when he was Naval Attaché in Washington. My mother came from South Africa, and he met her in Simonstown there. So she must have been a debutante about 1900."

I began to wonder if the lunch was going to finish without my hearing why Winston had sent for me. So I said: "How are you getting on with the *History of the English Speaking Peoples* which you told me about?"

"That is what I wanted to discuss with you after lunch."

I asked Winston if he had ever considered the flying saucers.

"I don't know what they are," he said.

I suggested that we had a good deal more evidence of the saucers than of the V.1's and V.2's in the war.

"We were very well informed about that — two years before," he said. "It's all in my book."

"I know," I said, "but most of it was from a single example smuggled out of Eastern Europe, wasn't it?"

"They fired one on some island in the Baltic."

This led to some talk of flying bombs — and it turned out that Winston's sister-in-law and I had both seen our first one near Godalming while Carmen described their appearance in South Kent. (She was driving a canteen wagon for the Y.M.C.A. then.) All this while Winston relapsed into thought.

Then I said, "Everybody missed the point about the new Elizabethan Age, when the new Queen came to the throne. Last time it was the surge across the Atlantic to the New World. This time, if she lasts for fifty years on the throne, it will be the break out into space, to the New Worlds."

"I wouldn't want to go," said Winston. "Blackpool and Brighton are far enough for me."

Carmen asked him if he was going abroad for a holiday, and he said, "I should very much like to go. And I could fix it, as the guest of some magazine. But there would be so many questions asked just now. I shall have to go to Chartwell."

When I opened the door for the women to leave, Mrs. Churchill said, "Would you like to go to Mars, then?"

"I think so," I replied.

When the women had risen and gone, Winston went to a door in the corner and said: "Norman, bring me that envelope which I left on the chair."

A young man came in with a large cream foolscap envelope full of stiff proof sheets, and these Winston laid on the dining-table before him.

I pulled my chair round and sat beside him.

"I thought it might interest you to look through the early part — especially the bit about Caesar. I worked on this in a great hurry for a year — I had undertaken a contract for Cassel and as I had been foolish enough to take the advance I had to deliver the manuscript. However, they seemed to like it."

"When was this? 1938 — 39?"

"Yes. Just before the war."

"But it never came out?"

"No. We came to the war. Then I had other things to think about. But I wrote it all myself. Of course, I got a good deal of help from people. It is about 800,000 words."

"How many volumes do you think it will take?"

"About the same as the present one."

He turned up the first page of the synopsis; and began to read, his dark horn-rimmed glasses firmly on his nose, in a voice which is familiar to millions, long extracts.

"Well," he said, reading from the top page of the proof. "This is the summary." The page was headed 'proofed out 28.3.52' (the luncheon was on the 8th of April). "Book 1. During the thousand years from the Roman Conquest, successive waves of invasion gave to the British Island a race and a general body of custom and fundamental law. There was a broad assertion of the rights of the individual, and of limits to the functions of the State or ruler. There were also established the moral conceptions of the Christian faith as enshrined in the Catholic Church. The whole body of moral, social, and political usages constitutes the root inheritance of the English Speaking Peoples, and is exemplified through all recurring courses of history, and find their most resolute and definite expression at the present today."

He turned over the page.

"What do you want me to do about it?" I asked.

"I thought you might care to read it. Especially the first part. When you have read it, come and see me again. Don't write. Scribble down what you like. But come and have a talk about it."

I confess that I felt a little bewildered by his attention to my opinion. All this seemed a very big hammer to crush and extract a very small nut, and Carmen afterwards described him as being 'up to something', looking at me, all through lunch, and sizing me up. What for? It seemed as if his eyes rested on me with particular speculation when he spoke of Caesar leading a life of absolute dissoluteness in his youth, and 'all this greatness emerges from it later.' Or it may have been that he was puzzled to find a politician whose mind, when focused on historical subjects, arrived independently at exactly the same conclusions. Where he described Cassivellaunus as a Fabius Cunctator, I had likened him to a Kutusov. No doubt I flattered myself — and assumed that he genuinely felt that I could help him with his history.

264

"Was all this written about 1938 then?" I asked.

"Yes, I dictated it all then. Of course I had a good deal of help. But it is all my own stuff."

As indeed it appeared, when he read it out. Every now and then I was sharply impressed with some phrase, as of Henry VIII: 'He was the expression and the hammer of all the social, political and religious forces which were breaking loose from the long restraint of the Middle Ages.'

And at the head of the summary of Book V. 'By the end of the reign of Queen Elizabeth England was mistress of her future.' And I said so. He paused at the section on spelling with special reference to Canute.

He now turned to Chapter I and began with its title 'Britannia'.

"In the summer of the Roman year 699, now described as the year 55 before the Birth of Christ, the Proconsul of Gaul, Caius Julius Caesar turned his gaze upon Britain." He read on, his large head, with a slight patch of excema or rubbed place on the side of the jaw. His skin was still smooth and unwrinkled, but not as pink as it was. Indeed it was pallid. On account of Court mourning he wore a black tie knotted and dependent, not a bow tie as usual. The voice read on. I was impressed by his insistent use of the word Britannia instead of Britain, as I had once advocated this in a speech in the House as a compendious simple name for the Commonwealth and Empire.

" . . . Refugees from momentarily conquered Gaul were welcomed and sheltered in Britannia." He turned the pages, looking for Cassivellaunus.

"Ah yes. But the British had found a leader in the Chief Cassivellaunus, who was a master of war under the prevailing conditions. Dismissing to their homes the mass of untrained foot soldiers and peasantry, he kept pace with the invaders' march by march with his chariots and horsemen . . . . "

On the next page he picked up the narrative again: "Little is known of Cassivellaunus, and we can only hope that later defenders of the island will be equally successful, and that their measures will be as well suited to the needs of the time."

"All this of course," I put in, "being written before the war?"

"Of course." And Winston went on: "The impression remains of a prudent and skilful chief, whose qualities and whose achievement, but for the fact that they were displayed in an outlandish theatre, might well have ranked with those of Fabius Maximus Cunctator.

"The afterglow of his fame was no doubt arrested by the tremendous civil wars which racked the Roman Empire amid which the obstinate Island of Britain was happily forgotten."

Next his eye lighted on Boadicea. "She owes her name," said Winston, "to a clerk's mistake. It was really Boudicca." And again he paused at the final subjugation of Britain.

"The decisive battle was named Mons Graupius, which many authorities identify with the pass of Killicrankie."

The next passage he read was of Roman civilisation of Britain.

But he explained to me, "The Romans contributed nothing new to the economy of Britain, like the Saxon plough."

"They must have had a plough of some sort," I said. "Because when they were digging up a Roman villa at Chester they found an anagram — it is rather a remarkable one, which reads exactly the same each way 'Arepo, the sower, guides the wheels in work'. Let me write it down."

I saw a pad of notepaper and pencil, laid on the further corner of the table beside a bell and a small box which contained toothpicks. (I knew, for I had opened it when trying to find him a match.)

After one or two shots to make the words come in the right places, not much assisted by the brandy, I got it right.

S	A	T	O	R
A	R	E	P	O
T	E	N	E	T
O	P	E	R	A
R	O	T	A	S

But he was obviously not much interested and was waiting for me to finish. He had found another good bit.

"Before the Roman system lay troubles immeasurable, squalor,

266
slaughter, chaos itself, and the long night of barbarism which was to fall upon the world.

"Nothing," he read on, "could stifle indefinitely the demand for equality, at least of status and of opportunity. The Christian ideas, subversive, Communist,* as we should now call them, frayed the fabric and fire of Roman society, while from outside the uncouth barbarians beat upon the barriers. Here on the mainland were savage, fighting animals woven together in a comradeship of arms, the best fighting men and their progeny being leaders. In the rough-and-tumble of these barbarian communities, with all their crimes and bestialities, there was a more active principle of life than in the majestic achievements of the Roman Empire. We see these forces swelling like a flood against all the threatened dykes of the Roman world, not only brimming at the lip of the dam." (How well Winston's voice, saying this, comes back to me.) "Cold steel and discipline and the slight capital surplus necessary to move and organise armies constituted the sole defences. If the superior nature of the legion failed, all fell. Certainly from the middle of the second century, all those disruptive forces were plainly manifest. However, in Roman Britain men thought for many generations that they had answered the riddle of the Sphinx. They misconceived the meaning of her smile." Winston concluded with a smile no less inscrutable.

"The next chapter," he said, "is called the Lost Island. But the Romans sent expeditions several times to help us." He went on turning back the long stiff proof sheets, which were loosely fastened by a green thread through holes in the top left-hand corner. He came to Chapter III and read with relish (and no wonder).

"A red sunset; a long night; a pale, misty dawn! But as the light grew it becomes apparent to remote posterity that everything was changed. Night had fallen on Britannia. Dawn arose on England, humble, poor, barbarous, degraded and divided, but alive. Britannia had been an active part of a world state; England was now once again a barbarian island. It had been Christian, now

*I subsequently wrote to Winston pointing out that, as leader of the Conservative Party, he might find his reference to the early Christian Church as Communist embarrassing, if quoted out of context; and he eliminated it from his published version.

it was heathen."

I had been leaning forward toward the paper, following the lines and I leant back, dazed.

"What do you expect me to add to that?" I exclaimed.

"Well, I thought you might like to look through it all."

Winston's eye lighted on a nautical fact and picked it out of the dying Roman Empire.

"Such a fleet, the Classis Britannica, had been maintained from the first century. Tiles with an Admiralty mark show that it had permanent stations at Dover and Lympne."

There was more to come. He was searching for the Vikings.

"Ah yes: The Soul of the Vikings lay in the long ship. They had evolved, and now, in the eighth and ninth centuries, carried to perfection a vessel which by its shallow draught could sail far up rivers, or anchor in innumerable creeks and bays, and which by its beautiful lines and suppleness of construction could ride out the fiercest storms of the Atlantic Ocean.

"We are singularly well-informed about these ships," Winston read on, adding first, "I went to have a look at one of them in a Museum when I was in Norway: Half a dozen have been dug up practically intact, the most famous was unearthed at Gokstad in Norway in 1880, from a Tumulus. It is complete in all respects, even to the cooking pots and draught boards of the sailors. This ship was of the medium size, eighty feet from stem to stern, seventeen feet beam, and drawing only four feet amidships. She was clinker-built of eight strakes of solid oak planks, fastened with tree-nails and iron bolts, caulked with cord of cow-hair plaited – and so on . . . . "

I noticed that nearly all of the passages which he read out to me were scored in the margin, as if by the base of a fountain pen, or gold pencil. I think they were prepared beforehand for easy selection. He was really trying them out on the dog.

He dwelt a good deal on Alfred the Great. Indeed it might almost have seemed that the whole reading was designed to lead up to him:

"It is the sublime power to rise above the whole force of circumstances, to remain unbiased by the extremes of victory or defeat, to persevere in the teeth of disaster, to greet returning fortune with a cool eye, to have faith in men after repeated betrayals that raises Alfred far above the turmoil of barbaric wars to his pinnacle of deathless glory. From his example may be drawn all the rules that a soldier or a statesman needs."

Winston paused where he had referred to Alfred's Book of Laws or Doom Book, and indicating the words said: "Alfred inverted the Golden Rule. Instead of saying 'Do unto others, what you would that they should do unto you' he said 'What you will that other men should not do to you, that you do not unto them.'

"He was a great man. He was the father of the English Navy," said Winston. "He did great things with ships. He built the first Dreadnought."

"He is the only English ruler to have been called the Great so far," I mused.

"Yes. That is so," Winston agreed, and found the passage he was looking for: "But his fame rests largely upon his creation of the British Fleet. He saw the vision of English sea power, and that to be safe in an island it was necessary to command the sea. He made great departures in ship design, and hoped to beat the Viking numbers by fewer ships of much larger size."

He picked up the second batch of proofs and glanced at the Chapter headings — The Wars of the Roses, The Tudors, The Civil War.

He swept the second part aside and handed me the first part from which he had been reading.

"Take it along with you, and come and see me when you have read it."

He got up and I followed him along to the drawing-room. As we went I told him how his telegram about *Caesar* had arrived simultaneously with the baby (Carlo), and somewhat unnerved the doctor.

"I am sorry if it caused any inconvenience," Winston said.

"On the contrary," I assured him, "I regard it as an auspicious omen. Perhaps he will enter Parliament one day."

In the drawing-room I found Carmen with Mrs. Churchill and the sister. We hastened to take our leave. It was after half-past three. Winston embraced the sister and shook us by the hand.

Mrs. Churchill came out into the corridor, where I had left my hat and umbrella, and Carmen her fur coat (it was a drizzly day) and I showed her the green leather edition of *The Golden Carpet*, which I suggested leaving with her to arrange for Winston's promised signature. She glanced at the title page and Wavell's signature.

"Why not get him to do it now?" she said and led us back into the room. Winston seated himself good-naturedly at a small desk, and I indicated the somewhat narrow position left by Wavell at the top of the page.

"I want to get the chain of command," I explained again.

Winston signed his name and, standing stiffly to attention with hands at his side (a legacy from his military days, I suppose) and leaning slightly forward with a benign if slightly puck-like smile, in a gesture of farewell, watched us depart.

Mrs. Churchill saw us to the lift and we descended to find the sister in the hall just leaving for Godalming in a blue limousine, with a chauffeur, summoned for her by Mrs. Churchill.

We got into our own car and drove off past the considerable throng in Downing Street, which gathered every day in the hope of seeing Winston emerge.

We stayed up in London to dine, with the Editor of the *Sunday Express*, then we motored back to Blickling.

It loomed up, like a fabulous fairy palace in the morning mist as we approached, and we were greeted by the dawn chorus of the birds.

CHAPTER 22

The Still Afternoon

At the famous cocktail party given by Sir Bernard Docker at The Royal Thames Yacht Club (designed as Lady Docker said, to float that building from Knightsbridge to Hyde Park Corner), I ran into Sir Alexander Korda. His eye alerted like that of an eagle which sees some unexpected quarry far below it. "Somerset de Chair," he said, "you have written a wonderful book about Caesar."

"The book was written by Caesar," I pointed out, "which may account for any excellence it possesses."

"Winston Churchill was telling me about it. He was immensely impressed by it. I should like to buy a copy."

"That will cost you twenty-five guineas," I said. He recoiled a step but said bravely, "Ask them to send it to me."

"Shall I have it sent to Claridges or the office?"

"The office. You know, I have always wanted to make a film about Caesar. Not the battles; but something intimate. Have you read Thornton Wilder's book, *The Ides of March*?"

"Certainly. It is admirable. You might try your film of Caesar in the last year of his life with Cleopatra established in a villa across the Tiber."

"I was going to make a film of Churchill's life," Korda said, "with Churchill acting in it himself. But his return to Downing Street has put an end to that."

Korda was one of the enigmas of the twentieth century. He lived permanently in a suite, consisting of a whole floor, of Claridges, the most expensive hotel in England. Whenever the film industry in general and his own company in particular was going on the rocks, there would be another dinner party and another million pounds would be raised.

I wondered if he wanted me to write a scenario of his life's dream of a film of Caesar. But I never heard any more of it.

This was for me an idle time, but the idleness was not of my choosing. Apart from these minor diversions, life passed happily enough at Blickling.

It was as if, in the early afternoon of my life, I was left to take a little enforced nap after luncheon. Upon the modest fortune secured from the sale of the Chilham Estate I was able to sustain the Norfolk house in its accustomed grace, punctiliously meeting my obligation to admit the public to the house on certain days and in other ways doing my best to fulfil the spirit of Lothian's bequest to use the house in the pursuit of cultural ends.

What we first see of it, as Mr. Christopher Hussey has written, satisfies the most romantic conception of an English country house. Suddenly it is there. A chord is struck in the peaceful sunshine: the eye looks between giant walls of clipped yew, down a vista of gabled outbuildings, towards the symmetry of the house. It is not symmetrical in detail but the effect is symmetrical. The whole wealth of detail in the stone figures above the gables, the cutting of the date 1620 under the string course, the old lead rainwater heads; the stone escutcheons on the porch, and the quaint old stone bulls roaring in silent defiance across the Norfolk landscape; all draw each other into a unit of perfect harmony. The façade of the house is flanked by slender towers of old rose brick and these are topped with graceful lead cupolas, mellowed to silver by three hundred winters.

It is upon the stonework of the gateway and the great window above it, where little birds are carved inconspicuously, and upon the quoin-stone edges of the towers that the weather has been kindest, creating a great variety of colours from grey to gold.

Not to be understood in an afternoon is the magic of the place. But magic there undoubtedly is; for all who approach it are aware of it. And those who have lived with it are the most conscious of it.

The buildings are of mellowed brick trimmed with weathered stone. Withal there is a brown aura; as of classic violins. Stradivarius could have worked there in one of the deserted rooms in the line of outbuildings from which now comes the strident screech of a peacock. There are four gables on each of these side wings, which enclose the forecourt; a triumph of graceful Dutch curves, surmounted by a broad triangular pediment, owing much to the new ideas imported by Inigo Jones about that time.

These outbuildings are joined in the corner turrets of the house by a low arcade of slender rounded arches. There are three

Dutch gables on the front façade of the house, and above the middle one a centre piece has been added to the house in the form of a tall three-tiered tower, higher than the flanking towers and from the top of which a bell chimes out the hours with a musical note upon the still air. It creates a momentary sense of surprise to discover that it is a later addition. But the clock bell in it has survived from earlier days, for around the rim of it is written in Latin: 'Sir John Hubbert caused me to be made — 1628'.

Well, there it is: The great house standing serenely beyond its lawns and brooding in the sunshine, with ancient yew hedges tended carefully.

The rainwater heads on the east front carry the date ANO 1620. This is also the date carried proudly over the main entrance gate, with its bull's head knocker. It was a time of peace and broad acres. The turbulent reign of the Tudors had been followed by the Union of Scotland and England under James I and the Civil War between Charles I and Cromwell was still a quarter of a century away. In Prague they might be throwing people out of windows in the opening phases of the Thirty Years War, but not in England. Here the wealthier of the Flemish weavers who came to East Anglia and who brought with them Dutch ideas of architecture, created an atmosphere in which a house could be built on the spacious lines of Blickling.

To build him his new house, Sir Henry Hobart chose a master builder of genius — Robert Lyminge, or Leminge, who had just completed the building of Hatfield House for the Earl of Salisbury. At Hatfield the design is more cumbersome and sprawling.

The difficulty with houses of this kind is that most people inevitably see them with a crowd swarming through the staterooms and milling about the gardens. There have to be pillared ropes to prevent thousands of people a year treading down the carpets or fingering the curtains. All this creates a museum atmosphere even in the most lived-in houses. To savour their charm, one must imagine them on the still days — during the breathless early mornings of summer. A cyclist on his way to work whirrs past the gates. The clock up in the tower chimes seven: the old butler who has worked in the house for over forty years, comes out of his cottage behind the stables, passes through an arch in the yew hedge and crosses over to the arcade where the western tower joins the house to the outbuildings in which the head housemaid, the chauffeur and the head gardener have their houses, much modernised; where the gables are dated 1624 and the old kitchen and the laundry used to be. The butler disappears through the arch on his way round to the stewards' room door which gives him access to the pantry.

Somebody is crossing in the opposite direction to unlatch the door of the peacocks' house in the east line of outbuildings, and after a startled honk or two, the sapphire neck and crest of the male bird pops out, looks cautiously this way and that, then sweeping his long green tail with dazzling medallions of blue and gold, begins to run towards the empty moat. Into this he dives with a flouncing of wings and scampers across the grass at the bottom of it, under one of the arches of the drawbridge and then begins to slow up in a sunny corner. Presently, the hen bird emerges and stalks more sedately to join him. She flops down also, a little heavily for she will soon be laying her four eggs.

Gardeners are moving across the façade of the house; carrying their brooms or going in search of implements in the tool sheds. The days of enormous retinues of servants are gone but thanks to the ingenuity of Lord Lothian who was responsible for the National Trust scheme of preserving the Stately Homes of England as homes rather than museums, by admitting the public to them at stated times and relieving the Trust of Death Duties and income tax, an adequate staff of gardeners is maintained. In 1953 a staff of seven indoor servants and seven gardeners kept the place inside and out in a condition which awed the crowds who paid to see it. This system was a partial answer to the new social revolution. It proved that people could live in ample surroundings under conditions of high taxation without departing from the standard set by such a place; and the occupant of the house could gaze out upon gardens as far as the eye could reach in any direction. For these had been skilfully laid out to give broad and soothing vistas. If, over the centuries, the more rowdy forms of revolution should occur and the rabble were to charge up the drive with clenched fists, shouting, "A bas les riches," there was the perfect answer. "Why hurry? It belongs to you. Go round to the north-east turret door; pay 1/-, wipe your feet — and then only on Thursday and Sunday afternoons in the summer from 2 till 5."

Such a compromise with the spirit of the age had an element

of genius. If the aristocrats in France at the time of the French Revolution had been able to say as much to the Sansculottes who rushed to their front doors much inconvenience to both parties might have been avoided. And so the house stands there still, defying the corrosion of time and manners; indeed the brickwork a little better pointed than before, the roof more securely laid. In April the first camellias, red and pink come into bloom. In May a giant rhododendron bush near the orangery bursts into flame, followed soon by the beds of azaleas, which border the long walk up to an eighteenth century summer house. As the weeks go by, fire seems to creep along the edges of the lawns, so rich is the colour of the azaleas. There are cool avenues of stately oaks, and at the end of each, one graceful stone urn. It is all very soothing. In June and July the great arrangements of herbaceous flower beds at the four corners of the main lawn, before the eastern façade of the house, begin to rise into fountains of colour. This side of the house is very pleasing, when the sun throws deep shadows from the line of tall bays which stand out along it under five curved gables tipped with little stone statues. There is the glimpse of a cedar tree over the brown roof tiles: and away to the north sweeps the placid lake, beside which rises a tall group of beech trees.

To appreciate the peace and dignity of Blickling one should go up into the attics and gaze down from what seems a great height upon the gardens in summer. From these gable windows, the garden takes on the appearance of a glorious carpet with symmetrical patterns. Climb out upon the leads above the Peter the Great room on a hot summer's day. There is a bees' nest under it and the bees fly in and out, as they have done thoughout living memory. Here one can examine the stone balustrade, already covered with golden lichen, which was inserted in the eighteenth century alterations. Up here you are far from the world. A gardener far below buzzes along on the seat of a motor mower, getting the tennis court ready. Another gardener is crossing into the dining-room turret door with an armful of almond blossoms to prepare the flower decorations inside the house. From the roof the lake lies serene and open, and swans can be seen nesting in the bulrushes by the lawn. Out on the blue water two new arrivals, a pair of black and white Canada geese cruise about uneasily, not sure of their reception by the English swans; and honk stridently. But very magnificent and welcome they are. Just occasionally, a kingfisher appears near the lake; but you must watch by the water's edge for that.

In this still afternoon of life at Blickling I took to oil painting. For practice I obtained a permit from the National Gallery to copy the head of the angel in Leonardo's Madonna of the Rocks, and in a plum coloured fisherman's canvas jacket (bought in Yport on the Breton Coast) and with my easel erected on Friday mornings, I spent the three months which followed my departure from Parliament in November, 1951, painting the angel's head, while amused crowds surged around me, like a stream dividing at some unexpected boulder. "Thou shalt not put a blue line round thy mother," said one earnest young woman to a crowd of students, and I, having just begun to outline the angel's head in that particular colour on the panel which I had primed with white about the area of the face, felt needlessly embarrassed. When this picture was completed there were not lacking neighbours in Norfolk who wanted to look like angels; and some of these I tried to paint.

I spent seven years at Blickling, all needed to lay the ghost of its perfection; which would otherwise have haunted me. By 1955, when my lease was breakable, I could contemplate moving to a house of my own; and, leaving my elder sons to make their home at Blickling, bought St. Osyth's Priory in Essex, a congeries of ancient monuments of the thirteenth, fifteenth, sixteenth and eighteenth centuries.

My edition of *Caesar's Commentaries* was too expensive for general release, but *The Times Literary Supplement* gave it the dignity of a full Editorial Article, under the heading of 'The First European'. Caesar, they felt did not respond to this unveiling process with the same alacrity as did Napoleon Bonaparte. But they were grateful for the shift of focus. And the review, a very witty one,* went on to discuss the extraordinary gulf between the legend of Caesar, the immaculate god, and the realities of his rumbustious career in one of the toughest societies of all times.

'The legend of this god-like creature became also the legend of a being untouched by human passion, remote, four square, unstained, invincible. This would have greatly surprised his intimates.

*By the Rt. Hon. Walter Elliot, M.P.

'The real Cleopatra, after all, had an early, an intimate and lasting acquaintance with the facts of life. As for Caesar, sex no doubt, was not his main interest; but he was not called the husband of all wives and the wife of all husbands, for nothing. Yet in Shaw's play Caesar and Cleopatra live under the same roof for months on end, without a line, without a situation which could bring the curve of interrogation to the eyebrow of the mildest governess. One is left with the impression that Caesarion, the baby, must have been some foundling by the bulrushes, brought to Cleopatra as a pet, probably by the stork.' And so on.

These weighty and serious reviews of my work were a great consolation for the missing years, cut out of my life by bullet and knife. I remember, when the Commons were sitting in Church House, staggering into the tea room, after the shattering news that the Army Medical Board had finally graded me Category E and thrown me out of the army altogether – at the very pith and moment of the war before D-day; threw me, I felt, on to the scrap heap like so much discarded junk. I sat down heavily at a table with Walter Elliott and Megan Lloyd George, who were sympathetic. Walter consoled me: "Never mind. That phase is over. That target is down. The sights are down. Another target goes up. Bang at the bull's-eye." All of life is a competition in some uncomfortable rifle butt or other; and whatever it is, there is satisfaction and even excitement to be gained by hitting the bull's-eye. In some shooting ranges this rings the bell as well. And so it does in life. I may have started out to be a Disraeli, but that target like the military one, was down. It requires almost as much physical energy to be a statesman as a paratrooper. Instead, at 41 I found myself taken with increasing seriousness as a writer.

"You are the only man," laughed Walter Elliot when I was giving him a lift one day in Berkeley Square, "who has ever made any money out of belles-lettres." The test, the barometer, I always felt was *The Times Literary Supplement*, and three times now I had been given a whole page – the front page for *The Golden Carpet*; a whole page for *Napoleon's Memoirs* and the Middle Editorial for *Caesar*. My novels, by comparison had been lightly dismissed; and I was driven to the conclusion that fiction, except perhaps for an occasional light political satire like *Red Tie in the Morning* or *The Teetotalitarian State*, was not my forte. But the combination of diverse forms of writing on the International

Situation (forecasting the Second World War and a European Union without Britain) in the *Impending Storm* and *Divided Europe*; *Peter Public*, a play of abstractions; the two light political satires; — the more serious novels (*Enter Napoleon* and *The Dome of the Rock*); the historical studies; and the non-fiction writing in *The Golden Carpet* and *A Mind on the March*; superimposed on normal political and army careers, seemed to bewilder the public, if they ever paused to consider me at all. Ian Spence, one of the heroes of *The Golden Carpet*, driving to dine with me at the House gave a lift to an old friend who asked whom he was visiting in that dim museum. "Somerset de Chair," said Ian.

"Ah" said his friend, "a mythical figure."

Now why mythical? Confusing, contradictory perhaps. But surely, I felt, when Ian recounted this to me as we sat down to the sparse wines and victuals of the Harcourt Room, no man was ever more directly in touch with the facts of life. My acquaintance with them might not have been as early or as intimate as Cleopatra's but nevertheless there were many who could testify to my un-mythicalness. Yet even my own party seemed to find it hard to accept me. "You are not fundamentally a Conservative," Quintin Hogg would say, not unkindly. And Aneurin Bevan, hailing me in the street as I passed along Cliveden Place, would say, "Why don't you join a decent party?" I was reminded more and more of the dictum of Erasmus. 'I have too much respect for my intelligence to belong to any party.' And so I was left at 41, somewhat in mid-air as a politician, and cloven-footed as an author, barely touching the ground.

Perhaps I would sprout wings, mechanical, not angelic, and take off — who knew where — to outer space; and outer darkness, whence we all emerge and whither all are bound.

Parallel with Trerice in the West Country I took to sailing. I had
settled on a 56 ton ocean-going ketch with a steel hull called the
Harebell, which was fortunate, and in the course of buying her in
the River Dart I had made the acquaintance of Trevor Hampton
who agreed to sail her for me the first summer. Trevor knew the
Harebell intimately. He was going to lay up his own yacht *Ling* in
a mud berth at Moody's, fit out *Harebell* for me, and sail it into
the blue; the further the better. His ambition was to go around the
world. All the cordage was rotten and would have to be replaced
with new Italian hemp. Otherwise she was in fair condition and
since the painting of the boot-top and top-sides at Galampton,
looked reasonably smart.

We planned to get away on my birthday, August 22nd. I had
a lot to see to at Chilham and returned on the hot afternoon of
August 22nd to find Trevor in his khaki shorts and battered sun
hat, leaning back disconsolately against the railing of the jetty.

"It's all over," he said, "I went up the mast," (he was never
happier than up in the rigging) "and pulled armfuls of pulp out of
the mast, under the sheathing. We can't get away for weeks."

There was nothing else to be done but have a new mast fitted.
But the men in the yard set to with a will, and all day and far into
the dusk they planed and sandpapered and finally varnished till
all was ready. Up she went in the derrick and an old and owl-like
rigger lowered the mast, through the hole in the deck and I put
half a crown ('a piece of silver') under the foot before it was
stepped. We were not thus delayed more than a week and in the
meantime accompanied Trevor to marine suppliers of various
kinds in Southampton, where charts of the Channel were bought;
a patent log to be trailed aft and record the day's run; tide tables;
sliding rulers, an Aldis lamp (for signalling in emergency. It was
badly needed one day). I bought a yachting cap, and Trevor wore
one ashore, but he set the tone of the cruise — a workmanlike

279

business, in shorts without any nonsense about blazers and suede shoes. He knew his way about the oceans and was primarily concerned with making landfalls, not with what happened after. He took us to Buckles in Southampton where they deluged us with stores for three months — Dundee cakes and all. Carmen's eyes bulged. It appeared that the Lords of the Admiralty, even under a Socialist Government, while rationing was still in force, encouraged the amateur yachtsman, for they obtained thus a well trained R.N.V.R. at no expense to themselves. Moreover the *Harebell* was over 40 tons and therefore ranked with the *Queen Mary* as an ocean going vessel at the Board of Trade, for purposes of carrying whisky, cigarettes and such-like bonded stores for consumption outside the three mile limit, duty free.

At last we were ready to sail, and went down river under the power of our diesel engine; with Trevor, bare to the waist, calling gleefully from the wheel to his friends on ships we passed, that we were off to Melbourne. He believed in 'shooting a line' and his favourite slogan was from the Air Force — "Bang on. Pay no regard."

We had been joined at the last moment by Grose, formerly my soldier servant in the Blues. I had found him at a loose end after the war and he and his wife were running Trerice for me, since the tenants had left. Thus there were five of us aboard — and none too many to handle a 56 ton gaff ketch in rough weather.

I took a lot of Trevor's skilled navigation for granted at this time. It was not until I had run aground off the Needles without him that I appreciated his knowledge. We sailed past them now with a wave of the hand and he was calling to Gwyn Harding* to help him raise the mizzen sail. She wore a long pointed red woollen cap with a bobble on the end, like the women who knitted at the guillotine. But her face was full of sweetness. She took life exactly as it came. Soon we began to hit the first waves of the open Channel; but the *Harebell* was a stiff boat, with an eight-foot-six draught; and even I was not much disturbed. Trevor took her well out to sea, before turning west, so as to give the Portland Race a wide berth. We could see its leaping tongues of foam; a mile or two away to starboard.

Trevor was happy at the wheel and for the first night he promised to be on watch with Gwyn or Grose all the time, so

*A neice of the Field-Marshal

that Carmen and I could rest. I became a much more active seaman in time, but for the moment enjoyed the opportunity to relax and, with an unstable stomach, preferred the horizontal position below.

In the morning we were off the entrance to the Dart; and would have entered it; but all of us had seen more than enough of that river and decided to make straight for Falmouth. It was a sunny morning and the coast of Devon glided by in coves and headlands, peacefully. It was midnight when we approached Falmouth and Trevor sailed the *Harebell* into it, like a man unlocking his own front door. He preferred to enter harbours at night, when there were a recognized number of flashes to identify the lighthouses. The channels were buoyed with lights and all, seemingly, clear to him.

We did not intend to spend the rest of our days in Falmouth. We browsed about the town, while Grose went overland to Trerice to see his wife and came back for us in the jeep, which was kept there. I was glad of the opportunity to see the place again and talk reassuringly to the gardener Dingle, who scratched the back of his head, with a hand holding his cloth cap and said, "I doan't know, Zur," whenever I made a suggestion.

I realised that a casual observer would have considered me a very rich man with my castle in Kent and an old Cornish manor seemingly handy when my yacht put into harbour in the West Country. But it was precariously balanced and, like the best conjuring tricks, not maintained without strain. It was as if the Great Pyramid had been balanced upside down on a penny. But it was fun while it lasted. And if you substitute Blickling for Chilham and find yourself unable to sell the Cornish manor or the yacht, the illusion, perforce, persists. Sometimes I wonder how all this was financed. I already had my hands full with the buildings and gardens and outbuildings of Chilham. Thelma mercifully, paid the staff indoors and fed us all. I had never regarded myself as a millionaire: but there were bank managers in those days who understood the requirements of the leisured class before the days of Tory Government and the Credit Squeeze. If you told your bank manager that you needed a yacht, he expressed some pained surprise that you had not already got one, asked how much it would cost, and when you said six thousand, or ten thousand, or whatever the price might be, he nodded thoughtfully and asked,

"What security do you suggest?" And you said, "Why, the yacht, of course." And he rubbed his hands together gleefully, saying, "Why, of course," and the cheque was honoured at once. But in those days we had the Socialist administration of the people's representatives, like Sir Hartley Shawcross, who had two yachts. Of course there was still petrol rationing and food rationing. But for yachtsmen — petrol to run their electric light plants, their out-board motors: yea, spilling over into the petrol tanks of motor cars: with red-printed coupons galore.

"You are fitting out for a cruise to the Azores, Sir, or Tripoli, or the Antipodes? You require three months', six months', a year's stores? Dundee cake off the ration, Sir? But for you, Sir," a deferential glance at the cap badge of a well-known yacht club, "for you, Sir, twelve Dundee cakes, large and round and pressed tight with currants, raisins, almonds, bits of cubed fruit. God knows what."

"And if we don't get to Tripoli or the Antipodes? If we get seasick and turn back at the first fist-smash of the Atlantic gales, what then?"

"Why, you will have a lot of stores to eat up in harbour."

"And no doubt the trolley along the jetty to the old home town."

"No doubt at all, Sir."

"Tell me, good ship's-chandler, joking about the egalitarian state we live in, apart: just why is all this spread before yachtsmen of all people?"

"Their Lordships, Sir."

"Their Lordships?"

"Yes, of the Admiralty, Sir. They reckon that you gentlemen are training yourselves for them, when the next war, or the next Dunkirk evacuation comes along, free gratis and for nothing. You don't cost them a penny."

"Hence the Dundee cakes and the whisky at 6/6 a bottle and the cigarettes at 10d a packet straight out of bond once you clear the three mile limit?"

"Precisely so, Sir."

"And do many of these cheaply bought cigarettes and spirits find themselves into the hands of low and unauthorised persons in foreign ports?"

"It has, I fear, been known to happen, Sir."

"Too bad."

Now we were swinging out past St. Mawes and soon Falmouth and the Cornish coast sank, like Atlantis, into the memory behind us. We were out in the real Atlantic; and here began the puzzle as to why anyone with my interior should have let himself in for this type of life. The deck was never more than two feet from the water, and the boat reared and plunged into the oncoming sea. It was a day of dazzling sunshine and in other surroundings I should have admired the foam, blown like glass particles off the crests of the waves, and the upward sweep of indigo blue from the long Atlantic roll.

'There is' wrote Emerson of the Englishman 'in the workings of his mind a long Atlantic roll, not known except in deepest waters.' There was very little in the workings of my mind just then but a desire for death. I lay upended across a coil of rope in the after parts of the ship, vomiting into the waves, which all but washed my mouth out afterwards. There was no thought in my mind of sailing through the Bay of Biscay. I had received a cablegram, mercifully, inviting me to attend the first Pan-Europe Congress which was to be held in Gstaad in a few days' time. Was not Europe to be saved as well as de Chair? Dawn found us off Ushant and the maze of rocks and reefs which challenge the best of navigators. Some go right round the outside to approach Brest from the south. We went in through the rocks; and were happily unaware that our charts were obsolete since the Germans had strewn the channels with mines. The only thing that mattered to me was that the sea was calmer now. The rocks slid by underwater, often within inches of the hull; and Tevor studied the landscape ahead with growing bewilderment. The lighthouse which he expected to find, all white or black and white, was barred with red. What did this mean? Was it another lighthouse or was it the same one painted differently? It might be all-important. Grose and I, accustomed to navigate from desert maps, looked over his shoulder.

"That, surely," I said, "is the village of St. Mathieu ahead of us. This must be quite a different lighthouse. Look at this headland — and that reef — look." Yes there was plenty to look at. The everlasting rocks, with the water seething around them, on both sides of us. It only needed a scrape. The mainsail was down now and we were cruising under power; but the maximum speed was 5 knots and once the tide turned, the Goulet de Brest would disgorge us on a seven knot tide, whatever we tried to do. Suddenly across the middle distance we saw a liner speeding across the view. That must be the channel. Once we got into the wake of the big ships we were all right. We were glad enough to reach the fairway.

Brest was devastated from much bombing. Here the *Scharnhorst* and *Gneisnau* had been pounded – by Trevor among others. Amid the ruins near the harbour a township of prefabricated houses had grown up. The French received us enthusiastically and there were few formalities. We were advised to make our way to the Doge's Bar, where we sipped aperitifs in comfort. Carmen and I left for Paris by the night train, while Trevor, Gwyn and Grose took the *Harebell* up the Chatelan river. It was, they said, the most beautiful spot they had ever visited; a fast flowing river between steeply wooded banks. The *Harebell* was easily identified at a distance by her white mizzen mast; for Trevor had painted it thus over Bullock's beige, before the mainmast was renewed in varnished pine. They took a photograph of her in the Chatelan river, with the dinghy beached on the gravel shore, and made us envious with it, when we rejoined them later.

Carmen was caught up in the excitement of the Rue de la Paix and emerged from Paquin beautifully attired. There was a succession of saucy white hatboxes and we went on to Switzerland, appreciably poorer. Most people mistook her for a Parisienne with her very dark colouring.

The Pan-Europe movement had now reached the point at which astute statesmen were prepared to take it out of the hands of the man who had preached the idea up and down Europe for twenty years. This was Count Coudenhove-Kalergi, an Austrian Count whose mother had been a Japanese. His wife had played Cleopatra in about 1902 to frenzied audiences in Vienna. They now lived in an attractive chalet in Gstaad. The conference was held at a large hotel and thither assembled such Europeans as Paul Reynaud and Louis Bohle. The British delegation, like all the others, seemed haphazard. Its members were those who had responded to the invitation sent out by Coudenhove-Kalergi. It consisted of two Socialist members of Parliament, R. G. W. Mackay and King, the new member for Falmouth and Penrhyn (we could have offered him a lift). The Tories were represented from the House by Sir Peter MacDonald, Member for the Isle of Wight (who might also have been collected on our way) and Sir Walter Smiles. Outside the House were Duncan Sandys and myself. From the beginning Sandys began lobbying the French and Belgians to get the Secretaryship of the European movement away from Coudenhove. Madame Coudenhove was very outspoken on the subject. She burst out at the astonished Sandys in front of all: "You come here, trading on the name of your great father-in-law and you try to turn my husband out of his lifelong work." For all that, Coudenhove took the chair at the meetings. Before we assembled, the British delegates met privately in Peter MacDonald's room. It had been proposed that Mackay, representing the governing party in the House, should speak for Britain. But when he submitted what he proposed to say, we learned that he wanted Britain to leave the Commonwealth and enter a binding European Federation.

"That will never do," we told him.

"It is the only logical step," he insisted doggedly; the more inappropriately since he came from Australia. "Take that out and there is no point in my speaking at all."

We agreed that there was no point and King, the other Socialist, spoke for us instead. He said nothing untoward. He was a schoolmaster.

We now trooped into the conference room and sat at the front table, covered with green baize, which was marked 'Great Britain'. I found myself sitting next to Sandys. Coudenhove began the proceedings by reading out telegrams of good wishes from distinguished statesmen.

"I have just realised," whispered Sandys, "that there ought to have been one from Winston."

"You had better prepare it quick then," I laughed.

He proceeded rather laboriously to draft a message of good wishes from his father-in-law. He passed it to me. It lacked the Churchillian sparkle.

"You must make it more convincing," I said and added a phrase about 'this ancient and famous continent of Europe.' Sandys liked that — so much so that he used it subsequently in a letter drafted for Winston's signature to supporters of the United Europe Movement in England; and I received an appeal some months later signed by the great man asking me to support his efforts to unify 'this ancient and famous continent of Europe'. In the meantime Sandys sent the amended 'telegram' up to

Coudenhove-Kalergi, who jumped to his feet, threw out his chest and cried, "I have a message from the man who saved civilisation in 1940." The delegates cheered this ancient and famous continent to the echo.

We had got off to a good start. Duncan Sandys and I were not allowed to speak, as the delegates were all supposed to be members of their own National Parliaments. We were observers. I was glad to meet Coudenhove again, whom I had last seen in Vienna when he lectured on United Europe there in 1934. He had written many books on the subject and had also written a book which Duff-Cooper likened in the House of Commons to Rousseau's Social Contract. It was called *The Totalitarian State against Man* and enunciated clearly the central issue of our time. I had brought with me from Paris the new French translation of my book. It was called in French *Le Tapis Doré* and I gave copies to Coudenhove and Paul Reynaud. 'You are what a man should be,' wrote Coudenhove flatteringly after reading it, 'an artist and a hero.'

There was precious little entertaining among the delegations. At this time Englishmen were allowed £75 each on the Continent; but even that pinched at the end of a journey across Europe. We had no idea what restrictions on travel were yet in store for us. Certainly it was already damaging to our prestige. Walter Smiles said that he had made his calculations down to the last franc, so that by carrying his suitcase out of the hotel himself, and thus not having to tip the porter, and by travelling third class, he and his wife would just be able to visit the Jungfrau. This was not how Englishmen did the grand tour in the eighteenth century. Carmen and I retired hurriedly to France, by way of Mont Blanc, gazing in wonder on its bald splendour. We tramped in the summer heat along the pine shaded walks to the Pras de Chamonix; and travelled second class, without sleepers, northwards, not daring to pause again in Paris, till we reached Cherbourg. We gave our last francs to the porter who trundled our bags across the cobblestones of the harbour. We had cabled to the *Harebell* at St. Peter Port in the Channel Islands to meet us this very day in Cherbourg. What if wind and tide had played false; or they had not yet reached Guernsey? Where would we sleep the night? There was the white mizzen mast moored in a line of yachts; and we shouted from the quay, "Harebell ahoy!" Grose stumbled sleepily on deck and helped us aboard with the bags. The crew were full of the Chatelan river and St. Peter Port. We decided to make for the latter; and cleared harbour in the forenoon. The battleship *Richelieu* was lying alongside the quay of the main basin as we coiled the long warp on deck.

Carmen and I were very tired after our sitting-up journey from Chamonix, whereas the others were rested in their gentle voyaging. So we retired early to sleep after entering the race of Alderney and heard little of the excitements of the night. Trevor had intended to get through the race with the west flowing tide, but we made slow going and soon the seven knot tide began to drive us back upon France. This he did not wish to suffer; and tied the anchor on to twenty fathoms of thick rope. This kedge and warp was heaved overboard (a hundred and twenty feet of it) and held us precariously to the bottom till the tide turned. When the warp came up in the morning its three inch diameter was drawn as tight and thin as a pencil and came up hot over the side. We were stationary beside a bell rock, from which a dismal tolling came all night long on the starboard beam, a few yards away. Next the auxiliary engine stalled within sight of harbour, a place most difficult to approach, where a crew of distinguished amateurs had recently impaled their yacht on a jagged reef. Trevor tried in vain to restart the diesel engine with a great handle – I heard his clanking and curses through the bulkhead drowsily. It was of no avail. The dinghy was lowered with its outboard motor and a tow rope, which nearly sawed Grose out of the boat, when it started to pull, for it then swung the outboard away violently sideways under his feet. But, thus drawn, the *Harebell* limped into the deep outer harbour of St. Peter Port where there was just water enough for her at low water in the middle. All round, other yachts were lying half over as the water receded. Inside the main harbour, the smaller yachts were provided with stilts upon which they remained standing precariously. Trevor advised a very long rope for the dinghy. Even so we found it hanging, like a corpse on the end of it, when we came back from the town. The water had run out of the inner harbour as if somebody had taken the bung plug out of a bath. The tide had fallen twenty-nine feet in six hours. It seemed unbelievable. We walked out along the mole to see if *Harebell* was all right. She was within two inches of touching bottom. We waited for the tide to rise and then yelled to Grose for the small dinghy, which he was able to pull in to the end of the mole. These are fierce tides. We stayed a few days in St. Peter Port, where we got a much needed new carpet laid in the saloon; thick and blue to replace the damp worn brown of Bullock's floor covering. We set sail, with a stiff westerly breeze for Falmouth; but Grose was at the wheel much of the time and his mother, whom he wanted to visit, lived near Brixham. He said afterwards that there was an error of 15° in the compass. The wind got up, rising to gale force. The *Harebell* had all sails set and Trevor eyed the western horizon anxiously. He reefed down the mainsail, and the old ship was now heeled right over, till the water was in the scuppers. The sea was white all over — not a patch of blue to be seen. "As white as a Christmas card," said Grose humorously. The ship was slashing across the wind at ten knots. The gale was only fresh to strong, about thirty miles an hour; but it was all we could stand comfortably. We shot across to Brixham in six hours and arrived after nightfall. But the auxiliary engine would not start. And here we were charging into the harbour at 10 knots under full sail. Under the lee of Berry Head the wind dropped, but we were still moving all too quickly in the confined space. Trevor put the wheel over and began circling round to find a berth. The great boom swung over; all of us ducking as it went. Then "Anchor overboard" and over the bows it went, with a rattle of chains and the ship pulled up, with a jar. We all rushed for the mainsail peak and throat halyards, to bring the sail down billowing and flapping about us. We wrapped the mainsail, all wet, along the boom and fastened it with canvas ties. Then the mizzen sail. That was easier. When all was over, about one in the morning, we went below for cocoa. And now Trevor missed his cat. A word must be said about this animal which chose my cabin deck-light as its urinating ground and had in other ways made its presence aboard seem quite unnecessary to me. But Trevor and Gwyn were devoted to it. Now they eyed me suspiciously. Had I taken advantage of the scuffle in the dark to throw it overboard?

"Of course not. Why should I wait till now, when we have reached England again? Why not at Cherbourg, or St. Peter Port?"

They were not reassured; and Trevor, wearing his old white duffle coat, grey with use, rowed himself to the mole, where a red light marked the end of the pier. Perhaps pussy-cat had swum towards that beacon light. He searched all up and down the mole. No pussy-cat. Next day an atmosphere of strain prevailed. A customs officer came aboard, consumed a lot of our whisky and went away again. Still no cat. Next morning was fine and clear. The wind had abated and we chugged lazily along the coast towards Falmouth again — using the mizzen sail and the auxiliary engine. We came thus in good order to Falmouth. By now Trevor had reconciled himself to the loss of his cat, but I thought that he still eyed me darkly. In Falmouth we had leisure to unwrap the wet mainsail for drying, before flaking it properly and putting on the sail cover. We undid the ties and heaved out the hurriedly crushed folds. Out tumbled pussy-cat, none the worse. Not a mew, not a murmur for three days. Trevor and Gwyn wept. I was absolved at last.

There was still some cruising weather left and Trevor wanted to show us Frenchman's Creek so, when all was tidied up aboard, we left the harbour again. A Russian ship of the old square rigged type — a grain ship — had anchored in harbour and the men were working up in the rigging as we passed. I thought this a good moment to practise my Russian. So I shouted to one of the men aloft "Kak Pashevaite?" The answer came back across the water, quite distinctly and to the great mirth of my companions: "Very well, thank you," in flawless English. We rounded the head and coasted south for an hour or two until the Helford River opened up to starboard. We turned into it, and moved upstream past the Ferry Boat Inn, to a point in the river above Helford. We rowed ashore and wandered across a small bridge and through the tiny village, till we mounted a street. At the end of it were passion flowers growing on the wall of a cottage. They were strange and wonderful flowers — five waxy blue-white petals, with a fiery circle in the centre, across which was placed the white cross of stamens. I picked one, thinking these flowers grew thus wild hereabouts, only to learn later that they were lovingly cultivated by the old lady on the other side of the wall. How could I fasten her passion flower to the wall again? It would have died. And if, one distant day, I am hauled before the Judgement Seat to answer for my crimes, and marched up to some celestial orderly room, left, right, left, salute and St. Peter looks up with a twinkle in his eye and says: "What are you here for?" I shall say, "I stole the Flower of the Passion from an old lady on the other side of a wall." And St. Peter will say irritably — "Yes, yes. Confined to Heaven for 28 days," and turn wearily to the next case.

We dined at the Ferry Boat Inn, where the management eyed some of our sea-going rig askance. But when I said, "Is this an inn within the meaning of the Act?" they served us with lobster in the dining-room, which was filled for the most part with residents in evening dress. After dinner we returned to the ship. Grose was no longer with us, having returned for a day or two to help his wife who was looking after Trerice alone in his absence. Now the moon was rising and we rowed silently over water like still mercury, towards the dark wooded entrance to the smuggler's creek. There was a spit of sand on which the dinghy grated gently and we rowed on, very quiet. Gwyn was at the oars.

"Make music Gwyn," whispered Trevor softly and Gwyn, responding to his mood, lifted the oar blades in the moonlight and let the drops run tinkling off into the water. It was a priceless moment of time — such as Beethoven had captured in his *Moonlight Sonata*. The four of us sat entranced. Then gently Gwyn dipped the oars again and we slipped silently under the ebony shadow of the trees, hidden from the moonlight, up the still reaches of Frenchman's Creek. Thus no doubt, but stealthily for different reasons, many a light craft had put off from an ocean-going ship in the Helford River in years gone by and, rowing with deadened rowlocks and oars dipped quietly into the water, had gone up this creek to deliver smuggled goods. We stole out again in the moonlight, not wishing to break the spell, and spoke softly when we clumped aboard the yacht again. And at intervals during the night, I looked out upon the mercury surface of the broad river, which clung about the hull; and saw the moonlight white upon the houses in the sleeping village, then dip behind the woods upon the hill; and all was dark.

In the morning the seagulls dived for fish and it was not the same at all. We sailed away and put into Fowey, perched raggedly upon its hills. There we left Gwyn and Trevor in charge of the boat, which they would take slowly, as weather permitted, up the coast to Bursledon again; while we obtained a car and drove overland to Trerice; where there was hot water and baths and comfort after the cramped grime of the ocean life.

CHAPTER 24

My researches into domestic architecture were in vain. 'How are the Mighty Fallen on Their Feet' did not reach the bookstalls. The difficulty was that each time I submitted a chapter on some house to the owner, he would say, "This is extraordinarily interesting about the house but perhaps you could leave out the bits about us." I was thus back to the bare boards which had already been scrubbed pretty clean by such architectural experts as Christopher Hussey; and the real interest of the book, in the anniversary year of the Festival of Britain 1951, was how the mighty were still standing up to it all. I decided therefore, that the book should be left intact till the next centenary exhibition, in 2051, rather than published in a mutilated form now.

In Norfolk a new and gay element was settling down in the county – the Forbes at Easton, the Fosters at Lexham (which I remembered as a Victorian house in my old constituency of S.W. Norfolk), now rebuilt, white without and beautiful within. The Richard Allhusens at Bradenham and the Derek Allhusens at Claxton. Sonia and Julian Melchett were anchored at Blakeney to an experiment of Julian's in crop drying. Into the old rectory which they had rented from Aubrey Buxton, they squeezed half the county at a champagne bottle party which set a new level in entertainment to this staid neighbourhood. The dancing was confined to the carpeted floor of a tiny sitting-room, and the light, such as it was, filtered in through the door of the dining-room beyond, which the hostess shut negligently in passing if she happened to be dancing with a particular friend. In the corner, as dawn came in through the windows, Julian, tired by now of everybody's company but his own, did a pas de seul, occasionally spinning like a top.

We expected to be away in our yacht during August, and had agreed to Blickling being opened to the public on August Bank Holiday, when it would normally be shut. Owing to being shipwrecked off the Needles we found ourselves at home, with the prospect of sharing the garden in the afternoon with a large selection of the public. From this predicament Sonia and Julian rescued us and we spent a bizarre afternoon with them at the Blakeney Bank Holiday Fair instead, riding on the dodgems, the switchbacks and the whirligigs. Jean Dawney* was staying with the Melchetts and we were accompanied by Harold and Mary Keeble who were staying with us over the Bank Holiday. Mary was very beautiful and I painted her portrait in between the strenuous bouts of tennis which Harold played with her. He was now Editor of the *Sunday Express* and was becoming more and more like Beaverbrook every day.

Towards the end of August (1952) Harold and Vita Nicolson arrived at Houghton in Norfolk, where they were dazed by the accumulation of press reviews of *King George V*. They came to lunch at Blickling. Apart from picking up *The Times* one day to read the first leader, and discovering that it was about Harold's book, Vita said they had seen no reviews, as they had been touring the remote parts of the island. Harold seemed completely dazed by it all. Success had come to him possibly in the wrong field. I had known him in the 1935 Parliament, which he entered with me. His ambitions, carefully steered along the narrow ledge of the National Labour Party, had not led him to the Foreign Secretary-ship. In the war he held subordinate office at the Ministry of Information but did not feel that it had added much to his renown. "I have been put in the shop-window," he said ruefully, "and withdrawn." I had never been displayed at all, I pointed out in reply. "Ah," he sighed, "you rush forward with your fresh laurels held out, and then you let them droop." But what should I have done about them? I never knew how to follow up successes. Now we were both in the wilderness; and both writing; although his fame was far ahead of mine. He kept up a sparkling commentary every week in *The Spectator*; and reviewed books for *The Observer*. How he turned it out so fresh for so long was a miracle. It welled up from a deep spring of cultured scholarship. He seemed astounded by the popular success of his *George V*.

"It was intended primarily for the scholar," he chided me, when I complained of the welter of footnotes, which ought, I

*Later Princess Galitzene

thought to have been incorporated in the text. He said it had been anxious work getting the book approved in high places. King George VI had passed it only a week before he died; and if anything had happened to Queen Mary before its publication there would have been a long delay. There was only one bottle of Napoleon brandy in the cellar – but this seemed the occasion, if ever, to drink it. Harold had written *The Congress of Vienna* and I had edited *Napoleon's Memoirs*. Wyndham-Ketton Cremer, a Norfolk historian, close friend and neighbour at Felbrigg would have joined us but his mother had just died. Humphrey Hare, an authority on Swinburne and translater of de Vigny's *Splendeurs et Servitude Militaires*, living with his sister, Diana Astley, at Elsing not far away, joined us and Sonia Melchett took a photograph of the three authors on the bridge after lunch. It was a pity that Vita Sackville-West was not in the picture but she and Carmen were walking round the garden in which Vita expressed her usual horticultural interest. I asked her what her next book was going to be. "A novel, this time," she said, *"The Easter Party."*

"I enjoyed *The Edwardians* so much," I told her, "I hope it is like that."

"This one is really about a dog."

I was painting Sonia too. Both she and Mary were appearing in a book of drawings by Nicholas Egon called *Some Beautiful Women in our Time*. The title turned their heads; but the drawings by no means flattered them.

Towards the end of the year, Allison Owens flew in from the Far East via Fifth Avenue. Reggie, shortly due to be Vice-President of Park Davis, hastened on round the world to the East, but Allison stayed in England, where she had settled her children firmly in school.

"I have been put inside once by the Japs, Somerset; and I'm not going to be put inside by the Chinese. In fact, I would rather go back to the Japs. It's just like 1941 out there all over again. Everybody knows it's coming. But nobody does anything about it. They still haven't built the aerodrome they were talking about when you were there. One day I got the notion I would pull the children out, while I could do it easily. I simply took them aboard the first aeroplane – that was in 1950, do you remember? – and brought them over here."

"Do you realise," I said, "that it is five years since I first met you out there in Hong Kong, and we have never quarrelled once?"

"Didn't you know," she laughed, "I am famous for it. I never quarrel. I always give in."

She seemed to have grown more beautiful and certainly more sophisticated, always with the latest thing from Paquin or Jacques Fath. She was now 31, and her lovely grey hair looked as startling as ever. She stayed in Norfolk with us.

The cook had married the old butler's son in July and seemed irreplaceable for a while. This was a common lament among our friends — who had to do the cooking themselves. As the festive season approached, I felt that Carmen must be freed from this preoccupation, and we heard of a young chef who had just left the French Foreign Legion. He was a Norfolk man of 30, who when interviewed, showed his citation for the Croix de Guerre, signed by de Lattre de Tassigny. He had been fighting the Viet Mihn in Indo-China. "That is all right, so far as it goes," I said "but does it help us with the crêpe Suzette?"

"I can do that too," he laughed.

He had found life in the Foreign Legion hard. He had to fight all day and then cook for the officers' mess in the evening. He had fought in the Commandos during the war. I asked him about the war in Vietnam.

"It could go on for another two years at the present rate. Both sides have American equipment. And the Viet Mihn are very skilfully officered — mostly by Germans who joined the Legion and then deserted to the other side when they found they were offering more pay."

"Was the discipline in the Legion very severe?" I asked.

"You were all right, so long as you kept your nose clean. There was no appeal beyond the Sergeant. After you had been in the clink once, you did not want to go in again."

With the hors d'oeuvre, artistically arranged in star-like patterns with a lot of garlic, onions and gerkins, he would send up captured Viet Mihn documents in Chinese, but written in Western script. Allison, who could speak and read Cantonese, tried to read them but was baffled.

What with Allison in the house over Christmas and this man in the kitchen, we were very well informed about the Far East that winter.

It was a grim war in Indo-China. "The French are very cruel," the chef confided to me. "One day we picked up an old man, who had a couple of cartridges on him. They had nothing else against him; and it wasn't as if they were trying to get information out of him. But the French hung him up by his two thumbs and burnt him over a fire. It took an hour and a half for him to die. And when he would not burn properly they threw more petrol over his legs."

I was appalled. "What possessed them to do that?"

"Just boredom," he said, "the French were very cruel. They just did it to amuse themselves."

"And you saw all this?"

"Yes, I was there. But I couldn't do anything about it."

"Did not this lead to very savage reprisals when they captured any of the Legion?" I asked.

"They seemed to respect the Legion," he said. "They treated our prisoners quite well. In fact one lot were given some revolvers, by an officer on the other side, to protect themselves with. But the Communists were very ruthless with their own people — the coolies and peasants. Especially the women. They would usually lop off stray parts of their anatomy, to start with, and in the end — chop, chop, right through the head."

Clearly the human race had advanced nowhere at all. Nothing worse than these episodes, from both sides in Indo-China, had been perpetrated in Hitler's Reich.

Carmen thought that it probably went on in all armies, but that one did not often hear about it. I feared that she might be right.

The chef, Easter, had a high opinion of de Lattre. "He shook them up when he arrived in Hanoi. Soon there wasn't an officer left in the place. He had them all up at the front. When his plane was about to take off, he inspected the crew and one of them had a beard. He looked at the man, then his watch and said, 'in the army men are properly shaven. We leave in ten minutes time'. The man was back by then with it off. The men thought the world of de Lattre. But you know that his son was killed, and that seemed to break him up. He got ill, and was flown back to Paris for an operation of some kind. He died there. But some think he may have been done in."

Easter had been born in Norfolk, where his mother had been a cook in domestic service (and he had started his own career as kitchen boy at Weasenham, for Elise Coke, just after I gave up that house) — but it was not to be expected that a man who had been fighting in the Foreign Legion and seen what he had seen, would prove a soothing influence in the household. He was all right so long as he had plenty to drink; but would get very temperamental during dinner parties. He would begin to throw knives about the kitchen, and the rest of the staff would not dare to go into it. We were giving a dinner party for the West Norfolk Hunt Ball, upon which we had decided to release Allison, like a secret weapon; and there were some ten people for dinner — the Melchetts, Hargreaves, Allison and a Hungarian. It was Julian's birthday, and we were trying to keep him supplied with his staple diet, champagne. There was the worst fog of this foggy winter and two of the party, from London, (Sonia's sister, Bunty Kinsman and Julian's sister) did not reach the ball at Westacre till two o'clock in the morning. The main dish came up very depressed. I had told Doris, the head housemaid to warn the ageing butler, Sidney, to open up a bottle of Burgundy in the back regions to lubricate the domestic machinery; but Sidney, who had been in the house since he started as hall boy, fifty years earlier, was getting a little forgetful and had not yet got the bottle out of the cellar. I went down to the kitchen to find Easter, with a cloth wound round his neck, striding up and down with his black eyes as dark as unlit coals. I asked him if he had heard about the Burgundy.

His eyes changed from coals to diamonds; and I went in search of the wine. After that the savoury was a dream. But such instability was an anxiety. The nanny and under-housemaid never knew whether he was going to tease them good-naturedly or send a knife whizzing past them into the table. He was only with us temporarily, over Christmas and the New Year, while waiting to hear, after a medical board, whether the British Army wanted him. He had been invalided out of the Marines, suffering from some kind of shock. He had been aboard the *King George V,* and seen the *Bismarck* go down. "Churchill came aboard and addressed us," he told me. "He spoke for three-quarters of an hour. It was wonderful — but he did not tell us anything." I had no doubt that Winston had been careful not to do so.

Pat Hornsby-Smith would have been with us for Christmas also, if duty had not retained her in her constituency, visiting hospitals on Christmas morning, a gesture much appreciated there. She arrived the day after Boxing Day; and over dinner, Derek Allhusen pointed out that no less than three of those present, had served during the war in S.O.E. (Special Operations Enemy). Jean Foster as a driver had driven many a doomed man to his embarkation. And Pat had been private secretary to Top Selborne. She told us the story of the blowing up of the Heavy Water Plant in Norway.

"We had always maintained that it was a job for S.O.E. But the War Office tried to do it with a glider and airborne troops. Naturally there was a reception committee waiting for them and the men were all captured and shot. Then we were allowed to do it. We sent two men, who worked with two Norwegians. They hid up in the mountain and would come down on skis, to watch the plant for six weeks, until they had the timing of the sentries' movements down to split seconds. There was just an interval of so much between rounds. When the day came, they slipped in, planted their charges and were a quarter of a mile away when it went up. Hitler refused to believe that it could have been done without the connivance of the guard and he had them all shot."

She told us the tragedy of Yeo-Thomas too. "He was always such a gay and jolly fellow, when he came in to the office. He would sit there cracking jokes; a big robust hearty fellow. But we knew the Germans were on to him; and Selborne would not let him go back the last time. But Yeo-Thomas appealed to the Old Man, over the Minister's head; and he was allowed to go. The Germans treated him abominably. Between the Metro where they caught him and the Gestapo headquarters, which is no distance, they had broken both his arms. Then they tried the water torture on him. They hung him upside down in ice cold water, till he actually drowned. Then they would revive him with artificial respiration, hoping that in this dazed condition as he came to, he would give them the information they wanted. But he gave them nothing. Then they sent him to Belsen. He was to have been shot, with seventeen other prisoners of ours. But we paid four million francs, to bribe a guard there to replace him with another corpse. There were plenty of corpses available there. But we did not know what had happened to him till Ivor Thomas said in an interview that he had met another Thomas, 'Yeo-Thomas'. Selborne rang him up at once. Somebody said he was in bed and could not be disturbed. 'Then get him out of bed,' demanded Selborne. Ivor Thomas could not imagine what he had done, but came to the telephone. 'Come round for breakfast now,' Selborne urged him. 'I want to know if you have really seen this man.'

"We sent an aeroplane over to fetch him. It was all we could do to get him to come near the building. Colonel S- - -ᵗ - - said 'It's all right, Yeo-Thomas, you are among friends now.' It was pitiful to see him so changed. He was completely broken, thin, emaciated, looking furtively around him. So different from the jolly, hearty fellow we had known before."

I felt, listening to Pat, and watching her cheerful, animated expression, with her colourful red hair, that all this experience of war behind the scenes had qualified her in a way I had not realised before, for considerable responsibilities. She was obviously moved by what she described; but retained with it all a singularly robust detachment from the individual aspect of so much tragedy — an attitude of mind which I had noticed in Churchill, but not often in others. She would understand but she would not worry. She told us how the Danes had sent an S.O.S. when some of the leaders of the resistance there had been imprisoned. "They wanted us to bomb the gaol. It meant, virtually picking the lock. We had a lot of trouble with Bomber Harris, as he would never spare aircraft, if he could help it, for our work, which, after all, was just as important as bombing the German civilians. Anyhow we got what we wanted. What we did not know was that a lot of top-ranking Nazis happened to be visiting the gaol and were holding a conference in the main hall when we hit it."

About the Heavy Water Plant she said, "We had exact information about the extent of the damage because the engineer employed by Hitler to report on the results of the explosion was one of our sympathisers; and passed a carbon copy of his report to us before sending it to Hitler. So we were able to send it to the Old Man with his comment: 'You are getting this before Herr Hitler.' I typed the memo."

Pat and Carmen and I saw the New Year in alone, hoping that it would be brighter than the old. Allison telephoned from London, to which she had returned a day or two before, with her three children, Madeleyn (born in the Jap prison camp) Reggie and Tim. We spoke with her in turn.

"Kung - Hai - Fat - Choy," she said to me. "Happy, Happy,

New Year. This is going to be a successful year for you, I feel sure." I could see no signs of it, but was glad of her assurance.

Allison returned to us for the West Norfolk Hunt Ball and came out shooting with Jack and Monica Hargreaves. Bill Forbes, a great admirer of the girls, said to Carmen, "I could understand any man falling for that."

Allison stood behind me while we waited, in line on a canal bank, for partridges to be driven over; and waited a long time, for the beaters had gone off in the opposite direction. There was more liquid mud in the lanes around Jack's house at Twyford than Allison or I had seen this side of Siam, and I gave her a piggy-back ride, in between stands. Carmen and Monica ploughed ahead, Norfolk-wise, through the slush, gossiping.

It was not to be expected that many birds would have survived for long within half a mile of Jack's murderous gun, and the snares of the fowlers over the Christmas season. But one pheasant, Archibald, was thought to be still about. Allison and I stood by the barn, waiting for the solitary pheasant to fly over. Charles McLean* down from Duart, who was staying with Bill Forbes was posted further out in the field, wondering where the famous Norfolk pheasants were. Allison and I talked again of her experiences in Stanley Camp.

"I have often felt," I said, "that perhaps you did not tell me everything about what happened to you there. It would be no discredit to you, if the worst had happened."

"I suppose not," she said, with a far-away look in her eyes, the look I had been trying to capture in a portrait.

"There were some bad moments, when one thought 'this is it'. But I got by, somehow. At first we were living in our own house for six weeks, with the Japs wandering in and out. But Reggie, being civilian, was with me, and nothing happened. Drunken Jap soldiers would come to the door, demanding to look round. They would ransack the place; often sticking a bayonet into a sack of rice and leaving it there. Then we were all rounded up, as I told you, and taken down to that brothel." She shuddered, "Ugh, I shall never forget that dark little room. And people looking in on you all the time. Out at Stanley it wasn't so bad. Once they got to realising I was really having a baby they were quite kind. The Japs

*Later Chief Scout

are funny that way. They adore children. But they took our dogs away. I had a dog I was very fond of and I wanted to keep it. But one day I ran into Tarda in the camp. He was the tall Japanese, a magnificent looking man, who had come in the delegation to demand Hong Kong's surrender. He spoke perfect English. He said 'If you try to keep the dog, it will only be taken away from you and be killed. Let me keep it for you.' I let him have the dog, and in return he used to send me a little food sometimes. That was the worst suffering, Somerset, the starvation."

She put out her two tiny hands to hold a few imaginary grains of rice.

"Two bowlfuls of rice a day. Eileen Bliss was having a baby in the camp too. She had a dreadful experience. She had married a young man in the internment camp. Her husband was trying to steal her some sugar from the Jap store; and they caught him. She was dragged out by them to watch him being beheaded. She lost the baby after that."

"Why drag her out to watch it?" I asked in despair. "What was the point of that?"

"Oh we were all taken out to see it. But she was very much pushed forward in the centre of the line. It was a regular performance; which we were always made to watch. If anyone was caught they would starve us for three weeks afterwards. Sometimes people would get away, and they would starve us for that too. But we said 'good luck to them' and starved cheerfully. There was a book about Madeleyn being born in that camp, called *Prisoner of the Japs* by Gwen Dew. I ought to get a copy for Madeleyn's sake."

(Allison later showed me the Hong Kong newspaper, printed in English, after it was taken over by the Japs. 'Imperial Forces occupy Hong Kong. Rising Sun raised on Government House Flag Staff.' These were the headlines across the front page; with a photograph of the harbour and Victoria Island. All this had been very hard to bear.)

The lone pheasant, Archibald, flew suddenly over the barn, and I gave him both barrels, absent-mindedly, without effect. It was so difficult to visualise it all, standing there in the keen east wind on an estate in Norfolk, surrounded by friends; and lunch waiting for us indoors, with mulled claret and port to follow. And I reflected once again, on the extraordinary insecurity of the world in which my generation had grown up — Allison, born under the British Flag in Australia, only to see it hauled down in surrender from the Governor's flagstaff in Hong Kong, and taking her children away from the rising storm in Asia; Jack Hargreaves and Bill Forbes and McLean, and I, who had fought away our youth all across the world, in battles for sheer personal survival. Nothing else. For when you stripped away all the glamour of the wars for democracy and the badges and standards under which we motored into action; you were left with the knowledge that defeat meant the prison camp for girls like Allison. And already the familiar landmarks, like Shepherds in Cairo, were going. There was going to be no easy peace. The barbarians were at the gates of Rome once more.

CHAPTER 25

I have noticed that when I secured one of the properties that really mattered to me, I felt a great sense of excitement and relief when I heard that the contract had finally been exchanged. One dreaded, up to the last moment, some hitch or backsliding. This was particularly so in the case of St. Osyth, which had passed into the possession of a Friendly Society called The Loyal Order of Ancient Shepherds; and the place was occupied by a formidable woman, weighing 18 stone, called Miss George. You could hear her 3 corridors away berating some gardener caught stealing potatoes. The headquarters of the Friendly Society was in Ashton-under-Lyne, a respectable organisation, and they were not at all happy to find their branch in Essex established in a large country mansion; with the peaches and cream coming in every day. Their Newmarket solicitors had pointed out that the Acts of Parliament providing for the conduct of charities covered few, if any, of the activities going on. The late branch secretary, Mr. Titmarsh, had set up his two daughters in what he considered suitable circumstances there. One was married to a tailor in the East End of London, who was rapidly appointed farm bailiff. The other was a State Registered Nurse, and the main house was conveniently organised into a Convalescent Home, around her. The branch secretary, Titmarsh, also thought of converting the chapel into a war memorial and applied to the relatives of Essex fallen for subscriptions, which later had to be returned. Mr. Titmarsh died, leaving his own secretary, Miss George, in charge. She was difficult to dislodge, and had her own ideas as to who the purchaser should be — a contractor who no doubt knew more about the gravel deposits than I did at the time. After the sale to me had been accepted by her superiors, I asked a carpet dealer in London to bring down an Agra carpet on approval to try out in the drawing-room. Miss George stood in the doorway, which her 18 stone bulk completely blocked, and refused him admission. We had to lay the carpet down on the lawn under a cedar tree. When Knight Frank and Rutley were taking the inventory of the contents which I had agreed to buy lock stock and barrel as part of the purchase price, numerous items were found to be missing; stuffed lions in glass cases; panelled oak gates. When they came to the Georgian wing, which Miss George occupied, the connecting doors were sealed and they were told that everything in it, including a set of 12 Chippendale chairs had been given to Miss George personally by Mr. Titmarsh. The agents telephoned me for instructions. If Miss George hoped by this action to make me drop the purchase and leave room for her friend, the contractor, she was disappointed. I try to keep a grasp of the essentials.

"Forget the contents of Miss George's wing," I told them. "What is important is the property."

No wonder I felt a sense of relief when Miss George finally departed; and that was not till she received confirmation on the telephone that the cheque for the purchase price had been cashed. I was relieved to hear that too. Coutts had not been too enthusiastic, as a mortgage had yet to be arranged; and 6 years of Blickling had drained most of the capital left me from the sale of Chilham and the paying off of the overdrafts there. Still, survival is the *specialité de la maison*; and I felt instinctively that if I could only get the deeds to St. Osyth, the genius of the place, would as usual assert itself. I have usually felt this about houses; they have a will of their own, and like people, some have genius. When in doubt or trouble of any kind, I would look up at the great façades of Chilham or Blickling or St. Osyth and murmur, "Let the genius of the place assert itself." Perhaps that is why they accepted me.

I had known about St. Osyth for a long time. It was in the series of volumes on historic English houses published from time to time by *Country Life*; and as Paul Getty pointed out to me, on one occasion, there are not that many of any significance within a radius of 70 miles of London — if you want to be within reach of the capital. Not everybody does, but most wives seem to want to be within easy reach of a hairdresser and when it comes to the castle with 37 bathrooms and the swimming pool heated out to the 3 mile limit on the coast of Wales these considerations seem to become cardinal.

I had noticed with some distress the sale of St. Osyth by

General Kincaid Smith to the Loyal Order, shortly after I had decided to move from Chilham to Blickling; and I was surprised to see it advertised in *Country Life* again just when I was selling Trerice to the National Trust. Carmen and I decided to make a detour on the way back from Cornwall to Norfolk to inspect the property.

We spent a night in London with an old friend from Hong Kong, who had stayed with us at Blickling and Trerice — Allison Owens, who was thus intrigued by the new development. I also persuaded my old friend and accountant Randulph Barker, without whose advice I would not have bought a new property, to accompany us and we drove down to Essex. Randulph was one of those massive and imposing people, fond of food and wine, who inspire confidence — even in tax inspectors.

In those days, 1953, the road from Colchester to St. Osyth was a quiet country road without building developments or caravan camps, so that the approach was not as disturbing as it has gradually become over the years, reaching a sort of crescendo as we lurched into the European Community. Liverpool Street Station had not yet become the gateway to the Golden East.

The first impression made by houses is, I think, always decisive. You either gasp in delighted astonishment or you feel a sense of disappointment. What I had not foreseen, as I skirted the park fencing, and then the massive high walls of the old Abbey, built by the Augustinian Monks 500 years earlier, was the dominating size of the great gatehouse. I had already decided that this building, if it lived up to expectations, was to be the principal residence of the estate; but I was not prepared for its majestic, towering lines, topped by castellated battlements of the period; so very different from the bogus eighteenth century attempts at castleification on the front of the Jacobean house at Chilham. Here the defensive purpose of the medieval building was apparent. It was built, incredibly, of squared flint bricks, interspersed with tall narrow bands of golden stone. A row of grinning gargoyles looked down from a great height, and over the high Gothic arched gateway, in two spandrels were exquisitely carved panels of a dragon with a knot in his tail; and St. Michael hacking at it across the point of the archway, with his sword raised over his shoulder. He was authentically clad in fifteenth century stone feathers; reminiscent of the angels over a fireplace in the brown drawing-room at

Blickling brought from an earlier house. (Baddlesmere)

In a flash I registered that the whole edifice was authentic and a masterpiece of the period. No wonder *Country Life* said it was unexcelled by any monastic remains in the country. There were three empty niches; one over the gateway, where a lead emblem of the Sun Insurance Company had been set as a seal by the trustees of the 3rd Earl of Rochford in 1790. The other niches flanked the archway. They were believed to have carried statues of St. Peter and St. Paul; while that of St. Osyth, above, had commemorated the remarkable woman in whose honour the Priory had been founded in 1121. These three statues had been torn down in the Cromwellian Revolution; as St. Osyth was then owned by a Roman Catholic, Lady Rivers, and the place had been brutally sacked.

To right and left of the great gatehouse, with its tall Gothic windows; stretched supporting wings. The nearest contained, inside, an original pointed gateway of about 1380 overlaid by the monks in the rebuilding of the main gatehouse in 1475. These dates are bandied about by archaeologists. The latter date seems to be based on the records of the Lady Chapel in Long Melford Church, which bears a close resemblance in design and texture to St. Osyth.

To the left of the main block of the gatehouse, and partly concealing the west wing was another high monastic wall at right angles capped by castellation. In it had been inserted an old Norman arched gateway; with the typical rounded Roman arch of the period, supported by pillars; contrasting with the pointed Gothic arch of the main entrance. The Norman arch led to the farm buildings which began, where the gatehouse wing ended, in a tiled tithe barn of incredible length. The walls on the south side were of tarred planking; those on the north were of chequered medieval stone; and the whole long roof was of timbered beams dating from Henry VIII's time.

It was difficult to take it all in; or believe that it was all still there; untouched by the centuries. The jumble of farm buildings round the corner were of stone or septaria, capped by attractive Tudor brick gables; and wavy tiled roofs.

We had not even penetrated the main quadrangle, which we proceeded to do through the main arch of the gatehouse, gazing unbelievingly at the medieval vaulting above our heads, embossed with stone carvings of St. Osyth, St. Sebastian and a host of legendary figures.

On the north wall of the stone gatehouse, above the arch and below some Gothic windows on the second floor, were the faded wooden funeral hatchments of the last Earl of Rochford. It was protected from the weather by a narrow projecting wooden gable.

Beyond us, now looking north across a vast square lawn, shaded by giant walnut trees and cedars, was another group of buildings, forming with the farm buildings and bailiff's cottage to our left, a quadrangle reminiscent of an Oxford or Cambridge College. The centre part of the façade was of Tudor brick, in the centre of which was a big oriel window, carved, we discovered, by Abbot Vyntner, with 182 escutcheons on the inside and the date, both in arabic and Roman numerals 1527.

To the right of this an extension of the building projected towards us partly in Tudor brick and partly in chequered stone and brown septaria, topped by a chequered octagonal clock tower of 1553 in the Georgian cupola of which a bell chimed 4 times stridently. It was time to pay our respects to the formidable Miss George. Before doing so, we turned right into the rose garden, where the roses were grouped in beds neatly edged by box hedging a few inches high. Tall clipped yew hedges at the far end of the rose garden (whose other sides were ceeeper covered stone and brick walls of the sixteenth century) separated it from the topiary garden of ornamental clipped yews, above which reared another astonishing building of chequered stone and brown septaria (septaria is a sort of hardened clay). This was the so-called Abbot's Tower, built by Lord d'Arcy as part of his extensions to the house in 1553. It had original stone chimneys of that date. Beyond this was a small chapel of which the ribbed vaulted ceiling dated from about 1225 and had formed the undercroft of the old monks' dormitory. Beside this were the ruins of parts of d'Arcy's house burnt down in 1645 — exposed Tudor hearths, high up in the air; some beautifully moulded brick Tudor chimneys, with criss-cross moulding. Birds were already pecking holes in them; and I later had to put scaffolding up to repair them, with the aid of a grant from the Ministry of Works. I pointed out that I must be the last man in England to be actually propping up ruins.

306

"I feel money rising up from the ground,"* Carmen said. She had gypsy blood from an ancestor in the eighteenth century — when one of the Earls of Shaftsbury had run off with a Basque gypsy from the Pyrenees. She was gifted with second sight. At Chilham, she had felt arms reaching out of the Henry VII linenfold panelling of the study, to welcome her; while the genius of the place had certainly appeared to do its best to repel Thelma, whose fey Scot's instinct had prejudiced her against the house from the outset.

Carmen was right about the money 'coming up out of the ground' but we did not know that then. We were awed by the surface appearance.

After the glorious façade which stretched in the opposite direction, to complete the quadrangle with a Georgian wing (housing Miss George); it was something of a letdown to discover that the hinder parts on the north front had all been a Victorian reconstruction dated 1866. The interior reflected this ungainly epoch when Queen Victoria ruled over a large part of the globe, and Osborne set the tone for architectural design. We were also engaged in the grab for Africa at that time, from which enigmatic continent, General Kincaid Smith had brought back the innumerable trophies, which dotted the walls of the dining-room — a white rhino, shot on the Blue Nile in 1911; hartebeest; kudu; gnu; impala. He must have been a crack shot; and under the glazed eyes of these innocent beasts, patients from the Welfare State ate their meals.

Miss George was not forthcoming. But on her desk (in General Kincaid Smith's library, with its pull-out maps of the world) beside a plate of figs and grapes just brought in from the hothouses, reposed the account books for the current month. Randulph, a commanding figure, but still yielding 40 or 50 pounds to Miss George in the ring, managed to get a look at the figures. The other books were all away at the solicitors, she said; and as mere buyers we could not be expected to have access to them.

Randulph whispered to me, "If these figures stand up for the rest of the year you have nothing to fear." They did not stand up

*She was right. Surveys carried out subsequently by gravel merchants, revealed deposits of sand and gravel amounting to 2,600,000 cubic yards for which they paid £189,000 as a capital sum. In 1984, 54 panels of brilliant fruit and flower paintings by Edward Ladell, were uncovered on the ceiling; painted in 1866.

for the rest of the year; but he was right. The organisation was geared to the Welfare State, and reflected over the next 30 years the erosions of inflation, so that the fee per patient of 7 gns per week paid by the North East Metropolitan Hospital Board in 1953; rose gradually to 120 guineas by 1983; and would no doubt continue to rise. As I was not, like the Loyal Order, a Charity, there need be no inhibitions about the peaches or cream or the 4 gardeners. At this time there was only a trickle of people allowed round the gardens and a shifty-eyed senior citizen took the money and kept most of it. According to him the takings for 1953 were less than £400. By 1983 this had risen in more expert and more honest hands, to £18,000 and the gardeners from 4 to 6. Beyond the gardens lay a park with avenues stretching fanwise in 3 directions. In the foreground was the first Lombardy poplar grown in England introduced by Lord Rochford who was an arborical enthusiast. He had also planted a white-beam in the park, now one of the largest trees of the species in England.

We walked up the central avenue of chestnuts and limes which cast a dense shade in August, and came to the Nun's Wood, where the remains of the Saxon Chapel still stood, on the door of which St. Osyth 'had left the marks of her bloody hands and there fell down'. This was after she had been beheaded by the Danes in 653 in the Grotto Wood a quarter of a mile away. She had carried her head the whole distance. It must have seemed a long walk.

Between the Nun's Wood and the Grotto Wood was a view of the estuary, and the property extended right down across the arable land to the marshes and the sea wall. It seemed unbelievable and my last anxieties disappeared. So often there is some snag in the background. But here the views were superb. We could see Brightlingsea in the distance, and the gleam of water at high tides in the creeks, which bordered the estate on two sides and led down to the North Sea. At this time I still had the ocean-going ketch, *Harebell*, and the prospect of being able to lay the gear up for the winter on one's own property instead of in some costly yachtyard was appealing.

On the way back to the gardens by way of the seal pond, we came upon a pair of fine shire horses, still used for ploughing under the eye of Cyril King, an indigenous and enterprising worker on the estate. At the north end of the park was a pair of rather rickety lodges of Strawberry Hill Gothic design, joined by a delapidated old coaching arch made of wood. Here the keeper, Craske, lived; already feeling the effects of rheumatism which was to drive him to seek a warmer climate and new lease of life in Rhodesia.

There could be no doubt about my intention to buy the property. Blickling had served its purpose. After 5 years the ghost had more or less been laid; and I had to face the fact that with 2½ tons of anthracite feeding the central heating boiler every week, and with the wages of 8 servants and all the rest of it, even if the National Trust contributed half the rates and some other expenses, there was no future in it for me. I only had a lease of the house and gardens. The effect of inflation would work continuously against me in a rented house, but would operate in my favour if I could own a congeries of ancient monuments with 560 acres on the Essex coast.

The Shepherds wanted £30,000 for the property. Fortunately Miss George had prevented their disclosing in the advertisement that it included the Convalescent Home as a going concern. *Après moi* the deluge. She could not believe that anybody else could or should keep it going. She summoned all the staff and dismissed them. I summoned them all back again and re-engaged them. I also visited the Hospital Board who were keen to keep it going, but said that the County Council would establish very different requirements for a private owner. With a Charity they had been powerless — even to insist on fire escape ladders. They were right.

I was back to my original £12,000 after the sale of Trerice for that sum to the National Trust with nothing to show for it but an expensive 57-ton yacht (old and difficult to sell) 14 years of pleasant living, and a new Rolls Royce on hire purchase. The £94,000 I had got from the sale of Chilham (£4,000 of which went in sales commission and solicitors fees) had been swallowed up in paying off Thelma's contributions to the Jersey herd, etc. the accumulated overdraft, relieving her of Trerice and its overdraft, and living comfortably but not extravagantly for the last 6 years at Blickling, 4 of them without Thelma's assistance inside the house. So there was the problem of raising a mortgage. George Judd, a partner in Strutt and Partner came to lunch at Blickling during the last summer of grandeur. He had been asked by the Agricultural Mortgage Corporation (who had advanced £30,000 against £42,500 at Chilham) to value the St. Osyth Estate. He came up with the surprising figure of £16,000, as the value for the whole estate. This was not enough for an advance of more than £10,000 and eventually the Church Commissioners obliged with £15,000 to be increased to £18,000 when the gatehouse was converted as a private residence. I really felt pushed to get the farm started and start with the restoration of the gatehouse. I remember a biting cold day in February 1954 when I casually laid down a Post Office Savings Book with my last £1,000 in it, as security for a farm loan at Barclays in Colchester, while Carmen walked up and down outside in her sheepskin coat keeping her freezing fingers crossed.

Fortunately, the agents who were selling St. Osyth, Percival and Company of Sudbury, were keen for me to secure the place; and when Miss George's friends made the mistake of a final offer of £26,500 they felt entitled and by law required to get the highest bid and closed with me rapidly at £27,000. Miss George was black with rage but the Shepherds in Ashton-under-Lyne signed with gleeful haste; and she left, with the furniture of the Georgian wing, as our car drove up.

It had not been easy to see inside the gatehouse, but perhaps Miss George had thought it would put us off, so she had allowed us in. The ceilings and floors had all fallen in. Jackdaws' nests were falling down into the Tudor fireplaces; the stairs were rickety chicken-house stairs. The building still looked as it had done when the troops gave up billeting it during the war. A depressing spectacle, but I noticed that the stonework of the bricked-up doorway in the hall was authentic, as was a piscina for throwing away Holy Water after the Mass, and a beggar's window open to the elements, through which pilgrims used to put in their hands for bread. It would take a lot of doing up, and we needed an architect. Sonia and Julian Melchett in Norfolk invited Darcy Braddell to meet us. He was a descendant of the Darcys, and proved a sympathetic and enthusiastic architect, insisting on riven oak laths behind the new plaster work, as in medieval times, designing oak doors of a pleasing appearance, two vertical ridged slabs of oak, side by side in panels, fitting well into the building. We met frequently on the site, an empty stone building unheated in the depths of an English winter. No wonder, poor man, that it was his last assignment. He was nearly 80, but he died happy to have had a hand in restoring his ancestor's building.

As soon as the sale was agreed in September 1953, Carmen and I started buying furniture for the gatehouse. I had in fact begun earlier with the sale of Trerice in mind and the need to fatten it up like a calf for the slaughter. Thus during Coronation week in 1953, when most people were at their village fêtes, a sale had taken place in Norwich of a deceased furniture dealer. Some of his pieces still needed repair (the loose pieces were mostly inside the drawers), and the local dealers got some bargains in a rather tight circle. My appearance was not popular. I bought a slightly damaged, William and Mary walnut bureau bookcase with original Vauxhall glass mirror doors, for £80. The repairs to my horror cost £35! (In 1971 an American dealer offered me £10,000 for it.) I also secured for £30 a Sheraton satinwood commode with Grecian urns inlaid on the 3 doors. In the Trerice sale a dealer in Swansea telephoned the auctioneers offering to go to £300 for it. As I took the message I felt bound to stick to the reserve of £250 and he got it for that.

At the sale of furniture at Hengrave Hall in Suffolk, we found a round Italian seventeenth century inlaid scagliola table in gorgeous colours, with the head of Medusa done in a centre plaque in fine mosaic, on gilt lion's paw legs. It was knocked down to me for £42 and was sold in 1984 at £6,500. It is fortunate that we still had just enough money or bank spending power to buy this sort of thing to start off St. Osyth. Nearly everything I owned in London or at Chilham had gone to Thelma, as part of the settlement to pay her off, or in the Trerice sale. Blickling was fully furnished with incomparable pieces; and I had not felt the need to keep more than was required to furnish the Cornish house sparsely as a summer residence.

In the end, just before we moved from Blickling, and I handed the lease over to Thelma, to renegotiate it, with the National Trust for the next 15 years, I took on a lecture tour of the North of England, through Christina Foyle, on the subject of historic houses; it netted me £25 a time and I was glad of the £300. Carmen was moving in, with the help, unknown to me, of the Naval Commander, who had navigated my yacht and was finally the cause of our marriage breaking up. I think Carmen later on sincerely regretted this. When I asked (after his successful promotion to the rank of Captain and a divorce) why she did not marry him, she exclaimed: "Marry that fat pig! I would sooner see him in hell first." Too much, too late.

It is not all that easy to take over a Convalescent Home, if you are not a medical man. I had first to find a matron. Miss George, without any medical qualifications, had called herself 'the Matron' and been accepted as such; reluctantly by the County Medical Officer of Health, who regretted bitterly the notion dating from Elizabeth I's time that a Charity was automatically capable of caring for the sick.

Fortunately help was to hand. My fourth son Carlo had just been born in the west turret bedroom at Blickling and the monthly nurse was a brisk and competent young SRN from Norwich called Sister Lyon. I suggested that instead of heaving babies out of the bath she would be better off shouldering the administrative duties of Matron in a Convalescent Home. She agreed to give it a try — and, although always 'at the end of her tether', lasted 12 years; and ran it so efficiently that we called her Lady Cowley — after the last lady of the Manor, who had lived in the big house.

*   *   *

The resoration of the gatehouse went on during our last year at Blickling; and it was possible to give a shooting party, using the still unconverted farm-bailiff's (ex-tailor's) west wing for lunch, and bringing the guests down from Norfolk. But it was a hideous wrench to leave the perfection of Blickling, and the first night we slept at St. Osyth, before the gatehouse was ready, was in the Convalescent Home, where the temperature fell to 12° below zero and I wept from the cold, wondering where I had finished up, and not realising that in our own bedroom at Blickling, in spite of the central heating, it was also registering 12° below.

The table from Hengrave, the walnut bureau bookcase, a panelled Baktiari carpet bought at Sothebys in a sale of Chester Beatty's carpets, all went into the Matron's drawing-room for the first year. Strutt and Parker took over the running of the farm, ploughed up the park and planted it all over with blue lupins to nitrogenate the ground. We lent the gardens to the Conservative Party for an address by the Home Secretary R. A. Butler. The audience of 4,000 spent most of their time turning to look at the sea of blue lupins stretching away behind them.

When George Judd lunched at Blickling he brought with him

Strutt and Parker's proposals for running the farm. I could either spend £24,000 with grain drier and all, which would show a profit of £2,400 (10% of the capital outlay) or £14,000 and lose £500 p.a. I chose the latter alternative and they only lost £5,000 the first year. Blue lupins merely have to be ploughed back into the soil. After that the farm only lost £2,500 a year for the next 20 years, under the care of Arthur Skinner, husband of the head housemaid at Blickling. The cottage at the corner of the quadrangle was rebuilt for them, and they moved in during April 1955. Arthur began every conversation with, "You please yourself, Sir, but . . . . " Doris, his wife, was of course a phenomenon, who not only carried over to St. Osyth the beeswax and turpentine standards of Blickling, but became responsible for the public showing of the interior too, as she had been at Blickling.

Darcy Braddell, had his blind spots, like most architects. The big drawing-room over the archway of the gatehouse had been used in Lord Rochford's time, towards the end of the eighteenth century, as a 'banketing hall', a sort of room for picnic banquets, I imagine; and it had been done up simply in the Georgian tradition. Darcy Braddell wanted to approach this room, from the ground floor of an austere medieval building, by a marble staircase with wrought iron banisters. This would not only have looked incongruous, but would have impinged on the very limited space in the main hall. I had the good fortune at this moment to hear of an original Charles II staircase, with the Queen's beasts of the period on the newel posts, in store at Knebworth, where it had remained since the death of 'Citizen Kane', the late William Randolph Hearst. He had a habit of picking up staircases or Burgundian fireplaces for St. Donats in Wales or St. Simeons in California. The staircase had come out of Costessey Hall, a Stuart house in Norfolk. This staircase and a 1520 Tudor stone fireplace from Ellens Hall in Lancashire, also left over from Hearst's time, I acquired from his executors. Darcy Braddell refused to have anything to do with the staircase. "It would be like falsifying a historical document," he complained and went off in dudgeon to Italy to study medieval villages; leaving me to put it in. Fortunately the builders, Everett and Sons of Colchester had a foreman called Hammond of remarkably sensitive artistic taste. Again and again he would make practical suggestions for preserving the original brickwork inside the window openings, or matching up original stonework. He produced a plan of the staircase well; showing the 4 walls spread out in sequence, with the existing doors and windows correctly placed. The problem was to fit in the Charles II staircase, so as to pass these at the correct levels. Already unexpected stone arched niches had come to light under the plaster. The staircase, when at Costessey, must have also ascended at a more gradual angle than was required by the cramped space inside the gatehouse. Each of the twisted 'barley-sugar' pillars of the staircase had to be altered top and bottom, to fit the new gradient. Everett complained afterwards that I had said, "All you have to do is to cock it up a bit." He asked for, and got, an extra £100 later. The staircase with its 8 Queen's beasts, each a work of art in carved wood of the Stuart period, had only cost £250. Hammond and I worked out the line for the treads and landings. It meant raising the narrow little medieval stone door of the ground floor water closet. This had obviously served the same purpose in the monks' time, because the door jambs had been cut away at hand level each side to take a wheelbarrow in and out when removing the nightsoil. Everett's carpenters were worried about the disappearance of the architect. "Who is going to design the mouldings under the stair-case?" "Mouldings!" I snorted, "I'll give you mouldings," and drew a few swiggles which satisfied their sense of priority and emerged in carpentered form to provide an edging to the supporting woodwork. When Darcy returned from his Italian villages he made no comment; but was later to be heard saying that some wrought iron lanterns on the landings were not worthy of such a fine staircase.

Why does one get married for the third time?

I was getting very disillusioned with Carmen at this period. As the popular song had it, 'She was a nice girl, a proper girl, but — one of the roving kind.' I went to a charity dress show at Terling Hall, where some famous models, Sylvia Shelly, Gloria Clarry and another were giving their services for nothing. I was sitting with a judge (Upjohn) in the window seat, when Gloria Clarry came down the catwalk. "That's a plump partridge," exclaimed the judge. Then Tessa appeared and I thought, that is the girl I'm going to marry. All I said was, "She is really beautiful." I knew the owner of the house — Ursula Rayleigh. Her husband was restrained for a while because he had a habit of standing up when the vicar published the Banns and saying, "I know just cause and impediment why she should not be married." This always caused maximum embarrassment. He was also said to keep a list of people he intended to sleep with, which was not popular in Royal circles. So on this occasion, he was not present when I asked Ursula to introduce me to the model. Ursula was in fact one of the trouts, of whom there was one always stationed in each county I had lived in, who had been at school with my first wife Thelma, at Miss Lewis's establishment, North Foreland Lodge. They all had standing instructions to keep an eye on me. Elizabeth Leicester had even refused to allow me to attend a dance at Holkham, although invited, because of counter-instructions received from her old school mate Thelma, while away on a course at the First Church of Christian Scientists, Boston, Massachusetts. However, as the Terling occasion was in aid of charity, Ursula introduced me to the hostess, (Margaret Screen) who was entertaining Tessa. I asked them all to come over for a drink the following day. Carmen appeared in a black riding habit, black slacks with a long black diamond cigarette holder, which I had given her. Barry Screen was impressed by the weight of Works of Art in the hall at St. Osyth. The front door and staircase were not yet installed.

Tessa, with her well-known slogan, "The best is good enough," took a favourable view of the building and agreed to have lunch with me in London. I thought it prudent, as I did with my next wife, to send her a copy of *The Story of a Lifetime* first. It is a slightly unconventional story of the experiences of Christ after the Crucifixion and before the Resurrection, based on a dream of Carmen's. It was published in a limited edition of one hundred copies by the Golden Cockerel Press, with alum-tanned sheepskin binding, and woodcuts by Clifford Webb. It is extremely sympathetic to the character of Christ — but as Carmen dreamt that she was three months pregnant by Christ at the time of the Crucifixion, it startled some believers. Tessa (or Pat as she was then known) was not dismayed. And the romance proceeded from there. By August we were lying under a haystack in Cornwall on a starless night with slugs falling on us; and by September she was in love — or so she said when she heard that I had sold Chilham for £94,000. It took me years and a divorce to discover that she sincerely loved me. In 1966, Carmen, supposedly tired of her Commander, was wringing her hands in the corner and pretending to go mad at the thought of my leaving her — I took her to see Rosamund Lehman doing the same thing in *The Waltz of the Toreadors*. After the annual service in the Chapel to commemorate St. Osyth on October 7th 1966, I left Carmen to join Tessa, and we departed next day in her Ford Anglia for Morocco and Spain. Carmen knew various coutouriers, like Speed and Joe Mattli, with whom she met a congenial naturalised Czech called Kaufler. The temptation to call him the Czech that bounced was too much, and this did not help the chances of reconciliation when I abandoned Tessa in Spain to rejoin Carmen and my sons for Christmas. The journey from Cadiz to Gibraltar with Tessa in the circumstances was sulphurous. I had paid all expenses for her Christmas and New Year at the Reina Christina in Algeciras with her son, and left her with the sapphire engagement ring. I was accused of doing everything on the scale of a butcher's boy.

It was not long before we met again and eloped a second time to Spain and Morocco. She had left her car conveniently garaged in Algeciras. I have never been able to resist women, so I suppose the marriage was inevitable — and it lasted eighteen years. My first one to Thelma lasted nineteen years. I expected to get an accolade from the Queen for such stamina. All I got was the bum's rush.

Tessa and I carried on the restoration and improvement at St. Osyth — much helped when the gravel seams were opened up in 1961. Thereafter, I bought her jewels, which she said she did not want — a 33.carat flawless cinnamon diamond, marquise shaped ring — a sapphire and diamond necklace, a sapphire and diamond bracelet, a 16.carat diamond brooch to match the cinnamon ring — and a diamond necklace and pendant (convertible into a ring) which she wore at the Mountbatten-Hicks wedding. Someone said they saw her wearing the Hope diamond.

Am I being unkind to Tessa? She took it all as no more than her due. Models tend to be arrogant. They are so used to attention; to being ushered to the best table in the best restaurants, that it all becomes a little difficult to unbend. But attractive and generous in her responses she always was.

When Tessa saw Darcy Braddell's conversion she pointed out that the only way to get from the main staircase to the rest of the rooms on the first floor was through the principal bedroom.

So Hammond was instructed to take the corner off the room, and form an internal porch in the Jacobean tradition; over the door of which he himself moulded my coat of arms in plaster and the date 1957. We were in Germany at the time and asked Doris on the telephone what it looked like. "It is definitely a work of art," she said. Later Hammond set himself up as a builder on his own and pottered about the place with 2 assistants, mending roofs and so on. He had developed a passion for fishing; and this seemed to take him away from the work a lot. He tried to placate us with a large golden carp which was slipped into the lily pond till winter came and the ice began to suffocate it, when my new stepson, without consulting me removed it to the deep 'engine' pond in the park; where its nose was seen once or twice rising excalibur-like to the surface. Since then it has never been seen at all; and if it lives as long as the one labelled by Frederick II of Hohenstaufen and caught 250 years later, it will outlive us all.

I am not trying to write the story of my life at St. Osyth or any of the other houses; except in so far as it affected my connection with them, or give some indication of the kind of life I lived there. The dramas were too fierce. I am surprised that the five-foot thick walls stood up to some of them.

We had to hack two tons of stone out of the wall on the top floor inside the garderobe to make room for a bath opposite the 'Rembrandt Room'. This room got its rather high sounding title from the series of original etchings by the master, shown to the public, in it. These cost from £60 to £120 at that time, according to their state, 1st, 2nd or 3rd state. Hammond helped me to hang them artistically when the plastering was finished. This plastering had been left half done when I had expected to introduce some panelling from Lullingstone Castle also offered to me by the same man who sold me the staircase. But I never bought the panelling and this meant that the finished plaster had to join the new plastering. I decided to make a virtue of this by having a band bordered by two neat lines drawn in the wet plaster. I then climbed a ladder and went round the room with a large nail scratching a series of letters in the wet plaster, which most visitors believe the monks to have done. I put a series of C's upside down to stand for Carmen; another wall was adorned with P to represent P for Patricia my third wife's official name. She was known to me as Tessa. Then on another wall I added a series of recumbent S's for

S to stand for Somerset. Later, after Kincaid Smith's retired farm bailiff, Murphy, who was living rent-free for the remainder of his life in the east wing, had died and I started the restoration of that part of the building, I repeated the motive with an S for Somerset and J for Juliet. So do our transient lives melt into the fabric of our buildings. Somebody mis-hearing this thought I said 'so do our transient wives melt into the fabric of our buildings', and she was not far wrong.

The restoration of the east wing was not begun till the autumn of 1969 and brought to light some startling features. Behind a Victorian cooking stove, was revealed a large stone Tudor fireplace, inside which was an original salt cupboard, where salt, then a precious commodity, was kept dry. One whole wall was found to be covered by a mural (partly defaced in the Civil War) with the Royal Coat of Arms showing the leopards couchant. On an adjoining wall were the 3 crowns in red which were the crest of the Abbey – and the vine leaves and bunches of grapes, probably introduced by Abbot Vyntner, who used the same motive in panelling, as a pun on his name.

Whenever I tried to reorganise a library with straightforward book shelves, the removal of the brown Victorian wallpaper would show up vertical timber-framed beams and plastering under which was the original wattle and daub – wattle sticks pushed through mud to reinforce it; like reinforced concrete. In one corner was a doorway of 1500. Upstairs we broke through the wall of a bedroom from the medieval turret beyond, where it had been walled up, and found two consecutive archways, so that we came out on a different wall from the one we had expected. It was all very exciting. This latest find lined the east wing to the staterooms on the top floor and virtually created a second house out of the building. Sometimes my son used to say irreverently, "In my father's house are many mansions." There certainly were; and all came in useful.

In 1960 we had completed the top floor by restoring the Calderon Room. This was named after the young Spanish artist, Fernando Calderon, who came with his bride on honeymoon, to paint a huge mural called The Running of the Bulls at Pamplona. Tessa and I had found him in the cold wintry church at Loeches outside Madrid, working for the Duke of Alba on an altar piece 51 feet high about the Apotheosis of Don Guzman to replace the

Rubens altar piece destroyed in the Spanish Civil War. He had always wanted to do something in England. For this stupendous mêlée of bulls and *aficionados* drinking themselves into a state of stupor during the feast of San Firmin he proposed to charge £600; which did not seem unreasonable even then. I had the canvas 28 ft long by 14 ft high, stitched together in two 7 ft widths by a sail-maker from Brightlingsea. It was laid flat on trestles inside the room, then hoisted into slots prepared on the east wall. We had last seen Calderon shivering on the scaffolding of the unheated church outside Madrid, where the Albas are buried. Young Alba, whom I had met with his wife Cayetana at Sutton when they were the Duke and Duchess of Montoros during the Sutherlands' time, happened to turn up, while we were there, to choose the ledge for his future tomb, in the high circular vault used by the family. An assistant had a large placard marked R I P, and kept jumping about with it from ledge to ledge like a monkey, until Alba decided on a comfortable resting place.

Fernando Calderon had been a bachelor at that time and we were somewhat astonished to receive a card from him on the way to St. Osyth from Venice on his honeymoon. He arrived with an attractive blonde Brazilian bride called Marly, whose parents had both been killed in an air crash. Work began at once on the picture; people streaming out of Pamplona in the top left hand corner, getting jumbled up in the middle and gored by bulls, of which about four were mingling with the crowd. They were all in seventeenth century costumes. Some were still drinking away in celebration of San Firmin, while bulls were tossing their friends about. The whole picture started on a gold background, in sepia. The only colourful figure was a matador squatting in the foreground with his back to the room, holding up a cloak to enrage some bull. His suit of lights was done in scarlet but Fernando did not feel satisfied with such ostentation and subdued it to brown and gold. The whole crowd scene was coming to life, when Marly announced that she was going to have a baby. Fernando, in the manner of Spaniards, was as proud as a peacock, until Marly told him that it was far too early in the marriage to start a family. The arguments began, in shrill tones, from which Fernando escaped to the mural on the second floor, mounted his ladder, and proceeded to take it out in paint. Everybody to the right of the picture began hitting everybody else over the head.

Barricades were knocked down. Clubs raised. The astounding thing to me, as an amateur artist who would by this stage have got covered in paint myself from head to foot, was that Fernando, working in a white sweater, under arc lights and drinking quarts of milk, obtained his effects without getting paint even on his fingers. Everything must be 'fuerte', he declared; but that did not mean bashing the brush at the canvas. When asked how long he expected his marriage to last, he clicked his heels together and said, "A la Muerte," and meant it. The doctor arrived and confirmed Marly's fears. Fernando's father and mother were notified in Santander, by telegram, and accompanied by a young friend, arrived on the next plane at Southend Airport. Nobody had remembered, or had time, to remind them that the traffic in England drives on the left. As there are no road signs in Spanish in England they ran over the policeman's feet at the first round-about. When the English bobby did his traditional bit about, "You can't do that there 'ere," they held up a card on which was written the mystic figures St. Osyth 492. The police telephoned. Did we know any Spaniards arriving at Southend? We did indeed. "Then get them the hell out of here before we arrest them."

The house seemed to be full of Spaniards, six if you count Marly, the Brazilian wife and her unborn infant. Two years later we saw the child at their flat in Madrid, flourishing except for having just swallowed a safety-pin. The Spaniards are very fond of children and another infant had joined the crèche by then.

The mural was completed in 6 weeks of July and August 1961. Fernando did a picture of Teresa, my daughter, on a swing in three-quarters of an hour. Also he started on the cat. He could draw anything, almost in his sleep, with the precision of a great master. When he was on a ladder he could be painting the top half of figures of which he would not even see, nor need to see, the bottom. In years to come there were periodical S O S's from Spain for photographs of the mural or the Calderon Room to illustrate the various books being published on his work. By then he had exhibited all over the world and done a lot of work in America. We saw them in Spain from time to time. He has remained one of my dearest friends; and his Christmas cards, reproducing his latest painting — perhaps the ceiling of the Chamber of Deputies at Palencia with 1,100 figures and horses, seen from underneath, galloping overhead usually add, in the Spanish manner, "Un fuerte abrazzo" from Fernando.

It is sad that many of my best friends were scattered so far apart – Pearl Levy in Sydney, Pantip Chumbot in Bangkok, Fernando Calderon in Madrid, Carlos de Salamanca in Marbella, Gillie Rumsey in Los Angeles, Paul Getty in Surrey, Charles Bellows in Pennsylvania, Randulph Barker from the Madelena Islands, Bill Forbes in Perthshire, Dick Alhusen in Norfolk, Anne Hale in Gloucestershire, Palmer Kennedy and John Hinkley in Delaware County, Francesca Ruspoli in Morocco and Allison Werner in Capri (both Godparents to my daughter, as Charles Bellows was Godfather to my daughter also); and if it were possible I should add to this list Carlo Fountaine, George Churchill and Miles Killearn from 'that undiscovered country'. One day I would fly them all to some central rendezvous at the same time. We would have a grand reunion.

I have recorded the painting of the mural at St. Osyth, because it is so large and difficult to remove that it has almost become part of the fabric of the building.

There was also the episode of the burglar. My wife had just taken delivery of a new Ford Corsair in London; and the exhaust system had fallen off with a clatter in the East End of London and was dragging its guts noisily down the Mile End Road. So we had to abandon it in a car park and take a train and taxi back to St. Osyth. We had scarcely returned by one o'clock in the morning and I was not in the best of temper; when young Matron Lyon telephoned from the Convalescent Home across the lawn to say that there was a burglar on her landing with a cloth cap and a torch. She and the red-headed Sister had just looked out of their rooms and seen him.

"I'll come and deal with the bastard," I said; rushed downstairs in my pyjamas, grabbed my double-barrelled shotgun, (a Purdey somewhat wasted on burglars) shoved two cartridges into the breech and loped across the lawn, to the Convalescent Home. Entering the patients' dining-room, I could faintly make out in the dim light from a corridor beyond, the antlered heads and gleaming eyes of Kincaid Smith's many victims. I peered into the shadows beyond the billiard table, and yelled, "I can see you. Come out of there you bastard." But nobody emerged. I then joined the Matron on the landing of the Georgian staff wing, the same which the redoubtable Miss George had occupied. One wondered what would have happened to the burglar if Miss George had been there to intercept him. Matron Lyon was also a woman of considerable backbone and was not afraid to do a tour of the building with me, peering into the darkest cellars. From the medical room I put a call through to the village police station. The constable's wife said her husband was out on his rounds but would be telephoning her a routine call at 2 a.m. I asked her to tell him what was happening; and the Matron and I then returned to her landing, where she let out a yell, "There they are," and pointed through the window at the end, overlooking the garden. Torchlights were flickering about the lawn beyond the cedar tree, held by two men wearing white shirts. So I threw up the sash window, shouted, "I'll teach you to burgle my house," and discharged the 12-bore into the night; aiming at the lights through the downward sweeping fronds of a great cedar of Lebanon.

There was a yelp of pain and an answering shout: "It's the police you fool and you've shot one of us."

This was surprising. How had they got there so soon? And in white shirts? However, I said as urbanely as possible: "That's all right. We have a medical room here. You can have it attended to at once."

The police constable felt justifiably aggrieved. "You are not really supposed to shoot the police," he said. I agreed. "But it would be easier to distinguish you from the burglar if you wore uniform." But at 2 in the morning he had not been so attired and, happening to telephone his wife just after my call, came straight towards the sound of the guns. In the meantime, the burglar, having armed himself with one of the brass stair-rods and 2 billiard balls (which he jettisoned later) could be heard laughing from the bushes, and all the way up the Colchester Road. Fortunately there were only a few pellets in the constable's forearm, and these were deftly removed by the Matron in a matter of seconds. One could scarcely offer quicker service. But on the whole it was not a successful evening. The burglar, who had probably mistaken the house for the main residence, returned ten days later and stole all the loose silver in the gatehouse without even waking us up. He left a weapon beside each piece of furniture he broke open. He wrenched open the door of my desk, to extract 9 gold sovereigns, but scattered all Winston Churchill's letters over the floor, without realising their value or importance. I felt upset for days by this violation of my property, as I had done by a similar robbery at Chilham, when the burglar was seen by the cook getting out of her window and down a ladder.

The only thing I recovered from the silver burglary was a silver medal awarded to me for the best sample of malting barley in Essex. This was the joke of the year. The farm at St. Osyth is somewhere around mid eighteenth century. Stanley Kubrick, after the 2001 Space Odyssey, looking for a location for an eighteenth century film, was delighted to find that the farm buildings had never been modernised. What happened was that the winter of 1962/63 was so severe that the ground froze solid, no water came through the pipes for 6 weeks, and everybody else's barley seed froze in the ground. As we were, as usual, six weeks behind everybody else, Cyril King was to be seen ploughing the Lodge Piece and seeding it in late March. So ours was the only sample that survived. The medal inscribed to Somerset de Chair for this feat, was handed in by the burglar at a pub in Hackney, well pencilled over to hide the inscription. The innkeeper gave him seven shillings for it. Eventually Donald McCulloch, who had interviewed me on television about the capture of Baghdad and who was now public relations officer to Watneys Brewery, asked me to lunch at their headquarters and returned the medal. Curiously enough the burglar had also spared a silver salver, inscribed to me by my constituants in Swaffham after my victory at the 1935 election, and a silver christening bowl inscribed to Somerset de Chair from his Godfather, Earl of Carrick (after whose son, Somerset Butler, I was named). Although this particular burglar got away with it, the subsequent news in the underworld that I was prone to shoot policemen and might be expected to do worse to burglars, spared me any further visits for several years.

CHAPTER 26

I knew a woman, Nell Luddington from Norfolk, who was buried under nine floors of a hotel in Agadir where the earthquake took place. She left a baffled husband and nine children. People questioned the workings of providence and Agadir recovered only slowly as a tourist attraction.

We drove there from the Gazelle d'or at Touradant – a pleasant oasis; on the way south to the Sahara. We wanted to see the camel market on the desert at Goulemine, but it was to take at least two attempts before we got there.

Tessa got the impression from a receptionist at the hotel desk in Agadir that there was a fine parador in Tiznit on the way; where we could break the journey for the first night. His cousin ran it. I might have guessed.

We drove down a straight road towards the south and the Sahara; reaching Tiznit in the dark. We found a maidan of beaten earth with a fort-like structure on one side which had been the army headquarters during the French occupation. We asked for the Hotel de l'Univers. Nobody seemed to have heard of it.

We found a café on one side of the square and sipped black coffee, mocha; named after a town in the Yemen, where the bean is grown, I have been told. There had to be a hotel somewhere. We drove slowly round the square again; and a small boy on a bicycle drew alongside us and said, "Hotel de l'Univers?" with a wide grin. "Follow me."

He darted down a side alley and we followed him, till we came to the forecourt of a disused garage where twenty or thirty Arab children were clustered in the forecourt, watching a black and white television propped up in the cavernous interior of the garage. The small boy ushered us importantly through the throng, shooing his friends out of the way. "Hotel de l'Univers," he announced proudly.

"This?" we quizzed. There was a manager leaning over a sort

of improvised bar. A heavy man with sleepy eyes. "Your cousin — " I suggested, "at Agadir."

"There is a room," he conceded and led the way, out of the garage and up some rickety stairs. There was a small room almost completely occupied by a double bed, and a basin in the corner, with a single tap, from which no water ran. Tessa inspected the sheets.

"Very clean sheets," said the manager.

"I think not," said Tessa, between clenched teeth. There were unmistakable signs of recent occupation, probably during the afternoon.

"There is another room," said the manager, wearily.

It was even worse. We went back.

"I change the sheets," he said.

"And pillow cases," said Tessa firmly. "Where is the bathroom?"

"Bathroom — ?" The manager looked hurt. "In Tiznit? A bathroom?" This was asking too much — even for the Hotel de l'Univers.

"There is a Water," he said. He went out on to the landing. It had a high-up cistern with a chain to pull. But a stick had been pushed under the lever arm. "No water at night," he explained.

There were some twelve other guests in the bedrooms — all Arabs. During the night the lack of water became awkward.

The bed sagged in the middle like a hammock, as soon as we both got into it, making us sit bolt upright. We had to laugh. But not for long — there was a large tear in the mosquito screen — and we began to get bitten; wondering if they were malarial of the anopheles variety.

It was a sleepless night and we came down to a breakfast, in the garage, of coffee and rolls; deciding that we would postpone our visit to Goulemine and return to Agadir.

Everything is relative: In Marrakesh at the Mamounia we gave a lunch party for Field Marshal Auchinlech who lived in Marrakesh. Francesca Ruspoli, Teresa's godmother, was there having taken over the top floor of the hotel for a year, while building her Palazzo in the Ourika Gorge; I was amused to hear from Auchinlech that he too had stayed at the Hotel de l'Univers at Tiznit; and that Thesiger, the explorer and author of *Desert Sands*, had come up that way from the Sahara and considered it unbelievable luxury after the sands of the desert. His mother had met him there, but had not been equally impressed. It struck me that the manager of the Hotel de l'Univers had been entertaining angels unawares. He should have kept a visitor's book; it might have been quite valuable one day.

The roads in Morocco were very much more primitive in the south when we first visited it in 1957 than they have become since the French left. When we first came to Morocco, Tangier in the north was still a free port — with no customs duties and a remarkable freedom from currency restrictions. Money changers had their booths up all along the street, with boards behind them, marking the fluctuating currencies, like bookmakers at a race meeting. You could go down the line, till you got the highest rate. Women's most exotic watches in the jewellers' shops would have tempted a saint to smuggle one home.

The British still had their own post office, with a red pillar box, marked V.R. for Victoria Regina.

The hinterland up to a certain distance was still Spanish Morocco. A well-known man in the story of Middle East espionage, called Meinertshagen ran a small hotel there. Or perhaps it was his son.

Further south the French were pulling out of French Morocco and there were only fifteen guests in the Manounia at Marrakesh. A sullen atmosphere prevailed in the south. A number of Frenchmen had been murdered on the way out. Most of the petrol stations were abandoned.

We drove over the Atlas Mountains, to the Gazelle d'or, where the proprietor, a French Count, was said to maintain an excellent cuisine. At the top of the pass we were enveloped in mist, and Tessa was convinced that a car behind us was trying to get to the Gazelle d'or and would secure the last room. So she plunged down the twisting road in the mist; vertiginous glimpses to right or left; till we reached the town; and found that the Gazelle d'or was outside it in a thicket of bamboo. There was crimson floodlit bougainvillaea growing all over the portico and we were allotted a bungalow. An Arab soffragi padded ahead of us, showing the way. We awoke in the morning sunshine to find camels grazing outside the window — and down a winding path a swimming pool — not heated and somewhat chilly in March.

In Taroudant we found an old walled Berber town, on the filled in moat of which Berber horsemen were carrying on some tournament of their own – charging at each other in their blue gowns with old brass mounted flintlock muskets levelled at each other, and raising these in the air and firing them at the last minute as they passed.

The road across the southern part of cultivated Morocco was interspersed with great mud walled castles, many turretted and castellated – where the Foreign Legion had once reigned over a restive countryside.

From Ouazza Zat to Tenerir, the road disappeared altogether, becoming a traverse across untreated rock; which jolted us into a sense of incredulity for 70 kilometres. Half-way along it we diverted into a picturesque gorge, where Arab children threw themselves down in front of the car – expecting and receiving baksheesh. At Tenerir at last, was a comfortable hotel; and the road resumed a more normal surface. We were told that we should have come from the other direction.

We did not reach the Camel Market at Goulemine till some years later; and this time we started a lot earlier, leaving Tiznit and the Hotel de l'Univers out of our itinerary.

Goulemine was a small frontier town – on the frontier of the Sahara proper, and a good dinner of French cooking was served to us, with appropriate Moroccan dishes eaten on divans in the Arab style. We were awakened before dawn by a roaring outside our window; and opened it onto a spectacle of primitive colour – there must have been a thousand camels, herded into the market place before us – with Arab dealers in their gowns of white or black or blue going round tapping the knees and hindquarters of camels to test their soundness; making them kneel or get up. No wonder they were roaring.

We spent the morning wandering about among the throng. This was the weekly mart for half a continent. The camel routes and caravans wound up to it from as far south as Timbuctoo (she of the knotted navel).

Outside the hotel I noticed the arrival of a young couple – the man, possibly French, obviously disconcerted by the price quoted for a room. They had a jeep laden with camping gear. But the girl startled me – so obviously a fair haired American of good family. She wore an Arab shift, and her feet were bare in the dust of the street. But her toe-nails were still neatly manicured. She looked at me with candid blue eyes, slightly defiant. She had obviously decided, as so many had in the 1960s to go hippy – and I wondered what anxious parents she had abandoned in Baltimore or Massachusetts to lead this wandering life. I was on the point of asking her if there was any message she wanted me to convey to parents or relatives at home, when her lover came out of the hotel and shook his head. They drove off in search of cheaper accommodation of which there was nothing else above the Tiznit standard in Goulemine.

By this time Tangier had been absorbed in Morocco and was just another town; and the frontier post between the former Spanish and French parts of Morocco stood abandoned and desolate. King Hassan's photograph hung over every reception desk; and he seemed extremely popular. But monarchs were becoming scarcer in the Arab world – one would have to fly over Algiers, Tunisia, Libya and Egypt before coming across another survival of the species in Saudi Arabia and further north in Jordan.

The only monarch I had met in the Middle East was young King Feisal II whom I had found at the age of six in the Palace of Roses, outside Baghdad with his uncle, the Regent Abdul Illah. They had both been shot and dragged through the streets of Baghdad in a subsequent Revolution. One wondered at times for what or whom we had been fighting. Survival, I suppose. The King was necessary to us then. And I learned years afterwards from a most unexpected source, where he had been guarded. The Conservative agent for the Harwich division of Parliament had been a naval officer on a cruiser in the Persian Gulf, where the young King with his English Nanny and the Regent had been guarded till we could refurbish his throne, after Raschid Ali al Gaylani's coup.

Now it is all gone – the dominion over palm and pine. And one with Nineveh and Tyre. It is difficult for a person who knew Kipling and grew up in a world of which a quarter was painted red on the map, to adjust himself to being a British tourist at the bottom of the queue. I wonder what history will say of us – and the French and the Belgians and the Dutch and the Portuguese who survived the assaults of Germany on our possessions in two world wars, only to throw them away; handing over two thirds of the world's surface from law enforcement and stability – to emergent nationalisms with corruption and political murder at regular intervals. No wonder the standards of law and order have fallen throughout the globe. One is reminded of the children who suffered an air crash on an island without grown-ups, in *The Lord of the Flies*. Primitive disciplines and appetites soon surfaced.

It was Winston Churchill who wrote the epitaph of the western world — 'We were so glutted with the fruits of victory that in our folly we threw them away.'

Was he perhaps right, even over India?

I remember my first appearance in public life — at a meeting of the Conservative Council, when I was a prospective candidate for South-West Norfolk, aged 23. Winston and old Lord Salisbury were pleading for Britain to retain control of defence and foreign policy in the future shaping of India. I stepped to the rostrum and shouted; "While you old tigers are fighting over the carcass of India the jackals of Socialism are entering your lairs and stealing the cubs." Heilger who followed me, a Suffolk member, said he always felt like the smoke after the bomb. Perhaps I should have pursued my political career further than I did. But in the end it was the flesh-pots that got me — or the women — or the bullets.

CHAPTER 27

On the 9th December 1962, an event half expected, and long dreaded by my first wife Thelma and me, occurred. Our second son Peter, committed suicide by shooting himself through the mouth, with the shotgun which I had given him for his twenty-first birthday.

Useless to apportion blame now, or indulge in recriminations. He had contracted rheumatic fever at Eton, and it was quickly diagnosed. Thelma, recently divorced and confident in her ability as a Christian Scientist to handle the situation, did not consider it necessary to inform me as Peter's father. She took him to a specialist, who said that he should be flat on his back in hospital having oriomycin injections. Thelma demurred and sought the advice of another specialist who was on holiday. By the time I heard about it, three precious months had elapsed and he was in St. Thomas's Hospital, with his wrists as thin as sticks. He was condemned to spend Christmas in hospital, before his slow and partial recovery began.

When he returned to Eton, he was not allowed to play games. Two valves of his heart had been burned out by the disease, and this was before the days of heart surgery and Doctor Barnard's discoveries. I got permission for Peter to have my mare at school, and he was allowed to ride this in Windsor Park. He began to feel isolated from his fellows, who teased him about this lordly pastime, when they were not allowed to ride. He wrote something saucy on one of the Headmaster's notices – sacred ground. He had to own up and be caned, rheumatic fever or no rheumatic fever. Fair enough. He could not have been allowed to trade on his disability. He was fifteen years old.

As he grew older, he lived with certain inhibitions. Doctors warned him that he must not contract a common cold. One is reminded of the Tsarevitch and his haemophilia, precluding the slightest bump for fear of bleeding.

Once or twice Peter began talking of suicide. He said that in Scotland, his hostess had said something so awful to him that he had decided to shoot himself — tactfully, of course, in a car outside the front door, so that it could be driven away by the police, without leaving a mess. I asked, "What on earth had she said to you?"

"She said, I was treating her house like an hotel."

"I expect you were. There was nothing very awful about that."

He never told his host about his disability, so when stalking or shooting grouse, would often, as the youngest member of the party, be sent the long way round with the ghillies. This led to over-exhaustion. The loss of two valves prevented the blood being pumped properly to his brain, at which times he suffered from some derangement.

At St. Osyth he wailed, "Nothing is ever what it seems." His mother had recently remarried, an amiable breeder of Lucas Terriers, who had been in the House of Commons with me. Peter, who had at first, after my departure, been placed at the head of the table, opposite his mother, felt his nose put somewhat out of joint. Thelma bought a lonely farm in a moat, in the most desolate part of Suffolk, for him, and there, after three years at Cirencester Agricultural College, he commuted to a job as a land agent in Ipswich. A couple looked after him, but the husband had been trampled in a cavalry charge of the Life Guards on manoeuvres on Salisbury Plain, and his head had been crushed. His wife cooked plain meals, which Peter pretended to eat, then threw into the moat at night.

I began to worry about his frame of mind and his isolation at the farm. He sought my advice on Chinese Works of Art, which he had started collecting, but he did not fit into St. Osyth, with my third wife, Tessa, "Dripping in diamonds" as he observed.

When he said, "Nothing is ever what it seems," he was referring to the gun, made by Purdey. Jocelyn Lucas, his stepfather, had pointed out that the barrels had been shortened and 'recessed' as a process needed to compensate for the effect of shortening the barrels on the bore. No doubt. But it was still an accurate and expensive gun, which had been nitro-proofed.

The last time I saw Peter, was when I went over to the farm, an hour's drive from St. Osyth. He lived near Eye. He wanted me to see a Wei Dynasty pottery horse's head, and a marble carving of a horse, with head down, very possibly of the Tang period. I took a decanter of vintage port with me; and he shared some of this. It was the last time I saw him. I hope it did not affect his heart. But I was worried about his increasingly morbid condition, and on my return, had urged Thelma, by telephone, to give up all her other commitments for two months, and move in with him. I knew I could not be of sufficient help to him for more than a few hours at a time. He would soon begin to get querulous. Thelma said it was quite impossible. She had people coming to dinner – a big party for fourteen – in a fortnight. Then she and Jocelyn were committed to staying in Buckinghamshire with Bertie Buckinghamshire – a long prearranged house party. And so on.

So she was staying with Bertie Buckinghamshire, and Tessa and I with George Spencer-Churchill at Northwick, in Gloucestershire, when the telephone rang just before lunch at Northwick.

Beware of hubris. I had just been reading in the *Sunday Times*, the leading review in the fiction section on my new historical novel *Bring Back the Gods*. The article was headlined 'Frequently flows the Rubicon' and referred to the gilded sewer of the Roman World.

George Churchill also had a large luncheon party of fourteen or sixteen people due to arrive at any minute. The call was from the police at Eye. "There has been an accident, I am afraid Sir." My heart missed a beat.

"What sort of an accident?"

"Well, sir, I don't know how to say it, but I am afraid your son has been shot."

"You mean he shot himself?"

"It looks very much like it, sir."

The blow so long dreaded, was nevertheless too much to bear, and my only desire was to get away from the people who were arriving, and hide myself in my room, till I could get over it, or collect myself enough to face the guests. But George (who had been left for dead in the First World War) and my wife Tessa, who believed in self-control and the stiff upper lip, insisted that I go through the luncheon party, listening to the small talk of my neighbours, as if nothing had happened. On a later occasion, Tessa, was to describe my habit of having flowers put on Peter's grave on the anniversary of his death, as "amateur theatricals." These were hard English people, and perhaps they were right. Face up to it at once. Don't give in. So, for their sakes, and the social conventions, I bottled up all my feelings of guilt (for having failed him as a father) and misery, and went through the motions. So I am prone at unexpected times, but especially around the anniversary of December 9th, to dissolve into tears. Is it so surprising?

The events of the next few days were a nightmare. I arrived from Gloucestershire at the farm in Suffolk, on a cold winter's day, for the inquest, dressed in a black hat and long overcoat. Thelma, also in black, arrived almost at the same moment, and gasped. She scarcely recognised me; or was reminded perhaps of our first reunion on the quayside at West Loch Tarbert, when I had returned, wounded, from the Middle East, and she felt that she was seeing a ghost.

Her solicitor, John Barstow, asked me to identify the body. It was lying inside the coffin, and the face was puffed and waxy — perhaps even repaired with wax. I could not honestly say that I recognised my son. "Surely there must be something," he said desperately.

"Well, I think I recognise the hands."

"That will have to do."

And the lid of the coffin went down. Oh God! Do we really have to go through these things in life? We start out so gaily; so optimistic, and then — Wham! — out of clear sky — bullets and air cannon-shell. Or this. Our whole lives are subtly altered. We are never the same again. It is as if an express train were racing along and somebody switched the points without warning, and you are slowing down, with screaming brakes into a siding.

After the inquest, I returned to St. Osyth, and developed discoid excema on my back and upper arms. The local National Health doctor diagnosed it first on the telephone as ringworm. But Mitchell Hedges, in Harley Street, knew what it was at once — the result of intolerable nervous strain, when something has to give, and the body cracks rather than the mind. He recommended no baths for six weeks, and a complete holiday in the sun. By chance, the great freeze started on Boxing Day. Everybody combined to make Christmas cheerful — Carmen sent both Rory and Carlo to spend their first Christmas since the divorce with me, and there was Teresa, four years old, so after their birthdays in January, Tessa and I flew to Egypt, determined to see the great temple of Abu Simbel on the Nile, before it was raised to a new position to make way for the High Dam.

Visiting Egypt in 1963 was very different from my recollections of it in 1946, when Miles Killearn ruled from the British Embassy as a latter-day Cromer – the last of the British Pharaohs.

Now we were dogs; who had, only seven years before, been at war with Egypt. Our passports, instead of being waved aside as unnecessary, were heavily scrutinised. A Levantine, who was organising our tour; a smooth man, in a grey suit, looked over the official's shoulder to see how much currency was marked on the last pages of our passports. "Only £90 in traveller's cheques, that won't go very far," he sneered.

"We are supposed to have paid for the whole trip in advance," I explained. A mirthless grin from the Lebanese. While we were waiting to collect our baggage, an Egyptian boy of about ten, in a grey jellabiah, nicked the signet ring off my little finger and slipped through the crowd, like an eel. The police shrugged their shoulders.

We were next embussed and arrived, instead of at the hotel advertised in the brochure, at a low down hotel in the brothel quarter. By this time, most of the guests, after a five hour flight were too tired and depressed to argue. But this is where Tessa's character comes into its own. She was 'not prepared to be thrown into a doss house,' and the Levantine's feeble pretences that all the promised accommodation was unaccountably unavailable, were scornfully rejected. He was marched to the telephone, and sighing for the delicious profits he was foregoing, made reservations for us at a decent hotel. He took it out of us at later stops on the journey. Next day we moved to the old-fashioned Semiramis, where Tessa was startled and somewhat reassured to find Sudanese servants, garbed in white, standing guard outside the doors of the bedrooms all night.

At Aswan, we saw the Nile steamer, on which we were to make the final journey up river. As it was not sailing till next day, we decided to spend the night on shore at the Cataract Hotel, from which we had a view of the Aga Khan's mausoleum across the river; with triangular sailed feluccas gliding by – a restful sight for the spirit of that old man who had the world to choose from for his resting place.

By the time we joined the ship for the first night of the voyage we found that the cabin and shower we had paid for, had been

334

commandeered by two travelling Englishwomen — Polly Bruce and Betty Pollock, who seemed reluctant to relinquish their comforts. So we were relegated to a single cabin, over the engine room, in which an upper berth had hastily been installed. I took the upper berth as a matter of courtesy, but Tessa, looking up at its flimsy supports, doubted its stability, and with good reason. The frame was of immensely heavy square mahogany; and the whole thing gave her an uneasy feeling.

We bathed in the Upper Nile, from the bank, in spite of gloomy prognostications of some fellow passengers about bilharzia. But that bug is normally confined to the sewer-polluted waters of Cairo, and the Lower Nile.

At dinner we met a couple called Armstrong. He was suffering from the same complaint as I — discoid excema; which came out in the form of small circles the size of the silver sixpence, then in circulation; with unsupportable irritation. He had good cause for it too. He had built up the Ribena business, and half the blackcurrants in England went into producing this invogorating red liquid. Then, one morning without any warning, he received a letter saying that Birds-Eye had bought a majority of the shares and taken over the business, but would be delighted if he stayed on as General Manager. His mind, after years of thinking of himself as Ribena in person, suddenly could not take in the enormity of its being controlled by anyone else. So he too had been recommended a cruise up the Nile, to get away from it all.

We glided down on Abu Simbel in the dusk. There is nothing like it in all the world; and taking it to pieces and reassembling it on an eminence above the lake, to be formed by the High Dam, then under construction, was an act of sacrilege against the ancient Gods of Egypt, and man's aesthetic genius, which no modern economic advantages could possibly outweigh.

Every so often in history, buildings are constructed which seem to express the sublimer aspirations of the human spirit. They arise almost effortlessly out of the ground — like Angkor Wat or Chartres cathedral. The Alhambra in Spain; even a fairy palace like Chenonçeaux, spanning the river Cher; or Compton Wynyates, resting like a ruby in a fold of green velvet.

Abu Simbel was like a stage set for *Aida* — but far more intimate than I had expected. The thing was only four yards away, separated from the water by a narrow beach of reddish sand. First came the four figures of Rameses' wife Nefertari, brought to life out of the dead rock. It is not the rock that is living. She stands there fourfold – two statues each side of the rectangular doorway. The figures are about four times life size, twenty or thirty feet, seemingly smaller because only a third as high as the neighbouring figures of her husband. No women's lib here. Twelve yards further along the gently shelving beach, reared the four fantastic figures of Nefertari's husband, Rameses II. Vanity in stone, perhaps; red sandstone. Hewn from the cliff, these majestic seated figures brooded with more permanence than the severed head of Ozymandas abandoned on the desert of Shelley's imagination. Even here, in spite of the size of these sixty feet high figures with the effigy of his wife knee-high beside him, the whole effect was intimate. You could reach out and touch it. A finely carved falcon guarded the entrance to the inner shrine.

We were told that at sunrise the sun shone directly through the entrance and lighted on the head of Amon Ra, seated with three fellow gods inside the shrine. So, after wandering about the knees of the statues – only one of which is headless – and all the rest preserved by the rainless atmosphere of upper Egypt for three or four millennia, we returned to the ship for supper.

Before dawn, we were filing down the gangway in the dark, and being guided into the stone passage in the centre of the temple, towards the inner sanctum, which the rising sun was supposed to penetrate. The sun rose outside, but did not penetrate the interior at all. It obliges only at the winter and summer solstices. So we were reduced to taking flash photographs; and retired somewhat sheepishly on board.

It was now that one of the Ancient Gods reached out a hand to protect Tessa, for she decided to slump down in a wicker chair on the deck, outside the cabin, to continue feasting her eyes on the marvellous façade, while I, not overjoyed at having risen before dawn in vain, went inside. I climbed up the ladder and flung myself down on the upper berth. The whole contraption collapsed with the suddenness and precision of a guillotine on to the bunk below; where Tessa might have been lying, and would certainly have been crushed to death; or at least maimed and disfigured for life. Her famous beauty marred for ever. The shock, both for me in crashing down so unexpectedly, and for Tessa outside, seeing what might have happened to her, was enormous.

But my first reaction was one of rage at the callous inefficiency of Egyptian workmanship, and the risk the Company had taken with our lives. I roared for the Captain of the ship; who took one look at the disaster — the two bunks closed as neatly together as a clothes press — and said — "Two whisky soda, I think, yes?" I said, "Yes, indeed," and these were brought, also carpenters with shame-faced expressions. After this, it was difficult not to recall some of the comments on Egyptians, I had heard from Miles Killearn. "The paste is rotten" and other comments during the paling rays of British sunset over Cairo. Certainly, independence did not seem to have improved their efficiency or attention to detail, and I remember Faroukh's cousin comparing them to an aircraft with a ceiling of nought feet. Nevertheless, it was an Egyptian pilot and crew who had flown us safely to Cairo — and in spite of gleeful prophecies to the contrary, Egyptian pilots had been found fully capable of navigating the Suez Canal after Nasser had nationalised it.

We returned down the Nile, to Luxor, where we regained some of the luxuries of civilisation in the Winter Palace Hotel, surrounded by its lovely gardens.

From this much safer base, we visited the Valley of the Kings, and another of the wonders of the world, the Temple of Karnak. When Napoleon's army extended his authority by sending a regiment up the Nile, and came in sight of Karnak, the troops presented arms, instinctively, without a word of command; so awe-struck were they.

Here again there is nothing else remotely like it in the world. I have described it elsewhere — a forest of stone, in which the trees had succeeded in growing up to the sky. And having visited it as a second lieutenant — I need not dwell on it again, except to say that Tessa was suitably impressed. The best was indeed good enough. So we decided to hire a gharry to return by moonlight. Unfortunately, the poor old nag, drawing the open vehicle, was so thin and bony, we thought he would never make it. Nevertheless, we reached the legendary avenue of Ram's-headed sphinxes, and wandered about in the dark. This was before the days of son et lumière. There was no moon, but the starlight was enough. The vast columns of lotus headed pillars disappeared mysteriously in the darkness above us.

The driver seemed determined to return along the Nile road at a gallop, which was the final torment for the poor old nag, who collapsed and died in the shafts in front of us, much to our distress. There is a story in Spain of a man who complained that he had only just succeeded in teaching his donkey to work without food, when the patient beast died on him. The Egyptian fellahin still had much to learn, and seemed to us, only to be on the bottom rung of the ladder, which ascended to the heights scaled by the builders of Abu Simbel and Karnak. When we were finally returned to the hotel in the dark, and paid the driver, I did not examine the change he gave me, which, I discovered next day, included a meal token on some Scandinavian railway.

The Syrian or Lebanese organiser of the tour was still trying to get his own back on us for the business of the hotel accommodation in Cairo. So we should not have been so pleased when told that our first class supplement on the sleeping car from Luxor to Cairo necessitated our leaving the hotel before dinner and hastening to the station. There we sat on upturned packing cases for two hours, while various trains, which we were not booked on, arrived and departed. After two hours, the rest of the tour, looking well fed and rested, arrived in a hotel bus, and were immediately put on a train, while we were told that ours, with special sleepers – the old Cook's Wagon – Lit – would come in due course. It did, and after forty years in constant use, had nearly rattled itself to pieces. Desert dust came in through chinks everywhere, making breathing difficult, and we were glad eventually to reach the American haven of the Nile Hilton at Cairo in the morning.

Here we ran into the woman I had proposed to as a girl, (Dot Collins) in Douglas Fairbank's swimming pool at Pickfair in Hollywood, when I was eighteen. Dorothy Willard-Brown, now widowed, was still a Christian Scientist, and as delightful as ever. Advised by Tessa to wear slacks when climbing the pyramid above a lot of staring Arabs, she accompanied us in a hired car to Giza.

The last time I had been here was when Quintin Hailsham and I had sat at the base of the great pyramid and drunk coffee before separating, to be shot on different battlefields. I had felt much more secure then with the British Army based in the Kasr Nil barracks and controlling every road and canal in Egypt.

We started to climb the ten foot high stone blocks, and Dorothy Willard-Brown, and I, who were of the same age, realised by the time we had ascended a third of the way to the top, that it was a long way and time since Pickfair, so we were content to sit in the shade of the stones while Tessa climbed to the very apex of the pyramid, and took a photograph of its shadow in the slanting sunlight stretching almost to the Nile.

Having seen the gold sacophagus of Tutankhamun in his tomb, in the Valley of Kings, and his gold and glass inlaid mask in the museum, to add to all the other wonders of Ancient Egypt, we felt we could return to the regions of the coldest winter in England, where the water pipes were still frozen underground. It did not worry me as I was still within the six weeks for which the skin specialist had prescribed no baths – but I felt better and more relaxed for having been laved by the waters of history and the Nile. Also, I had fulfilled, for a fourth time, the repeated saying that once you have tasted the waters of the Nile, you will return.

The travels began early – up the Moselle while waiting for our daughter Teresa's arrival. Then when she was only a month old, and her mother forty-one, a flight to Tangier and a hired car up into the mountains at Xauen. The baby howled while we were exploring the Soukh, and the Arabs (who are accustomed to babies being wrapped tight in swaddling clothes for three months after birth) thought she was dying and sent a boy in search of us.

By the time we had crossed over to Spain and reached the Marbella Club Hotel, (in those days, little more than a converted set of farm buildings, with a small reception office in the corner), Tessa had a serious haemorrhage. Fortunately Lady Cynthia Payne and a dentist friend in the next room offered assistance; and a competent Spanish doctor arrived promptly and stopped the bleeding. But it was a premature journey.

Fez; Granada; magical cities. Who can visit them without failing to be excited? We had been to Fez before – and were to go there again. A walled city, with cobbled stoned streets; only donkeys and no wheeled vehicles. A thousand minarets. At every turn some hidden courtyard, and a glimpse of some scene out of the Arabian Nights. And in the ramparts, the Palais Jamail – once residence of the Vizier. Now the most exotic of hotels.

Granada. Can there be a more romantic spot in all the world – with its Moorish palace and the patio of the twelfth century lions, splashed with water; the garden of the princesses and the wing where Washington Irving immortalised it, perched over a gorge. Here, Teresa was probably conceived, in the Parador de San Francisco, in the chapel of which were laid in State the Reies Catholicos, Ferdinand and Isabella, who conquered the Moors and sent Christopher Columbus to discover a new world. Across the valley the Generalife (spelt like an insurance company, but pronounced Heneral Leefey). Surely one of the most beautiful and satisfying buildings in the world – the summer residence of the Moorish rulers, with its arch of fountains in the patio.

Tessa and I grew up in love in these glorious surroundings. I have a photograph taken of her in her sleep, leaning against a wall, on a bench, in the shade of the Generalife; she could never have looked more beautiful, with those perfectly balanced features, eyelids closed above shadowed cheeks, and the perfect jaw line. Why is such beauty given to some and not to others? Perhaps because if it were given to all it would not be at all remarkable.

And of her, it could truly be said, as it was of Cleopatra, 'age cannot wither her, nor custom stale her infinite variety.' At sixty, people thought she was thirty-five or forty, but in the end, as my discerning daughter said, I settled for contentment, and married for the fourth time, into a life of untroubled bliss; and received the blessing of another daughter, born in due course to comfort the waning hours.

Marriage is an institution we have inherited from the nineteenth century. Now people no longer count on the freehold, and are content with a lease, renewable on either side at ten, twenty or thirty years. In the end it is clash of temperaments that usually causes the break. Not true in Carmen's case, that was betrayal and infidelity – the same faults I had displayed in my own marriage to Thelma.

At Granada, I was impressed by the immense self-confidence of Charles V, who had dared to add a square Renaissance building with its round central courtyard, and eagle-held rings in bronze, to the intricacies of a Moorish palace. The union is successful and explains much in the Spanish character which combines the subtlety of the Mahommedan with the rigidity of the Spanish Inquisition.

What treasures there are in Spain – from the Escurial, or the chapel at Toledo, with El Greco's Burial of Count Orgaz, to the Vaille de los Caidos, where Franco built a cathedral underground to the memory of the fallen in the Civil War.

We only knew Spain in Franco's time – an orderly country. I remember a night in Malaga, during the Semana Santa. We were renting a villa at Torremolinos (before it was spoilt) with a mile of foreshore, from Manolo de Salamanca. His brother, the Marquis, asked us to join him in the Mayor's room in Malaga to watch the procession. There was much sherry and Spanish wine where we crowded to the balcony as the heavy statues were borne by on the shoulders of devout Catholics. Some robed in the scarlet of the Inquisition with their pointed hoods. And suddenly amid the hubbub of the crowded street came the wailing of the Faena, a gipsy voice, intoning in a rising and falling cadence all the melancholy and history of Spain.

"Listen, listen," cried Carlos de Salamanca, holding up his hand. And suddenly the whole city was still, as the sad sound of the singer's voice wailed over the heads of the procession. They passed by – the Virgin, encrusted with jewels, innumerable saints, each borne on the shoulders of sweating penitents – and still this sad immemorial crying sounded over the roof tops. Who was the singer? No one knew. Some descendant of the Moors, driven out of Spain in 1482.

In Granada are the tombs of the Catholic Kings, in a vault, impressive in their marble immobility and there are pictures of piety by the great artists in the Church above them. Memling and others.

Spain is still a deeply religious community. At the age of three Teresa got loose during a procession headed by the Bishop in the Cathedral at Burgos and the priests were overjoyed, took her in hand and carried her along. She was named Teresa after St. Teresa of Avila that fabulous walled city, surviving from medieval times. The Spaniards delighted to call her Terecita. Muy Guapa; as indeed she was. Her mother was hermosa, which is something different.

All these early travels in Spain must have gone into building Teresa's character somehow. She certainly has all the intolerance and steel of the Inquisition.

There were other journeys – especially to America, when we acquired the American farm, and after one look at it, went on to Calgary and Lake Louise in Canada.

By that time Teresa was seven, and riding with cowboys down in the corral – she was also difficult to extract from the swimming pool. We had to wait three days before the snow had cleared sufficiently for us to reach Lake Louise. My father and mother had visited it on their honeymoon and talked much of it.

They had also visited the Grand Canyon, and stayed at the Bright Angel, which was full. They had been offered the billiard table (in 1902). My mother said she did not mind the billiard table so much as the twelve Chinese sleeping on the floor round it.

342

Tessa and I also visited the Grand Canyon. What wonders, after that, are there left to visit?

Lake Louise came up to expectation, except for the weather which was cloudy. The glacier was sometimes reflected in the lake when it was unruffled enough. I was reminded of Mapourika Lake in the South Island of New Zealand where the ice-blue Franz Joseph glacier is reflected in the water also.

Perhaps I have been everywhere that matters, except South America and Mexico. Looking back over my life, I find that it is the far places that loom largest. I remember Stanley Spencer saying to me at Cliveden on the subject of his always painting check trousers – once he started on them, it was like buying a loaf of bread on the way to China. Buying a loaf at the corner shop in London was insignificant, but as soon as you bought one on the way to China, it became important. The same with my travels in the Middle East. Riding an Arab mare in Essex is not quite the same as in the Egyptian delta.

One of our last journeys before the divorce was to Cambodia. The elephant passed sedately through the garden, casually dropping a bright yellow turd, round and large, like a football. The bungalows of the Auberge des Temples slumbered in afternoon sunshine. It was February (1970). Bodies were to be seen floating down the Mekong river; but so far the fighting had not disturbed the ancient temples of Angkor Wat and Angkor Thom.

Outside on the tarmac road dividing the hotel from the moat of the great five-towered temple, a Cambodian water carrier, with water in tall bamboo jars suspended from a pole slung over his shoulder, chaffered with a customer.

The temples brooded in their surrounding jungle. The mere proximity of such awesome beauty acted as a magnet, and I roused my wife. Not that I was the energetic member of the partnership. She was always the one to climb to the top of the Cathedral. But we had travelled a long way from Bangkok, via Phnom Penh Airport and the airstrip at Siam Riep, nearest to the temples. We had already done the tourist's regulation visits to the three temples, marvelling especially at the approach to Angkor Thom, guarded by giant stone faces of the Khmer Gods; each head ten or twelve feet high.

Now we wanted to wander up to the main temple of Angkor Wat. There is nothing quite like it in the world. The façade presents a tall tower, tapering towards the top, all intricately carved, flanked on each side by two lesser towers, also carved in stone, or it appears that way. They are really four corner towers.

A vast staircase rises towards the central tower. Steeper ones descend at the sides of the temple; creating a sort of giddiness at the idea of going down them.

It is always stimulating living with a model, before or after marriage. But when you have married someone for their beauty, it is not always comforting to find a tendency to pontificate, and a determination always the be right. I told her — "I know what epitaph will be on your tomb — I have decided." She was immensely practical, tidy and loyal. It was a pity I could not live up to it all, or be prepared to repeat more often the three little words which mean so much to a marriage — "I was wrong." She could have used them once or twice herself during a marriage of eighteen years!

We had come together for this journey in Bangkok. She on her way to visit her sister in the Solomon Islands, I to the Imperial Museum in Taiwan. She had spent a week alone at the Beach Hotel in Pataya and we were welcomed in Bangkok by our old friend Princess Chumbot; the first woman in Thailand to preside over a bank, and achieve many other distinctions unknown to women in the Orient. Her husband had been Crown Prince; and she had erected in his honour, in her garden, a seventeenth century lacquer pavilion, wrenched from the reluctant grasp of some Abbot in an up country monastery. The lacquer panels inside showed French soldiers in the uniform of Louis XIV's time. Pantip Chumbot's brother-in-law, Mai Discul, showed us the sights of Bangkok. The temple of the Reclining Buddah, and the temple of the Emerald Buddah. We sailed in the early dawn up the river to the water market. My telephoto lens was stolen on that boat. At this time, Tessa's sister, Nobby Aveline, also going to the Solomon Islands, was with us. I always felt happy in her company, and our friendship, like that of Tessa herself, survived our divorce four years later. Nobby had gone on to Hong Kong, to wait for us there, while we took the somewhat more expensive detour through Cambodia — just in time — as it transpired. We were almost the last Western visitors to the Temple before the Khmer Rouge closed in, and the air strip was cut off.

We wandered about the great temple — as dusk came on —

running our fingers over the endless bas reliefs of the inner arcades and peering into the dark recesses of the upper towers. Tessa was higher up as usual, and although not afraid of heights, or spiders, recoiled a step when she realised that the whole floor of a darkened chamber was moving — it was a living carpet of spiders. Bats clung to the domed ceiling in great numbers and flew twittering out into the gloaming around our heads.

One evening we took a gharry — one of the horse-drawn open cabs, used for sightseers, to drive round the whole circumference of the moat. Each side was a mile long, and the water was about two hundred yards wide. At a watering place, buffaloes were floundering in the shallows and swimming out into the depths. Further round, in the sparse jungle — the trees are not very dense here, and there are leaves on the ground; a Buddhist monk in his saffron-coloured robe, sped past us on the dusty track on his motor scooter, hastening perhaps to his evening prayers.

In the bus taking us one morning to the third temple, Bantai-Serai, deep in the jungle, a large black tarantula crouched over the window, and was hastily brushed outside. This temple was smaller than the others, but the carving was of a far higher standard, and could stand comparison with the doors of Ghiberti or the work of the Renaissance in Italy, three centuries later.

Who were these extraordinary Khmers, with their high standard of architecture and carving? A million of them had lived in the area; and all decamped suddenly — almost certainly because of malaria, which would not have been understood or curable by them. After that, the jungle took over — until the French archaeologists arrived in the nineteenth century. They went on with their restoration, even during the fighting which followed our visit — bicycling between the front lines, where the guns were tactfully covered over as they passed. Then came victory for the Khmer Rouge, and the blood bath, which is believed to have killed half a million people. We live in savage times, where genocide has been practiced on a scale not known since Genghis Khan.

I had only been able to finance this trip and Tessa's round the world via the Solomon Islands, by getting an advance of £25,000 from MacAlpines, against some future contract for extracting gravel from the estate at St. Osyth. In all, I took £195,000. Moreover, I had persuaded Kenneth MacAlpine to let me transfer £27,000 of Corporation of London Stock, (held in trust as a reserve against the possibility of a shortfall) into a recumbent Jade Horse of the Ming period, costing £27,000 (at Spinks in 1969). The Corporation of London Stock had already wilted, but the Horse was valued by Christies in 1976 at £120,000. So on balance, I seemed to have come out favourably. But my overdrafts soon caught up. This is how we lived in the twentieth century; if you had access to counsel's opinion and could sell your sand and gravel under a licence for a capital gain, free of tax.

Along these lines, Tessa and I had been able to live fairly comfortably since 1961, when the first excavations were paid for. We had travelled a good deal, and the highlights of our marriage are undoubtedly the journeys and the combined effort at collecting, under the fatherly eye of one of the greatest collectors of them all — George Spencer-Churchill, with whom we stayed four or five times a year at Northwick.

See p 331

When in time it came to another divorce, and setting Tessa up in a suitable house "The best is good enough". It was a beautiful house on the river, at Strand-on-the-Green, an exquisite stretch of Georgian houses, laved at high tide by the Thames, with a lovely garden behind it and a garage for three cars. There she was able to throw a Champagne party, with a butler and six footmen with striped waistcoats, during Teresa's coming out season. My new wife Juliet and I floodlit St. Osyth for a dance on one of the long hot nights in 1976, which could never be repeated. It all seemed to have worked out for the best, and the best was good enough.

CHAPTER 29   *The Farm in New York*

In June 1973 I bought a silver Monteith punch-bowl at the Grosvenor House Antique Dealer's Fair. It was dated 1708 in the reign of Queen Anne. I regarded it as a piece of respectable antiquity in the realm of silver, although it was still in pristine condition with lion-mask handles, and the sterling marks of 1708 still clearly visible. Yet this was the year when Queen Anne, some say through the error of one of her clerks, who thought that 2,000 acres must be too little, granted a patent for 2,000,000 acres, comprising the whole of the Catskill Mountains in New York State to Johannis Hardenberg and seven associates. This was the famous Hardenberg patent which was the subject of legal disputes for nearly 100 years, and prevented the land-hungry immigrants arriving in America from getting their hands on upper New York State as early as they did in other parts of the Eastern seaboard. The area became known from the Hardenberg Patent as the Patent, and later as God's Patent. Old ladies could be heard mumbling that they had looked for a lost thimble all over God's Patent. As late as 1973 I asked my neighbour in the Western Catskills, Dorothy Hinkley, if she had ever heard the phrase God's Patent and she said, "Oh yes, sure."

It has always seemed to me a good name for the area. It certainly contains within its 2,000,000 acres a high proportion of God-fearing folk. There are seven churches in each village and no public houses; which is the exact opposite of the situation in England where there is possibly one church and seven pubs. When I arrived in 1965, the nearest town was 'dry' — It still practised prohibition 40 years after everybody else in America had given it up. There was a single liquor store 8 miles in the opposite direction, at Hobart.

English names, Stamford, Hobart, Norwich, Cooperstown, Binghampton, Albany. I have often speculated on the appearance of the name Hobart so close to the farm. Is this a link with the

Hobarts who were building Blickling in 1620? Did some younger son come out to America at about the time the Monteith bowl was being engraved in 1708?

Well, it is a long story, whatever happened. There were Indians still in the Catskills, Mohawks and Iroquois mostly, who chaffered with the land speculators, or disputed more violently the boundaries of the Hardenberg Patent which was breaking up their old hunting grounds.

Alf Evers in his book on the history of the Catskills describes them thus: 'They were things of mystery, things which asserted their influence over the manor folks in subtle ways which were past puzzling out. Rainstorms and windstorms, for example, plainly formed about the heads of the mountains and from these swooped down to revive or destroy crops. In the fall the snow whitened the Catskills while summer still lingered on the manor as if to warn those below to get their pumpkins in and heap leaves and straw about the foundations of their houses in preparation for the coming winter. Every change in temperature or humidity brought a corresponding change in the look of the mountains. Sometimes they seemed to advance, at others to retreat; their deep blue colour changed in a few moments to lavender or grey. On a summer afternoon they seemed soft and green, and in the winter when the foliage of their oaks and beeches fell, they displayed hard rocky faces capped by the evergreens showing black against the snow.' In the fall the maple-covered hills turned scarlet and gold. They seem to catch fire in the setting sun.

I used often to use the throw-away line, "My farm in New York," leaving people to speculate as to where exactly between the Empire State Building and the Statue of Liberty you could fit a farm of 400 acres. Very few people outside of America think of New York as anything but a city like Paris or London. It is only in America that New York is recognised as a State into which the British Isles, with a little bending, could be fitted comfortably.

The farm is in Delaware County — the very western fringe of the Catskills, and still beyond the boundaries of the Reservation — as some people call it — that is to say the Jewish Reservation, because the Jews have replaced the Mohawks up to a distance of 90 miles from Manhattan. 'Common consent,' writes Evers, 'accepts the country around Stamford in Delaware County as forming the Catskills' northwest corner. From here the common-consent

348

line runs southward through as lovely a farming region as the eye of man may rest upon. There the gurgling of brooks is everywhere, in early summer the air is heavy with the fragrance of wild strawberries, pasture after pasture soars upward toward the forest-crowned hill or mountain top. Cows outnumber humans.'

My farm was right in the middle of this enchanted valley 13 miles south of Stamford; therefore 'by common consent' the north-west corner of the Catskills. My attorney in Delaware County, was also the district attorney (and was used to being called out at 3.30 a.m., when a woman of 39 stabbed her 24-year-old husband in the right ventricle and rang up the police at midnight to say he had fallen on a knife). Palmer Kennedy is a benign bear of a man; slightly bald, with a wide-ranging reputation as one of the nicest and straightest guys in the County. "Palmer Kennedy is tops," said my farming neighbour John Hinkley. Only twice otherwise have I heard him use this supreme accolade. "Gregory is tops with tractors." Gregory runs the local garage, and complained during the temporary fuel shortage, that my friend Paul Getty left him short of gas, towards the end of the month, and sold no petrol (gas) on Saturday mornings. There was then a notice on the pumps 'No Gas'. Paul Getty, to whom I reported this, was rather amused but he said that he thought that the shortage would continue and indeed get worse. Dr. Flint, a physician in Delhi (America not India) near by and whose son made me a cash offer of $100,000 for the farm in 1971, was also described as tops. These are presumably the summits of the local range of personalities.

Palmer sits, drinking Scotch, his favourite beverage, on my porch and gazing out at the range after range of blue hills: "The finest view in all Delaware County. How come, Somerset, that you find a nice little white house like this, set back on a hillside, up a private drive; while I live here and spend all my time looking for just such a place, and all I get is a house on the road? God-dammit all the farmhouses are on the dirt roads because of the snow in winter. How did you find this?"

"I did not find it. It found me. I bought it on the telephone without ever seeing it."

"You must be kidding."

"Not at all. We were having lunch at St. Osyth — it must have been quite a good lunch, I remember the Binnys and Carrick-Smiths, were the guests, who were neighbours of ours in Essex, and over the port I read out to them an advertisement from *The Times*. This was in October 1964, just after the Labour Government had been elected. '303 Acres. Farm in New York State on edge of village. Thermostatically controlled central heating. T.V. Two tractors. Station Wagon. Lock stock and barrel £12,000.' "

"Buy it sight unseen," Lindsey Carrick-Smith had said and this was echoed all round the table.

So, feeling rather vain and inebriated, I went to the telephone and cabled the owner in Pompano beach, Florida, saying that unless there were any snags not disclosed in the advertisement, I would buy the farm.

My wife Tessa, in the way of wives generally, wanted to go and look at it first. But I knew that if we did so, we would not buy it. Also I feared that unless I lodged an immediate application with the Bank of England to convert the necessary pounds into dollars, the new Labour Chancellor of the Exchequer, Jim Callaghan, would clamp down on all foreign investment. Which he did after his Christmas holiday, but just after I got a letter from the Bank of England dated January 4th giving me permission to transfer the advertised price.

So I acquired, at one and the same time, a dollar investment outside England, and a farm in New York State.

The owner, was I believe an Englishman, who had lived in U.S.A. or Canada for some years. He sounded American. "Quit stalling." He would telephone me from Forida where the temperature was in the eighties and say, "How is it with you?" As I had just got out of the bath, to take the call and was dripping all over the carpet in a temperature of about 55° I said, "Freezing."

He lied about all the wrong things. The 'thermostatically controlled' central heating, was thermostatically controlled, and acted in the summer, drawing air from a cool basement, as an air conditioning. But it was wood-fired for heat.

He was obsessed by the T.V. nonsense; and we found disintegrating sets in various stages strewn all over the basement. Reception in the hills was, in any case, nil; in spite of an aerial which attempted to rise above the mountains.

I asked him about the fences: "You could put 40 Herefords in there tomorrow." When I arrived I found 2 miles of road fencing absolutely flat on the ground, and it took me years with limited dollar resources and a helpful neighbour to get the fences built.

I asked Joyce (the vendor) if there was an aerodrome near by. I feared the noise of jets, or some other disturbance, from a nearby aerodrome. He was evasive. He thought I must be a tycoon who wanted to land his private plane near by. "I guess there are plenty within easy reach, if you really want them."

Eventually, when details were getting rather obscure, and the New York Title Guarantee Company found there were only 281 acres and that 15 were missing, I offered, under pressure, to go over in March. It would have been an appalling time to see the farm and Joyce knew it. He begged me to postpone my first visit till June, which I did.

*   *   *

All the way through those beautiful Catskills the rivers really did wind peacefully through valleys topped by maple woods, and the houses were graceful white colonial type wooden buildings, standing in unfenced lawns, and as we drove west, the farms became more beautiful, with outlines like castles, from their tall round capped silo towers. I began to fear that the view would run out before we reached the farm. The name of the village was not attractive – Bloomville, which sounded vaguely suburban. It would have been better in the Anglo-Saxon – as Flowertown. We spent the first night in a pleasant little wooden motel, with a round swimming pool at Fleischmans, on the edge of the Reservation. Teresa, my daughter aged 7, revelled in the pool, and could scarcely be dragged away.

This was the moment of truth. We passed through Margaretville, where the railroad crosses the road with nothing more than the letters RR to warn motorists. Andes, the next village, was like a Wild West town out of the movies – with its single old colonial hotel. From there the road climbed up towards skiing grounds before dropping down towards Delhi, a sleepy town pronounced by the inhabitants Dell-High (which may very well have been its original spelling – it is spelt here Delhi), and now passing the old brick courthouse of 1866 and the graceful white Baptist church with its wooden clock tower topped by a gilded dome, and the Grecian portico of the Delaware National Bank, we were out on

Route 10, heading up the last valley towards Hobart and Stamford. We came to an old covered snow bridge, crossing the lazy trout stream which eventually becomes the massive Delaware River. The bridge enchanted us, with its notice that anyone passing it at more than a walking pace would be fined 5 dollars. Next to it was the Christian Science Church, a neat white edifice in wood, with pointed spires and a tower. Here the river wound through low meadows, and on either side rose sloping pastures, on which black and white Freisians grazed, or sought shelter from flies in the trees higher up. The heat was oppressive, in the nineties, and gave me the illusion that the area could offer instant heat in June. Alas this was not always so; but even in the hottest heat wave, there is a breeze up in the hills, and the temperature drops at night.

So we came, after 8 miles, to a notice saying Town of Kortright. There was no sign of a town of any kind but I knew from the title deeds that the farm was 'situate in the parish of Kortright.' Bloomville was a small cluster of wooden houses; needing a coat or two of paint. The post office had a swinging fly door, and a benign white-haired Post Mistress, Miss Dibble, pointed the way up Maple Street, to the beginnings of Scotch Hill Road on which the farm was situated. On a balcony, above the stars and stripes, over the post office, Miss Dibble's lingeries was hanging out on the line to dry. We had definitely reached the hills – 166 miles from New York City and about as far as Shropshire or North Wales is from London.

Beyond the post office was 'Olsen's Meat Store', and Miss Dibble explained that after climbing 'quite a way' we would come to some trailer caravans belonging to Olsen, where Scotch Hill Road and Irish Hill Road forked. "I guess where you folks are going, ought to be called English Hill," she cackled. Like many Americans she recognised and professed to like "your English accent."

The first sight of Olsen's Caravansary was not reassuring. But I have come to accept the Great American Trailer; which is but a small irritant in a very large landscape. There is an awful lot of wilderness in America, and as Governor Rockefeller said in the introduction to his State brochure 'Wilderness is necessary to man.' There is little of it left in England.

So we passed Olsen's Caravansary on our right; and I knew from conversations with Joyce that I would be asked to supply him with water from the estate. I did so — for a dollar a year. It became quite a joke when I went into his store every summer and collected my dollar, which eventually I took in silver dollars. "Now I know summer has arrived," he would say. He was a hard working young Dane; and his daughter's horses used to graze in my pasture, also in the summer, to our mutual convenience. America is a place where it is a good thing to know your neighbours.

After passing the caravans, the road rose steeply to the left, in a curve. We were already 2,000 feet above sea level. I assumed, correctly, that the park-like dip on the right of the road with its huge maple trees shading the rough pasture, dotted with thorn bushes, belonged to me. I saw with dismay, the flattened and delapidated fencing. Then we crested the hill, and, propped like a little white doll's house half-way up the slope of a wide hill, crested with woods, was the farmhouse. In a flash I realised "It is all right." For in these matters it is the position which is everything. We drove on to the two white cart wheels which Joyce had told me flanked the entrance to the drive, and proceeded to turn into this. The surface was indeed rugged, and as we approached it the large square barn on the left, which in photographs had appeared as brick, revealed itself as a wooden barn, with — ye Gods — brick-patterned paper, pasted over it. O Joyce, where is thy sting? From further up the drive, the eastern side of the barn was even more depressing — because the paper was peeling off and hanging in strips. It cost me $109 to have it completely stripped off that one side, to reveal a rather pleasing Swiss type of vertical wooden planking.

The house was charming, but it too needed repainting. But we paused and gazed at its little 4-pillared portico with dawning affection. Much would have to be done — but still. Joyce had strung a barrier of stake-fencing across the drive with a notice Private Property — Keep Out, and it took us some time to untie the cord from the base of a fair sized maple tree, which cast some shade. There was another on the lawn — and between them I eventually squeezed a swimming pool 30 feet long.

We had collected a key to the house, from Jim Johnstone, the insurance agent in Delhi, who also acted as Joyce's agent. He told us that one, Walter Zeller, had been keeping an eye on the house. This individual appeared, unexpectedly, behind 5 cows, which he was pushing up the drive so that they could 'stray', as he put it, in the meadowland above the house, which was the subject of an astonishing soil conservation contract under which Uncle Sam paid the owner $1,000 a year, not to farm the land. At least the hay was supposed to be cut, but it could not be gathered or grazed. It rotted back into the soil, and acted as compost.

Walter Zeller was simple minded, and continued to prod his cows into the forbidden pasture. My one anxiety was that there might be poisonous snakes. "No Siree. Never did see one of them." In fact they dislike the cold winters; and all we have are one or two harmless 'garder' snakes who protect the house from flies and other insects.

Inside the house, the furniture was comfortable – in the sense that 3 of the beds were modern, and the chests of drawers practical. But the wallpapers and upholstery were in a somewhat Kingston Bypass style. Mrs. Rossler in Delhi soon produced agreeable patterns of blue-rosed cretonne, suitable for a cottage decor. And Jim Tucker, also from Delhi, replaced most of the wallpapers to match, in time.

The kitchen was a pleasant surprise – with a workable de luxe Westinghouse Laundry Machine, which lasted another 7 years, a refrigerator which survived 9 summers until it started crying steadily inside itself; there was also an electric cooker and sink unit. Upstairs on the landing there was a bucket to catch rain coming through the roof; and it was evident that rain had been seeping down the old chimneys through the walls of the bedrooms. There were buckets everywhere.

The extra large bath, promised by Joyce, turned out, by English standards, to be an extra small one. The lavatory cistern pedestal exuded damp on a discoloured linoleum floor. I thought it prudent to remove my wife and daughter to Lake Louise in Canada as quickly as possible, and leave the problems of rehabilitation till our return. We allowed ourselves 3 days at the end of the journey for this. I was also waiting for the survey map of the property – due from an attorney's office in Stamford, and not yet ready. The only map I had was a sketch map of the Soil Conservation Contract, which gave a very restricted impression of the boundaries. I thought from this that the land ended at the crest of the fields on either side of the house. I could not have been more wrong. Admittedly the pasture immediately to the west of the house, with a fence only six feet from it belonged to

Passuello. At the corner of the house it turned away westwards, leaving the barn and a lot of rough land in my part. But my wife was quick to point out the dangers of having someone else's land come so close up to the building. She was right of course; and I was relieved the following year when John Hinkley wrote to say Passuello was giving up to go bear hunting in Alaska and was prepared to sell me 90 acres adjoining the house. It was a snip. I got those 90 acres for $4,500 in 1966 and increased my holding to 371 acres. Later in 1970 I straightened the boundary by selling off 9 acres for the same sum.

* * *

The great help for an Englishman in dealing with Americans is that they talk in terms of acres, or pounds to the square inch (when blowing up your tyres) or miles; and even rods poles and perches. They do not torture you with kilometres, or kilos, or hectares. Whoever thought up the idea of Anglo-Saxon Britons joining the European Economic Community must have been a Germanic sadist.

'Tops' Gregory got the old tractor going, and with it for a number of years I did my best to qualify for the soil conservation grant by cutting a meadow or two of hay.

My recollection of the people I had to deal with in those early days is classified by the code names I remember them by: 'Ground-to-air-Evans', 'No-hard-liquor-Garcia', 'I wouldn't-burn-anybody-that-hard-Frazier', and 'The buyers from Utica'.

First came 'ground-to-air-Evans', a builder from New York City, who had set up at Hobart and was recommended by an electrician there, who stared unbelievingly at the connections of the electric cooker and said that Joyce must have been trying to burn the place down to get the insurance. Evans arrived in a shooting brake, and had scarcely alighted when a light plane flew overhead and he leapt back into the front seat, grabbed a microphone and said "Ground to air over." I am not sure whether this was intended to impress me with his high powered business methods. He estimated $1,800 to repaint the whole house, put on a new roof, make and paint storm shutters; install a second bathroom on the first floor; block up the old chimneys and make good. Even in 1965 this sounded reasonable enough. He had close-cropped hair and an alert face. He pointed out that as I would be recrossing the Atlantic, he would like half the money in advance to pay for materials. This also seemed reasonable and I gave him the money.

When we arrived for a short visit next year, we found nothing accomplished but a few felt tiles on the front side of the roof and yawning gashes in all the bedroom walls, where the chimneys had been excavated but not yet filled in or papered over. It was very depressing and he promised to do better.

After we had got back to England we heard that he had suffered an accident and this slowed matters up even more. His wife did not explain in the correspondence the nature of his accident or I would have felt more sympathy. He had cut off his penis on a circular saw, and according to Palmer Kennedy, an interesting point of law arose in the industrial court as to whether this incapacitated him for work.

Eventually he recovered sufficiently to complete the bathroom, with a blue bath. My eldest son, Rodney, in the Royal Navy, had snatched a few hours from his ship, while in New York and came up to the farm in time to stop him installing a beige-coloured bath. The roof tiles were also of a different colour from the dark blue we had ordered. Ground-to-air-Evans was inclined to make use of what he could get cheap. Of the painting of the house and the storm shutters or the hinder parts of the roof was no sign, and I was glad to get the bath system and what he had done for the original estimate of $1,800 and sought out Jim Tucker, an alert and more reliable builder from Delhi, with piercing blue eyes, who painted the outside of the house for $1,100.

'No-hard-liquor-Garcia' belongs to the unsuccessful cattle raising period. The Director of Barclays Bank in New York, John Basford, gave me an introduction to him, as he was a successful breeder of beef Angus cattle. He lived near Cairo, 50 miles to the east, and it was a long hot drive. On arrival he asked if I wanted a drink, which I certainly did. "No hard liquor, mind." So I went inside the house, where his wife opened a cocktail cabinet full of hard liquor and said, "What do you want? Gin and tonic?"

"That would do fine," I replied and rejoined Garcia outside. He stared at my glass. "What is that?"

"Gin and tonic."

"I said no hard liquor."

Happily I am glad to say this was not American hospitality as I came to know it. Garcia had made his money the hard way. He showed us his herds and Angus bulls. But he would not sell any of the progeny. He had a haymaking machine costing $1,500 which cut, squeezed, baled and flung the hay into a trailer all in one process. "Saves labour."

We eventually bought 14 Angus cattle through a young cattle dealer in Bloomville. We bought them in the spring when everybody else was buying and sold them when everybody else was selling in the fall. So it was not surprising that we lost money. After the auction at Oneonta, I saw Frazier in an open-necked check shirt in the village and said, "They reckoned at Oneonta that you must have taken 35 dollars off each of those beasts." He looked at me with aggrieved innocence. "I wouldn't burn anybody that hard."

The sale had been a surprise. On a sweltering hot day in October, the cattle were driven with difficulty by John Hinkley and the driver, Mr. Coager, into a van. When they were let into the ring the bidding ceased abruptly and was suspended for thirty minutes, while they stood with dripping tongues, losing condition. I went along the bench to find out what was happening. The auctioneer said he was waiting for the buyers from Utica. These arrived in pork-pie hats, with blondes on their arms, having lunched well on the way, while the steers' tongues were lolling out. They formed a tight ring around the beasts. Results of grazing beef cattle for 6 months. 50 dollars loss on each.

After that I let the grazing for a couple of seasons to old Elmer Murdoch. He had heart trouble. He paid $400 for the whole season, which did not seem a lot, and scarcely paid the school taxes. He kept the calves from the mothers, by locking them inside the barn, to accustom the mothers to being miled twice a day. As a result the calves started to roar for milk at 5 a.m., which was disturbing. Then Elmer would arrive at 7 cursing the decrepit old cows, "Come on Blackie, I can see you, you old sod. Where's Brownie?" And so on, in anything but a subdued voice. When he peeled 200 dollars off a roll one evening to meet half his grazing rent, the Hinkleys thought they had heard of a miracle. But poor Elmer; the first year he got Shippon Fever and lost 20 cows. Next year he had about 160 cattle of all kinds, and dealers were always coming up and down at odd hours to collect a few. He had 20,000 dollars tied up in it all; and John thought he came out on the wrong side. I found him lying in the long grass near the barn once, getting his breath back. His heart was giving him trouble. "But I ain't dead yet," he said.

Now he is gone, I miss the calves roaring or the cows bellowing to get at them and old Elmer roaring at both of them.

I could never have coped with the farm without the help of the Hinkleys next door. During the 3 days we spent at the farm in 1965 I took Teresa round to all the neighbours. Nobody let us in; possibly they were too busy milking to pay us any attention. Except the Hinkleys. John Hinkley had been sitting beside a cow milking. He was a thin wiry dark man, without an ounce of fat on him. His wife was just as thin, they worked from 5.30 every morning till dark. Their 3 daughters and (in those days) their 11-year-old son, Jim, helped too. In the evening John and his daughter Joyce came up to the farm and apologised for not having given us a better welcome, "If there is anything we can do to help, just let us know," there was a lot to do; and over the years they took over the care of the place when we were away and had the house ready for our return. They got the fencing built; and the swimming pool installed. It was a joy to see the children enjoying it. In 1973 I got John to arrange for the pool to be heated. Elmer was not to be persuaded to part even with 400 dollars again, so I let John and Dorothy Hinkley cut all the hay for themselves and store it in the barn. They were doing this all through the hottest days of July and August — Dorothy, a diminutive figure on a huge tractor going round and round the field across the road at the bottom of the drive, rowing up the hay while John followed on another tractor with the bailer. Then the girls, Jan and Jane, would come over and after an electric elevator had been connected up to the house, the bales were shot up to the first floor of the barn. Some of the family cooled off in the pool: 14-year-old Jan with her flaxen hair and pale blue eyes. The crying fridge, having been demoted to the basement, provided cold cokes and 7-up. It was a good healthy open-air life. The tractor seemed to have given up the ghost — but I mowed the lawn, vacuumed the pool and hoovered the carpets inside the house. So grateful was John for the hay that he insisted on adding a diving board to the pool. It meant anchoring the supports in concrete; and this involved excavating rock-hard earth in the heat of August. "I know Erwin Gramlich doesn't work on Sundays," said John with a chuckle and the two Gramlich brothers, who did much of the building work inside the house, spent their Sunday, free, delving and setting concrete in time for my daughter's arrival next day. It is a good community. John Gramlich with a deaf aid said he was supposed to be installing a barbecue pit for some people who were giving a lunch party at 1.30. He left at 12, saying, "I'll get it done. But I'll have to say you detained me."

The farm detains us all. No one ever seems to want to leave; to descend from the cool heights and stupendous views to the turmoil of the world.

In the summer of 1973 I arrived to find that the rocky driveway had mysteriously smoothed itself without any assistance from me, financial or otherwise.

Now they are looking for Natural Gas and may well find it in these hills. They bring us contracts made up entirely of small print offering a dollar an acre to explore. One wonders what effect that will have on the neighbourhood, if they find it. I have never discovered where the sewage goes to. Perhaps for years it has been going to some bottomless pit; and one day some bright prospector will drop a match down it; there will be a loud explosion of methane gas; and reports of gas in them thar hills.

*　　*　　*

Driven up into the hills, by the overpowering heat of the valleys and plains further south, a humming bird came and hovered beside me on the terrace in front of the farm yesterday evening. It was the first humming bird I had ever seen in this part of the world. Dusk had already fallen and his feathers looked a dark olive green — the colour of spinach — green jade. No doubt in sunlight the humming bird would have flashed with an iridescent emerald colour. He hovered for a few seconds, looking at me sideways out of one black bead of an eye, his long beak questing in vain, in these pastures, for some luxuriant honey-laden flower. Then he was gone, down the drive, to where the dog roses still carried an occasional bloom.

All week the hills had been lost in a haze of heat; one had been reduced to eating lunch standing up in the shallow end of the swimming pool with a straw sombrero and a towel over one's shoulders; but yesterday a light breeze had carried it away, and the hills across the valley leapt into life; blue vales, and wooded hills, with here and there a bright clearing of grazing land. In the foreground the rough pastures of the farm resembled an African savanna, with long browned grass and thorn bushes. The sun had shone down all day, with the temperature in the nineties. That is one of the first pieces of information you hear on the radio – 92 degrees under sunny and partly cloudy skies, at Albany Airport. This is XYK calling. They do not torture you with centigrades. Stand by for an important announcement. A white and black collie dog has been lost from the home of Mrs. J. Barber on Main Street, I repeat, an important announcement. You do not hear anything about England or Europe. In 1973 the news came from as far as Washington where the Watergate hearing was dragging on all summer. I suggested to John Hinkley that it was becoming a sort of entertainment. He jumped up off the porch, stuffing away his pipe. "I don't find it entertaining," he said bitterly. Honest Americans were deeply shocked by the revelations as to the whole way their Government has been carried on.

I followed the path the humming bird had taken down the drive. There was no sign of him. No flowers in Bloomville – or even a mile and a half from it. But I traced the line of blue spruces struggling up through the long grass. Ladybird Johnson, the ex-President's wife, had persuaded the Government to give a grant of 80% for beautification – including any trees planted within sight of a highway. So in 1968 I had planted 1,000 blue spruce seedlings along the boundaries of the property, with the help of an enthusiast in the department of Agriculture and Forestry at Stamford, Ron Bernard. He and an old tree supplier, Mr. Ballard, did all the planting for me in the winters while I was away in England. I also planted 10,000 Scotch firs and other pines on waste ground with an 80% grant. Their enthusiasm was extraordinary. When Ron Bernard moved on to another job, his successor came over, and took only a perfunctory interest in further projects. President Nixon, after he was elected, soon stopped the beautification nonsense. So no more trees within sight of highways qualified for 80%. The blue spruce were very slow in growing up. Each year I expected to find an imposing avenue, only to have to search in the grass for them. In America they don't recommend clearing the grass away too much. It provides moisture and shelter from the sun. After five years the tallest were just over three feet and topping the grass. I halted along the line in the gloaming, kicking the grass away with my feet. Across the dirt road, the grass was bright green where Dorothy Hinkley had cleared the hay. A woodchuck poked his head up from his hole and watched me warily. They are tubby creatures, like beavers but without a tail. Under some light aspen trees fifty yards across the meadow two wild deer were standing, one foreleg poised for flight. They turned and loped away towards the fir trees on the slope above them. Their white cotton tails showed brightly in the fading light. They were light chestnut in colour without the dappled marking of our tame fallow deer. Unlike the deer in England escaped from private parks like the one at St. Osyth, these were born wild and were part of the natural fauna of the area. Ferrucio Passuello told me he once came upon a small black bear in the woods, that I bought from him. And up there, when my niece was staying, we had seen three black masked racoons up in the tall trees.

After a time everything about the place seemed to become sacred – as if one had penetrated some secret Shangri-la. Even the worst of Joyce's atrocities acquired an affectionate respect. The tall drinking glasses ornamented in black and red with pheasants, the plates decorated with fir cones, brown and green; the old-fashioned sound radio in its large varnished box case, from which the varnish was peeling, gave out local music for some years: 'Those were the days, my friend. We thought they'd never end. We thought they'd last for ever and a day.' Then the old time valves began to give out; and could not be replaced. The oval floral patterned porcelain ceiling lamps, each holding two naked bulbs on the corridor landing and my dressing-room, were retained. But the circular hanging light, like a flying saucer, on a pulley in the main living-room had to go, replaced by a more graceful candelabra. Gradually the brown porcelain table lamps, in the shape of weird gourds decorated with white ivy were relegated to a room at the back; which became a sort of Joyce Museum.

I kept the ancient (1948) shooting brake, on its deflated tyres, with its ripped upholstry in the garage to act as a sort of burglar prevention device.

When my son Carlo first came to visit the farm he said, "The engine is still going." That seemed surprising after three years. He opened the bonnet. The humming was coming from a wasps' nest! He rehabilitated the vehicle, to the extent of getting it to go, but as the brakes did not work, he gathered momentum towards the bottom of the drive and had to swerve into the dirt road abruptly. In time the Parish Council voted enough money to surface the road up from the village for one mile with a hard top; and this ceased abruptly about 70 yards from the gate. After that every car passing towards Drake's house and Wosnik's further along Scotch Hill Road, sent up clouds of red dust — fortunately far enough away from the house not to reach us.

The house had been built at the turn of the century for the school mistress. The school house itself had stood near the entrance of the drive; but later the school was situated in the village, in a larger wooden house, and later still transferred to a majestic new brick building near Hobart to which the children were driven in yellow buses. The old schoolmarm's house at the bottom of the drive had been dragged up on skids to join the Davidson's hen houses; and when I first saw the place it filled me with unnatural gloom — dilapidated, leaning drunkenly forward, its windows without glass, the floor broken in, and only two old-fashioned lavatory pans in cubicles each side of the door, at one end, to remind one of the former pupils. It proved, however, a tough obstacle to demolish. Various builders tried pulling it down with two ropes from tractors without effect. I thought at one time of reconstructing it, as a studio, with a famous tapestry of lions and unicorns occupying the whole of one wall. But Mayorcas wanted $100,000 for the tapestry in New York; and I could not organise that in America. In any case it would have been a crazy idea abandoned in the winter with five feet of snow on the ground. So in the year when Carlo and my stepson Nicholas were both there, 1970, they made a determined assault on the building, and I took films of it going down heavily like a broken backed elephant. Soon only the white porcelain pedestals anchored by long iron rods to some mysterious plumbing device in the bowels of the earth, showed above the grass to mark the end of the old school-house.

There was one shed in the lower pasture where about 1,000 old buckets for collecting maple syrup survived from a time when maple syrup had been a thriving trade in these parts. Now it is hard to come by — except in branded bottles in supermarkets.

362

Occasionally there is a roadside sign outside a farmhouse – Maple Syrup for Sale.

There were some surprisingly good restaurants in the neighbourhood. One, near Hobart, was an old converted Boat House, run by an elderly and rather precious pair of Danish ladies. They provided Dublin Bay prawns, freshly flown from Boston, and renowned steaks. But every time we tried to get a table at first, by calling in, there were rows of Cadillacs outside – they asked us primly if we had made a reservation by telephone. As we had not yet succeeded in getting the telephone reanimated since it was cut off after Joyce's departure, it took us 3 years before we could get a table. As years went by some restaurants improved and other declined. The old ladies sold out to the proprietor of the local beer garden. The Hidden Inn across the bridge in South Kortright improved, after its owner, Tuffy Clarke, who used to come and put his arm round the necks of his guests in a rather hearty manner, took his profits and retired to Florida. The building was a fine old eighteenth century coaching inn. This was taken over by a friendly couple, and continued to prosper. Part of the fun of a holiday at the farm was the evening sortie to one or other of the chosen restaurants within a radius of 40 miles. For lunch one ate salads by the pool, unless business took one into Delhi and one had a bacon, lettuce and tomato sandwich with a milkshake in the air-conditioned Delhi Diner, where one was likely to meet the builder, the Bank President, the Insurance Agent or Palmer, sitting on a stool democratically at ease with each other.

An annual event in the area which revealed a lot about the American character at its best was the Walton Fair. The Hinkley family always looked forward to seeing this with us. In 1973 my daughter and I were accompanied by Juliet Bristol, who had obtained a divorce from her husband, and was enjoying the peace of the New York hills which she found strangely reminiscent of the Wicklow mountains, where she lived at Coolattin with her mother, Olive, Countess Fitzwilliam. Juliet and I had spent a lot of time in antique shops, seeking out old Boston rockers, with the original stencilling on, or Hotchkis's chairs, decorated by some old Senator's widow within living memory. In Oneonta at 4 o'clock we had bought a modern glass coffee table on chromium supports and were astonished to find it already delivered on the porch of the farm, 25 miles away, by the time we got home after dinner.

We were amused to hear the lady who runs the Hidden Inn telling some Americans in the next room, "We have a lovely Englishman out here who has a farm. They are trying to get married and we pray for him." It was not clear whether they were praying for me because I was trying to get married or to help me get married and I hasten to add that the Americans use the word lovely in quite a different sense from the way we do. There were also expeditions with Teresa to the new drive-in supermarkets in Oneonta, which supplied everything from jeans and curtains to washing machines and refrigerators. Juliet's favourite phrase, "I don't want to influence you, but . . . " came into play a good deal over the old crying refrigerator; and as Grants of Oneonta were offering a double discount for one week, we got a king-size refrigerator and the latest non-vibrating washing machine for $560 and a credit of $54 in the food department. It was great fun going round the food department with two wheeled trolleys and such a large credit. I threw in all the tins I could lay hands on of Campbells beef boullion, as this mixed with vodka makes a nutritious and refreshing drink which we had discovered at the Bullshead Inn in Coblestill called bullshot. I grabbed packets of frosted flakes, detergents, frozen sweetcorn, anything that came to hand, relying on the subconscious mind to keep tally and on arrival at the pay counter with my 54 dollar coupon the cashier was electrified to discover that the total load of two trolleys came to $53.98c. To that Governor Rockefeller added $1.75 tax, as most of the items were in food which is untaxed. Sometimes we made purchases further afield. One autumn in Arizona we bought pictures of cormorants being dashed in spume against the rocks at Terra del Fuego painted by an Argentinian artist called Huertas or a snow scene of some lonely barn by Jessica Mitchell. On the last day of the Walton Fair we collected Jan Hinkley and Jim Arnold, Palmer Kennedy's new stepson who was Teresa's age, before leaving for the Walton Fair. The drive of twenty miles is down the continuing Delaware Valley and even with the fair at the other end there were few cars to spoil the ease of motoring, so unlike the constipated roads of Britain. In Walton approaching the fair of course we had to join a queue of cars trying to get into the fairground. We parked in about the fifth row — I say the fifth because all American cars look alike and when we returned to the parking area in the dark we could not find the car for half an hour. The Hinkley parents were due to join us at the grandstand at 8 o'clock to see the Demolition Derby but the seats were already sold out and I had some difficulty at the other end of the stand to get 5 seats for ourselves and the children. They went off on a round of the sideshows while Juliet and I visited the largest steer in the world – a friesian – or as the Americans would say a holstein bull – standing over eleven feet high at the withers and weighing eleven thousand pounds. No kidding, as they say in America. One can see almost anything at the Walton Fair. One year I saw a calf with two heads. I kid you not, as Humphrey Bogart used also to say. At 7.30 an announcement said that the Demolition Derby was beginning. This was the main event. In earlier years draft horses dragging increasing weights had been the big draw. Now there were lines of old cars drawn up facing each other in reverse. The drivers wore crash helmets and certainly needed them. The only safety rule seemed to be an embargo on smashing the driver's door. At the drop of a flag the cars charged backwards at each other like knights of old chivalry in armour jousting in the lists. The crashes were shattering. The announcer's voice came over clear, "We've got John Dean, John Erlichman, Bob Haldemann and John Mitchell (the chief Watergate witnesses) all lined up here this evening and are going to sort this Watergate mess out once and for all." The cars kept on revving up and slamming into each other till only two were left in action and they kept on crashing into each other till both were wrecks. The audience were asked to decide the winner by their cheers and to a deafening ovation the final winner was able to drive his car from the lists. The rest were periodically towed away by pick-up lorries. By now it was nearly dark and Juliet and I started towards the car. We could not find it and when Teresa and Jim arrived we were horrified to see that Jan was not with them. She had wanted to stay on. But we sent the two back to fetch her and then Jan managed to stay on by finding some friends who agreed to drive her home later. But as she did not reach home till 1.15 a.m. at the age of fourteen I felt that I had failed in my responsibility; but in Delaware County the parents did not seem unduly perturbed. All was well. I remember an Italian industrialist buying the farm above the Hinkley's on Irish Hill Road one year and spending a lot of money on it. I asked him what brought him up here. He replied, "In New York my wife can't leave the apartment without a guard dog and a bodyguard." I suspected him of belonging to the Mafia. "Here the Hinkleys can walk two miles down the road to Bloomville without a single street lamp." He sold out after two years when his wife said she preferred the apartment in New York and a guard dog and possibly also the bodyguard and the farm was sold to a Swiss bachelor who milks 150 cows morning and night through the milking parlour. So in Delaware County the cows continue to outnumber the humans and we can lift up our eyes to the hills from whence cometh our salvation.

CHAPTER 30

Paul Getty

Between 1959 and 1975 (when he died) the American Jeal Paul Getty became a significant figure in England, not so much because he was the richest man in the world, as because he acquired Sutton Place in Surrey from the Duke of Sutherland and had a great deal of personal charm.

I first met him at a dinner party given by the Killearns before a dance at Herstmonceux Castle for their daughter Jacquetta. Jacqueline had persuaded a somewhat reluctant Astronomer Royal to lend this rose-brick fifteenth century castle in its moat for the occasion.

In May or June 1973 my current publisher Ben Glazebrook of Constable & Co., gave me lunch at the Savoy Grill. The news was all of Nixon bugging people's telephones.

Glazebrook said, I thought rather wittily, "Does that make him a bugger?"

At lunch he said he was tired of publishing books by me about people no one had ever heard of or wanted to hear of like Galla Placidia and Alaric, or Frederick II of Hohenstaufen. Why couldn't I write the official biography of someone like Chairman Mao or Paul Getty, whom people had heard of? I replied that I did not know Mao Tse-tung, that I did not speak Chinese and was most unlikely to get near him, even if I travelled the 8 or 9,000 miles involved. But I had known Paul Getty for over 10 years and could always ask him.

So, I telephoned Paul. I had his ex-directory telephone number, after he had taken me to his desk during lunch one day to take a call my accountant Randulph Barker had succeeded in putting through to me there. I told Paul that I had thought of a splendid title for a biography of him: 'The Life and Dimes of J. Paul Getty'. My publisher wanted me to do the book. He gave a chuckle at the title (which he subsequently suppressed) and agreed to my coming down to Sutton for lunch to discuss it. The lunch took place in September 1973 and he agreed to start the sittings (almost as if I were painting his portrait) in October. To the surprise of his secretaries he agreed to my bringing a tape recorder, and the book finally emerged as *A Man in a Billion*. When it was nearly completed I took my fiancée and literary executor Juliet Bristol, down to lunch and subsequently to run through a recording of my interview on television about the book. He also wanted to add some observations on the inequalities in the distribution of wealth that he considered inherent in any human society.

The luncheon took place on 7th November 1973 and the 'Epilogue' sessions on 27th March and 30th April 1974. Paul came in and sat down in the chair which I usually used when interviewing him, and started to ask me my opinion on the subject of Marshal Grouchy. He had been reading my 'Waterloo Campaign' published by the Folio Society.

I said: "Grouchy's instructions were to follow Marshal Blücher and bring him to battle but Blücher in fact got away from him. Napoleon, in his memoirs, reproached him for not having come towards the cannonade of Waterloo. One of Grouchy's generals came to him and said that he had served with the emperor during the Italian campaign, and added, 'I have heard the general enunciate a hundred times that you should move towards the sound of the guns. The emperor is at grips with the enemy at this moment, and we should proceed towards the battlefield.' But Grouchy stuck to his orders, as he had read them, and continued in his vain search for Marshal Blücher."

At this point Paul observed: "There was no real reason why Grouchy should not have moved as fast as Blücher. The Germans were men, just the same as the French, and presumably Blücher was able to move fast enough."

I pointed out that Napoleon had, himself in his memoirs, stressed the slowness of Grouchy's movements, even referring to the fact that they were waiting for the soup to be made, and so forth. Paul then launched out on the subject of underlings.

He said, "One is very nearly always let down by underlings. They may be all right for eighty per cent of the time, but for twenty per cent of the time they do something quite incredible. If you ask them to show caution, they go and do something reckless. If you ask them to be bold, they show extreme caution. And this is what makes it so difficult for leaders and great men to rely entirely upon subordinates."

I think he was speaking very much from his own personal experience. He went on to refer to Napoleon's failing judgement during the five years prior to the Battle of Waterloo, and quoted the case of the Russian campaign.

He said, "I sometimes worry whether my own judgement can be failing. For example, I feel that I'm running scared, because one cannot be certain that one is making decisions with the same certainty of touch."

When Paul was talking before lunch about the tendency of leaders like Napoleon to fall into the error of lack of judgement towards the end of their career, he referred to President Nixon and thought that he had recently been showing lack of judgement. For instance, he thought that if the tapes were to be handed over at all, they should have been handed over earlier. This I found interesting in the light of what he had said to me in the tapes about Nixon. He had then defended Nixon fairly vigorously and said that it would be very wrong of him to hand over the tapes of private conversations because this would compromise the privacy of all presidential conversations.

We then had a very pleasant lunch with some extremely good claret and port to follow. I noticed that Getty, who drank comparatively little, did drink a small amount of white wine which was served with the first course — a very good hock — and also did drink a glass of port. During lunch he talked to Juliet about horse racing.

We got on to the subject of other horses, and he referred to the King horses, as he called them, which had been memorable in the past, and referred in particular to a horse ridden by a Mexican bandit called Joaquin Murietta. Getty told the story.

"Murietta was being chased by the American army, and came to an enormous chasm. He managed to jump the chasm with his superb horse, but both the other horses and riders with him balked at the chasm. He could have got away on this superb horse but for the fact that a sharpshooter in the army brought him down and the horse."

I think we all felt that this was rather sad after such a gallant leap.

"There is a place," he said, "called Murietta's Leap. On

another occasion, there were some customers in a dance hall in San Francisco gathered together with a pile of gold, and they were boasting about what they would do to Joaquin Murietta if they caught him, as there was a large price on his head. And it so happened that Murietta was in the room. He came forward and said 'I'm Joaquin Murietta. Just exactly what would you do?' At that moment the lights went out, and when they came on again there was no sign of Joaquin Murietta or of the gold that had been heaped upon the table."

Paul chuckled a good deal at this story himself.

I asked him a little bit more about his hobby of weight-lifting, and he said that the heaviest weight he had succeeded in lifting from the ground was two hundred and thirty pounds. This is of course a colossal weight, and I asked him why, in particular, he had chosen weight-lifting. He said:

"Well, you can't cheat yourself, you can always ease up a bit or say that you weren't feeling well or that the other fellow wasn't too good or did too well, and so on. But when it comes to lifting weights, you can't cheat yourself. If you get, say, two hundred pounds up in the air and you struggle with your hands to raise this," and there at the end of the table he was making a gesture of lifting both his hands up, struggling to raise an enormous weight, "and you succeed in doing that, then, if you add another five pounds to that, you've got to make an even greater effort to lift it up, and this is, in fact, a final test of your endurance."

And I felt that somehow this hobby may have presented Paul with the sort of challenge of character that he enjoyed. I asked him how long ago it was since he had lifted a weight of that kind, and he said, "Well it must be forty years."

I asked him if he knew Heini Thyssen well. He said that he was a friend of his, and I told him an amusing story that Heini Thyssen had told me; that when he invited Paul to the Villa Favorita on Lake Lugano, the villa began to get so full of Arab oil sheikhs and others coming to see Paul about his business deals that eventually Heini had to move out himself.

And I had said to Heini, "Why don't you move into Sutton?"

Paul laughed a lot at this, and admitted that the story was true. Juliet asked him about the island that he owned in the Bay of Naples, and Paul said that he had leased it the previous year to Fulke Warwick for four months.

I said, "Fulke Warwick is a strong character, isn't he."
Paul agreed.

We also got on to the subject of inheritance of titles through the female line abroad, because in England, if Juliet had been a boy, she would have been the present Earl Fitzwilliam. I said to Getty:

"You know Nell Gwynn was an ancestress of hers? I never know what the connection is."

Juliet interposed, "From that source springs our bad teeth and probably many other problems too. But she was quite a girl, Nell Gwynn."

Paul observed, "As Napoleon said, the only thing he ever inherited from his father was a bad stomach."

"How do you go back to Nell Gwyn?" I asked.

"Well, there's a certain relationship. Through her son and Charles's son, the Earl of St. Albans. There's a charming story, Paul, that you may know about Nell Gwynn," Juliet said. "Unlike Charles II's many other girl-friends, she never asked for anything for herself. She asked for a pension for her mother, and the money to found Chelsea Hospital, and eventually a title for her son, but she did not ask for anything for herself. But Charles rather liked Nell because she differed from his grasping girl-friends, who always wanted this, that and the other. And one day he came to see her at Newmarket, where he'd established her in a little house. Charles arrived unexpectedly, and asked Nell if he could see his son. So Nell yelled up the stairs – she probably spoke with a very broad cockney which I can't imitate, 'Come hither, bastard.' So Charles said, 'Sweet Nell, call not our son by this name.' And she looked him straight in the eye and said, 'How can I otherwise, since your Majesty has given him no other?' So he took the hint and gave the baby an Earldom, and hence sprang the name of St. Albans, from whom we're descended."

Paul thought that women's lib would eventually see that women were entitled to inherit, as well as men. I did not think he sounded very keen on the women's lib movement. This came through during the discussions at lunch. The table in the dining-room at Sutton is an immensely long refectory table which, he said, had formerly belonged to Randolph Hearst. He said, "Hearst and I shared a liking for long tables." Indeed, the one at Sutton was really extended by a second table, which went pretty well the length of the room. Paul sat at the end of the table, nearest the door, with Juliet on his right, and myself on his left, sitting on Charles II chairs, and we had a quiet private lunch, served by the butler.

After lunch Paul showed us round the house, and when we came to the Throne of Juliano de Medici, on which the prince could be flanked by two admirers, he said, "It reminds me of a story my father used to tell me, about a rich man who lay dying, and he sent for his two lawyers. So they came, rubbing their hands. And he said to one of them, 'Stand on this side of the bed.' And to the other, 'Stand on the other side of the bed.' And they just stood there, you know, hoping for his blessing. And he said, 'And now, like the blessed Lord Jesus, I lay me down to sleep between two thieves.' "

On the 27th March, 1974, I drove down to Sutton in the afternoon. After we had been through the whole typescript, Getty laid the book down on his knee.

"Now I don't think it's in this book, but I thought that I'd say a few words about wealth on this series. About great discrepancies in the amount of wealth that people have. Talents and rewards are not equally distributed in any field. For example, in politics, I've known men who were very intelligent, very hard-working, very honest, very able in every way, good speakers, and yet they never got beyond the City Council. And another man becomes Governor of the State, or President of the United States, or Prime Minister, and what is the explanation of that? Why does one man, who seems qualified to be in a high political office never make the grade? And we find that in the field of entertainment; we find some people that seem to have all the qualities for a movie star. I've known girls, myself, that had looks, personality, were photogenic, were hard-working, were good actresses, and yet they never got beyond an 'extra' part. And some girl that maybe wasn't so good-looking, didn't seem to be such a good actress, becomes a great star. Then we have that in the field of painting; some of the best painters that ever lived, more or less starved to death because they couldn't sell their paintings. They died bankrupt."

"Like Vermeer, and Rembrandt died in poverty."

"Yes, and Van Gogh. And so it is in business. As I said, whether it's an Iron Curtain country or in the West, there's always the best hotel in town, and the best room in the best hotel in town, and there's always somebody in it. And there's always the worst hotel, and there's always the worst room in the worst hotel, and there's always somebody there."

"Yes, you're dead right."

"It might seem disproportionate that some people make a great deal of money in business, and some people who seem equally able, equally hard-working, equally competent, never make more than a small amount of money and haven't very much success. But that seems to be the way the world goes. It's true, not only in business, but in politics, in art, in the entertainment world."

"I can understand your analogy with the entertainment world, but when you compare making a success in business and making a lot of money, with the fate of people like Rembrandt who died in poverty because they were not sufficiently recognised at the time, as artists, surely there is a difference here, because you have a very clear yardstick of success in business. The yardstick is the financial success, on the whole. Of course, it also includes the ability to organise and to run an efficient business, but when you're talking about a person who accumulates a vast fortune by his own efforts, there is a visible standard by which you can measure that. It's not a question of opinion, like an expression of art."

"Yes. Look at the case of the Coca-Cola company. The man who started Coca-Cola didn't live long enough to see it develop into a great company."

"So he may have died in comparative poverty."

"Yes. And so that should be true of other businesses, and I'm thinking of, too, the question of responsibility, what the consequences would be if people were levelled out, and I would think that if you divided all the money and property in the world at three o'clock this afternoon, in half an hour afterwards there would be a lot of people that had nothing. The people that had given theirs away, had lost theirs, had gambled theirs away, or for some reason or another didn't have it any more. And you'd have practically as great a discrepancy in wealth in half an hour as you have today. It may be some exaggeration in that, but not very much. I think that nature works on the principle of inequality, and it's hard to change it. Why should some people live a long and happy life, and others die very young after great suffering?"

"Do you think it is a basic factor of nature?"

"Well, I think that nature doesn't create people equal.

Certainly we don't all have a singing voice like Caruso, do we? Or Nellie Melba. But I think the business man who had made a fortune generally has made it honestly. It's hard to make money in business. It's very difficult. You've got to serve the public, and if your reward is relatively great, that's the way nature works. I don't see it's any more extraordinary for a man in business to accumulate a large fortune than it is for a man in politics to attain a very high office."

"I think that's a very good analogy. We can't all be Prime Ministers."

"No. A Prime Minister may not have as much money as a successful business man, but he has a great deal more power, and a great deal more position. But why should one man be Prime Minister and another man should be on the County Council; why should one man be a millionaire and another man should be a very modest business man?"

"But you're appealing to a slightly different electorate, aren't you?"

"Yes."

"In the one case, in a democracy, you're appealing to qualities in people that respond to oratory or to persuasion of one kind. In business, presumably, you're appealing to a more discriminating or intellectual audience."

"Yes. But you've got to perform a service to the public. And in a free country you've got to face competition, which is remorseless."

"Paul, to come back to another subject, and one that was raised by the Editor of the *Daily Express* in writing to me – to put on record what your real anxieties were during the kidnapping case of your grandson."

"No, I'd rather not," he replied firmly.

"You'd rather not? No, well, then, we'll leave it. I fully appreciate your feelings about it."

"It's an unsavoury topic."

"Well, I'm glad we've been able to clear up the various points."

"We've made some progress."

"Oh, I think so, yes. Do you find the book readable?"

"Yes, I think so, yes. You'll probably be in touch with me."

"I'll be in touch with you in a few days, Paul. Goodbye."

This recording took place at Sutton Place on Wednesday, 27th

March, 1974 between half-past three and five o'clock, when Paul and an under-butler showed me to the door and let me out as usual. While I was pausing in the drive to add this information on the tape, as I usually did for the record, a blue car came long and the driver stopped and said, "I am the security guard. Do you mind my asking what you're doing?" I explained to him that I was writing Paul Getty's biography and that the picture of him with the Queen Mother which I'd got with me had just been taken by me with Mr. Getty's consent for reproduction in the book. But it did show what a tight guard he had around him at this time, which was only to be expected in view of the attention which had been focused upon him as the richest man in the world, during the kidnapping of his grandson; and now that even Princess Anne had been the victim of a kidnapping attempt I had no doubt that special precautions had been stepped up to watch over him.

On April 30th Juliet and I visited Sutton again, to play a recording for Getty of my interview on BBC1's 'Look East' programme which had been televised on March 19th. He was in high good humour and in very good health and spirits. I suggested that two of his secretaries, Barbara Wallace and Carole Tier, should join us in the drawing-room to hear the recording. He listened to it attentively and did not demur when I answered the interviewer's question as to the extent of Getty's private fortune by estimating it at between $1,000 million and $2,000 million. After the recording Carole Tier left to resume her work, while Barbara Wallace remained behind Paul Getty's chair, to make corrections as he read through the whole of the transcript of our last recorded session on the revision of the book on March 27th.

He thought my remarks on *Time Magazine* would lead to my being 'writted' for what I had 'written' and these were modified. He was also overjoyed by a misprint over the Villa de Papyri at Herculaneum — the finest villa that was *never* found. He told us of a case in the newspapers where a man was referred to as a 'bottle-scarred Veteran', instead of a 'battle-scarred Veteran'. Complaints were made to the newspaper, which tried to correct it but made another error in describing him as a 'battle-scared Veteran'.

Altogether it was a good afternoon in bright sunshine, Sutton looking at its best. At the front door, with a security guard undoing the bolts, he told me that he was very pleased with the book and was obviously fortified in this by a letter from his New York attorney Lansing Hays, who said it was the first biography of Paul he had read in which he appeared as a fine man; and that he, Hays, recognised Getty from the book because I let him talk. He made some detailed suggestions for amendments, but nothing serious.

Paul told my fiancée, while I was out of the room fetching the secretaries, that he was much amused by my letter saying that in future I would stick to people like Caesar and Napoleon who had no attorneys or accountants in New York.

After reading right through the epilogue, which included his philosophy on tax inequalities in business as in politics and the arts (an excerpt from which was used by the BBC in my interview), he initialled the bottom of the last page and his secretary dated it, April 30th, 1974. This concluded the book, so far as the conversations were concerned.

Getty was something of an enigma. Because he had had his face lifted around the age of sixty, he always looked rather drawn and miserable in his photographs. But he had a great sense of humour. Few Americans seemed to realise that one of his ancestors had laid out plans for the city of Gettysburg, named after him. They tended to think of him as a self-made man. In fact his family had come from Ireland to America, by way of France, in the eighteenth century. Also, his father left over five million dollars, of which Paul received 500,000. Nor was he a Jew, which many Americans seemed to believe. On the whole he was much better received in England than in America or Italy and that, I think, is one reason why he happily spent the last fifteen years of his life here. I count him among three or four of the most remarkable people I have known, including Rudyard Kipling, Winston Churchill and Major F.R. Burnham, DSO, the American who showed me at Pasadena in 1930 the rifle with which, in a secret cave in the Matoppos, he had shot the M'Limo and thus ended the second Matabele war in Rhodesia.

376
Inscription on the flyleaf of Major Burnham's own book *Scouting on Two Continents.*

To my young friend
Sommerset de Chair
who is reefing sail on the
Ship of State in preparation for
the coming Storm *
Yours sincerely
F. R. Burnham
1930

*A reference to my first book *The Impending Storm* published that year in New York.   Somerset de Chair

POSTSCRIPT

As I have said, in an earlier volume, when an author starts writing an autobiography, he is dipping into his gold reserves. For where does his art come from but his experience and observation of life? It is the same in business. As Paul Getty said to me, when I was writing his biography and taping conversations with him at Sutton Place, "No man's judgement is better than his information."

This story of my own life carries me up to the respectable age of 63. In that year (1974) I married for the fourth time; Juliet, the only child of Peter Fitzwilliam, the 8th Earl, who was tragically killed with his companion Kathleen Kennedy (sister of the future president) in a private plane in France. My life since then has been active enough; but it has been devoted to helping her reorganise the Fitzwilliam inheritance, including the rehousing of its world famous collection.

I was fortunate in remembering, from my Chilham days in Kent, a large Queen Anne mansion called Bourne Park. Following my mother-in-law's death in 1975, and the sale of the Fitzwilliam property in Ireland, we were able to acquire Bourne and do it up, at the trustees' expense. Wentworth Woodhouse had already been let by my father-in-law on a 99-year lease to a college; and only a part of it kept for private use. With the death of my wife's cousin the 10th Earl, the house and 20,000 acres of the estate in Yorkshire passed to a distant connection. The entire collection, originating from this 365-roomed house (longer than the Houses of Parliament put together) reverted to my wife. We were able first to accommodate all the paintings by George Stubbs at St. Osyth. A drawing-room in the Georgian wing was especially adapted to take the life-sized portrait of the stallion Whistlejacket. (We had to lower the floor nine inches to accommodate him.) The principal Van Dycks and some of the best furniture by Langlois, Chippendale and James Moore, all went to St. Osyth. We lent four Van Dycks to the Van Dyck exhibition at the National Portrait Gallery and

377

seven Stubbs to the Tate Gallery exhibition, followed by the Stubbs exhibition at Yale, and a number of items to the Treasure Houses of Britain exhibition at the National Gallery of Art in Washington.

These are not the sorts of preoccupation for which one gets much sympathy — but they do take up a lot of time and energy, to which must be added my wife's absorbtion in bloodstock and racing; which, if not exactly a lucrative preoccupation, requires a lot of attention. I must have stood on more damp manure heaps than any man in East Anglia.

So my later years have not been idle; but I feel that the acquisition of Bourne and a house on Lake Otsego at Cooperstown in New York State, with the reorganisation of this world-famous collection, cannot be listed among my own achievements; and belong more properly to my wife's autobiography.

My first wife, Thelma, died in 1974, (six months before I married Juliet Bristol.) She had moved back to Blickling when I bought St. Osyth; and saw out the remaining fourteen years of the National Trust lease. Then she moved to a delightful George I house in Hampshire, where our eldest son, Rodney, lives the life of a retired naval officer. She also left him some property in the South of France.

The eldest son born to Carmen and me, Rory, revealed a certain genius for invention, working first for the Rolls Royce Aero Division at Derby and Filton. He invented a new type of jet engine — a combination of ram jet and turbine — known as the Rory Rambine. Rolls Royce patented it in 23 countries; but it never got off the ground, possibly because research costs of getting it into production were put at £100m. He was then chosen out of 185 candidates to deal with the problem of pollution during the building of the Drax B power station in Yorkshire, and still works for the General Electricity Board.

His younger brother, Carlo, followed me in the Blues. He served for a term in Northern Ireland; and nearly got engaged to a Cypriot giantess. He is at present working out, in Australia, the formula: "Have widow; will travel."

My elder daughter, Teresa, who inherited much of Tessa's beauty, was married, on a blazing day in July, at St. Osyth, in the parish church, to an amiable hunting baronet from Gloucestershire who had been an exact contemporary and friend of my son Peter at Eton, Sir Toby Clarke. We had more trouble parking the helicopters than the cars. Shortly afterwards I accepted an offer of $2,900,000 for the property from an American from Locust Valley on Long Island.

I may not have achieved all I set out to do. At the age of 12 I was deeply impressed by Sir Austen Chamberlain as Foreign Secretary, in his top hat and monocle, emerging from the Treaty of Locarno with the Knighthood of the Garter, and decided to emulate him. And but for circumstances largely of my own making, and the attentions of the Vichy French at Palmyra, I might almost have made it. But I console myself that the accolade I received from my seven-year-old daughter is worth all the honours and material reward I might have received by a more steady application to the paths of duty:

To Daddy

you are the most wonderful daddy in the world.

Lots of Love
Helena
xxx

Can one, at the age of 73, ask for more? And whatever impression to the contrary this book may give, it makes me feel that I cannot be wholly bad.

In the evening of my life, I am surrounded by a host of friends; and on New Year's Eve of 1984/5, we were able to seat 149 of them round the swimming pool at Bourne for dinner under a marquee, followed by dancing in the ballroom. The Queen Anne house and surrounding trees were floodlit, and towards midnight we stood outside, in the mildest clear weather, as the figures 1984 in Catherine wheels turned to 1985; amid a blaze of fireworks.